NAVIGATING THE INTERNET WITH OS/2 WARP

Herb Tyson

SAMS
PUBLISHING

201 West 103rd Street
Indianapolis, Indiana 46290

Of all the interfaces ever conceived, the human interface is the only one that counts. This book is dedicated to the patience, love, and non-computerness of Karen and Katie. Day after day, they prove that computer stuff, although interesting, is no substitute for the human interface. Computers can't hug. Or, if they can, I don't want to hear about it! Karen and Katie: I love you. Thank you for making Earth a nicer place to live. —HT

Trademarks

OVERVIEW

CONTENTS

12   Additional Internet Applications and Related Utilities   345

Appendixes

ACKNOWLEDGMENTS

I would like to use this space to acknowledge the contributions of the many people who helped make this book possible. First, thanks to Mark Taber, who persisted despite the fact that I thought YAIB (Yet Another Internet Book) was stupid. Thanks to Artch Griffin, an Internet veteran and fellow cpcug.org user who was kind enough to entertain a number of my stupid questions, and who never once openly said *Gee, what a dummy!*—at least not loudly enough for me to hear it. Thanks also to Mike Shacter, whose HyperView program logged record usage during the course of this book, and whose comments were invaluable. I also would like to thank the hundreds of people who posted their problems and questions on the Internet, thus giving me material for this book. Let's see, there's Andy, and Sue, and Amy, and Dave…well, y'all know who you are! Thanks, folks!

I want to extend a different kind of thanks to my family—Karen and Katie—who once again put up with a two-month siege. They endured not only 12 to 18 hours a day of my staring into a computer screen, but 10 to 15 hours a day of having the phone tied up. Now that I'm nearly done, they keep asking, "What's that ringing sound?" Fortunately, they aren't asking, "Who's that strange man?"

ABOUT THE AUTHOR

Herb Tyson is an internationally respected consultant, developer, and writer. He is a consultant to OS/2's I.V. League, for which he has prepared, evaluated, and reviewed technical materials. Oddly enough, he also has been awarded the status of MVP (most valuable professional) by Microsoft Word's technical support team for his contributions on CompuServe's MSWORD forum. He is the author of a number of books for computer users, including *Word for Windows 6 Super Book*, *Your OS/2 Warp Consultant*, *XyWrite Revealed*, *Word for Windows Revealed*, and *101 Essential Word for Windows Tips*. He also was a contributing author to *Using OS/2 Warp*, *OS/2 Warp Unleashed*, and a number of other books. His articles appear regularly in *OS/2 Professional* (his adjectives and verbs, however, appear elsewhere). As a Team OS/2 member, he also is an active participant and moderator on forums on FidoNet and the Washington, D.C., Capital PC User's Group BBS (the MIX). Tyson received a bachelor's degree from Georgetown University and an interdisciplinary doctorate from Michigan State University.

INTRODUCTION

So, you saw the Warp commercials on television, heard them on the radio, and read them in the newspapers. Then you grabbed a fistful of money from the ATM machine and marched down to your local software shop or computer superstore to get Warped. Congratulations! Are you ready to get Netted, too? That's the next step, you know. First you get Warped, then you get Netted. *Inter*netted.

If you're brand new to the world of the Internet, you're probably about to ask yourself a question—the same question I asked. *How could all of this Internet stuff be going on without my knowing about it?* A virtual world of data, business, personal relationships, talk groups, electronic mail with long-lost classmates and relatives, museums, libraries, catalogs, and even access to and information about your government, are all right there on your desktop or laptop computer, within easy reach.

Just how big *is* this Internet thing? As the comedian said, *It's really really big*. Is it just for computer nerds and technojocks? Nope. It's for almost everybody, just like television eventually was for almost everybody. Why? For the same reason—business.

Corporate America—no, make that Corporate Earth—has discovered the Internet. It's the new way to do business. It's so pervasive that you practically can guess a company's Web address and be correct. One evening, just to see what was really out there, I tried out some WWW (World Wide Web) addresses. I was shocked and amazed to discover that almost every one I tried worked—although sometimes I didn't get the companies I expected. Do you want to see what's happening at IBM? Try `http://www.ibm.com`. Care to see what Microsoft (remember them?) is doing? Try `http://www.microsoft.com`.

How about *The New York Times*, the *Washington Post*, *TV Guide*, and *Reader's Digest*. Do all of them have their own addresses on the Internet? I don't know. However, if not now, then soon. I just checked on a box of Post Raisin Bran. There's an 800 number you can call with questions, comments, or suggestions. Look on almost any product, and you'll see an 800 number you can call. Right now, almost every computer and electronics company in the world can be reached just as easily over the Internet. I'm betting that, in a very few years, all kinds of companies all over the world will be including their Internet addresses on products they sell.

Do you want to go shopping? Don't leave home, shop the Net. Do you want to buy a computer book? Visit any of dozens of bookstores and publishers on the Internet. For example, did you know that you could have bought *Navigating the Internet with OS/2 Warp* over the Internet (and for a 20 percent discount)? It's true. Just point the WebExplorer to `http://www.mcp.com` (mcp is Macmillan Computer Publishing—not male chauvinist pig). Check out *Your OS/2 Warp Consultant*, while you're there!

Until recently, getting onto the Internet was a rather daunting proposition. First, if you wanted to really get into it, you needed to go out and buy some TCP/IP software to take advantage of it. A full suite of Internet access software typically costs anywhere from $150 to $500. Second, you might have needed to get the telephone company to install a dedicated line for access to an Internet provider. That kind of hookup typically costs from $100 to $1,000 *per month!* At those prices, to get onto the Internet, you really had to have a need.

Enter Warp. With Warp, suddenly hundreds of thousands of people are discovering that they can get onto the Internet using just their modems. Moreover, they don't need to go out and buy a bunch of extra software. Everything they need comes with Warp. And the whole package can be bought for less than $100. Better still, using the stuff that comes with Warp is a whole heck of a lot easier than spending the next year learning all about UNIX.

If It's So Easy, Why Write a Book About It?

Well, some parts are easy and some aren't. Moreover, there's a lot of capability that comes with the Warp IBM Internet Connection for OS/2. Even when the individual parts aren't hard to understand, taken as a whole it can be a bit overwhelming. If you're like most users, you want a way to get a handle on what you have and how to use it. That's what this book is for. It's your handle on using the Internet with OS/2 Warp.

One thing some Warp users discover—once they're Warped and Netted—is that local Internet providers can give them Internet service that better meets their needs than the IBM Global Network can. Not everyone needs the kind of polish and first-class service you get from the IBM Internet Connection. And, although connecting using the IBM Global Network is quite easy, setting up to use another Internet provider often proves quite a challenge for even the most sophisticated users. One purpose of this book is to help meet that challenge so that the decision of which provider to use can be made calmly and rationally, rather than defaulting to the only provider that works.

Another thing Warp users discover is that the applications that come with Warp are real software. To get the most out of them, you either need a ton of time to experiment, or a good book. I can't help you with the former, but I hope you're holding the latter in your hands right now!

Who Should Get This Book?

Everyone on the planet should get this book. Even Windows users should get this book so they'll know what they're missing by not getting Warped. Even people without computers should get it because it makes a great coaster. A glass of iced tea could sit comfortably on this book for weeks without getting the coffee table wet.

In addition to *everyone*, this book is especially for people who want to get the most out of Warp's Internet access tools. If you need to know how to get a complete list of previously-read articles in a newsgroup but can't find out from reading the Help file—you need this book. If you need to know why Ultimedia Mail/2 Lite thinks your password and mail ID are wrong—you need this book. If you wonder why you can't FTP from the WebExplorer—you need this book. *If you wonder what the heck the preceding three sentences mean—then you definitely need this book!*

Have you ever wondered:

◆ Why does NewsReader/2 sometimes refuse my articles with Error 441?

◆ Why doesn't my mail show up in the In-basket?

◆ Why does FTP-PM pester me with Relogin errors?

◆ How can I keep from having to type my password each time I start the IBM Internet Dialer?

◆ How can I start Ultimedia Mail/2 Lite without its checking to see if I'm already online?

◆ Where do I go to download shareware and freeware for OS/2?

◆ How do I write a letter to Santa Claus on the Internet?

◆ How do I decode dirty pict..., er high-quality artwork that's UUEncoded?

◆ What the heck is a spoiler alert?

◆ What does IAK stand for?

If you've ever wondered about any of these burning issues of our time, then you've come to the right place. I've spent the past several months getting intimately acquainted with the OS/2 IAK (Internet Access Kit, a moniker that was applied to the IBM Internet Connection for OS/2 during beta testing, and which stuck because IAK is easier to type than IBM Internet Connection for OS/2). During that time, I've hit a *lot* of snags. Each time the path became rocky, I took notes. I worked through the problems so I could share the solutions with you. Each time I discovered a cool trick, I said, "Neat!" (really!) and wrote it down. Each time somebody asked a difficult question on comp.os.os2.networking.tcp-ip (*the* newsgroup to frequent when you have questions or comments about Warp's Internet software), I took notes.

What you have here is the result of over 2,000 hours of digging into all the nooks and crannies in the Warp IAK. If certain aspects of using the Internet under Warp have left you with a migraine headache, then try this book as an antidote. If you feel like you're lost and need something solid you can sink your eyes into (how's that for a revolting image?), then this book is just the ticket.

About This Book

In Chapter 1, you'll see a little bit (not too much, hopefully) about what the Internet is, where it came from, and where the OS/2 Warp Internet Access Kit (IAK) fits in. In Chapter 2, you'll survey the main resources on the Internet and the OS/2 software designed to help you tap into those resources. In Chapters 3 and 4, you'll see how to use the IBM Internet Dialer or the Dial Other Internet Provider dialer to get set up to log on to the Internet using a SLIP or PPP account, or using a SLIP emulator program such as TIA (The Internet Adapter).

In Chapters 5 through 11, you learn all about the individual programs that comprise the IAK—Ultimedia Mail/2 Lite, NewsReader/2, OS/2 Gopher, the WebExplorer, FTP-PM, Telnet, and a variety of smaller programs and utilities. In Chapter 12, I show you some OS/2 alternatives to the IAK offerings, some of which you might want to take for a test run.

Along the way, I throw in numerous tips and warnings about various sidetrips you can take, as well as dives and potholes to avoid. Throughout this, keep in mind that even though OS/2 version 3 is called Warp, I've never personally seen any of the later Star Trek television shows (*The Next Generation*, *Deep Space Nine*, and so on). So, if I'm a little weak on appropriate metaphors, you'll have to forgive me. You see, it's impossible (for me, at least) to watch television and write computer books at the same time. So, if my jargon seems hopelessly stuck at the level of the original Star Trek series, that's why!

> *Scotty, beam me aboard. Scotty, why did you just send me a two-by-four?*
>
> *Lieutenant Uhura, check Ultimedia Mail/2 Lite to see if Star Fleet has left any messages for us. See if you can find out why we can receive mail, but can't send any. Spock, see if you can figure out how to get the Dial Other Internet Provider dialer working. I think it requires some Vulcan logic. Bones, have some acetaminophen standing by.*
>
> *Chekov. Set a course for the Internet. Warp factor 3.*

Conventions Used in This Book

The design of this book uses special typefaces and other graphical elements to highlight different types of information.

Four types of "boxed" elements present pertinent information that relates to the topic being discussed.

Notes	You're reading a note right now, as you can tell from the special icon. Notes highlight special details about the current topic.
Sidebars	A sidebar contains information that you might find useful, interesting, or at least entertaining, but it isn't required reading. Sidebars have headings rather than a special icon.
Tips	A tip informs you about a shortcut or a trouble-saver for performing a specific task. Tips also have a special icon.
Warnings	A warning contains information that is a must-read. Warnings are supplied to help you avoid making decisions or performing actions that can cause trouble for you.

The first few occurrences of new terms, such as *URL*, *newsgroup*, and *ping*, appear in *italics*. New terms are followed immediately by a definition or explanation; you also can find them in the book's glossary. In addition to new terms, italics are used for proper names of books, other titles, and for emphasis.

When I point out options on menus, I designate them using the items you see in the menu, like so: File|Open. This indicates that you select File from the menu, and then choose the Open command.

Several items are presented in a monospaced font, which can be plain, boldface, italics, or bold-face italics.

`plain mono`	Applied to commands, filenames, file extensions, directory names, Internet addresses, and text you would see on the screen or in part of a dialog box. For example, OS/2 commands such as `COPY` and `DIR` appear in this font.
`mono italics`	Applied to placeholders, which are generic items for which something specific is substituted as part of a command or as part of computer *output* (what a program displays on-screen, not what you type). For instance, the term represented by `filename`, would be the real name of the file, such as `myfile`.
`mono bold` and ***`bold ital`***	Applied to any text that you must type on the command line or in a dialog box. Placeholders for which you must substitute something specific as computer *input* also can be mono bold. Here's an example of a typical instruction: "Type them as ***`envvar=setting`***, as in **`path=/usr/mypath`**."

The following example illustrates these fonts. The gray background used here indicates that an example contains an interactive session, that is, the session shows input by you and output by the system.

```
SunOS UNIX 4.1 (cpcug.org) (ttyp7)
login:tyson
Password:password
Last login: Tue Jan 24 15:11:47 from tyson.cpcug.org
SunOS Release 4.1.3 (CPCUG) #1: Thu Sep 15 13:09:59 EDT 1994
```

Note that most of the Internet is case-sensitive. If you see a directory named `Pub/os2`, then you must type it exactly that way for it to work: uppercase "P" and the rest lowercase.

Filenames and program names appear in capital letters, except under the following two circumstances:

◆ When they must be typed differently in order to work.

◆ When the way you'll usually encounter them on your computer is lowercase.

That is, when this book writes about a command, it will be capitalized. When it shows how to use a command, it very often will *not* be capitalized. An exception, however, is many of the Internet commands that work from OS/2. Commands such as ping and host, for example, are names that you'll almost never see capitalized. In fact, if you have HPFS (high performance file system) drives on your system, you won't even see them capitalized when you display a directory. As a rule, commands you see capitalized in this book are normal OS/2 commands that aren't part of the Internet tools. Commands that are not capitalized are Internet-specific OS/2 commands and UNIX commands.

A Note About Mouse Buttons

In this book, rather than saying right and left mouse button, I'm using IBM's convention of mouse button 1 and mouse button 2. That's because which is right and which is left depends on which hand you're using and whether or not you've changed OS/2 Warp's default behavior (in the OS/2 System Setup folder's Mouse settings object). If you're a typical right-handed mouse user, mouse button 2 is the right mouse button, and mouse button 1 is the left. If you're not typical, then you probably already understand all this and are halfway through the next chapter by now. Right? Right?? Hey, where'd you go???

CHAPTER ONE INTRODUCTION TO THE INTERNET

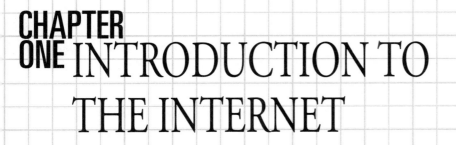

The Internet is rooted in national defense, academia, and science. It has its own culture, its own traditions, its own values, and its own customs. The customs on the Internet might strike many newcomers as odd, especially if they expect the Internet to be like BBSs they've used, or like GEnie, America Online, or CompuServe. Knowing at least a little about why the Internet is the way it is and how it got that way can help new arrivals fit in better. I know you want to get started on the Internet, so I'll keep this short. If you want to skip ahead, I'll understand.

Okay, now that the history-phobes are gone, here's a two-paragraph history of the Internet. The Internet came about from two aims. One was to build a computer network over an extremely wide area in order to link the work of researchers (defense researchers in particular). The other aim was to build a network that would be robust enough to withstand multiple links being interrupted or destroyed (such as, "What happens if somebody nukes some of the computers on the network?"). The Earth's volatile natural history of earthquakes and hurricanes, coupled with its combative human history, has taught us that anything important *can* be destroyed. If computers were to be a vital link in our national defense, it had become evident, it was folly to entrust it to one, two, or even three computers.

The Internet began in 1969 with the creation of *ARPANET* (Advanced Research Projects Agency, which later became *DARPA* for Defense Advanced Research Projects Agency). At the outset, ARPANET used four computers and was essentially just a feasibility study, that is, to show that such a network was possible. Just three years later, when ARPANET was unveiled to the public, it already had grown to include some 50 universities and research organizations with defense projects. As the old joke goes, *Once upon a time, there were two bunnies.* **Now** *look how many…!*

What Is the Internet?

Electronically, the Internet is a network made up of networks. It comes from *inter*, meaning between or among, and *network*, meaning a group of computers that are connected. Thus, the Internet is many computer networks that are *inter*connected. Each time another network joins the Internet, another collection of information becomes potentially available to Internet users. One ambitious goal is to connect as many computers and computer networks as possible to create something called the *information superhighway*.

I said *electronically* because, in some sense, the Internet really is more than the computers and networks connected to it. It's also the people and the efforts that go into making the Internet a useful resource. For better or worse, there's a real chance that the Internet will merge with other communications and commercial industries throughout the world. In fact, that's already happening.

> ### Grammies on the Internet
>
> Last night while cruising the Web (I'm writing this the day after the Grammy awards), I found a URL (Uniform Resource Locator—you'll learn more about those in Chapter 8, "Navigating the Web with WebExplorer") which indicated that the Grammies were being hosted on the Internet. So, I followed the trail and indeed discovered a Grammies home page where someone was providing information to "The Net" backstage at the Grammies. "How weird!" I thought. It's happening.

Just as television is more than antennas, transmitters, cables, and receivers, the Internet is more than computers. There's television, with a little *t*; and there's Television, with a capital *T*. There's the internet, conceptually with a little *t*; and there's the Internet, conceptually with a capital *T*. And, just as Television means the industry and people who surround that electronic resource, the Internet rapidly is becoming the industry and people who surround all of these millions and millions of networked computers.

To some, the Internet is synonymous with the information superhighway. Many don't agree, however. At its most fundamental, the information superhighway (also known as the "Iway") refers to the rapid exchange of all computerized information. As such, the Iway is at best a goal toward which we are making progress, which is aided by the Internet. Whether the internet (with a little *i*) ultimately is the connecting fabric, or whether some other, better-organized structure serves that purpose, we don't know. At the moment, however, thousands of new users are joining the Internet (with a capital *I*) each week, all over the world. For better or for worse, for now at least, the Internet might as well be the information superhighway.

How Does the Internet Work?

The networks on the Internet include governmental, educational, religious, political, commercial, and private interests. They are from every corner of the globe. Different networks connect to the Internet via *gateways*. A gateway just means a way of connecting different, and possibly incompatible, computer systems. The primary communications tool that lets all this work together is something called *Transmission Control Protocol/Internet Protocol* (TCP/IP). Perhaps you've seen advertisements for TCP/IP in various computer magazines. TCP/IP is a set of computer programs that allow different computers to exchange information. TCP/IP packages are available from a number of different software companies, including IBM. The *Internet Access Kit* (IAK) that comes with OS/2 Warp was based, in fact, on IBM's TCP/IP 2.*x* for OS/2 package.

The foundation of the Internet is hundreds of computers electronically connected to one another. Connections are made using dedicated high-speed transmission wires, telephone lines, microwave links, and satellites. At any end of a transmission line, communication is handled by TCP/IP using a set of *protocols*. A protocol is computerese for a method of exchanging information. By using known protocols, the computers at each end are able to make sense of information. Different protocols are used for establishing a basic connection, transferring messages, transferring data, and so on.

The set of protocols used for TCP/IP is often referred to as the TCP/IP *stack*. Don't let the term worry you. It's just jargon. Imagine, if you will, a system of roadways comprised of superhighways and primary, secondary, and tertiary (neighborhood) roads. Neighborhood roads are connected to houses with driveways. For entering the roadway to and from driveways, you use a specific set of maneuvers—protocols, if you will. To go from your neighborhood to secondary roads, another set of protocols is used, usually involving stop signs. To go from secondary roads to primary roads, still other protocols are required, including traffic lights, stop signs, and traffic circles. For going from primary roads to superhighways, you often need to use onramps and toll booths. Think of the various methods for getting from one point to another as different protocols. Taken all together, they are conceptually stacked in a way that prioritizes them.

In a similar way, different components of the Internet are linked together by protocols. To move out into the neighborhoods (smaller networks) of the Internet, you move up the stack. To get closer to the core of the Internet, you move down the stack. Fortunately, this is the last time I'll talk about the stack of Internet protocols. Because the word stack is thrown around from time to time, however, it helps to have an idea of what's being said so that you don't get frightened off thinking it has something to do with assembly language.

This Time We Almost Made the Pieces Fit...

The Internet comprises a number of subunits. The largest subunit is the *domain*. A domain is a network that is connected to the Internet. Some examples are ibm.com (used by the IBM Internet Connection), nmsu.edu (New Mexico State University), nasa.gov (National Aeronautics and Space Administration), and cpcug.org (Capital PC Users Group). Note the domain name endings: com, edu, gov, and org. These endings denote the type of domain. Major Internet domain types are

com	Commercial organizations (businesses)
edu	Educational institutions
gov	Government (other than the military)
mil	Military organizations
net	Major network facilitators
org	Other organizations

In addition to these, you'll often see two-letter country code abbreviations (such as uk for the United Kingdom, ca for Canada, au for Australia, ch (yes, really) for Switzerland, and nl for the Netherlands).

Within each domain, there usually are subunits called *subdomains* and *subsubdomains* (yes, it does go deeper, but you get the point). A subdomain is a dedicated offshoot from a domain. For example, at nmsu.edu there are a number of special-purpose subdomains. Of interest to OS/2 users, however, is a subunit called os2.nmsu.edu. Usually called Hobbes, os2.nmsu.edu is a subdomain dedicated to OS/2. Among other things, Hobbes is an FTP (File Transfer Protocol) site where many OS/2 users obtain files—updates, fixes, and shareware—for OS/2.

Note the periods between the different parts of the subdomain name. The periods derive from the UNIX operating system, wherein periods are used to separate distinct parts of filenames. It's not unheard of for an Internet name to contain six or seven subparts, all connected with periods, such as the following newsgroup:

```
alt.binaries.pictures.erotica.bestiality.hamster.duct-tape
```

Yes, it really does exist, but I don't even want to *think* about what goes on there!

How Does the Warp Internet Access Kit Fit In?

So far, we've been talking about networks and their subunits. The second smallest conceptual subunit on the Internet is the *host*. The smallest subunit is an e-mail address—something like tyson@cpcug.org. Many Internet users log on to what are called shell accounts and never go beyond being the smallest subunit. The OS/2 Warp IAK provides the means for your computer to become one of the second-smallest subunits, or hosts, using a SLIP or PPP connection (more on these later in this book).

Note

> A shell account is a way of accessing the Internet using a modem and ordinary communications software. A shell account in itself provides access only using programs installed on the UNIX host system.

For many setups, although your e-mail address might be *name@host.suffix* (which enables you to receive mail even when you aren't logged on to the Internet), when you *are* logged on to the Internet, your computer will be visible as *name.host.suffix* (for example, tyson.cpcug.org), without the @. As a direct Internet player, you can connect your Internet client software to Internet servers for direct use of Gopher, FTP, and the World Wide Web directly on the Internet.

As a host, what exactly are you able to do? Does this mean you have to throw parties? No. Host is just one of those silly jargonistic terms. I'll warn you that its use is hardly standard, and you're likely to see it used in ways other than that defined here—and those other ways will be correct too. Very often, you will see the word *host* being used in a way that is synonymous with *server*. A server is a computer or computer program that provides an operating platform for client software. In the world of Internet, you'll hear about Gopher, FTP, World Wide Web, newsgroups, and mail servers. There are other servers as well. You will sometimes see these servers referred to as hosts.

At some point, it all boils down to the fact that a host is really an individual destination or address on the Internet. For receiving mail, pinging, fingering (no, this doesn't involve hamsters and duct tape), and doing a wide variety of other activities using the OS/2 Warp IAK, you are a host. In order to do some of those activities, however, you will have to log on to another host.

Looking now at the *server* meaning of the word *host*, the OS/2 IAK comes with a number of *client* programs for running on the Internet. They include NewsReader/2, the WebExplorer, FTP-PM (and FTP), TelnetPM (and Telnet and 3270 Telnet), Ultimedia Mail/2 Lite, as well as a number of small Internet utilities such as Ping and Finger.

The OS/2 Warp IAK is designed to work with SLIP (Serial Line/Internet Protocol) or PPP (Point-to-Point Protocol) accounts. SLIP and PPP accounts are connected to your computer using some kind of serial interface device, such as a modem connected to a communications (COM) port. You call your Internet provider's modem bank, issue the appropriate user ID and account number, and a set of electronic switches connects the data stream from your modem directly to the Internet. From then on, during that session, your computer can *talk* to any available computer on the Internet. In fact, you can literally *chat* with thousands of other users who are attached in the same way—see the discussion of Internet Relay Chat in Chapter 12, "Additional Internet Applications and Related Utilities," for details.

The Internet Culture

The Internet is a living, breathing example of libertarian democracy in action. Although you will find proponents of virtually every political, economic, and philosophical point of view represented, the Internet is amazingly tolerant. You will find pornography and art, bigotry and philanthropy, divorces and marriages, worthless crud and data goldmines, Jay Leno fans and David Letterman fans, all side-by-side on the Internet. It's a juxtapositionist's dream come true. All of it is crowded into one virtual universe.

For some reason, however, although you'll find a copious supply of diametrically opposed, opinionated rantings and zealotry, you will discover that one of the few things established citizens of the Internet won't tolerate is censorship. My own theory is that this is because of the academic roots in the Internet. Although academics come in all sizes, shapes, colors, flavors, and persuasions, they seem to agree on the *need* for the free flow of information and ideas.

Internet veterans tolerate newcomers. You are expected, however, in exchange for that toleration, to read something you don't know about, and something you might have to ask where to find: FAQs. An FAQ is a Frequently Asked Questions list. There are FAQs for virtually everything on the Internet. If you venture into an Internet newsgroup and ask a question that zillions before you have asked already, you will be told to RTFFAQ—*Read the &@*#-ing FAQ!* If you ask where to find it, you'll probably get a half-dozen copies e-mailed to you. So, to spare yourself *that*, keep your eyes open for the letters FAQ in everything you read. When you venture onto a Gopher, World Wide Web, or FTP site, be on the lookout for FAQs. Chances are good that there's an FAQ with exactly what you need to know.

How Does This Book Fit In?

The Internet is a virtual universe. It's a universe for which maps are almost useless because the landscape or netscape (if you allow that term in a generic way) changes hourly. The Warp IAK is a set of navigation tools designed to get you onto the Internet, and to let you cruise around once you're there. As maps are nearly useless in a fluid universe, you'll instead need some navigation aids: a compass, a sextant, and a telescope.

This book is a navigation aid for using the Internet from OS/2 Warp. I've written it to aid in your foray onto the Internet. I hope this book will help keep you from getting too terribly lost or bogged down in those tiny little backwaters known as bugs, often masquerading as features. I hope, too, that it can show you shortcuts and detours that keep you from getting sucked into black holes—such as "Password or UserID is invalid, return to your starbase."

CHAPTER TWO
THE OS/2 WARP
INTERNET ACCESS KIT

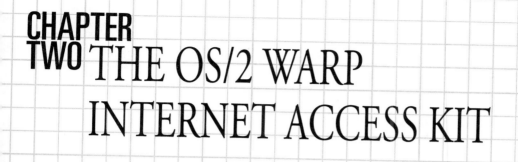

The IBM Internet Connection for OS/2 Folder

The OS/2 Warp Internet Access Kit Applications

The Internet is a network of computer networks. Armed with the appropriate accounts and passwords, you could cruise around the Internet, logging in here and there, obtaining whatever information you sought. To do this, however, you would need to be skilled at using UNIX and UNIX programs from the command line. That's because most of the systems that are on the Internet are UNIX-based. As difficult as learning DOS or OS/2 was, learning UNIX represents another magnitude of difficulty, largely because it's a very powerful and different operating system. It takes some users months before they really feel comfortable using it.

Rather than go through all that, however, there are a number of programs and utilities that make using the Internet much simpler. OS/2 Warp's Internet Access Kit comes with OS/2 versions of the most popular Internet tools and utilities, as well as some unique programs that provide access to electronic mail and other Internet features. The major tools provided are

Ultimedia Mail/2 Lite	Mail program for retrieving, reading, writing, replying, and sending electronic mail.
WebExplorer	OS/2's answer to Mosaic and Netscape, for navigating the World Wide Web.
Gopher	OS/2 program for navigating Gopher sites.
FTP-PM	OS/2 GUI program for downloading and uploading files.
NewsReader/2	OS/2 program for reading and replying to articles on the Usenet.

In this chapter, you'll take a short tour of the major features and tools in the IBM OS/2 Warp Internet Access Kit and also will learn how to get the WebExplorer and updates to other components. I offer some suggestions about how you might want to set up the IBM Internet Connection for OS/2 folder and show you how some of the applications work.

The IBM Internet Connection for OS/2 Folder

Depending on how you install the Internet Access Kit (IAK), there will be a folder called either the IBM Information Superhighway or the IBM Internet Connection for OS/2 on your OS/2 Desktop. If you have only the Superhighway folder, the Internet Connection folder will be in that folder. As shown in Figure 2.1, the default IBM Internet Connection for OS/2 folder contains the objects described in Table 2.1. If it's not already open, open the IBM Internet Connection for OS/2 folder. If you have not yet installed the IAK, see Appendix A, "Installing the OS/2 Warp Internet Access Kit."

FIGURE 2.1.

The Internet Access Kit tools are in the IBM Internet Connection for OS/2 folder.

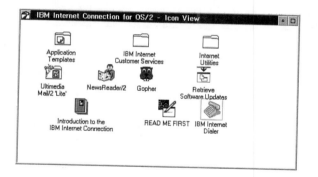

Table 2.1. The IBM Internet Connection for OS/2 folder contains several objects.

Object	Explanation
Application Templates	Folder containing templates for creating new objects for Telnet, FTP-PM, and 3270 Telnet.
NewsReader/2	OS/2 PM program for reading Usenet newsgroups.
Internet Utilities	Folder containing: Dial Other Internet Provider, Telnet, FTP-PM, and 3270 Telnet. For most users, the Dial Other Internet Provider dialer will be of more use than IBM Internet Dialer.
Gopher	OS/2 PM program for navigating Internet Gopher sites.
Retrieve Software Updates	Object for obtaining the WebExplorer and updates for other OS/2 Internet software.
Introduction	OS/2 .INF file containing an introduction to the IBM Internet Connection.
READ ME FIRST	If you're adventurous, don't read this!
IBM Internet Dialer	Dialer for accessing the Internet via the IBM Internet connection. If you are not using IBM as your provider, you should use the Dial Other Internet Provider dialer instead, in the Internet Utilities folder.
IBM Internet Customer Services	Folder containing Registration Services and Customer Assistance objects. If you register for this service, this folder also will contain

continues

Table 2.1. continued

Object	Explanation
	Account and UserID objects. *This folder is for users of the IBM Internet Dialer only.* If you use the Internet from a different provider, such as the Dial Other Internet Provider dialer, then the contents of this folder should not be of interest to you.
Ultimedia Mail/2 Lite	Folder containing an UltiMail Information folder and the four main components of Ultimedia Mail/2 Lite: Names and Addresses (Address Book), New Letter, Mail Cabinet, and In-basket.
WebExplorer, WEB README 1ST, and WEB README objects	OS/2 PM World Wide Web program and information. These objects (not shown) might not be present, depending on your version of OS/2 Warp.

Where's the WebExplorer?

Depending on which version of OS/2 Warp you have, the WebExplorer might not have been included, as *not shown* in Figure 2.1. The WebExplorer can be obtained online using the Retrieve Software Updates object. Follow these steps:

1. Double-click on the Retrieve Software Updates icon. After a few seconds, the dialog box shown in Figure 2.2 should appear.

2. Install the Descriptions item first, if desired. If you download that item, you will have to rerun the Retrieve Software Updates object after you're done. Then click on the WebExplorer item.

3. Click on the Install button.

4. The Update program will now download the update and install it on your system. After it's finished, you will be admonished to shut down and reboot. For installing the WebExplorer, this is not really necessary. For some other updates, however, it might be.

The process can take anywhere from 5 to 20 minutes depending on the speed of your hardware (including your modem) and on how busy the Internet is. When you're done, the WebExplorer, WEB README 1ST, and WEB README objects are added to the IBM Internet Connection for OS/2 folder.

Under some circumstances, the Retrieve Software Updates object will tell you that it couldn't find anything. Usually, opening the Retrieve Software Updates a second time will solve the problem. If that doesn't do it, you usually can fix the problem permanently by removing the `linkup.exe` program from the process. Open the Retrieve Software Updates object's Settings notebook. Replace `linkup.exe` with `update.exe` in the Path and Filename box. In the Parameters box, delete `update.exe` and the space that follows it, leaving just `/h updates.gopher.ibm.com`. Note: if you're uncomfortable modifying the built-in objects, then copy the Retrieve Software Updates object and modify your copy.

FIGURE 2.2.

The Retrieve Software Updates tool.

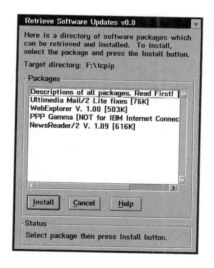

Setting Up Your Internet Access Kit Workspace

Depending upon how you use the Internet tools, you'll probably want to rearrange the furniture a little. For starters, if you choose to use a non-IBM Internet provider, you might do well to move the IBM Internet Dialer object into the IBM Internet Customer Services folder, and drag the Dial Other Internet Provider object (or a shadow of it) into the main IBM Internet Connection for OS/2 folder.

You might also want to put shadows of FTP-PM and Telnet into the IBM Internet Connection for OS/2 folder. The Ultimedia Mail/2 Lite components might also be handier from the IBM Internet Connection for OS/2 folder. You could, at the same time, drag any unused objects to a subfolder—such as Internet Utilities—so that they're out of the way. Likely candidates include the various Readme files (after you've read them) and the Introduction file (after you've been introduced).

For Experts Only

This information is designated for experts only just in case you mess something up and because it might involve more tinkering than most users are willing to do.

Caveat: Make a backup copy of everything before doing any of the following. Heck, if you can afford it, buy a duplicate computer and do this only on the duplicate.

Another useful thing you might want to do is make the IBM Internet Connection for OS/2 folder a *work area*. By designating a folder as a work area, each time you open the folder, all objects contained therein automatically open (depending on your folder settings). This makes it possible, for example, to open just the IBM Internet Connection for OS/2 folder, and have all of your OS/2 Internet tools laid out before you, ready to go. In fact, if you're using the IBM Internet Dialer, it can even hit the ground dialing (unfortunately, there does not appear to be a built-in way to get SLIPPM (the Dial Other Internet Provider object) to dial upon startup).

There is a problem with the work-area approach, however. As installed by IBM, all of the Internet clients—except for WebExplorer—use the `linkup.exe` program to start. The `linkup.exe` program checks to see if a SLIP or PPP connection is active before launching the respective programs. (If SLIP or PPP is *not* active, you are informed of that fact via the dialog box shown in Figure 2.3.) When the IBM Internet Connection for OS/2 folder first opens, a SLIP or PPP connection has not yet been established. This means that any SLIP clients you left open the last time will now grumble as `linkup.exe` tells you that SLIP/PPP is not active.

There is a way around this problem, however, if you're determined to make it work. You would need to modify all of the programs that use `linkup.exe` so that they no longer use it. Or, clone each of the objects, remove `linkup.exe` from each, and then use the clones for your Internet activities. For example, here's how to modify Gopher so that it doesn't gripe about the lack of a connection:

1. Open the Settings notebook for the Gopher object.
2. In the Path and Filename box, replace `linkup.exe` with `gopher.exe`.
3. Remove `gopher.exe` from the Parameters field.
4. Close the Settings notebook.

For each of the following objects, you would replace `linkup.exe` with the program name shown in the Parameters field:

Gopher	`gopher.exe`
NewsReader/2	`nr2.exe`
Retrieve Software Updates	`update.exe`

For FTP-PM, Telnet and UltiMail, however, you would need a different approach. The built-in FTP-PM and Telnet objects' Settings notebooks do not have a Program tab. You can, instead, create new program objects based on `ftppm.exe` and `telnetpm.exe`.

Create these objects using the regular Program template in the main OS/2 Templates folder rather than using the FTP-PM and Telnet templates in the IBM Internet Connection for OS/2 folder's Application Templates folder. The new objects will lack the FTP-PM and Telnet-specific controls that the original object have. However, they won't be hampered by linkup.exe. See Chapter 9, "Sending and Receiving Files with FTP," for more about creating new FTP-PM objects.

For UltiMail, you would create a program object using umail.exe as the executable file. Unlike with the Telnet object, you don't really lose anything when you create a UMAIL object, because the default Mail Cabinet object doesn't have an object-accessible Settings notebook. Instead, Mail Cabinet settings are available only after Mail Cabinet is running.

To make the IBM Internet Connection for OS/2 folder a work area:

1. Open the Settings notebook for the IBM Internet Connection for OS/2 folder.
2. Click on the File tab.
3. Click to enable the Work area checkbox.
4. Close the IBM Internet Connection for OS/2 folder.

Now, when you open the IBM Internet Connection for OS/2 folder, everything in it will be opened up exactly as you left it (except for UltiMail objects—see the next paragraph). When you close or minimize the IBM Internet Connection for OS/2 folder, everything is closed or minimized. You should repeat this procedure for all subfolders contained in the IBM Internet Connection for OS/2 folder, as well. That way, their programs will be closed too.

Why don't the UltiMail programs close? For some reason, perhaps related to the kinds of objects that the Mail Cabinet and In-basket are, they do not close when the Ultimedia Mail/2 Lite folder closes, even if (as you should) you make the Ultimedia Mail/2 Lite folder a work area. You can, however, create a normal OS/2 object for UltiMail, which will then open and close with the UltiMail folder.

FIGURE 2.3.

The linkup command tells you that you're not connected.

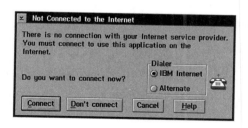

The OS/2 Warp Internet Access Kit Applications

The Internet Access Kit comprises more than 60 executable programs. Of these, six garner the most attention. Let's take a brief look at each. For complete information, see the full coverage in Chapters 5 through 10.

Ultimedia Mail/2 Lite—Electronic Mail

Ultimedia Mail/2 Lite is an electronic mail (*e-mail*) program for OS/2. E-mail is the computerized exchange of private (well, semi-private) messages among Internet users. Suppose that you wanted to send an e-mail letter to the White House. You can. Just address it to feedback@www.whitehouse.gov. Will they answer? Who knows?

The Ultimedia Mail/2 Lite program is accessed from the Ultimedia Mail/2 Lite folder, shown in Figure 2.4. Ultimedia Mail/2 Lite provides tools for reading incoming e-mail (In-basket), creating outgoing e-mail (New Letter), managing your e-mail (Mail Cabinet), and maintaining a list of correspondents (Names and Addresses). For detailed information on using Ultimedia Mail/2 Lite, see Chapter 5. For information on some alternatives to Ultimedia Mail/2 Lite, see Chapter 12, "Additional Internet Applications and Related Utilities."

FIGURE 2.4.

The Ultimedia Mail/2 Lite folder.

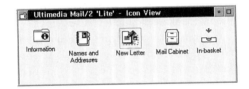

NewsReader/2—Newsgroups

One of the most popular hangouts on the Internet is something called *newsgroups*. Newsgroups are open discussion areas in which almost every imaginable topic is discussed. As I'm writing this, there are over 10,000 newsgroups just waiting for you. In newsgroups, you'll stand side-by-side with some of the world's leaders in the areas of government, computing, education, science, and religion. You'll also be shoulder-to-shoulder with crackpots, anarchists, ax murderers, pornographers, and politicians. It sends shivers up my spine just thinking about it.

The OS/2 Internet Access Kit's NewsReader/2 program gives you quick and easy access to all this, and more. You'll also be able to read David Letterman's Top Ten lists and find out close-up what Sirajul and Mujibar are *really* like. For complete coverage of NewsReader/2, see Chapter 6.

OS/2 Gopher—Gopherspace

There are many ways of looking at information on the Internet. A few years ago, some enterprising programmers at the University of Minnesota did the Internet community a favor by developing an easy-access method called *Gopher*. Using Gopher, you can access tons of information on hundreds of Gopher servers all around the world (sometimes called *Gopherspace*). Gopher also gives you access to files, pictures, and noises, as well as the latest in OS/2 fixes and patches. For complete information on the OS/2 Gopher program, see Chapter 7.

WebExplorer—The World Wide Web

In competition with Gopher for providing easy access to the resources on the Internet is the *World Wide Web*. The World Wide Web is an ambitious attempt to make all of the public resources available on the Internet accessible from a single, graphical (usually), easy-to-use interface. Using OS/2's WebExplorer, you'll be able to visit art museums and libraries, see weather maps, read newsgroups, visit Gopher sites, and participate in online surveys. Visit the North Pole home page and send a letter to Santa. Visit the White House and listen to Socks meow, or… was that Bill, playing the saxophone? Whatever it was, see Chapter 8 for the full scoop.

FTP-PM—File Transfer Protocol Sites

On the Internet, you have access to thousands upon thousands of files. In these files you'll find data, programs, and information. You'll find games, shareware, freeware, and even something called underware. (I'll leave it to you to discover what that is.) The OS/2 access kit gives you both PM and text-mode FTP programs for accessing all that information. See Chapter 9 for a full exploration of FTP and FTP-PM, as well as useful places to get OS/2 files.

Note

> PM stands for Presentation Manager. PM refers to the graphical API (Applications Programming Interface) that underlies OS/2's GUI (Graphical User Interface). OS/2 users and developers often contrast *text-mode* programs that don't use any graphics (such as telnet and FTP) with *Presentation Manager* or PM programs that do use graphics for display (such as TelnetPM and FTP-PM).

TelnetPM—Netfind and Other Telnet Hosts

Although Gopher, the World Wide Web, FTP, Ultimedia Mail/2 Lite, and NewsReader/2 all provide easy ways to access many of the Internet's most popular and important resources, there remain some things for which comparable easy-access tools have not yet emerged. If you have a typical (non-IBM) Internet account, for example, some administrative chores—such as changing your password—can be performed only from an interactive telnet session (or a session using some other terminal-emulation program).

Another terminal-only activity involves using something called *Netfind*. Netfind is a way to try to locate someone on the Internet. It is a program that searches the Internet for someone for you—using the `finger` command, which you'll learn about in Chapter 11, "Other Warp Internet Tools and Programs." There are about a dozen Netfind servers on the Internet, worldwide, and you're most likely to find them while Gophering or Webbing. When you do find them, however, you'll see a little picture of a terminal. That's your reminder of just how much the Internet has changed over the past few years (from an archaic system where you pound the terminal keyboard at the UNIX command line to a refined system that uses sophisticated tools such as the WebExplorer). To get Netfind to search, however, you'll have to feed it information the old-fashioned way (that is, pounding away at the keyboard).

You'll also find games and other programs that can be accessed only using Telnet or 3270 Telnet. So, when you're surfing the net at warp speed, and you suddenly see a Telnet icon, that's your signal to get out and walk the WebExplorer across the intersection. For full information on the wonderful world of antiques, see Chapter 10, "Connecting to Other Systems Using Telnet."

CHAPTER THREE

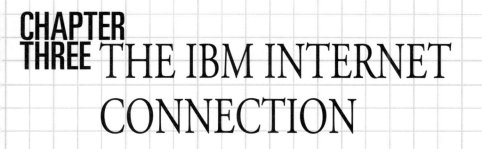

THE IBM INTERNET CONNECTION

The easiest way to get onto the Internet is using the IBM Internet Connection (IIC) through the IBM Global Network. The IIC provides high quality international access to the Internet. If you don't need the extra services and international coverage provided by IIC, it's probably worth a few minutes of your time to shop around for the best possible rate. However, if you need a reliable provider, with easy setup, and without the hassles of busy signals, then the IIC just might fit the bill.

What Is Advantis?

You might hear a number of OS/2 users on the Internet refer to the IBM Internet Connection as Advantis. IBM will tell you that, technically, that's not exactly correct. Advantis is the U.S. provider for something called the IBM Global Network, one of whose "products" is the *IBM Internet Connection.*

In this chapter, when I mention Advantis or the IBM Internet Connection, I'm talking about using IBM as your provider through Advantis—I'm *not* talking about the whole Internet Access Kit for OS/2 Warp, despite the fact that the folder installed by IBM is called the IBM OS/2 Internet Connection (which sometimes invites confusion). Note that one has the term *OS/2* in it, and the other does not. If you're confused about the naming, you're not alone.

However, regardless of what the IBM Internet access service is called, the purpose of this chapter is to describe using the Internet through the IBM Internet Connection, which is handled by the IBM Global Network. If you are connecting using a different provider, such as Netcom or Digex, see Chapter 4, "Connecting to Other (Non-IBM) Internet Providers."

The purpose of this chapter is to save you a little time and to save you from surprises. If you read through this whole chapter before you connect with the IBM Internet Connection, you'll know what to expect, and you'll know how to make the most of your three hours free trial when exploring what the Internet has to offer.

Note

If you must access the IBM Internet Connection with an 800 access number, there is a $6-per-hour access charge, even during the three-hour trial period, according to IBM. However, when I tried the 800 number during my trial subscription, I never got billed for the 30 minutes or so I used it (not yet, at least), and they didn't even know I was writing a book about it at the time! Just the same, you can't count on not being charged, and so be prepared for it to show up on your credit card statement.

Registration and Setup

Getting up and running with the IBM Internet Connection is extremely simple. If you're in a hurry to get started with the Internet, using IBM as your provider often is much faster than obtaining a SLIP or PPP account from another Internet provider. When I got my SLIP account from my current provider, it took about three weeks for the IP number to get assigned, and another week to get all of the software set up correctly. In contrast, when I signed up with The IBM Internet Connection, I was up and running within a matter of minutes.

Registration

To register to use the IBM Internet Connection, open the IBM Internet Customer Services folder in the IBM Internet Connection for OS/2 folder. Then open the Registration object, as shown in Figure 3.1. Your choices are as follows:

◆ *Open a personal account*—Choose this option to begin the registration process for an individual.

◆ *Open a business account* (not available at this writing)—Same as above, but for businesses rather than individuals.

◆ *Learn about the Internet*—A brief description of the Internet.

◆ *Learn about this service*—A description of the different types of services offered by the IBM Internet Connection.

◆ *Learn about the IBM Network*—Surprise! It's the same as the preceding choice.

FIGURE 3.1.

The Registration object.

Telephone Support for the IBM Global Network Technical Support (1-800-727-2222 in the U.S.) is available as follows:

◆ Connection question and problems—24 hours a day, 7 days a week

◆ Technical assistance—10 a.m. to 2 a.m. (Eastern U.S. time), 7 days a week

◆ Billing and administrative assistance—9 a.m. to 7 p.m. (Eastern U.S. time), Monday through Friday

For other times, open the Customer Assistance object in the IBM Internet Customer Services folder, and click on Ask for help.

After reading through about the Internet and IBM, click on the Open a personal account option. This begins the registration process, as shown in Figure 3.2. The first window (IBM Internet Service Terms and Conditions, window 1 of 5) alerts you to the fact that there are charges associated with registration. Read the description carefully before proceeding. Then, if you agree to the terms, click OK.

FIGURE 3.2.

Opening an IBM Internet Connection account.

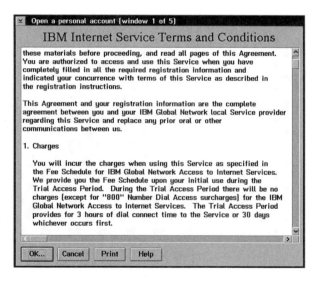

The first page does *not* tell you the pricing for the IBM Internet Connection access to the Internet. That's because it's subject to change. The IBM Internet Service Terms and Conditions page mentions a Fee Schedule that you will see when you register. There's a catch-22 in that you can't find out the fees until you go through the registration process. If you're leery of sending your credit card number without knowing the prices, relax. You will have ample opportunity to say "no" if the terms don't meet with your approval.

If you still prefer to know in advance before transmitting your credit card number, then—in the U.S.—you can call 1-800-727-2222 for the current pricing. After you find out the current pricing, you also might want to do some comparison shopping to see if other Internet service providers offer a better deal. Just as a point of reference, fees from other providers typically range from $20 to $50 per month for SLIP access, providing four to six hours of daily connect time (some provide unlimited connect time). See Appendix C, "Internet Resources for OS/2," for a list of other Internet providers.

Do You Really Need 800 Access to the IBM Internet Connection?

One advantage of the IBM Internet Connection system is that there are local access numbers in most urban areas in the U.S., as well as in urban areas in a number of other countries. If you *do* have to access the IBM Internet Connection using an 800 number, then the cost might be prohibitive. To find out if the IBM Internet Connection access will require 800 access, if you're in the U.S., call 1-800-727-2222. Follow the voice prompts to enter your area code and dialing exchange (if your telephone number is 1-804-555-1212, for example, then you'll enter 804 and then 555, when prompted). You will then be given your "least cost dial number."

After you click OK, the Registration object shows you the second window (Owner Account Information, window 2 of 5). Fill out all the data requested, as shown in Figure 3.3, and click OK. Once you click OK to this screen, all your registration information so far—except for your credit card number—is saved to \TCPIP\ETC\ADVANTIS.INI. If you cancel (during the current registration session) or choose the Register some other time option, you will have to re-enter only your credit card number.

FIGURE 3.3.

Owner account information.

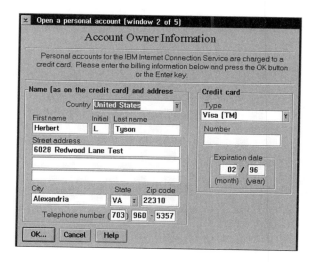

ADVANTIS.INI is an OS/2 system .INI file that cannot be edited with a text editor. You should not need to edit it. I'm only telling you about it so you'll know where your registration information is kept, just in case you need to be satisfied that your credit card number isn't being stored on your hard disk. Also, it lets you know what file to back up if you want to preserve your registration information. ADVANTIS.INI is a hidden file. Like other OS/2 .INI files, it is renamed with an extension of .!!! whenever TCP/IP is running. It can be backed up, however by using xcopy advantis.ini *backupfile* /t. The /t switch enables copying files that have the system attribute; for example:

```
xcopy advantis.ini advantis.bak /t
```

When you click OK in the Owner Account Information window, the next window (Modem Configuration, window 3 of 5) is displayed, as shown in Figure 3.4. Choose your modem, a registration telephone number appropriate for your country, the COM port to which your modem is connected, a dial prefix (many business phone systems require a number or code to get an outside telephone line), and the type of dialing (pulse or tone) required. Then click OK.

FIGURE 3.4.
Modem configuration.

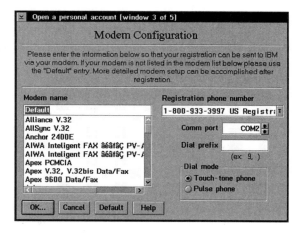

Modem information for the IBM Internet Connection registration is kept in a file called \tcpip\etc\modem.1st. Some of the information in this file might be wrong for your modem, especially if you don't find an exact match. If the settings for your modem don't work, then try the Default entry. If that doesn't work, then make a copy of modem.1st (such as modem.old) and then open modem.1st with a text editor. Before doing this, make sure that the Modem Configuration page of the registration object is not open (but you need not close the registration object altogether; it rereads the modem.1st file each time the Modem Configuration page is loaded). Find the entry for your modem, and—using the documentation for your modem—edit the setup string so it is correct for your modem. Make a copy of the modified version of modem.1st (such as modem.new), and then retry Registration. The reason you need to make a copy of the modified version is that when you finally get onto the Internet, the software will update your modem list—along with some of the other Internet software. You'll want to keep your modified modem file around just in case IBM's modified list still isn't correct for your modem.

After choosing modem configuration information, the User ID Preferences (window 4 of 5) is displayed, as shown in Figure 3.5. This perhaps is the most important window so far. This will become part of your e-mail address on the Internet. This is the name by which you will be known on the Internet. The most popular choices often are just a last name, or a first initial and a last name. If you want people to recognize your ID easily, try to include an element of your first and last name. For example, I might choose htyson. The IBM Internet Connection limits you to 5 to 7 characters. Choose your ID preferences and click OK.

FIGURE 3.5.
User ID preferences.

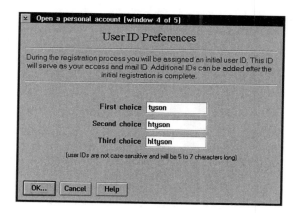

Now you're down to the home stretch: Registration Confirmation (window 5 of 5). Following are your options:

Send registration to IBM	This option dials the telephone and sends your registration information to IBM.
Review information	This option steps you back through windows 1 through 5.
Register some other time	This option saves most of your registration information in ADVANTIS.INI, and takes you back to the main IBM Internet Connection Service Registration window.

When you click on Send registration, the registration process dials the telephone, showing the progress, as shown in Figure 3.6. If you don't get an answer, then keep trying. The registration servers (the computers that perform registration) are supposed to operate 24 hours a day, 7 days a week. If the phone answers but registration doesn't work, then back up and check your modem settings carefully.

FIGURE 3.6.

*The Dialing Progress
window.*

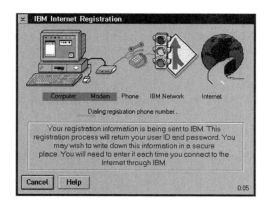

When your modem connects with the IBM Internet registration server, it will take about a minute before anything concrete happens, depending on how busy the system is. You will be shown the current fee schedule, as shown in Figure 3.7. If you decide not to proceed, click No. If you decide to go ahead, then click Yes.

FIGURE 3.7.

*The IBM Internet
Connection shows you the
current fee schedule when
registering.*

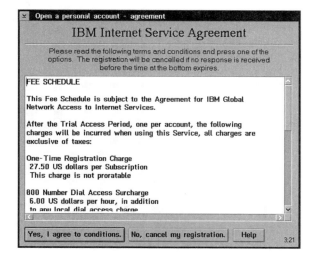

Note

Don't Panic. When you click Yes, the telephone will disconnect almost immediately. The usual reaction is to get alarmed and think that you've been cut off, wondering now whether you've been registered correctly. Relax, after a few seconds (if you're panicking, it actually will seem like about an hour), the Registration Complete message will appear on screen, as shown in Figure 3.8.

FIGURE 3.8.

Write down the information from the Registration Complete screen.

When you get the Registration Complete message, take a moment to write down all the information—or press the PrintScreen key to get OS/2 to print the information to a piece of paper—and put it in a secure place. Although the software does write most of the information on your hard disk, this does not provide protection if you have a disk crash before your next backup. Once you've reviewed the information, click OK to proceed.

> Write your password down! The software does not save your password to disk. You must write it down, memorize it, or press the PrintScreen key.

The registration program next displays the Access Phone Number Selection screen for you to select the telephone numbers from which you will access the IBM Internet Connection, as shown in Figure 3.9. If you are calling from a large metropolitan area, there often will be multiple numbers to which you can connect without incurring 800 access charges. Select your first choice in the Primary phone number section, and your second choice in the Backup phone number section. Try not to make your backup phone number an 800 number unless it's necessary. Note that the backup number also can be the same as the primary number, which means simply that the dialer will keep trying the same number.

> Depending on your location, it often is necessary to edit the telephone numbers to eliminate the 1 and area code. In my area, for example, the Primary phone number was within my dialing exchange. I certainly didn't need to precede it with the area code.

After making your telephone number selections, click OK. All the numbered registration windows will be closed, and you will be returned to the main Internet Registration window. Click Close.

FIGURE 3.9.

Choose your access phone numbers carefully; don't use the 800 numbers unless absolutely necessary.

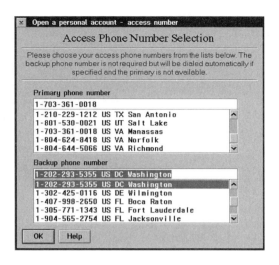

Registration Information

After you complete registration, your account information is stored in the IBM Internet Customer Services folder, as shown in Figure 3.10. Note that your password is *not* stored there. The other information is stored on disk, but you either must write down or memorize your password (but, see "Connecting to the Internet the First Time After Registration" for a way to avoid having to type your password each time).

FIGURE 3.10.

Your account information is stored in the IBM Internet Customer Services folder.

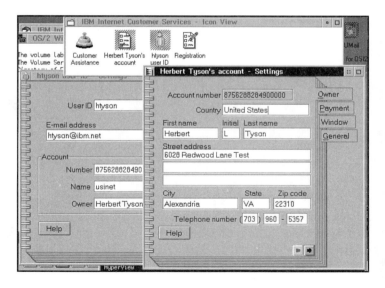

Making the Most of Your Three-Hour Tour

Once you are registered, you have three hours of free trial (plus $6 an hour if you must call using an 800 access line) that begins when you connect to the Internet using the IBM Internet Dialer. Time flies when you're connected to the Internet, so use that three hours wisely. To avoid any charges at all—in the event that you decide to cancel your IBM Internet Connection account—the first three hours are crucial. Once you go beyond three hours, you not only in-cur a full month's charge, but the registration fee as well.

Connecting to the Internet the First Time After Registration

Once registration is complete, you can connect with the Internet using the IBM Internet Dialer, located in the IBM Internet Connection folder, shown in Figure 3.11. Start the dialer by double-clicking on the IBM Internet Dialer icon.

FIGURE 3.11.
The IBM Internet Dialer.

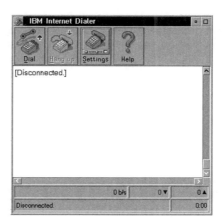

Tip

Before you open the IBM Internet Dialer, check the Dialer settings to make sure your mo-dem is set up to connect at the highest supported speed. If you have a 14,400 modem and if the IBM Internet Connection supports that rate, you typically would set your modem to a port speed that is much higher (often 38,400 or 57,600). How high you can set it de-pends upon a number of factors, including whether the modem is internal or external and whether or not you have a 16550UART-based I/O card. You might need to consult your modem documentation to determine an appropriate setting.

You should check the modem settings because, often, your connection and other param-eters have not yet been optimized. For example, if you chose the Default modem setup in the registration process, and if you have a modem capable of connecting at 14,400 or higher, you often will discover that the default baud setting is for 9,600, which is not opti-mum. Because connect time isn't free, you will benefit by maximizing your connect speed before proceeding. All the settings are covered in the section titled "IBM Internet

Dialer Settings" section presented later in this chapter. However, a few preliminary settings should be covered here:

1. Display the object settings for the IBM Internet Dialer (click mouse button 2 on the dialer icon and click settings). The Settings notebook opens, as shown in Figure 3.12.

2. If you want to have complete control, deselect the Dial when loaded and Minimize when loaded options for now. Otherwise, you will immediately lose visual contact with what you're doing when the dialer starts.

3. Click the Modem page, for the view shown in Figure 3.13.

4. Verify that the Modem, Command strings, Speed, and Comm Port are correct and optimal for your modem; make any changes that are necessary. To save your changes to the modem list, click Add to modem list.

5. Click the Logging page. By default, the dialer logs all connections with the Internet through the IBM Internet Connection. The default log size will record about 65 connections, and will then queue out old entries (about 30 percent of the list) when the log reaches the maximum size. When you're just getting started, it's useful to keep accurate information about connections so you can get an idea of how much the IBM Internet Connection is costing you. I recommend that you initially change the maximum log file size to at least 100KB. Once you've determined your operating habits, you then can set the size back down to something smaller, or disable the log altogether. See "IBM Internet Dialer Settings" for additional recommendations and reasons.

6. Make any other changes you see fit at this time, if desired, and close the Settings notebook (press Alt+F4).

FIGURE 3.12.

The IBM Internet Dialer — Settings notebook; the Phone page.

FIGURE 3.13.

The IBM Internet Dialer Modem settings page.

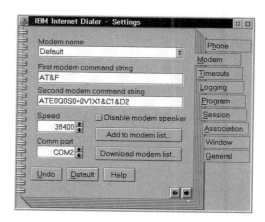

When you open the IBM Internet Dialer the first time, it hits the ground running by starting to dial the telephone. It also prompts you for your password, as shown in Figure 3.14. To continue at this point, type your password and press Enter. To cancel the call without closing the Dialer, click Cancel.

FIGURE 3.14.

The IBM Internet Dialer prompts you for your password. See the following sidebar to make it more automatic.

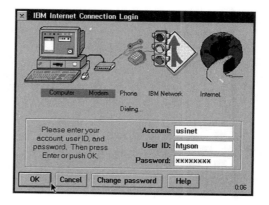

Automatic Password!

Some people think it's bothersome to have to type a password each time you call the Internet. If you are a SOHO (small office home office) or home user, all that cloak and dagger stuff really gets annoying after a while. Well, you don't have to put up with it! The IBM Internet Dialer object enables you to include your account (usinet in the U.S.), your user ID, and password (separated by spaces) in the parameters field. So, open the Settings notebook for the Dialer, click on the Program page (see Figure 3.15), and inscribe your information so that you don't have to memorize (although, that's still not a bad idea) and type your password each time you call the Internet.

If you use this tip, keep in mind that your password will be visible each time you display the Program page of the IBM Internet Dialer Settings notebook. Thus, you should use this tip only if security is not an issue for you.

FIGURE 3.15.

The IBM Internet Dialer Program page.

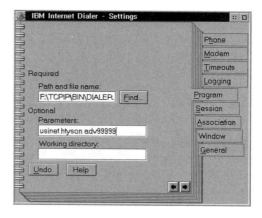

Tip

Do you have more than one user on your account? For example, you can have distinct user IDs for yourself, your spouse, your kids, or your pets (hey, I wonder if Socks has an account—try socks@whitehouse.gov). If you do have multiple user IDs (or even multiple accounts) you can create separate dialer objects for each user. Just follow these steps:

1. Click mouse button 2 on the IBM Internet Dialer object and then click on Copy. The Copy dialog box will appear, as shown in Figure 3.16.

2. Type a distinct name for the new dialer object (such as *Bob's IBM Dialer*), choose an appropriate folder (such as the IBM Internet Connection for OS/2 folder), and click on Copy.

3. Now open the Settings notebook for the new dialer object, and click on the Program tab.

4. Type your account name (usinet in the U.S.), your user ID, and your password into the parameters field, separated only by spaces.

5. Close the Settings notebook.

FIGURE 3.16.

The Copy dialog box.

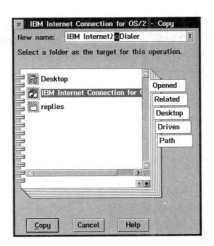

If you type your password and continue, the Dialer displays the window shown in Figure 3.17. Note the parts of the window and the information or function they provide. Note also the mouse button 2 popup menu in the Connection dialog box. If you want, you can use the mouse (or keys) to select text in the dialog box and copy it to the Clipboard or to a file. This sometimes is handy if an unusual message is displayed. Once the connection is ready, a message to start your SLIP software appears.

FIGURE 3.17.

The IBM Internet Dialer window shows the connection dialog box.

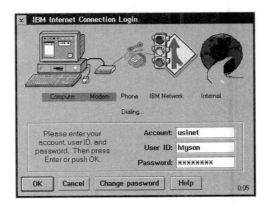

Waiting for Authentication

It's not something you've done! On occasion, the IBM Internet Connection gets disconnected. When the Internet part of the IBM Global Network is not functioning, your modem might nonetheless connect and your account (usinet in the U.S.) and user ID will be accepted. When your password is entered, however, the system then will discover that the connection to the Internet is not working. It will sit there, possibly for several minutes, displaying the message Waiting for authentication.

Mercifully, the Dialer is less patient than I am and eventually comes back with a message that suggests you might have done something wrong—such as entered a bad password, dialed the wrong phone number, had bad breath, or cheated on your taxes. Relax. The authentication problem is almost always a problem with the system. Such interruptions usually are short lived (IBM will tell you such interruptions are *growing pains*, and it must be true because alternate providers will tell you the same thing).

If, however, you always get that message—over the course of several days—then maybe it really *is* your breath. To find out, call 1-800-727-222 (in the U.S., click the Customer Assistance's Help box to find other numbers) and ask whether or not the system is having a problem. Tell them that you're having a `Waiting for authentication` problem, and they'll know what you're talking about. If it's a problem on your end, they'll also know how to fix it (usually).

Once you're online, you also might take a look in `ibmnet.news.admin` using NewsReader/2. You'll get a wealth of information from other users and representatives from IBM. Reading the news there for a day or so will help you get a better feel for the IBM Internet Connection, letting you know what's common and what's not. It's also a good place to get questions answered.

To Update or Not to Update—That Is the Question

When you connect to the Internet the first time after registration, you invariably will be informed that your Internet dialer and other data (modem and phone lists) need to be updated, and that the process will take from 3 to 20 minutes. At connect speeds of 9,600 or higher, the process usually takes about 10 minutes or less (now you see why it's important to set your speed up before you connect). It's usually a good idea to go ahead and update the dialer software at some point—but read the next paragraph before doing so.

If you aren't sure you're going to keep your IBM Internet Connection, and if you want to use as much of your three free hours as possible for just looking around, then you can say No to updating the dialer. If you do, you always can go back later and retrieve the updates using the Update Software option in the Customer Assistance object in the IBM Internet Customer Services folder.

If you agree to download the updates, the whole process is automatic. Just cross your fingers and hope that you don't get disconnected during the process (if it does disconnect, you'll have to do it all over again). After downloading the software, you'll be prompted to confirm the installation directory (usually `TCPIP` on the drive where the IBM Internet tools are installed). Click Install to proceed. You will be prompted to confirm closing the Internet Dialer before installation can continue. Click Yes.

Depending on the speed of your system, the Installation dialog box will linger on your screen for a few seconds, tempting you to click on Install again. *Don't click on Install again.* It's not necessary. After a few more seconds (perhaps 20 to 40 depending on the speed of your system), you will see another dialog box telling you to shutdown and restart OS/2. Click OK, and then click Close to close the Installation dialog box. Then shut down and reboot—it's necessary for the reinstalled components to work correctly.

Connecting the Second Time After Registration

The second time you connect to the Internet after registration, you will receive many notices about new services, rates, or other features. They are presented in dialog boxes. If you see any that interest you, write down the information. The bulletins will not be repeated until and unless information in them changes. Once you've disposed of the preliminary messages, you now can start any of the following Internet client applications:

◆ Retrieve Software Updates—While it seems a shame to expend your three hours free trial on a possibly unnecessary download, you might need to exercise this option if you want to try the WebExplorer. Depending on the version of OS/2 Warp you have, you might not have the WebExplorer yet. The latest version can be obtained using the Retrieve Software Updates object. See Chapter 11, "Other Warp Internet Tools and Programs," for additional information.

◆ Ultimedia Mail/2 Lite—Use UltiMail (as it's called) to send and receive e-mail. See Chapter 5, "Handling E-Mail with Ultimedia Mail/2 Lite," for additional information.

◆ NewsReader/2—Use NR/2 to explore Usenet; over 10,000 discussion groups covering almost every conceivable topic. See Chapter 6, "Reading News with NewsReader/2," for additional information.

◆ Gopher—Use Gopher to explore Gopherspace, which is a collection of resources, pictures, information, programs, and data—all accessible using a very simple and fast interface. See Chapter 7, "Navigating with OS/2 Gopher," for additional information.

◆ WebExplorer—Use the WebExplorer, the Internet's slickest tool, to surf the cream of the Internet crop. Use it carefully, however, because it's addictive and it's easy to use up all of your free trial time in a single WebExplorer session. See Chapter 8, "Navigating the Web with the WebExplorer," for additional information.

◆ FTP-PM—Use FTP-PM to download and upload software from computers all over the world. See Chapter 9, "Sending and Receiving Files with FTP," or additional information.

◆ Telnet—Use Telnet to log on to remote systems (if you have dialup access to those sites through other means, however, you might consider using them rather than Telnet. When you use telnet through the IBM Internet Connection, your free trial time and, later, your hourly access (local and/or 800) charges apply. See Chapter 10, "Connecting to Other Systems Using Telnet," for additional information.

See Chapter 2, "The OS/2 Warp Internet Access Kit," for an introduction to each of these resources. See the specific chapters for more detailed information.

Are You Using Your Bandwidth?

You are not limited to using one application at a time while on the Internet. It's not uncommon for users to have more than one of the SLIP applications open at the same time. NewsReader/2, FTP-PM, the WebExplorer, Gopher, and Ultimedia Mail/2 Lite can all be open and working at the same time. For example, suppose you're downloading a file from Australia, and the throughput indicator on the IBM Internet Dialer (showing b/s, for bytes per second for the past 20 seconds) says that you're only averaging 500 bytes per second— hey, it happens. When you're working a link halfway around the world, data packets might take a little while to get from point A to point B.

In any event, if your modem is capable of data rates of 1600 bytes per second or higher, and the current download is dragging along at 500 bytes per second, then there is a lot of room in your Internet bandwidth for using some other applications. Why not open NewsReader/2 and see what's being said on `comp.os.os2.advocacy`; open the WebExplorer and see what's on tap at the Louvre (`http://mistral.enst.fr/~pioch/louvre`); or, refresh the In-basket in Ultimedia Mail/2 Lite to see if anyone has sent you mail?

The IBM Internet SLIP Connection

The IBM Internet SLIP connection you get uses a dynamic IP address. A different IP address is assigned each time you connect to the Internet. It sometimes might be the same, but that's not guaranteed. While you are connected to the Internet, you actually are directly on the Internet. However, you can't reliably give someone your IP address as a connection point. The assigned IP address is displayed in the dialer window, and is recorded in `\TCPIP\ETC\CONNECT.LOG`.

IBM Internet Dialer Settings

Once it's set up correctly, most users won't have to use the Dialer Settings notebook. In fact, many users never access the Settings notebook at all. In this section, you look at each of the settings and learn when and why you might need to use them.

You can open the IBM Internet Dialer Settings notebook in the following several ways:

◆ Click mouse button 2 on the IBM Internet Dialer object, then click on the Settings option in the popup menu.

◆ Press and hold down the Alt button and double-click mouse button 1 on the IBM Internet Dialer.

◆ Select the IBM Internet Dialer object and press Alt+Enter.

◆ Click the Settings button in the IBM Internet Dialer window.

When you open the Settings notebook for the IBM Internet Dialer, the Phone page is displayed (see Figure 3.18). Note that the IBM Internet Dialer Settings notebook is similar to that for most other OS/2 program objects, in that it has Program, Session, Association, Window, and General pages. In addition, however, it has special pages for Phone, Modem, Timeouts, and Logging, which is discussed in the following sections.

FIGURE 3.18.

*The IBM Internet Dialer
Phone page.*

Phone

Use the *Phone* page settings to set the primary and backup phone numbers. To select a phone number, click on the arrow to the right of the entry field, as shown in Figure 3.19. If the telephone number you choose is within your dialing area, you might need to delete the area code. If the entire phone number is selected, press the Home key to move the text cursor to the beginning of the entry field, and press the Delete key until 1-800 has been removed. If you are in a large metropolitan area, such as the Washington, D.C. area, you might need to remove just the initial 1-, since calling local 202, 301, or 703 numbers from within the DC area requires an area code, but not the 1-.

FIGURE 3.19.

*Click the drop-down arrow
to show the list of numbers.*

Using the mouse, click the drop-down arrow (to the right of the displayed phone number) to show the list of numbers. Both Primary and Backup lists contain the same telephone numbers—from PHONE.LST. If you make changes to the numbers, or if you add numbers that aren't on the list, you can save your changes. First, add some descriptive text following the phone number to explain what the number is (for example, Modified Manassas Number, as shown in Figure 3.20). Then, click on the Add to phone list option. The Add to phone list option adds your numbers to a file named TCPIP\ETC\PHONE.USR. Telephone numbers in PHONE.USR are included at the top of the drop-down lists of Primary and Backup phone numbers (from PHONE.LST), making your own numbers easier to select.

FIGURE 3.20.

Custom phone number entries in the IBM Internet Dialer – Settings notebook are stored in PHONE.USR.

Use the Dial prefix option to indicate any necessary dialing code for getting an outside line. Many businesses use 9. Use the Dial mode choices to indicate what type of dialing the modem needs to perform: Tone (the default) or Pulse (old-fashioned rotary dialing).

> Tone or Pulse? Even if you have a rotary telephone, most areas in the U.S., Canada, and Europe support both tone dialing and pulse dialing. Tone dialing is much faster and less error prone. Unless your system absolutely does not support tone dialing, do not use the Pulse option.

The Dial when loaded option indicates whether you want the dialer to begin dialing the telephone when you open the IBM Internet Dialer object. Dialing when first opened is the default. If you want this as the default, but sometimes don't want it to dial, you will have to remember to click the Cancel button when the Dialer window appears.

The Minimize when loaded option causes the IBM Internet Dialer to be minimized when the dialing window appears and the Dial when loaded option is in use.

You use the Download phone list button to initiate a download of the latest PHONE.LST file from IBM. This choice corresponds to the Phone List option available from the Customer

Assistance object. To get the latest phone list using the Customer Assistance object (in the IBM Internet Customer Services folder), open Customer Assistance, click on Update software, click on Download latest software, and then click on Phone List. The option to download the phone list can be exercised only if you are already connected to the Internet. If you are getting satisfactory results from your current selection, then don't bother with this option.

The Show detailed information option causes the Dialer to display the entire dialog as you are connecting to the Internet as ilustrated by the following. If you are experiencing connection problems, the Show detailed information option often can help you find the problem.

```
[IBM Internet Dialer version 1.2]
[OS/2 2.3.0  486  16M  CP 437]
[Sun Jan 15 07:50:28 1995]
['F:\TCPIP\ETC\DIALER.INI' used]
['F:\TCPIP\ETC\TCPOS2.INI' used]
[Opening the Comm port...]
[open 'COM2']
[Initializing the Comm port...]
[set comm port DCB settings]
[set line control to 8, none, 1]
[set speed to 38400]
[speed set to 38400]
[DTR off]
[DTR on]
[Initializing the modem...]
AT
OK
ATZ
OK
[Default]
AT&F
OK
ATE0Q0S0=0V1X1&C1&D2
OK
[Dialing...]
[361-0018 Modified Manassas Number]
ATDT3610018
CONNECT 14400/REL-LAPM-COMP
[Logging in...]
[Carrier detect on]
&
**************************************************
  Welcome to the IBM Global Network
**************************************************
Enter dial script version ==>
1.1
Gateway:IBMT6ZA0 Port:31
Select one of the following services:
INTERNET
Enter service ==>
INTERNET
Enter account userID password [/new_password]==>
[Waiting for password to be entered...]
usinet htyson <password>
[Waiting for authentication...]
```

```
129.37.4.31 is your IP address.
[129.37.4.31]
129.37.1.12 is the Gateway IP address.
Begin TCP/IP communication now.
[129.37.1.12]
[resolv files updated]
[Starting SLIP...]
[SLIP.EXE -com2 -speed 38400 -nocfg -p3 -rtscts
[ccc]-ifconfig 129.37.4.31 129.37.1.12 +defaultroute]
[Connected.]
[login closed]
[2 pings to reach 165.87.194.250]
[sending config server request to 165.87.194.250]
[connect log updated]
[received config server response]
[TCP/IP INI file defaults updated.]
[account number: 8756288284900000]
[mail domain server: ibm.net]
[news server: news-s01.ny.us.ibm.net]
[gopher server: www01.ny.us.ibm.net]
[smtp server: smtp-gw01.ny.us.ibm.net]
[pop server: pop02.ny.us.ibm.net]
[www server: http://www01.ny.us.ibm.net]
[name server 1: 165.87.194.244]
[name server 2: 192.124.113.30]
[config server 1: 165.87.194.250]
[config server 2: 165.87.201.250]
[reg server 1: 129.37.1.60]
[reg server 2: 129.37.1.60]
[FTP server 1: 165.87.194.246]
[FTP server 2: 165.87.194.246]
[Hang up pressed]
<connected 0:18>
<702 bytes received, 475 bytes sent>
<147 bytes/second peak throughput>
<no transmission errors>
[Dial thread ended]
[Password removed from TCP/IP INI file]
[resolv files restored]
[SLIP process ended]
[DTR off]
[DTR on]
[DTR off]
[DTR on]
[DTR off]
[close Comm port]
<disconnected>
[Disconnected.]
[connect log updated]
```

Where Is Script Version 1.1?

If you're an inveterate hacker, you might have tried to find script 1.1. Unless you looked inside DIALER.EXE, however, you didn't find it. The IBM Internet Dialer doesn't use an external script. Instead, it has the necessary components for the script embedded in DIALER.EXE. The version number simply tells the IBM provider connection what types of prompts the connecting software expects. Unfortunately, this pretty much ruins any chance of using the IBM Internet Dialer to dial your own provider. Why might you want to do that? Because the IBM Internet Dialer automatically dials the alternate number when the primary number is busy. The Dial Other Internet Provider dialer, however, is a one-shot affair, requiring you to click Hang-Up, confirm the hang up prompt, wait a few seconds, and then click Dial again.

Modem

The *Modem* page, shown in Figure 3.21, enables you to choose or customize your modem and port settings. Modem name enables you to choose your modem from a list of over 200 modems (the latest modem list contains over 200; the November 15, 1994 list that ships with the original version of OS/2 Warp Version 3 contains fewer modems). To select a modem, click the drop-down arrow to the right of the Modem name box.

FIGURE 3.21.

Choose your modem settings in the Modem settings page.

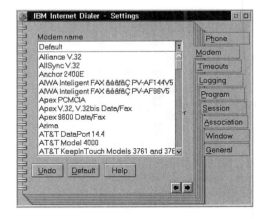

When using a drop-down list box, you can accelerate selection of items beginning with a letter by typing that letter. For example, to accelerate to modems starting with *p*, press the letter **p** on the keyboard. If you change your mind and want *z* instead, then press Backspace to delete the *p*, and press **z**.

The MODEM.LST file has two strings for each modem. The first string, usually AT&F, retrieves the factory settings for the modem (to return the modem to a known state). The second string then sets the modem for dialing the IBM Internet servers.

> Be cautious when changing modem strings. They're usually the way they are because they *worked* for whomever set them up. If you see something that looks wrong, and if you are very familiar with your modem settings, *and* if the settings shown don't work, then change them. However, do so carefully. If you make a mistake, it might be very difficult to find later on.

If you make changes to the modem settings, you should save your changes. First, add some descriptive text to the Modem name field so that you can better identify your modified settings. Next, click the Add to modem list option. This adds your settings to a file called MODEM.USR. When you display the modem list using the drop-down list, MODEM.USR modems are shown ahead of those in MODEM.LST.

You can use the Disable modem speaker option to turn off sound from your modem during the dialing and connection phase. This largely is a matter of personal tastes. Some people can hear when something goes wrong—a busy signal, ringing and ringing without an answer, the sound of a human voice, the sound of a FAX machine—and like to listen to their modem as it dials and connects. Some people would rather have their modem shut up. Some turn on the speaker only when trying to troubleshoot. Regardless of what you choose for this setting, the modem sound is turned off once a connection has been made.

You can use the Download modem list option only when you are connected to the Internet. This corresponds to the same choice you get when you choose the Update Software option from the Customer Assistance object in the IBM Internet Customer Services folder. If your modem already is connecting correctly and optimally, then you probably don't need to bother with this option. In other words, *if it ain't broke...*

Use the Speed control to select the correct speed for your modem. For most 14,400 baud modems (and faster), the speed can be set to 38,400 or 57,600 for negotiation of the highest possible connection. Use the Comm port option to tell the Dialer to use the port to which your modem is connected.

Timeouts

Timeout options, shown in Figure 3.22, are used to control whether or not the Dialer automatically disconnects the line after calls of a certain length or after a certain period of inactivity. You might want to use these options if you tend to get called away when using the Internet and don't want to waste connect time when you're not actually doing anything. Do you ever get a telephone call on another line while connected to the Internet, for example? If so, then you might want to use the Enable inactivity timeout option so that the Dialer will disconnect when the data flow has stopped for a certain period of time. Most users find a setting of 5 or 10 minutes keeps the amount of wasted connect time to a minimum. You are limited to just the time intervals displayed in the spin box (5, 10, 15, 20, 30, 45, 1 hour, and so on).

> This option also is useful when performing a long FTP file transfer. Even if you don't ordinarily have this setting enabled, you might want to enable it when performing a long file transfer. Keep in mind that data flows during FTP transfers do stop sometimes, but seldom for periods longer than a few seconds, and only very rarely for periods longer than a minute. So, you might safely set the disconnect for five minutes. That way, once the file transfer is done and the data flow has stopped for five minutes, disconnection occurs, and your access charges stop.

FIGURE 3.22.

Setting Timeout options wisely can save you money!

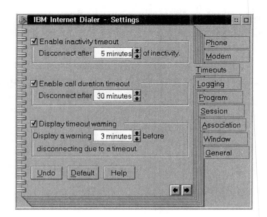

You can use the Enable call duration timeout to set an absolute limit for all calls, even if activity has not stopped. When budgeting the IBM Internet Connection's 6- or 30- hour pricing plans, you might want to set this timer so that you don't exceed your time budget.

> Don't be draconian: Although being able to set a cutoff for your connections is good, you don't want to be cut off in the middle of something. So, I highly recommend that you use the Enable call duration timeout option *only* in conjunction with the Display timeout warning option. Otherwise, the hatchet might fall while uploading or downloading mail or a file.

Use the Display timeout warning option to tell the Dialer to warn you when a disconnection is imminent. If you set it for 1 minute, for example, then you'll get the warning box shown in Figure 3.23.

FIGURE 3.23.

The IBM Internet Dialer warns you when disconnection is imminent.

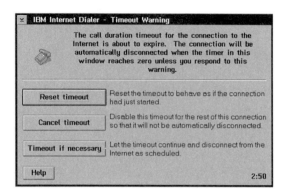

Logging

Use the *Logging* options, shown in Figure 3.24, to tell the Dialer whether to log calls, how large to allow the log to get, and where you want the log stored. By default, the Dialer logs all of your IBM Internet connections in a file called \TCPIP\ETC\CONNECT.LOG.

FIGURE 3.24.

Logging options have nothing to do with lumberjacks!

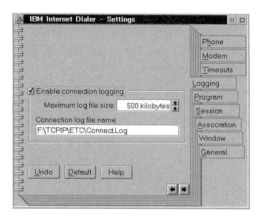

The initial default allows this log to reach a size no larger than 20KB. When about 95 percent of the Maximum log file size is reached, the Dialer makes a new log file, copies the most recent 70 percent to the new file, and discards the earliest 30 percent. If the maximum size is set to 100KB, for example, then the Dialer will rebuild the log each time it reaches 95KB. At that point, the first 30 percent (about 28KB) is discarded, and a new file is created that contains about 70 percent (about 67KB) of the most recent log entries from the old file. Thereafter, the log would be rebuilt in the same way each time it gets to 95KB.

Following is the beginning of a typical log:

```
IBM Global Network - Internet Connection Log

01/14 11:18:46
01/14 11:18:51 usinet htyson  dialed 17033610018  9600/REL-LAPM-COMP
01/14 11:18:51 Gateway:IBMT7TA0 Port:9 129.37.1.16  assigned 129.37.5.9
01/14 11:23:52 Disconnected after 00:05:03  0 errors  0 discards
01/14 16:22:55
01/14 16:23:01 usinet htyson  dialed 3610018  14400/REL-LAPM-COMP
01/14 16:23:01 Gateway:IBMT7ZA0 Port:8 129.37.1.20  assigned 129.37.6.8
01/14 16:23:26 Disconnected after 00:00:28  0 errors  0 discards
01/15 07:51:01
01/15 07:51:07 usinet htyson  dialed 3610018  14400/REL-LAPM-COMP
01/15 07:51:07 Gateway:IBMT6ZA0 Port:31 129.37.1.12  assigned 129.37.4.31
01/15 07:51:22 Disconnected after 00:00:18  0 errors  0 discards
```

By adding together the Disconnected after times, you can approximate your connect time to the IBM Internet Connection. Keep in mind that the log will show times a little longer than the times actually used for charges by the IBM Internet Connection, since the exact moment of connection doesn't occur until your password has been accepted, while the log records the time as of when the modem issues the Connect message.

Program, Session, Association, Window, and General

The remaining settings pages—*Program, Session, Association, Window,* and *General*—are identical to those of other OS/2 objects. The Program page, for example, contains the necessary path and filename to run the IBM Internet Dialer object—*x*:\TCPIP\ETC\DIALER.EXE, where *x* is the disk drive where \TCPIP is stored.

A useful option for the Program page (as noted in Connecting to the Internet the First Time After Registration) is to include your account, user ID, and password. That way, you don't have to type your password each time you connect. You also can create separate dialer objects for each distinct account and user ID.

Warning

If you work in a large business, frequently leave your computer unattended, are accountable for your connect time charges while logged onto the IBM Internet Connection, and if there's any chance that someone might use your account to call the Internet without your permission, then you should think twice about this tip. Although all the cloak and dagger password stuff might seem like so much nonsense to SOHO (small office/home office) users, it often (sadly) is necessary in larger businesses. You still might be able to use this convenient feature, however, if you use OS/2's password lockup feature (open the Settings notebook for the OS/2 desktop and click on the Lockup tab for settings and information). That way, when you're at the helm, you can use the system the way you want, and when you're not, your system generally (but not absolutely) is secure against unwanted interlopers.

The IBM Internet Customer Services Folder

Before registering with the IBM Internet Connection, the IBM Internet Customer Services folder contains Customer Assistance and Registration objects. After registration, account and user ID objects for each account and user are created, as shown in Figure 3.25. If you later terminate your account with IBM, those objects are automatically deleted.

FIGURE 3.25.

Account and UserID objects are created in the IBM Internet Customer Services folder.

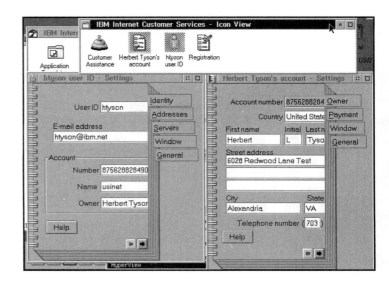

Customer Assistance

The *Customer Assistance* object is used to get Customer Assistance. It also is used to add or change accounts, add or delete user IDs to or from an existing account, update the IBM Internet Dialer software, or ask for help.

Open a New Account

When you registered, as described earlier in this chapter, you opened an account and you created a user ID for that account. Each distinct account is billed independently. Use this option to create another account with different billing.

Change or Delete an Existing Account

Use the *Change an existing account* option to change or delete an existing account (see Figure 3.26). Use the Change option to change any of the information you entered when you first registered. Use the Delete option to terminate your IBM Internet account. If you switch to another provider, for example, make sure you terminate your IBM account. You probably don't want to pay *two* different providers.

FIGURE 3.26.

Use the Change an existing account option to change or delete an existing account.

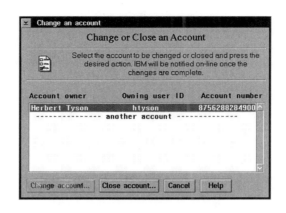

Both the Change and Delete options are available only if you are already online through the IBM Internet Connection. You cannot change or delete an IBM account while connected to a different provider.

Add Another User ID

Use the *Add another user ID* option to create mini-accounts for different users under an existing account. This enables different users to access e-mail under their own names, as well as have their own setup for Usenet newsgroups. To add another user ID, you must already be connected to the Internet through IBM. To add another user ID, follow these steps:

1. Click the Add another user ID button to display the Add another user ID dialog box, as shown in Figure 3.27.

2. Click on the account for which you want to add an ID, and click OK.

3. Enter the owner password and three preferred new user IDs for the other user.

4. Click OK.

FIGURE 3.27.

The Add another user ID dialog box.

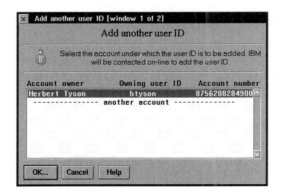

Delete a User ID

Use the *Delete a user ID* option to remove a user ID from an existing account. If you have an account with a number of employees, and one of them leaves, then remove them from the roster. To delete a user ID, follow these steps:

1. Select the account in which the target ID exists.

2. Click the Delete a user ID button to display the Delete a user ID dialog box (see Figure 3.28).

3. Click on the ID you want to delete.

4. Click OK, and then confirm the deletion.

FIGURE 3.28.

The Delete a user ID dialog box.

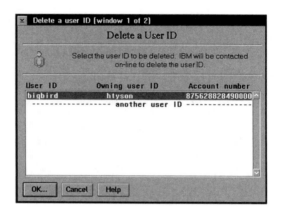

Update Software

You can use the *Update Software* option to do the following:

◆ *Download latest software*—Download IBM Internet Dialer and/or customer assistance programs, modem, or phone lists (the software that underlies the IBM Internet Dialer and the objects in IBM Internet Customer Services folder, for example).

◆ *Transfer configuration*—Copy the current machine's IBM Internet Connection Service configuration files to a disk for installation on another computer that also has the IBM Internet Connection Services software installed (use this option, for example, when you get a new computer).

◆ *Reinstall software*—Use this option to reinstall the software for the IBM Internet Connection Services folder; if you use the Download latest software option to install a new dialer or other IBM Internet Connection service software, then you don't need this option. Use this option only if you obtained the IBM Internet Connection Services software from some other source.

◆ *Recreate icons*—Use this option to re-create the object in the IBM Internet Customer Services folder. This usually is necessary only when you—for whatever reason—have to reinstall all or part of the OS/2 Warp Internet software.

The options in this section apply *only* to the IBM Internet Connection. These options cannot be used if you connect with other Internet providers. If you move to a different computer, for example, then you will need to copy manually the necessary support files to the new system, or re-create them. If disk references change in the process, the support files from the other system must be modified before they can be used on that other system. As a practical matter, it often is less problematic not to try to copy an existing setup, but to create a brand-new one instead.

Ask for Help

Use the *Ask for help* option to get Help, as shown in Figure 3.29. This is the place to look for phone numbers. It also is where you should go to access the following pages on the World Wide Web using the WebExplorer:

    IBM Customer Support   `http://www.ibm.net/support/menu01d.html)`

    Problem Notification   `http://www.ibm.net/support/notify.html`

The Web options work only if your modem currently is connected to the Internet.

FIGURE 3.29.

Help for the IBM Internet Connection.

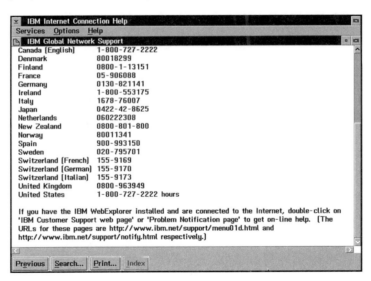

Should you use these? Unlike many of the other Customer Services functions, the Web page links work from other Internet (non-IBM) provider setups as well. However, these Web pages still are *only for IBM Internet Connection customers*, for example, users who are using the IBM Global Network (the U.S. provider of which is Advantis).

CHAPTER FOUR

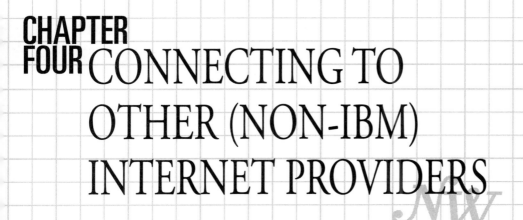

CONNECTING TO OTHER (NON-IBM) INTERNET PROVIDERS

Why Are SLIP and PPP Desirable?

Using the Dial Other Internet Provider Object

Using TIA

In the preceding chapter, I said that the easiest way to connect to the Internet is to use the IBM Internet Connection. However, it might not be the most economical way. Connecting to a non-IBM Internet provider sometimes requires more effort than using the IBM Internet Connection. However, it usually is worth the effort because of the lower cost.

In this chapter, you learn how to connect to the Internet using the Dial Other Internet Providers tool. In some cases, setting up the Dial Other Internet Provider is quite simple, once you've mastered the terminology. In other cases, it is a little more difficult. Following are three major options for using the Internet client applications in the OS/2 Warp Internet Access Kit:

SLIP	Serial Line Internet Protocol
PPP	Point to Point Protocol
SLIP emulators	TIA (The Internet Adapter) and others

Both SLIP and PPP require a special setup of some type from your Internet provider. Basically, your provider must make available a terminal connection to connect the modem that you call in on directly to the Internet. There is more on this later in the chapter. Recently, another way to run Internet client software has become popular, involving the use of a program called TIA (The Internet Adaptor).

Why Are SLIP and PPP Desirable?

Historically, the only way for IBM-PC users to access the Internet was directly from a host system connected to the Internet. Then came banks of modems connected to those hosts that allowed users to have dial-up access. Under the first arrangements, dial-up customers would be given UNIX "shell" (command-line) accounts that allowed them to work on the Internet using UNIX commands. Anyone who has spent much time working at the UNIX command line will tell you that it is very powerful, but very awkward. With time and patience, you can learn the ropes and develop macros to take out much of the awkwardness. Getting up to speed, however, is often enough of a challenge that most computer users couldn't justify investing the time.

Eventually, tools like Gopher, FTP, mail programs, and Web browsers were developed to make the Internet more accessible. At first, these tools were available only as programs that run on hosts connected to the Internet. You still used a UNIX shell account, but you didn't have to pound away at the command line quite so much. SLIP and PPP connections—direct connection to the Internet using communications ports—created the possibility of using Internet client software directly on user's own systems. Rather than dialing and using a provider's online versions of programs such as Gopher, FTP, and WWW browsers, you could use versions of those programs on your own system. Because much of the graphical control was handled locally (by programs running on the user's system), this opened up the possibility of developing applications with graphical user interfaces (GUIs) that further simplify learning and use.

Thus, a connection that puts you directly onto the Internet has an advantage in that it enables you to tour the Internet using programs that are easier and faster to learn. Because such connections require additional hardware on the host system, and because they're viewed as providing *premium* access to the Internet, users usually are charged a premium for SLIP or PPP accounts over straight UNIX shell accounts.

Help for UNIX Shell Account Holders—TIA

Not too long along, some clever programmers figured out they could devise programs that would provide nearly the same types of signals as an actual SLIP connection but that would use a regular shell connection instead. One such program is *TIA* (*The Internet Adapter*), which is a commercial program that runs on UNIX host systems. When TIA is running on the UNIX system, a dial-up customer using a UNIX shell account can use their SLIP and PPP client software. "It's a miracle!" someone said. Miracle or not, it provides a method for UNIX shell account holders to use the OS/2 Warp Internet tools.

Using the Dial Other Internet Provider Object

At some point, I assume that you will call or already will have called an Internet provider and set up a SLIP or PPP account. If you have only a UNIX shell account—no SLIP or PPP—then skip ahead to the section "Using TIA" to see if anything in this chapter is worth your time.

When you get your SLIP or PPP account, you will need a number of pieces of information from your provider—in fact, a number of providers provide a data sheet with this information. What you will need are each of the fields in the provider settings in the Dial Other Internet Provider (SLIPPM, which is SLIPPM.EXE) program. Rather than continuing to call this the Dial Other Internet Provider, from here on, it is called SLIPPM.

What Is SLIPPM?

SLIPPM is a 32-bit GUI program designed—believe it or not—to simplify connecting to a SLIP or PPP provider. The name, SLIPPM, actually is a misnomer because the current version also provides PPP access. Because SLIP came before PPP, however, it wins the naming contest. SLIPPM performs the following tasks:

- ◆ Acts as a repository for all of your SLIP/PPP connection data and settings
- ◆ Uses the SLATTACH command to dial the telephone and conduct a simple dialogue with your provider, passing it your SLIP/PPP user ID and your SLIP/PPP password
- ◆ Optionally uses a plain response file (.RSP) or a REXX program (.CMD) to handle SLIP or PPP connection
- ◆ Places mail ID, mail password, news server, Gopher server, name server, and other information into the OS/2 TCP/IP environment
- ◆ Starts either the SLIP.EXE or PPP.EXE program to allow you to use OS/2's Internet client applications (Gopher, FTP-PM, Ultimedia Mail/2 Lite, telnet, and the WebExplorer)

Information You Will Need

In order to use the Dial Other Internet Provider object (SLIPPM), you will need a number of pieces of information from your provider. If you have this information on hand, it will make doing setup a lot easier. Keep in mind that there are a lot of synonyms and ambiguous terms. If you need additional information about an item, jump ahead to the sections entitled "Login Info," "Connect Info," "Server Info," or "Modem Info" for a more complete description of individual items. Following are the items you will need from your Internet provider. If you write in the book, use a pencil!

Setting	Your Setting
Login ID	
Password	
Phone Number	
Login Sequence	
Connection Type	
Your IP Address	
Destination IP Address	
Netmask	
MTU Size	
VJ Compression	
Domain Nameserver	
Your Host Name	
Your Domain Name	
News Server	
Gopher Server	
WWW Server	
POP Mail Server	
Reply Domain	
Reply (Mail) ID	
POP Login ID	
POP Password	
Modem Speed	
Data Bits	
Parity	

Connecting with the Dial Other Internet Provider (SLIPPM) Object

To connect with Internet providers other than IBM, you use the Dial Other Internet Provider object, which really is a special object for controlling SLIPPM. To start SLIPPM, double-click on the Dial Other Internet Provider object, in the Internet Utilities folder, which is in the IBM Internet Connection for OS/2 folder. The window that appears is shown in Figure 4.1.

FIGURE 4.1.

The Dial Other Internet Provider dialer (in the Internet Utilities folder) is a special object for controlling SLIPPM.EXE.

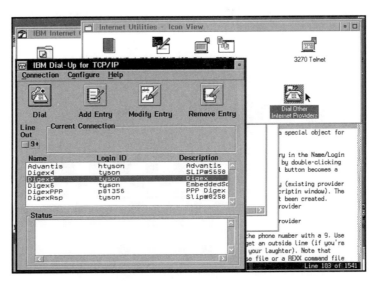

Following are the controls for SLIPPM:

Dial/Hang-up	Use this button to dial the selected entry in the Name/Login ID/Description window. (You also can dial an entry by double-clicking on the entry). When the telephone is connected, the Dial button becomes a Hang-Up button.
Add Entry	Use this button to create a new provider entry (existing provider entries, if any, are displayed in the Name/Login ID/Description window). The first time you open SLIPPM, no provider entries have yet been created.
Modify Entry	Use this button to change the selected provider configuration.
Remove Entry	Use this button to remove the selected provider configuration.
Line Out	Use this button to precede dialing the phone number with a 9. Use the Line Out option if you need to dial 9 to get an outside line (if you're an electrical engineer, please try to control your laughter). Note that this option does not work when using a response file or a REXX command file (see the section entitled "SLIPPM Settings").

Current Connection   This window displays the status of the connection.
                                  If it is empty, there is no connection. When you're
                                  dialing, it displays the message Trying *name*, to
                                  indicate which provider entry (*name*) you are calling.
                                  When connected, it displays the results of the actual
                                  modem connection, as shown in Figure 4.2. It also
                                  displays the Time Online for this call (from the
                                  moment the telephone goes off-hook, not from the
                                  moment of actual connection and not from the
                                  moment a SLIP connection is established), as well as
                                  the Total Time Online for all calls since the last
                                  time the time was reset (using Configure | Reset
                                  Connect Time).

Name/Login ID/Description   Use this window to select a provider to dial, modify,
                                  or delete. The Name, Login ID, and Description are
                                  taken from the Login Info page of SLIPPM's
                                  Settings notebook (see SLIPPM Settings). Note that
                                  as of SLIPPM version 2.0, revision 1.8a, the
                                  Description does not display.

Status   The status window displays the connection dialog
                                  box and any error messages. When first setting up,
                                  you will need to watch this window carefully for
                                  subtle clues about why things aren't working
                                  (assuming that it doesn't work the first time, heaven
                                  forbid!).

FIGURE 4.2.

*The Current Connection
window displays the status
of the current connection.*

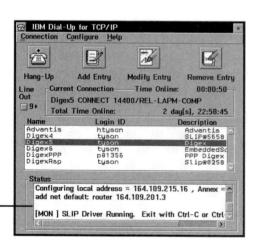

Status window

Why Doesn't It Redial?

When you get a busy signal, SLIPPM is not smart enough to redial. If you wait for it to redial, you will be waiting an awfully long time. When you get a busy signal, it usually will hang up after about four rings. It sometimes will even reset the Hang-Up button to Dial, but not always, however. If you're in a hurry, you'll have to do it the manual way. To do this, follow these steps:

1. Click Hang-Up.
2. Click OK to confirm the hang-up.
3. Wait five seconds (longer on slower systems) for the software to reset.
4. Click Dial.

If you click Dial too soon, you will get error messages similar to those shown in the Status window in Figure 4.3. Once you see those messages, even if the phone has started dialing, you might as well click Hang-Up, wait, and start over again. Those messages mean that the software didn't have time to reset and that all or part of your session is not going to work properly.

FIGURE 4.3.

If you dial too quickly after hanging up, the software doesn't have time to fully reset.

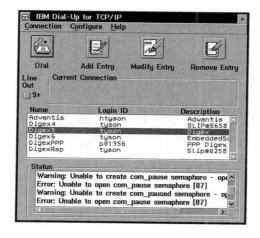

Once you have SLIPPM configured for your Internet provider(s), you can begin a connection by selecting the provider's name and clicking on Dial. Watch the Status window carefully. If all goes well, you will see or hear evidence of the modem working, and you will get a connection.

Turn on Your Modem's Speaker!

When dialing using a modem, it helps to know what the modem is *hearing*. Besides, most modems' speakers automatically turn off once a modem connection is established.

If the modem hears a busy signal, you'll want to know. If the phone line rings once and goes dead, you'll want to know that too. If the modem hears a fax tone, then you'll want to check the number you are dialing to find out what you're doing wrong. And, if the modem hears a voice saying, "Hello? Hello? If you keep calling and hanging up, I'm going to call the police. I've got caller ID, y'know!" You'll want to pick up the telephone and quickly apologize!

Aside from the obvious reasons for wanting the telephone speaker on, there are other reasons as well. After a few days of hearing those connect tones, you'll be able to hear if something goes wrong. A 28,800 connection sounds different from a 9,600 connection. If your 28,800 modem is connecting at 2,400, then you'll darn well want to know—immediately. Yes, you can always look at the Current Connection and Status displays on SLIPPM. However, when you hear it for yourself, you might be able to tell exactly why the results are what they are.

When connected, SLIPPM displays the messages `SLIP Driver Running. Exit with Ctrl+C or Ctrl+Break`, as shown in the Status window in Figure 4.4 (if you're using PPP, then you'll get an analogous message about PPP).

FIGURE 4.4.

Don't try to press Ctrl+C or
Ctrl+Break to hang up!

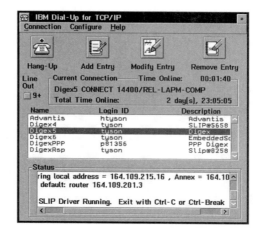

Don't press Ctrl+C or Ctrl+Break to end the session—it won't work in the SLIPPM window. That message comes from `SLIP.EXE` (or `PPP.EXE`), which SLIPPM is kind enough to launch for you. If you were to run PPP or SLIP from the OS/2 command line, then, yes, Ctrl+C is the way to end the session. To close a SLIP session from

> SLIPPM, however, just click the Hang-Up button. You do not have to enter **exit** or log out—just hang up. Although it might seem rude, just keep telling yourself, "It's only a computer; it doesn't know what rude is."

Once you see that SLIP or PPP has started, you now can move on to start any of your OS/2 Internet clients (Gopher, NewsReader/2, Ultimedia Mail/2 Lite, the WebExplorer, FTP, and so on). When you're ready to hang up, it usually is best to close all of your connection-dependent software, and then click on the Hang-Up button in SLIPPM. If you don't close the programs, you might get annoying messages such as the one shown in Figure 4.5. NewsReader/2 (NR/2) times out after a few minutes, and suddenly realizes that you're not connected anymore. If you reconnect within a minute or two, NR/2 usually won't skip a beat. If you hang up, having forgotten that NR/2 is running, however, it will yell at you.

FIGURE 4.5.

To avoid annoying messages, close your Internet programs before hanging up.

SLIPPM Settings

To see what information you need, start SLIPPM by double-clicking on the Dial Other Internet Provider object in the IBM Internet Connection for OS/2 folder. Then click on the Add Provider button to display the Login Info page (see Figure 4.6).

FIGURE 4.6.

The Login Info page in the updated Dial Other Internet Provider object.

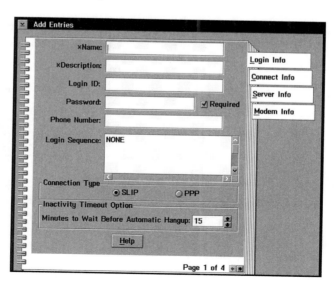

Update Alert!

Under SLIPPM's Configure menu, choose Add Entry or Modify Entry (if an entry already exists) to display page 1 of the SLIPPM settings. Which does page 1 in your SLIPPM settings look more like: Figure 4.6 or more like Figure 4.7? If it looks more like Figure 4.7, then you don't have the latest version of SLIPPM.EXE. Once you're connected to the Internet, you will be able to download the latest version by opening the Retrieve Software Updates object in the IBM Internet Connection for OS/2 folder. At this writing, the necessary update is disguised as the PPP Gamma (a gamma version of a program is supposed to be later than beta, and *almost* ready for release). Get the PPP Gamma anyway, however, because it fixes a number of problems with SLIPPM; it is not just for PPP. Besides, by the time you read this, it probably won't say "Gamma" anymore. If you have a PPP account, however, then you're going to have a problem because the version of SLIPPM that shipped with the original version of OS/2 Warp does not support PPP. If you do have a PPP account, you will need to obtain the update through other means or try to get it directly from IBM OS/2 support.

If you have access to the Internet other than through OS/2—which you presently are trying to set up, you can obtain the update that supports PPP via anonymous FTP from ftp.ibm.net. At this writing, the most recent version is listed as \pub\PPP\PPP.ZIP.

FIGURE 4.7.

The Login Info page in the original Dial Other Internet Provider object.

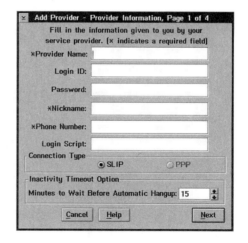

Always use exact case when FTPing.

Login Info Page

For the Login Info page, you will need the following information:

Name	Use the Name field for the identifying name (up to eight characters) you want to use as a label for the provider. This name will be used in naming your newsgroup settings and in holding your e-mail. You can make the name whatever you want, as long as the characters are valid for directory names.
Description	Description that is displayed next to the provider name in the SLIPPM window. You can use up to 11 characters to create a terse description of each provider.
Login ID	You can use SLIP or PPP ID. This is the user ID your provider's computer needs to see to know that your are a SLIP or PPP customer. If possible, try to get a SLIP ID that is the same as your UNIX shell or mail ID.
Password	Use a SLIP or PPP password. This is the password you use in conjunction with your SLIP or PPP user ID to log on to your SLIP account. If you leave this field blank and check the Required option, then SLIPPM will prompt you for your password when you click the Dial button.
Phone Number	Use the complete telephone number, including 1 and the area code (where applicable), for your SLIP provider. Note that this field is *not* used if you use an .RSP or .CMD file in the Login Sequence setting.
Login Sequence	This can be left blank or can be filled with the word NONE, the text of a simple send-expect login sequence, a file name (.RSP or .CMD) and login parameters, or the word slipterm. (Note: This field is the Script field in earlier versions of SLIPPM.)
Connection Type	Use SLIP or PPP, whichever is most appropriate.
Inactivity Timeout Option	Use this spin control to select a length of inactivity after which you want SLIPPM to automatically hang up.

The Login Sequence or Script field often is a source of confusion, especially in early versions of SLIPPM. This field tells SLIPPM how to handle the login, and is crucial for SLIPPM to work at all. In setting up SLIPPM, you should know that very often there are multiple ways to get it to work. It usually is not a matter of just one combination that will work for you. It is, however, a matter of one correctly setting up approach. Review each alternative and choose the simplest one for your situation. First, get it to work. You can go back and add frills later if you want them.

The Login Sequence or Script field can contain any of the following:

◆ A blank
◆ The word NONE
◆ A send-expect script (not a file, but the actual script)
◆ The name of a send-expect response file (.RSP)
◆ The name of a REXX .CMD file

Take a look at each possibility. These are presented in order of difficulty—from easiest to most complex. As you read through, try to determine whether or not an approach will work for you. Note that virtually *any* provider connection can be achieved using a REXX .CMD file. However, usually one of the simpler approaches will work as well, making less work for you.

Reader Alert!

If you think that you need to use a response file or a REXX command file in the Login Sequence field, *do not skip the following sections.* You might have been told or read that your situation requires a REXX command file or a response file. You probably were misinformed, however. Most users of the OS/2 Internet Access Kit don't need a response or REXX command file at all—especially if they obtain the updated version of SLIPPM using the Retrieve Software Updates object in the IBM Internet Connection for OS/2 folder. Many users don't need anything in the Login Sequence field at all— *period!* So, read through this and the following sections to find the minimum setup necessary. It can make getting onto the so-called *information superhighway* a lot less traumatic.

Blank

You can leave the Login Sequence field blank if both of the following are true:

◆ Your provider performs a very standard login: and password: dialog for a SLIP or PPP connection (the letters l and p are omitted to allow for the possibility that some systems capitalize the initial letter whereas others do not).

◆ You have been given two static IP addresses—*Your IP Address* and *Destination IP Address*—both to be entered on the Connect Info settings page.

Static?

IP addresses can be *static* or *dynamic.* Static means that they always are the same, such that they can be entered into the Connect Info page in the Dial Other Internet Provider Settings notebook. Dynamic means that IP addresses are assigned as available each time you connect.

Each computer on the Internet has a different IP address. The computer that provides you with your connection to the Internet is the *destination* or *gateway*. It also is sometimes called an *annex* system (all these synonyms are the source of endless confusion for OS/2 Warp Internet users). When you connect via SLIP or PPP, your computer also has its own unique IP address while you are connected.

With many large Internet providers, multiple computers are used to provide connection to the Internet. Your call can be connected to any of them, depending on which one is the most available when you call. Thus, your destination IP can vary when using a provider with multiple destination computers. For such providers, the Destination IP Address will be dynamic. If your provider uses a single IP destination for all callers, then your Destination IP Address will be static or fixed.

Some providers assign unique or static IP addresses for each account. This is a time-consuming administrative process that often takes several weeks. However, your IP address is always the same each time you call. Others providers have many IP addresses that they (their system software, actually) assign to users as they call in. Such providers usually can sign you up for a SLIP account without any wait or administrative delay. The IP number you get, however, varies from call to call, and is dynamic. If your provider assigns SLIP IP addresses dynamically, then you will need to use a response script of some type (embedded or a file), or possibly a REXX command file.

If you leave the Login Sequence field blank, then SLIPPM uses the information in the four settings pages to dial the telephone and configure your SLIP session, without any need for an embedded script, script file, or REXX file. In order to do this, all the configuration information must be known prior to dialing, including the IP addresses.

Can You Use the SIO Communications Drivers?

Maybe yes, maybe no. First of all, you'll need to add the following to your OS/2 STARTUP.CMD file, replacing *x* with the number of your COM port connected to your modem (such as COM1 or COM2):

```
mode comx dtr=on
```

STARTUP.CMD should be in the root directory on you OS/2 boot drive. If you don't have one, you can create one that contains just that line. STARTUP.CMD is analogous to DOS's AUTOEXEC.BAT file. Placed into STARTUP.CMD, the mode line sets DTR to ON each time you boot into OS/2. But, why do you need it?

The OS/2 COM.SYS defaults to DTR (*data terminal ready*) being ON, whereas SIO.SYS defaults to its being OFF. The IAK dialing and hang-up routines depend on DTR being ON, and assumes (because COM.SYS turns it on by default) that it will be ON. Usually, getting STARTUP.CMD to turn it on for you is enough.

For some reason, however, probably related to an interaction among SLATTACH, SIO, and some modems, turning DTR ON isn't enough. If you have an Intel 144/144e modem, for example, even with DTR ON, your modem might be hanging up immediately after the CONNECT message when using SLATTACH (SLIPPM's default) for dialing. This happens only when using certain modems, and usually only when using the SIO.SYS driver.

The result is that if you are using SIO.SYS, the Blank, NONE, and .RSP options sometimes do not work because they all involve using the default SLATTACH program. A symptom indicative of this problem is the presence of an error message, such as [MON] Error: Connection Failed, in the Status window of SLIPPM just after connecting to your provider. Sometimes the connection will drop immediately. The problem is not universal. However, if you get that error when using otherwise correct techniques, try switching back to COM.SYS and VCOM.SYS to see if the problems continue. If they do not, then you either must use a REXX .CMD file to connect (in the Login Sequence field), or you must revert to OS/2's default communications drivers.

The SIO drivers are high-performance replacements for the default COM.SYS and VCOM.SYS drivers that come with OS/2. They provide additional communications options, a utility called *Vmodem* that enables you to use a normal communications program (such as PMComm, TE/2, and ZOC) to connect with Vmodem sites on the Internet, and they often provide better performance for DOS programs running under OS/2. See Chapter 12, "Additional Internet Applications and Related Utilities," for additional information.

If your provider has a more complicated dialog than simply login: and password:, or if you don't have static IP addresses, then you will need to use a script of some type—an embedded response script, a response (.RSP) file, or a REXX command (.CMD) file.

What Happens When You Leave the Login Sequence Field Blank?

When you leave the Login Sequence field blank, each time you click on Dial, SLIPPM runs the SLIP.EXE or PPP.EXE program using parameters that, among other things, do the following:

- Start a SLIP or PPP session
- Issue the appropriate ifconfig and route commands using the Connect Info strings from page 2 of the Settings notebook
- Launch SLATTACH, which performs the following tasks (among others):
    1. Initializes the modem using the modem setting from the Modem Info page of the SLIPPM Settings notebook
    2. Dials the telephone number from the Phone Number field

> 3. Waits for the text `ogin:` from your provider, and then transmits the contents of the Login ID field
>
> 4. Waits for the text `assword:` from your provider, and then transmits the contents of your Password field
>
> And *Presto*, you're connected and ready to start any of the OS/2 SLIP/PPP client applications.

NONE

If you use the word NONE in the Login Sequence field, SLIPPM assumes that a PPP connection is initiated immediately upon connection, and that complete or partial negotiation of the login and IP addresses is done through PPP protocols. Some PPP providers will issue a single IP address or a pair of IP addresses. If you have those IP addresses (yours and that of the host system), they go into the IP Address fields on the Connect Info page, along with the netmask, if any (usually `255.255.255.0`). Note that the IP fields can be left blank if using the PPP option to accommodate different provider setups. If your provider *does* require a login dialog, however, then the NONE option is not available to you.

If you use the NONE option, SLIPPM retrieves all the information it needs, either over the PPP connection itself, or from the four Settings notebook pages.

Embedded Response Script

Another option is to embed a response script into the Login Sequence fill-in area—not a response file, but the actual script. When you include a response script in the Login Sequence field, SLIPPM starts SLIP and uses SLATTACH to perform modem setup and dialing using the telephone number field. Under most circumstances, this approach will work with both static and dynamic IP addresses, although setting up the latter can be quite tedious.

When would you do use this approach? You might use this approach when either or both of your IP addresses are dynamic, or when your provider's SLIP or PPP sign-on dialog cannot be handled with the *expect* strings `ogin:` and `assword:` (that is, the prompts that your script *expects* from the remote computer, minus the initial letter because it's sometimes capitalized and sometimes not). Suppose that your provider requires an additional selection or code of some kind to tell it that you're an Internet customer. This is not uncommon for some providers. To log onto the IBM Internet Connection (Advantis, in the U.S.), for example, your software must send a single & to get a prompt that your computer can understand, and then your system must send the word INTERNET. Next, the host system prompts for a script version. After that, the account name (usinet, in the U.S.), user ID, and password need to be sent. After all that, the system issues your IP address and the destination (or gateway) IP address.

You also might want to use a embedded script if your provider issues dynamic IP addresses each time you call. With dynamic addresses, you don't have numbers to enter into the two IP address fields on the Connect Info page. Thus, there must be some mechanism to obtain them from your provider's computer so that *your* computer can issue the appropriate `ifconfig` and `route` commands.

If your provider has a connect dialog similar to IBM's Internet Connection (but not identical, for reasons I'll explain in a moment), and/or if you have dynamic IP addresses, you probably can use an embedded script approach. Consider, for example, the following sign-on exchange, which requires more user input than the simple `login:` and `password:` dialog box, and in which the IP addresses are assigned dynamically. User input is shown in **bold**. Everything else is supplied by the provider.

```
<Enter>
ACME Gateway to the world:
Select one of the following services:
INTERNET SQUEEGEENET BARFNET
Enter service ==:
internet
account type:
ppp
userid:
htyson
password:
xxxxxxx
SL/IP session from (999.777.333.222) to 999.777.301.15
```

First, you must press Enter to wake up the system prompt (for example, **<Enter>** means to press the Enter key, not to type <Enter>). The system prompts you to select a service and an account type. After you choose `internet` and `ppp`, the system then issues the standard `login:` and `password:` prompts.

Where Are the Rules for Writing These Scripts?

The script is used by `SLATTACH.EXE`, not by SLIPPM. If you're searching through the SLIPPM help system trying to find script syntax other than \r, you won't find them. To get a list of the settings, enter **slattach -?** at the OS/2 command prompt, and you'll get the following (among other things):

```
<attach-script> [SendString ExpectString] [SendString ExpectString] ...
<esc-sequence>  [\d]      2 second delay
                [\n]      CRLF
                [\q]      toggle quiet mode
                [\r]      CR
                [\s]      space
                [^<c>]    Send Control <c>
```

In addition, you can use [PASSWORD] and [LOGINID] as send strings to send the contents of the Login ID and Password fields from the Login Info page of the SLIPPM Settings notebook. You can use the text **[$IPADDR]** and **[$IPDEST]** to parse the expect string for the Your IP Address and Destination IP Address fields.

Note that CR (Carriage Return) is just an ASCII 13, whereas CRLF (Carriage Return Linefeed) is an ASCII 13 followed by an ASCII 10. For most systems, however, both produce identical results on output, and \r usually is sufficient. To *read* a CR or a CRLF from the provider's data stream (as part of a prompt), however, you need to know which one is being sent. Also note that each send line also sends a CR. To send your user ID, do not include \r or \n at the end of it.

Another critical thing to know about using an embedded script is that you *must* use \s for spaces. The expected string for "account type" would be account\stype because of the way that SLATTACH processes the command line. Spaces on the command line are used to separate individual send and expect strings. Thus, "account type" with a space in it would be interpreted by SLATTACH as the expect string account, followed by the send string type.

Now, turn this into a script that can be used in SLIPPM's Login Sequence field. In Table 4.1, the script is shown at the left and an explanation is to the right.

Table 4.1. Embedded script for use in the Login Sequence field in the Dial Other Internet Provider Settings notebook.

Script	*Meaning*
\r	Send enter to get a prompt.
Enter\sservice\s==>	Wait for system prompt.
internet	Send the text internet.
account\stype	Wait for prompt for account.
ppp	Send the type of account.
ogin:	Wait for prompt for user ID.
htyson	Send the user ID.
assword:	Wait for password prompt.
[PASSWORD]	Send the contents of the Password field from SLIPPM's Login Info Settings page.
from\s([$IPDEST])\sto\s[$IPADDRI]	Wait for text from ipdest to ipaddr and parse the respective IP addresses. Everything between from and to is assigned to the Destination IP Address. Everything after to is assigned to Your IP Address.

In Table 4.1, note that the embedded script begins with a send string. Thereafter, wait for (or expect) and send strings are interspersed: wait for, send, wait for, send, wait for, and so on. Also in the table, \r and \s are highlighted to emphasize where they are. Note that each script item must contain no spaces and no blank lines. Thus, \r is used for blank lines, and \s is used for spaces. Note also that [PASSWORD] sends the contents of the Password field from the Login Info page. Optionally, you could use [LOGINID] to send the contents of the Login ID field. If your SLIP or PPP login ID is different from your mail ID, however, then you might want to see the following tip.

Use an Embedded Script as a Workaround for an UltiMail Problem

You also might use an embedded script approach to overcome a bug in the way Ultimedia Mail/2 Lite (UltiMail) and SLIPPM work. UltiMail takes your mail ID from the SLIP/PPP Login ID field in SLIPPM (version 2.0, revision 1.8a) at this writing. It instead should take your mail ID from the POP Login ID field on the Server Info page of the SLIPPM Settings notebook. When you try to get your mail, Ultimail erroneously uses your SLIP/PPP Login ID as your Mail ID, and—as you might expect—your mail server says that the wrong ID or Password is being used.

If your SLIP/PPP Login and Mail IDs are the same, then you won't encounter a problem. If you have different SLIP/PPP Login and Mail IDs, then you very likely *will* encounter this problem.

However, if you include your SLIP/PPP ID into the Login Sequence field (rather than using [LOGINID]) as part of the script, that then allows you to "lie" to the Login ID field by putting your Mail ID into that field. Because your script directly supplies the Login ID, the contents of the Login ID field won't affect your SLIP/PPP login.

Hence, you might want to use an embedded script even if you otherwise qualify for leaving the Login Sequence field blank. Assuming that your SLIP/PPP Login ID is s04321, you type the following into the Login Sequence field:

```
\r
ogin:
s04321
assword:
[PASSWORD]
```

Notice that the script uses the standard login: and password: prompts (minus the initial letter because some systems use a capital l and p, and others don't). Ordinarily, you could use the keyword [LOGINID] to supply the entry from the Login ID field, and the [PASSWORD] entry to tell SLIPPM to use the password that's filled out on the Login Info page. Here, we still use [PASSWORD], but rather than using [LOGINID], we use the actual SLIP/PPP login ID. We also put your *mail* ID into the Login ID field, as shown in Figure 4.8; that way, everybody's happy. If your mail and SLIP passwords are different, you can do the same thing with your password (such as put your mail password into the Password field, and put your actual SLIP login password (instead of [PASSWORD]) into the Login Sequence script).

FIGURE 4.8.

*You can put your mail
login ID into the Login ID
field, and put your SLIP
login ID into the Login
Sequence script.*

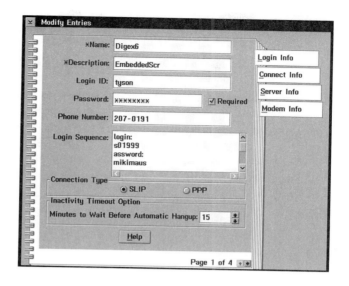

Response (.*RSP*) File

Another option for the Login Sequence field is to enter the name of a response file—a file that
contains a response script. To use a response file, your provider must use static IP addresses. If
your provider uses dynamic IP addresses, then you must use a REXX command file rather than
a simple response file. Although connections with such providers usually can work either by
leaving the Login Sequence field blank or by using an embedded response script, it sometimes
is more convenient to use a response file.

For example, it might make sense to use a response file if either of the following is true:

◆ Your login script is long or complicated

◆ The script will require frequent changes (such as for specifying different phone
numbers)

If your provider uses static IP addresses, you usually can use a response file (.RSP) rather than
a REXX .CMD file. Several sample .RSP files come with the OS/2 Internet Access Kit and are in
your TCPIP\ETC directory

To use a response file, include only the name of the response file in the Login Sequence field.
When using a response file, you must observe the following rules:

1. You cannot use a .CMD ending for a response file. You don't have to use the .RSP
   extension, but you cannot use .CMD.

2. You cannot use a directory specification with the name of the response file
   (myprov.rsp is okay, for example, but c:\tcpip\etc\myprov.rsp is not).

3. The response file *must* be located in your etc directory (as specified by the SET ETC=
   line in your OS/2 CONFIG.SYS file; usually it is \TCPIP\ETC on the drive where the
   Internet tools are installed).

[MON] Error: Connection Failed!

The number one reason for getting this error when trying to use a response file is that you haven't followed rules 2 and 3. If you include a path, or if the response file is not in your SET ETC directory, you will get this wholly uninformative error message. In fact, you can get that insipid error message for a variety of reasons. When using a response file, however, and the response file doesn't seem to work, the reason usually is because one of the rules was violated. Why doesn't SLATTACH like a path for response files? Probably because it is using the SET ETC environment string for the path, and doesn't understand where the heck `c:\tcpip\etc\c:\tcpip\etc\sample.rsp` is!

So, if that's the case, then why doesn't it give a more meaningful error? Beats me, but it doesn't.

When you use a response file, the modem initialization strings and telephone dialing commands (as well as the telephone number) must be provided by the response file, not by the SLIPPM settings. The IP Addresses, modem COM port, speed settings, data bits, and parity are obtained from the SLIPPM settings, but the rest is up to your script. Note that the IP addresses are obtained from SLIPPM's four-page Settings notebook when using a response file, and that this is different when using a REXX command (.CMD) file.

Tip

When typing modem strings, it is easy to make mistakes. If you need modem initialization strings, you can copy them to the OS/2 Clipboard from the Modem Info page of the SLIPPM Settings notebook. To do this, follow these steps:

1. Open the Settings notebook for SLIPPM (by clicking a Modify Provider button Although SLIPPM is running, or by choosing the Settings option from the Dial Other Internet Provider's popup menu).

2. Click on the Modem Info page.

3. Under Modem Type, select the modem you want to use. Notice that as you choose different modems, the settings in Initialization String 1 and 2 change.

4. Click the Initialization String field you want to copy.

5. Press the Home key to go to the beginning of the entry field.

6. Press Shift+End to select the field, and then press Ctrl+Insert to copy the string onto the Clipboard.

Once the string is on the Clipboard, you then can—using an editor from which the Clipboard is accessible—paste the string into the response file.

If you specify a file (such as MYPROVDR.RSP) in the Login Sequence field, the file must contain the complete telephone dialing instructions, your SLIP User ID, and your SLIP password. Whenever you use a file name, SLIPPM no longer dials for you.

A typical .RSP file contains a sequence of send and expect (or wait for) strings. IBM provides several sample .RSP files in the TCPIP\ETC directory. In those files, lines beginning with # are comment lines and are ignored by SLIPPM. Take a look at a common .RSP file in Table 4.2.

Table 4.2. A typical response file (.RSP) for use with the Dial Other Internet Provider (SLIPPM.EXE) application.

Response File	Explanation
# Reset the modem first	Comment that explains the line that follows (AT&F).
AT&F	Send command to the modem to reset the factory default settings for the modem. AT&F is a Hayes-compatible command.
# Wait for modem response, if none is received after 60 seconds, then the response file times out and SLIPPM issues an error.	Comment line explaining that the modem now has 60 seconds to issue an OK response to the AT&F command. If this response is not returned, there often is some type of a modem setting problem. It often helps (for external modems) to turn off the modem, wait a second and then turn it back on.
OK	Wait for Modem response.
# Dial the number, use the "9," if you need an outside line.	Comment line.
# Replace xxx-xxxx with the actual number.	Comment line that tells you for this script to work, you need to replace xxx-xxxx with the actual phone number. Here, xxx-xxxx was replaced with 1-800-555-5555 (dashes are optional).
atdt18005555555	Send Hayes compatible command to dial 1-800- 555-5555; (dashes are optional).
# Wait for name prompt	Comment line.
CONNECT	Wait for response from modem.
	Send a return (a blank line) to elicit a prompt from the remote host for user login.
slip login:	Wait for response from the remote host.

continues

Table 4.2. continued

Response File	*Explanation*
`# Send user name`	Comment line.
`sl1234`	`Send` SLIP or PPP user/login ID.
`# Wait for password request.`	Comment line.
`Password:`	`Wait for` response from the remote host.
`# Send your password`	Comment line.
`formula`	Send password.

Note that, aside from the comments, the contents of the response file are a dialog box of `Send` and `Wait for` strings, just as were the strings in an embedded script. You send `AT&F` and `Wait for` `OK`. You send `ATDT`*phone-number*, and `Wait for` the word `CONNECT`. As long as the modem or the remote host returns the expected text, the dialog continues. There is no provision for getting unexpected responses.

REXX *.CMD* File

If you use a `.CMD` file ending, SLIPPM will assume that it is a REXX command file rather than a response file. When you use a `.CMD` file, the IP addresses and several modem fields in the SLIPPM Settings notebook are unavailable for editing or selection. This is your *clue* that this information must be supplied by your REXX script.

What Is REXX?

REXX is a procedural programming language that comes with OS/2. REXX stands for—don't ask me why—**R**estructured **Ex**tended **Ex**ecutor language. Whereas DOS has BASIC, OS/2 has REXX. It is a powerful programming language that is integrated into OS/2. A number of applications even use REXX as their macro programming language. A number of other applications provide *APIs* (*application programming interface*) to use REXX in solving various problems.

Most users will be able to connect to the Internet using one of the previously described approaches. Although REXX is an option that is open to any user, it is not an option that is required very often. In general, you only need to use a REXX program only in two situations:

◆ When your logon session needs some kind of conditional logic; for example, the prompts from your provider vary from session to session

◆ When you need to issue a `MODE` port command or some other OS/2 command immediately prior to dialing

Because REXX is a programming language and can contain conditional logic commands (such as IF statements and so on), it provides a means to solve the problem of variable prompts and required responses. Suppose that your provider uses different networks to connect you to the Internet. If you connect to one provider, you get one set of send and expect strings, and if you connect to another provider, you need a different set of send and expect strings.

Note

Using Ray Gwinn's popular SIO replacements for the communications drivers that come with OS/2 is another known situation that appears to require using a REXX program. No one seems to know exactly why. A symptom that you are having this problem is when your modem hangs up as soon as it connects. You also will see a [MON] Error: Connection Failed message in the SLIPPM Status window.

When you refer to a REXX program file in the Login Sequence field, the rules for SLIPPM's settings are different than when you use other approaches (for example, as contrasted with putting any of the following in the Login Sequence field: an .RSP file, nothing (leaving it blank), the word NONE, or including an embedded script). In particular, when using a REXX program:

◆ You *can* specify a directory with the name of the REXX program in the Login Sequence field; if you don't specify a directory, then SLIPPM searches your OS/2 PATH rather than the SET ETC location.

◆ You can include in the Login Sequence field parameters with the name of the REXX program (such as d:\tcpip\etc\annex.cmd atdt555-1212 *mylogin mypassword*). It is up to the REXX program to parse the command line to decipher the parameters.

◆ When using a REXX program, the following SLIPPM settings are ignored: Line Out, Phone Number, IP numbers, Netmask, Modem Type, Dial Prefix, and both modem Initialization Strings.

When using a REXX program, dialing the phone, passing the login ID and password, obtaining the IP numbers, and issuing the appropriate ifconfig and route commands all must be done by the REXX program. The only thing that SLIPPM does is start SLIP, and the SLATTACH program is not used at all.

The IAK comes with a number of sample REXX programs located in the \TCPIP\BIN directory. To use one of the sample programs, you must carefully edit certain sections so that they work with your provider. In particular, you need to make sure that the send/expect sequences are correct. Look at the critical parts of CYBERNET.CMD, for example. Places where change usually are needed are noted.

Warning

> PPP REXX User Alert! If you use PPP rather than SLIP, all occurrences of REXX API functions that begin with `slip_` must be changed to `ppp_`. For example, the function `slip_com_output` becomes `ppp_com_output`. In the REXX code shown in the remainder of this section, those parts of the REXX programs that use the `slip_com_output` function are omitted because they usually don't require modification by the user. When modifying a REXX script that's been set up for SLIP, however, you will need to change the SLIP functions to reflect the different function names used by the PPP API.

The rest of this section presents an example of a REXX script. The script, which is 58 lines long, is presented in pieces with detailed explanations. The line numbers included in the code for this script are for reference purposes only and are not part of the script itself. Here is line 1:

```
1: parse arg interface , dialcmd username password
```

This line indicates that four parameters will be received by CYBERNET.CMD: *interface*, *dialcmd*, *username*, and *password*. The `interface` parameter is provided by SLIPPM. The other three parameters are ones that you include after the name of the REXX program in the Login Sequence field, such as **redial.cmd atdt3012200258 s09999 mikimaus** (see Figure 4.9). In the REXX program, the `dial` command, user name (SLIP or PPP login ID), and password are available as variables whose respective names are *dialcmd*, *username*, and *password*. Optionally, you could eliminate the need to include these as parameters in the Login Sequence field by deleting *dialcmd username password* from the `parse` line, and then setting those three variables directly in your REXX program file. To do this, you would include the following lines after line 1 of the script:

```
dialcmd = 'atdtPhoneNumber'
username = 'SLIP or PPP login ID'
password = 'Password'
```

FIGURE 4.9.

When using a REXX script, the dialing command, SLIP ID, and SLIP password usually are included in the Login Sequence field.

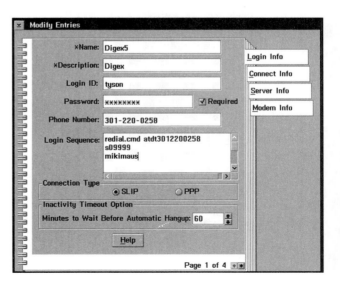

Replace *PhoneNumber*, `SLIP or PPP login ID`, and *Password* with the actual phone number, login ID, and password, as in the following:

```
dialcmd = 'atdt555-1212'
username = 'htyson'
password = 'xycabcd'
```

Lines 2 through 9 represent the beginning of the initialization and main script code.

```
 2: /*----------------------------------------------------------------*/
 3: /*                 Initialization and Main Script Code             */
 4: /*----------------------------------------------------------------*/
 5: /* Set some definitions for easier COM strings */
 6: cr='0d'x
 7: crlf='0d0a'x
 8: say ''
 9: say 'ANNEX - SLIP ANNEX Cybernet Server Connection Script ',
```

The text inside the single quotes in line 9 is displayed in the Status window of SLIPPM as the REXX program is executed. Although line 9 does not affect your connection, you might want to change this line to indicate who your provider really is, such as `say 'REXX program for connecting to DIGEX SLIP account ',`. The word *annex* often is a source of confusion to many OS/2 Warp Internet Access Kit users. The word *annex* is just jargon for your Internet provider (which itself is jargon); although, on some systems it actually *is* called an annex. Other jargon synonyms are your *destination system* or *destination site*, your *gateway*, or your *route*.

```
10:      '(interface' interface')'
11: /* Flush any stuff left over from previous COM activity */
12: call flush_receive
13: /* Reset the modem here */
14: /* You may need to customize this for your modem make and model */
15: call lineout , 'Reset modem...'
16: call send 'AT&F' || cr
```

Line 16 sends the Hayes compatible command to reset a modem to the factory setting (`AT&F`). If your modem is not Hayes-compatible, then substitute the appropriate modem command. "`|| cr|`" is a REXX way of appending a variable to output text. Here, the variable `cr` (which previously was defined as a carriage return) is sent following the `AT&F` command. The variable `cr` previously was defined as hex `0d`, which is ASCII character 13.

The `waitfor` subroutine in line 17 is used to tell the script to wait for the text `OK` to be sent by the modem:

```
17: call waitfor 'OK', 5 ; call flush_receive 'echo'
```

If your modem doesn't return the word `OK` by default (a few older modems, for example, might send numerical result codes rather than words), you would need to send the appropriate command to cause your modem to return text results instead of numerical results. You could add the text results modem command to the `call send 'AT&F' || CR` line. If your modem can send only numerical results codes, you would have to replace `OK` with whatever result code your modem sends to indicate that a command was accepted.

In the following code, lines 20 through 23 are for Hayes-compatible modem commands. Only in the rare event that your modem doesn't use these commands would they have to be changed.

```
18:  if RC = 1 then do
19:      call lineout , 'Modem not resetting... Trying again'
20.      call send '+++'
21:      call waitfor 'OK'
22:      call send 'ATHZ' ¦¦ cr
23:      call waitfor 'OK', 3
```

In lines 20 through 22, you would need to substitute your modem's equivalents for the following items:

+++   Switches the modem into "command mode"

OK   The default result code

ATHZ   Hang up (H), if off-hook, and restore the default configuration (Z)

Line 29 tells the script to wait for the word CONNECT. As noted previously, in the unlikely event that your modem sends a different connect signal, you will need to change CONNECT to whatever signal your modem sends.

```
24:    end
25: /* Dial the remote server */
26: call charout , 'Now Dialing...'
27: /* Wait for connection */
28: call send dialcmd ¦¦ cr
29: call waitfor 'CONNECT' ; call waitfor crlf
```

If your provider requires you to press Enter in order to start the login process, remove the /* and */ from line 32 to change it from a comment to an active line.

```
30: /* Handle login.  We wait for standard strings, and then flush anything */
31: /* else to take care of trailing spaces, etc..                          */
32: /* call send cr */
```

Lines 33 through 38 are the login dialog. Unless you're using CyberGate, you must change these lines to match the login exchange that takes place when you call your provider.

```
33: call waitfor 'CyberGate>' ; call flush_receive 'echo'
34: call send 'SLIP' ¦¦ cr
35: call waitfor 'Username:' ; call flush_receive 'echo'
36: call send username ¦¦ cr
37: call waitfor 'Password:' ; call flush_receive 'echo'
38: call send password ¦¦ cr
```

You sometimes can obtain this information from your provider. Usually, however, it is best to use an ordinary communications program (such as ProComm, PMComm, TE/2, HyperAccess Lite, and so on) to call your provider's computer, and capture the dialog to a file. Then, use a text editor (such as the OS/2 System Editor, E.EXE) to view the resulting file. Using the OS/2 Clipboard, copy into the waitfor quotes in lines 33, 35, and 37 the text the computer sends, and copy the parts you type into the send quotes in lines 34, 36, and 38.

For example, convert the following logon exchange to the necessary REXX commands (see Table 4.3). Note that each `call waitfor` line also has `; call flush_receive 'echo'` appended to the end. Because that part of the line doesn't change, however, it isn't shown in the table.

Table 4.3. Converting a login exchange into REXX commands.

Source	*<Enter>*	*REXX Command*
Host	Enter System>	call waitfor 'System>'
You	**internetslip**	call send 'internetslip'
Host	User ID:	call waitfor 'User ID:'
You	**jsmith**	call send 'jsmith'
Host	Password:	call waitfor 'Password:'
You	**hakensak**	call send 'hakensak'

This next section of code is required only if you have dynamic IP addresses.

```
39: /* Parse the results of the SLIP command to determine our address. */
40: /* We use the "waitfor_buffer" variable from the waitfor routine   */
41: /* to parse the stuff we get from the Annex after waiting for an    /
42: /* appropriate point in the data stream.                          */
43: call waitfor 'Your address is'
44: parse var waitfor_buffer . 'Annex address is' a '.' b '.' c '.' d '.' .
45: annex_address = a||'.'||b||'.'||c||'.'||d
46: call waitfor crlf
47: parse var waitfor_buffer  a '.' b '.' c '.' d '.' .
48: os2_address = a||'.'||b||'.'||c||'.'||d
```

If you have static IP addresses, you can delete lines 43 through 48 and directly set `os2_address` and `annex_address`. You set the `os2_address` variable to your IP address and the `annex_address` to your destination IP (also called gateway, route, or annex). If, for example, your IP is `999.888.222.1` and your destination IP is `999.888.201.3`, you could substitute the following two lines for lines 43 through 48:

```
os2_address = '999.888.222.1'
annex_address ='999.888.201.3'
```

If you don't have static IP addresses, you'll need to use some variation of lines 43 through 48 (although, it doesn't always require six lines). These are the lines that often give OS/2 users the most trouble. Once you're connected to your SLIP account, your provider sends a statement that indicates your IP numbers. The purpose of these lines is to read the IP statement and parse out your IP address and the destination IP address.

In the example, each IP address is parsed into `a`, `b`, `c`, and `d` components and then put back together using `||` operators. Very often, however, this technique isn't required.

The best way to proceed is to make an exact copy of the text your provider's uses to output the IP numbers. Following is a popular format:

```
SL/IP from 999.888.201.3 to 999.888.222.1 beginning
```

There are many ways in which to handle this. An easy way (assuming that the format is amenable to it) is to parse the line into the two IP addresses directly, rather than breaking it into a, b, c, and d and then putting it back together. The following example would directly parse the line shown into `annex_address` and `os2_address`:

```
call waitfor 'beginning'
parse var waitfor_buffer 'SL/IP from ' annex_address ' to ' os2_address ' '
```

Note that the `waitfor` command is a subroutine defined in CYBERNET.CMD (which is a subroutine not shown here). The command `call waitfor 'beginning'` reads the line that contains beginning. Everything on that line up to the `waitfor` string (in other words, everything up to beginning) is put into a variable called `waitfor_buffer`. You then can parse the `waitfor_buffer` for items contained within it—such as the IP addresses. Just make sure that the `waitfor` string is after the last item you need to parse.

Here is an easy way to avoid making mistakes when putting together the parse line:

1. Make an exact copy of the `SL/IP from` line, from the beginning of the line to the character that immediately precedes the first character in the `call waitfor` string (in other words, the space just before beginning).

2. Type over the IP addresses with the corresponding variable names (for example, replace 999.888.201.3 with *annex_address*, and replace 999.888.222.1 with *os2_address*).

3. Put single quote marks around each of the distinct components, other than the variable names ('SL/IP from ', ' to ', and ' ').

4. Add a single space before and after each variable name (' to ' os2_address ' ', for example, not ' to 'os2_address' ').

You undoubtedly will find many variations in how IP numbers are displayed. The IBM Internet Connection, for example, displays the IP numbers on successive lines rather than on the same line, as in the following example:

```
129.37.3.222 is your IP address.
129.37.1.11 is the Gateway IP address.
```

To handle this, you could use two `call wait_for` commands and two `parse` commands, as follows:

```
call wait_for ' is your'
parse var waitfor_buffer os2_address
call wait_for ' is the Gateway'
parse var waitfor_buffer annex_address
```

In the next section of code, you do not need to adjust lines 55 and 56; however, it is essential that they be correctly executed for your SLIP session to start. If everything up to this point seems to "work," but your OS/2 SLIP applications fail, it is likely that these commands were not executed correctly.

```
49: /* Flush anything else */
50: call flush_receive 'echo'
51: /* Now configure this host for the appropriate address, */
52: /* and for a default route through the Annex.           */
53: say 'SLIP Connection Established'
54: say 'Configuring local address =' os2_address ', Annex =' annex_address
55: 'ifconfig sl0' os2_address annex_address 'netmask 255.255.255.0'
56: 'route add default' annex_address '1'
```

To find out if this is the problem, see if you can read your IP address and the destination IP address in the SLIPPM status window. If you can, open an OS/2 command line session and issue the `ifconfig` and `route` commands directly, as in the following:

```
ifconfig sl0 ipaddr ipdest netmask 255.255.255.0
route add default ipdest 1
```

Replace *ipaddr* with your IP address, and *ipdest* with the destination (also called gateway, annex, or route) IP address. Then try your SLIP software (Gopher usually is the easiest and quickest to respond). If it now works, then take another look at the part of your REXX program that parses the IP numbers to see where it might be going wrong. It sometimes helps to make a small stand-alone REXX program that you can use to test the parsing. Doing this enables you to test the program logic without having to go through SLIPPM, as in the following:

```
/* IP Parsing Test Program */
waitfor_buffer = 'SL/IP from 999.888.201.3 to 999.888.222.1 beginning'
parse var waitfor_buffer 'SL/IP from ' annex_address ' to ' os2_address ' '
say 'My IP is 'os2_address
say 'Gateway IP is 'annex_address
```

The parsing line setup must be perfect. If you include a space in the wrong place, it will not work correctly. If you accidentally swap your IP address and the destination/gateway IP address, the resulting `ifconfig` and `route` commands won't work. Now you probably know why I stress using a REXX script as a last resort. Use it only when no other approaches work.

The last two lines of the script are as follows:

```
57: /* All done */
58: exit 0
```

Building a REXX command file can be extremely tedious and time consuming. As a programming language, REXX is very intolerant of any mistakes and is not always helpful in showing you what and where the errors are. Careful input can help you avoid many mistakes, as can developing a basic understanding of REXX. See the online REXX Reference in the OS/2 Information folder for additional information.

Sometimes it helps to create a stand-alone REXX program that you can use to test the parsing. That way, you can test the program logic without having to go through SLIPPM, as in the following example:

```
/* IP Parsing Test Program */
waitfor_buffer = 'SL/IP from 999.888.201.3 to 999.888.222.1 beginning'
parse var waitfor_buffer 'SL/IP from ' annex_address ' to ' os2_address ' '
say 'My IP is 'os2_address
say 'Gateway IP is 'annex_address
```

Put the preceding lines into a file (call it something like IPTEST.CMD) and enter **iptest** at the OS/2 command line. Does it correctly tell you your IP address and gateway IP address? If so, then great. Take the working parse line and copy it to your Internet REXX dialing script.

If it doesn't work, you must work on it. When trying to correctly set up the parsing line, it must be perfect. If you include a space in the wrong place inside the quotes, it will not work correctly. If you have mismatched quotes (you must have an even number of 's in a line of REXX code), the program won't work. If you accidentally swap your IP address and the destination/gateway IP address, it won't work. Now you probably know why I stress using a REXX script as a last resort. Use it only when no other approaches work.

SLIPTERM

Another option for the Login Sequence field is to use the word slipterm (must be lowercase!). The SLIPTERM program is a simple terminal program window that you can use to dial into your SLIP account. The use of SLIPTERM is entirely manual. It sometimes is useful because it is compatible with your SLIP site, and it shows you exactly what your script *sees* when logging on. It sometimes is more useful than using a regular communications program (such as HyperAccess Lite or PMComm) because you can actually start a full SLIP session from SLIPTERM, although you can't do this from regular communications programs (except for some, such as TE/2, which have been enhanced so that you can use them in this way).

To use SLIPTERM, just put the word slipterm into your Login Sequence field. When SLIPPM "sees" slipterm, the rules change. In particular, when using SLIPTERM, the following SLIPPM Settings notebook fields are not used:

◆ Phone number
◆ Modem type
◆ Modem dialing Prefix
◆ Modem initialization strings

The fields are not completely ignored, however. SLIPPM recognizes that if you're using SLIPTERM, you probably are using it for diagnostic purposes. Thus, when you use the SLIPTERM option, your settings for these fields are not blanked out.

When you use the SLIPTERM option, SLIPPM starts SLIP and then opens a SLIPTERM window (see Figure 4.10). Once open, the entire connection dialog is manual. You will need to type any modem setup strings, the command to dial the modem, your SLIP login ID, and so on. Fortunately, once you are connected, SLIPPM does issue the necessary `ifconfig` and `route` commands to configure the IP numbers.

FIGURE 4.10.

SLIPTERM looks like a regular OS/2 window in which you "talk" to your COM port.

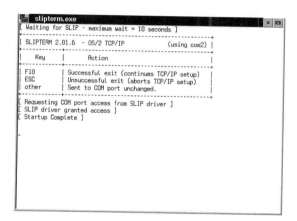

Unfortunately, if your IP numbers are assigned dynamically, you will have to enter dummy numbers into the Connect Info page fields in order to use SLIPTERM. Once connected and the correct numbers have been issued, you then can open an OS/2 command line window and issue the `ifconfig` and `route` commands manually, just to make sure that the SLIP session is working. There is more on this in a moment. Once you have your IP number (*ipaddr*) and the destination or gateway IP number (*ipdest*), you can run the following commands from the OS/2 command line:

```
ifconfig sl0 ipaddr ipdest netmask 255.255.255.0
route add default ipdest 1
```

Replace *ipaddr* and *ipdest* with the appropriate numbers. (If you have to do a lot of testing, you can turn these two lines into a command file.)

After you issue these commands, your SLIP session should be set up and ready to use. If you run UltiMail, however, you might be prompted to type your name or ID because SLIPPM hasn't really done a complete job of setting the TCP/IP environment. In any event, this mode of operations isn't intended to be a permanent way to connect to the Internet—it's just a way to try to nail down the place in which problems might be occurring, and to ensure that script elements are set up properly.

Note

In the following listing, user input (**send** text) is shown in bold and output from the modem and gateway system (*wait for* or *expect* text) is shown in italics. All other text is placed on-screen by the SLIPTERM program. Following is an example of a typical SLIPTERM session:

```
[ Waiting for SLIP - maximum wait = 10 seconds ]
+— — — — — — — — — — — — — — — — — — — — — — — — — — — —+
¦  SLIPTERM 2.01.6  - OS/2 TCP/IP              (using com2) ¦
+— — — — —+— — — — — — — — — — — — — — — — — — — — — — —+
¦   Key   ¦        Action                              ¦
+— — — — —+— — — — — — — — — — — — — — — — — — — — — — —+
¦  F10    ¦  Successful exit (continues TCP/IP setup)  ¦
¦  ESC    ¦  Unsuccessful exit (aborts TCP/IP setup)   ¦
¦  other  ¦  Sent to COM port unchanged.               ¦
+— — — — —+— — — — — — — — — — — — — — — — — — — — — — —+
[ Requesting COM port access from SLIP driver ]
[ SLIP driver granted access ]
[ Startup Complete ]

atdt555-55553
CONNECT 14400/REL-LAPM-COMP
Express Access Online Communications Service 301-220-2020
        Communication settings are Eight bits no parity.
        Don't have an account?  Login as new (no password).

access login:s0xxyyz
Password:abcdxyz
SL/IP session from (164.109.201.13) to 164.109.215.16
beginning....[F10][Shutdown Complete]
```

Note

> The typed password is shown in the listing. In the actual SLIPTERM output, however, the password does not appear. Also shown is the fact that the user pressed the F10 key after getting the SL/IP session from... message from the Internet provider system. [F10] does not show up in the SLIPTERM display, however.

So why use SLIPTERM? Use SLIPTERM when you can't get connected, or when you don't have any other means of displaying provider system output. Using SLIPTERM, you can see how a SLIP login session *should* go, which will enable you to determine whether you can leave the Login Sequence field blank, use an embedded script, use a response file, or have to use a REXX program.

The SLIPTERM program runs in an OS/2 window, which means that you can use the Clipboard to copy information from it into the Login Sequence field, other SLIPPM Settings notebook fields, or into an editor window to assist in setting up a script or REXX program. To copy information from the SLIPTERM window onto the OS/2 Clipboard, follow these steps:

1. Press the Alt key once and then press the K key. This places the window into marking mode.

2. Using the mouse or the keyboard (Shift+cursor-movement keys), select the text you want to place on the Clipboard, as shown in Figure 4.11.

3. Press Enter to copy the text onto the Clipboard.

Once the text is on the Clipboard, you can copy it to the place it is needed. Suppose that you have static IP addresses but don't have them written down anywhere. Use SLIPTERM to log onto your SLIP account so that the IP numbers appear on-screen. Next, copy your IP number to the Clipboard using the preceding steps. Then, open the SLIPPM Settings notebook to the Connect Info page and paste the IP number into the appropriate field. Repeat the procedure for the other IP number. When entering IP numbers, it is very easy to make mistakes, so use this technique to avoid typing errors!

FIGURE 4.11.

You can copy text from the SLIPTERM window to the OS/2 Clipboard.

Selected text ——————

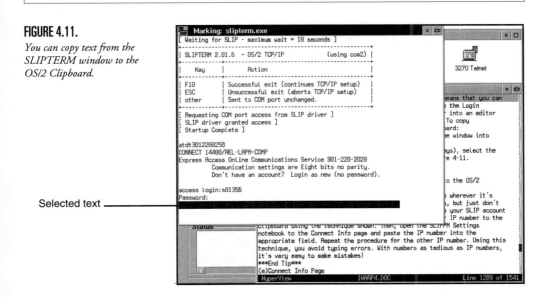

Connect Info Page

For the Connect Info page, you will need the following information:

Your IP Address	This is the IP number that is assigned to your computer when you are on the Internet. Ask your provider if your IP number is always the same, or if it changes each time you log onto the Internet.
Destination IP Address	This is the IP number of the computer that connects your computer to the Internet. This system sometimes is called a gateway, annex, or router.
Netmask	This almost always is 255.255.255.0. It sometimes is called a *Personal IP Netmask*.
MTU Size	Usually 1006 for SLIP and 1500 for PPP. Ask your provider what MTU size you need.
VJ Compression	Ask your provider if you're using CSLIP (compressed SLIP). If you have a choice between SLIP or CSLIP, choose CSLIP. If you have a further choice of PPP, choose PPP, and don't worry about the VJ Compression setting.
Domain Nameserver	This is the name or IP address of the computer that translates Internet names into IP addresses. This item sometimes is called the *primary name server* or just *name server*.
Your Host Name	This is the first part of your e-mail address. If your e-mail address is smith@acme.com, then your host name is smith.
Your Domain Name	This is the last part of your e-mail address. If your e-mail address is socks@whitehouse.gov, then your domain name is whitehouse.gov. And, here's a can of tuna for you!

Server Info Page

For this page, you will need the following information:

News Server	This is the name or the IP address of the computer that handles Usenet newsgroups.
Gopher Server	This field is optional. If you don't fill it in, Gopher will default to the IBM Gopher—os2info.gopher.ibm.com. If your provider has a Gopher site, however, you might want to explore it.
WWW Server	This is the default home page for the WebExplorer. If you don't fill it in, the WebExplorer will default to http://www.ibm.net.

POP Mail Server	This is the computer on which your mail resides. This often is the same as your domain name, but not always. It might be identified as the POP3 server, as well.
Reply Domain	This is the place in which replies to your mail are stored. This usually is the same as your POP Mail Server. Ask your provider if they are different.
Reply (Mail) ID:	This is the ID you use to send and receive e-mail. This and your reply domain, separated with an @ sign, usually form your e-mail address. For example, my e-mail address (at the moment) is tyson@cpcug.org. So, my Reply (Mail) ID is tyson, and my Reply Domain is cpcug.org.
POP Login ID	This is the user ID you use to log onto your POP Mail Server (and usually is not the same ID you use to log onto your SLIP or PPP server). Most of the time, your Reply (Mail) ID and POP Login ID are identical. If you have a UNIX shell account associated with your SLIP setup, this usually is the same as your shell user ID or login. If your provider gave you a data sheet, this ID might be called user ID, mail ID, POP mail ID, or something similar. If only one ID and one password is provided for a SLIP or PPP account, then it is possible that your SLIP and PPP user IDs and passwords are the same.
POP Password	This is the user ID you use to log onto your POP mail server. If you have a shell account, this password usually is the same as your shell password.

Modem Info Page

For the Modem Info page, you need the following information:

Modem Type	What type of modem do you have? If yours isn't listed, choose Hayes-Compatible.
Com Port	This is the port you are using for your modem (usually COM1 or COM2).
Speed	This is the maximum speed supported by your modem (you usually can set this to 57600 for 14,400 and 28,800 modems).
Data Bits	Check with your provider. This almost is always 8.
Parity	Check with your provider. This is almost always NONE.
Prefix	This is the dialing prefix for your modem (almost always ATDT). If you choose a modem under Modem Type, then this will be set for you.

Initialization String 1	This usually is AT&F. If you choose a modem under Modem Type, then this will be set for you.
Initialization String 2	This string varies widely. If you choose a modem under Modem Type, then this will be set for you, but can be wrong.
Dial/Answer	Choose Dial.
Call Waiting	If you have call waiting, enable this feature to prevent being disconnected while online.

Don't Take Modem Settings for Granted!

Modem setup sometimes can be crucial. The settings for my Intel 144/144e modem, for example, did not work correctly. Each time the second initialization string was sent to the modem, the modem returned the word ERRROR rather than OK. Experimentation revealed problems with the following string:

```
AT&C1&D2&S1&T5S7=60S0=2
```

By carefully trimming away one setting at a time, I discovered that the problem was the S0=2 command, which is used to put the modem into Answer mode (you might use this when connecting two computers with the Internet Access Kit together by modem). By removing that command, the string began returning OK. Unlike the IBM Internet Dialer program, however, the Dial Other Internet Provider program settings do not have an option to save user modifications. This means that you have to modify your modem settings each time you make a change that blanks out the modem type (when you use a script file, for example, the SLIPPM Settings notebook blanks out the modem type). If you later remove the script file and go back to using a different dialing approach, your former modem type entry will be gone.

If you don't want to edit your modem's initialization string each time you select your modem anew, you can modify it in the underlying list. To do this, first create a backup copy of TCPIP\ETC\MODEM.IAK. This is the list of modems that SLIPPM uses (rather than MODEM.LST, which, curiously enough, is used by the IBM Internet Dialer DIALER.EXE program). You can edit MODEM.IAK to change the initialization strings to whatever is appropriate for your modem. You even can add entries. Just copy the existing entry and give it a new name. For example, I started with the following:

```
[Intel 144/144e]
BAUD_RANGE=1200-115200
BAUD=38400
INIT1="AT&F"
INIT2="AT&C1&D2&S1&T5S7=60S0=2"
I copied that string and created:
[ Herb's Intel 144/144e]
BAUD_RANGE=1200-115200
BAUD=38400
INIT1="AT&F"
INIT2="AT&C1&D2&S1&T5S7=60"
```

Note two things. First, I added `Herb's` before `Intel`. The space before `Herb's` causes my modem to appear first on the modem list when SLIPPM sorts the `MODEM.IAK` list. Second, I removed the offending `S0=2`. Now, any time I choose a modem from the list, my modem is listed at the top. In fact, it is listed at the bottom, too. Once I have a working entry, I delete everything else in `MODEM.IAK`. (Remember, I created a backup copy; don't edit `MODEM.IAK` unless you have a backup copy). That makes SLIPPM a little faster, and eliminates the possibility of me selecting the wrong modem.

Using TIA

Even if you don't have a SLIP or PPP account, you still might not be out of luck. Using a program called *TIA*, it is possible to get most SLIP services using an ordinary Internet UNIX "Shell" account. In order to do this, however, the TIA program (or other SLIP emulator) must be present and available on your Internet provider's system.

What If TIA Isn't Available on My Internet Provider's System?

It can become available in two ways. It is increasingly common for providers to license TIA directly from Cyberspace Development, Inc. If it isn't on your provider's system, you might consult them to see if they're willing to get it. If that fails, however, single user trials and licenses are available. For additional information, use the `markeplace.com` FTP (use `marketplace.com` as the host, anonymous as the user, and your e-mail address as the password).

Once there, look for the `/tia/read.me` file. This file will contain all the information you need to get TIA working on your Internet provider's UNIX system. Note that there are different versions of TIA, and getting the correct one is essential.

Don't pay for a TIA license until you have verified that it works for you. Get an evaluation license and make sure that it works before you buy it. Don't buy a pig in a poke, as the saying goes.

If TIA is available on your provider's system, getting it started really is not much more complicated than connecting to a SLIP account. Most users can do everything they need by using an embedded response script in the Login Sequence field in SLIPPM. Assuming that TIA is set up for public access on your system, a variation of the following embedded response script usually is all you need:

```
\r
ogin:
[LOGINID]
assword:
[PASSWORD]
>
tia
```

To see if this will work for you, you will need to call your provider's system, and log onto your shell account. Do the system prompts match those shown here? On some systems, there might be an additional layer or two. On my provider system, for example, there is an additional login/ password dialog that comes at the beginning, during which I select a subprovider's host system.

SLIPPM Settings Notebook Setup When Using TIA

In addition to a script to start the TIA program, you also need a few other changes in the SLIPPM Settings notebook setup. The following entry fields will be different from a standard SLIP setup.

TIA Login Info

When using TIA, the following fields are different from standard SLIP or PPP:

User ID	The user ID should be your UNIX shell account ID, which usually is the same as your mail ID.
Password	The password should be the one corresponding to your shell account ID.
Phone Number	This is the telephone number for accessing your shell account. Note that whether the phone number is used depends on the contents of the Login Sequence field.
Login Sequence	This is a script similar to the preceding field, or a reference to a response file or REXX program. If you use a response file or REXX program, then you need to insert the necessary step to run TIA. Usually, your REXX program should *not* attempt to parse IP addresses because TIA does not usually provide any. In some installations, however, some TIA versions might provide the IP for the host (destination system). If so, then you might need to set up your TIA script to parse out the [$IPDEST] string.
Connection Type	Set this to SLIP.

TIA Connect Info

You will need the following information when using TIA:

Your IP Address	Most people using TIA don't have an IP address. Instead use a dummy IP. Try 192.0.2.1. If that doesn't work, then try 0.0.0.0.
Destination IP Address	This is the IP address of the computer in which your shell account resides.
Netmask	Use 255.255.255.0.

MTU Size	Use `1006`.
VJ Compression	Set to `Off` (unchecked).
Domain Nameserver	Use the IP address for your provider's name server. If you don't know it, then ask your provider. On most UNIX host systems, however, you can find the IP address of your domain nameserver by entering **`nslookup`** at the UNIX command line. It usually returns the name and IP number of your nameserver. To leave the NSLOOKUP program, enter **`exit`**.
Your Host Name	Type the first part of your e-mail address (if your e-mail address is `smith@jones.com`, then type **`smith`**).
Your Domain Name	Type the second part of your e-mail address (if your e-mail address is `smith@jones.com`, then type **`jones.com`**).

TIA Server Info

Use the same server information you use for normal SLIP or PPP (see "Server Info Page" earlier in this chapter).

TIA Modem Info

Use the same modem information you use for normal SLIP or PPP. Note that the modem fields used depend on the contents of the Login Sequence field in the Login Info page.

How TIA Differs from SLIP

For the most part, you can use TIA the same way you use SLIP. There are a few technical differences, however. The most important difference is that TIA users do not have their own IP address. This means that, unlike when you're running real SLIP or PPP, your computer is not actually *on* the Internet. Even so, most OS/2 SLIP client software—Gopher, Ultimedia Mail/2 Lite, the WebExplorer, and telnet—works just fine.

Notable exceptions to working "just fine" are FTP and FTP-PM. FTP servers usually insist on having an IP number for FTP users. The problem, however, is that you don't have one. Many users find that the OS/2 FTP clients do in fact connect to FTP servers, but only after a long (two to three minutes) wait. Some users also report better results using a local IP of `0.0.0.0` than `192.0.2.1`, and vice versa; so try both.

Another exception is the OS/2 Ping program. Ping is used to see if a computer is reachable from your Internet site. The command `ping ftp.ibm.net`, for example, will give you information about whether `ftp.ibm.net` is available for direct communications. Because `ping` needs a real (not a dummy) IP address for the pinger, you cannot use OS/2's `ping` command when running TIA. You can use `ping` on your host system; however, to do that you would need to use telnet to log onto your host.

There may be other programs as well that don't work or work differently when using TIA. Moreover, TIA is being improved in ways that might soon overcome some of the current limitations. So, if your version of TIA enables you to do things that I say you can't, it probably has been changed!

CHAPTER FIVE
HANDLING E-MAIL WITH ULTIMEDIA MAIL/2 LITE

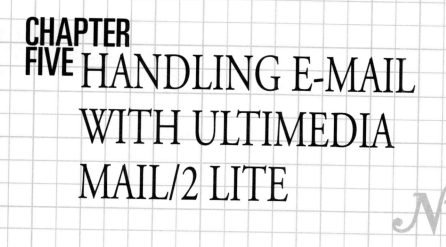

Ultimedia Mail/2 Lite (UltiMail) is a set of OS/2 objects that enables you to send, receive, and organize your electronic mail (e-mail). It is based on a fuller-featured Ultimedia Mail/2 that can be bought separately from IBM. (In fact, at the time of this writing IBM had announced a product called IBM Workgroups that will feature Ultimedia Mail/2).

Note

> Missing spelling? The full version of Ultimedia Mail/2 includes spelling capabilties. The UltiMail included with OS/2 does not have those capabilities, and the references to spelling in UltiMail's Help file are in error.

Using UltiMail, you can send and receive e-mail containing text, graphics, and binary files. In this chapter, you will see how to get UltiMail set up, how to send and receive e-mail, how to manage your e-mail, and how to customize your setup for productivity and efficiency.

UltiMail, loved by few and hated by many, is a very feature-rich e-mail package. It might or might not suit your needs or tastes. I happen to like it (but I don't love it), but I understand that among Internet veterans, liking UltiMail might alone be considered adequate grounds for being committed to a mental facility. Love it, like it, or hate it, however, UltiMail has zillions of features. Writing a complete how-to manual for UltiMail could easily consume the page count allotted for this whole book. Rather than do that, however (which would add to those commitment grounds mentioned earlier), this chapter covers UltiMail basics, showing you how to send and receive e-mail as well as how to recover from some known problems.

What Is E-Mail?

The term *e-mail* refers to private (sort of) messages between you and specific Internet users with e-mail addresses. Contrast e-mail with articles you might post to newsgroups. In newsgroups, postings are public and cannot be directed to a specific person. You can write "Attention: Bob Smith" somewhere in a newsgroup article or article header, but there's no guarantee that Bob Smith will see it. Moreover, messages in newsgroups are intended for public reading, not private. Your e-mail is not generally available for public view.

Don't be lulled into a false sense of security. I just said that e-mail is *sort of* private. Anytime you transmit a message electronically through a network controlled by others, absolute privacy cannot be assumed. In order for you to send or receive mail, it must be sent to various intermediate mail servers and routers. To do that, a disk file is copied from your computer to a mail server computer. It's then copied from there to another destination until it reaches the intended recipient. At any point along the way, whoever administers those computers can—if they are so inclined or motivated—intercept your mail. There are numerous opportunities for intruders to intrude.

As someone once said, *there's no reason to be overly paranoid,* which means, I guess, that you should be just paranoid enough, right? In reality, e-mail system administrators probably have no inclination to snoop—but they could if they wanted to, as could skilled (or even some unskilled) hackers. If somebody wants badly enough to see your correspondence, they very likely could arrange to do so—without you knowing. Where there's a will, there's a way. Forewarned is forearmed. A stitch in time saves nine. Trust, but don't trust. Is that enough aphorisms for one paragraph?

Thus, for your own privacy and security, never put anything absolutely vital into an electronic message. If you're moderately paranoid, there are encryption schemes you can use that provide a moderate amount of privacy. However, I wouldn't personally bet my life or my business on any of them. Of course, maybe I'm being overly paranoid (see above).

When you install the Internet tools for OS/2 Warp, the installation program creates a folder called Ultimedia Mail/2 Lite (which I'll call the UltiMail folder). The UltiMail folder, shown in Figure 5.1, contains the objects shown in Table 5.1.

FIGURE 5.1.

The Ultimedia Mail/2 Lite folder contains objects for sending and receiving e-mail on the Internet.

Table 5.1. Contents of the UltiMail folder.

Object	Explanation
Information	A tutorial, a readme file, and the UltiMail User's Guide
Names and Addresses (Address Book)	Object for storing electronic addresses of your correspondents
New Letter	Object for creating new letters
Mail Cabinet	Main mail object and container for all top-level mail folders
In-basket	Initial location for all incoming mail

The Mail Cabinet is the hub of the action. It manages each of the other active UltiMail components (Address Book, In-basket, and New Letter).

Getting Started with Ultimedia Mail/2 Lite

To start UltiMail, you should be connected to the Internet. You don't have to be, as you will see later, but for now, it helps if you are. So, to start UltiMail, first use the IBM Internet Dialer or the Dial Other Internet Provider object to connect to the Internet. Then, start UltiMail by double-clicking on the Mail Cabinet. You can also start UltiMail by double-clicking on any of the other UltiMail modules:

- ◆ In-basket in the UltiMail folder
- ◆ Address Book in the UltiMail folder
- ◆ New Letter object in the UltiMail folder

When you open the Mail Cabinet the first time, you'll get a view similar to that in Figure 5.2. The Received Mail and Sent Mail folders are storage locations for mail you receive and send. Mail you create is stored in the Sent Mail folder. Mail you receive shows up in the In-basket, but can be dragged to the Received Mail folder, if that's your preference.

FIGURE 5.2.

The Mail Cabinet contains Received Mail and Sent Mail folders for storing incoming and outgoing mail.

To see if someone has sent you any mail, double-click on the In-basket object. When you first open the In-basket, it automatically *refreshes* the In-basket. That is, it logs onto your mail server to see if there are any new messages for you. It then displays any new messages along with any older messages that you might have left in the In-basket from previous sessions, as shown in Figure 5.3. Letters in the In-basket are represented by envelopes. Letters you have not read are shown as closed envelopes, while letters you have read are shown as opened envelopes.

FIGURE 5.3.

The In-basket is where all incoming mail arrives.

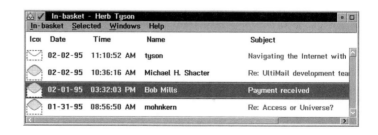

If you don't have any e-mail yet, you can send yourself a letter just to make sure everything is working. By sending yourself a letter, you can test sending and receiving in one fell swoop. To send a brand-new e-mail letter, double-click the New Letter object in the Ultimedia Mail/2

Lite folder. This opens a new letter window, as shown in Figure 5.4. Click the Name button. By default, before you've added any other names to the UltiMail Address Book, you should be listed in the Address Book as (ME). Click once on (ME) so that a To: appears to the left, and then click OK.

FIGURE 5.4.

When you choose New Letter, the new letter window is displayed.

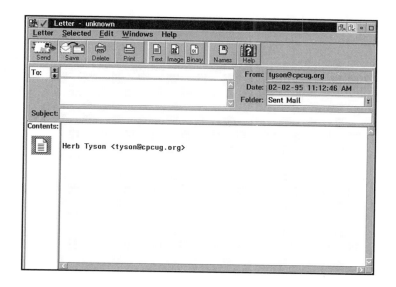

Under Subject, type **Test**. Now click in the letter area, just to the right of Contents:. Type yourself a simple test message, saying something like **Hi, Me!**

Now click the Send button. At this point, UltiMail saves the letter you just wrote to the Sent Mail folder. You can (and should) delete such test messages later on. It then tries to use the information you've provided to send the mail. Within a minute or two—usually sooner—you should get a popup dialog box that says that your letter was queued or sent successfully. If you're offline, it was queued and will be sent the next time you log on to the Internet using either IBM Internet Dialer or Dial Other Internet Provider. Once the letter has been sent, it should be available immediately in your In-basket. Open your In-basket to see. Or, if your In-basket is already open, then choose In-basket | Refresh from the In-basket menu.

If you use some other method to log on to the Internet—that is, if you use SLIP or PPP directly from the command line—you'll have to use Mailq to send your mail. The Mailq program checks the \tcpip\etc\mqueue directory and then launches the Sendmail program. To send the contents of the mqueue directory from the command line, just enter **mailq**. Check MAILQ.LOG to verify whether or not the command was successful. Then again, if you're using SLIP or PPP from the command line, you're probably already an expert at using Mailq and the rest of the OS/2 IAK command-line utilities.

Note

To read an e-mail message, double-click on its envelope to get the view shown in Figure 5.5. When you're done reading a letter, you can respond to it by clicking on the Reply button and composing your reply. To send a reply, click on the Send button. Or, in the case of a test message from yourself, you can delete it by clicking the Delete button. Note that doing this deletes the *received* copy of the letter, but not the *sent* copy. To delete the latter, you would need to open your Sent Letters folder and delete the letter there. For more detailed information on using these facilities, see "Using Ultimedia Mail/2 Lite" later in this chapter.

FIGURE 5.5.

Mail you receive is displayed in the received-letter window.

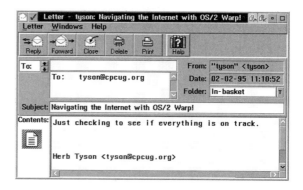

As you go through all this, does everything work okay? If so, you might not absolutely need to read the next section on UltiMail setup. If you did encounter problems—such as being told that the In-basket refresh failed, or that your password or login ID is wrong—you probably need to take a look at some basic setup issues.

Updates and Limitations

The version of UltiMail that ships with OS/2 has several limitations you might want to be aware of before undertaking some kinds of e-mail projects:

◆ The following MIME types aren't supported: enriched text, audio, and motion video

◆ Despite what the UltiMail documentation says, UltiMail Lite does not have a native ability to automatically alert you as new mail is received. The UltiMail In-basket must be refreshed manually either by explicitly opening the In-basket, or by choosing Refresh from the In-basket menu.

◆ The UltiMail Tutorial does not work from the UltiMail Help menu unless you copy `viewhelp.exe` from `\tcpip\bin` to `\tcpip\umail`. The UltiMail Tutorial does work when run from the UltiMail Information folder, however.

A complete list of known problems (or, at least all the ones that IBM is willing to document) is contained in the Read Me First object in the UltiMail Information folder. Check it out! These and other limitations and problems might be alleviated or fixed by updates available online from the Retrieve Software Updates object. You should check regularly for enhancements.

Updates to UltiMail also show up in other places. As this book is being prepared for publication, for example, an update to UltiMail is displayed in the Retrieve Software Updates object. However, it disappeared for three weeks and is back now. Fixes also show up in the following locations (the names keep changing, so look for files beginning with UMAIL and umail):

Walnut Creek   `ftp.cdrom.com`; in the `/.1/os2/incoming` directory, fixes were stored as `umail01.zip`, `UMAILD.EXE` and `UMAILD.TXT` (they're probably stored under a different subdirectory by now; check the file `/.1/os2/00index.txt` for a complete listing of files and where they're stored). Log in to Walnut Creek as anonymous, using your e-mail address as your password.

Hobbes   `hobbes.nmsu.edu`; in the `/os2/warp/patches` directory as `umail01.zip` and `umaild.zip`.

Don't jump the gun. Enhancements and updates are nice. Sometimes, however, they come out of the oven too soon. Unless you have a pioneering spirit (that is, you don't mind falling off the edge of unmapped cliffs), let others chart new territory. When you see a new update appear in the Retrieve Software Updates object, check `comp.os.os2.networking.tcp-ip` (using NewsReader/2) for several days before you install the update. If there are any problems with it that might affect your system or the way you work, someone else will probably trip over it without your having to take a fall yourself. So, who will do the bleeding edge testing? You can rest assured that OS/2 does not suffer from a lack of pioneers!

Using Ultimedia Mail/2 Lite

UltiMail provides tools for sending, receiving, and organizing your e-mail. The active UltiMail modules are as follows. In this section, you'll see what each module is for and how to use it.

In-basket   Mail folder where all of your incoming mail is first placed

Mail Cabinet   Main folder for your mail folders; must be active when using any other UltiMail component

Names and Addresses   Object for storing e-mail addresses

New Letter   Object for creating new e-mail

UltiMail itself is controlled by a program named `umail.exe`. You can start UltiMail by opening any of the active UltiMail modules, or by using `umail.exe` from the OS/2 command line. When you start UltiMail from any of the OS/2 objects in the Ultimedia Mail/2 Lite folder, the defaults for UltiMail are used.

Among other things, one important default is the use of the `umail.pro` profile. This file contains settings for each distinct UltiMail client. Although you can edit this file directly, most changes can be made with much less potential for error by using the settings controls from within the Mail Cabinet modules. If you choose to edit this file, always make a copy first for insurance.

> *Tip*
>
> Under some circumstances, the wrong user ID is inadvertently used to retrieve mail and the ID is changed subsequently. If you look at a listing of the subdirectories under `\tcpip\umail\mailstor`, you will see the wrong one along with several others, including the correct one. Although the messages retrieved previously are no longer available in the correct ID subdirectory, you can force UltiMail to read the errant ID directory, thus displaying a Mail Cabinet for that ID. You do this by setting up an UltiMail profile for the errant user ID. To do this,
>
> 1. Copy `umail.pro` to a new name (such as `other.pro`).
> 2. Using `E.EXE` or some other simple text editor that does not insert carriage returns at wordwrap locations, edit the new profile file (that is, enter `e other.pro` at the OS/2 command line).
> 3. In the `Session:` and `User:` sections, change both of the IDs to the errant ID. Save and close the profile file.
>
> Now, from the OS/2 command line, enter the following command, replacing *other.pro* as necessary:
>
> `umail /pro=other.pro`
>
> The messages stored under the older ID will now be available. Unfortunately, however, there is no easy, built-in method for copying those older messages into the newer Mail Cabinet.

Mail Cabinet

The Mail Cabinet, shown in Figure 5.6, is an electronic filing cabinet for all of your e-mail processed by UltiMail. The default Mail Cabinet contains just a Sent Mail and a Received Mail folder. Each new letter or response to someone else's mail you create is placed into the Sent Mail folder by default. You can change that default, as you will see.

FIGURE 5.6.

The Ultimedia Mail/2 Lite Mail Cabinet is the master container for all UltiMail mail.

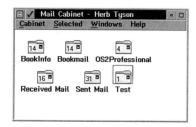

By default, the Received Mail folder is empty until you put something there. Many users open it expecting that mail that arrives from the In-basket will be put there automatically. Such is not the case.

Missing Mail?

One reason some users expect to find mail in the Received Mail folder is an occasional glitch in the way UltiMail works. If the address of an incoming mail message gets mangled, or if incoming mail mistakenly gets posted into your mail account (mistakes happen), UltiMail does not put it into your In-basket. When this happens, you'll see the message `Retrieving message 1 of 1` when you refresh the In-basket, but no mail is in the In-basket after the refresh. It's not in the Received Mail folder either. Instead, it goes either into the Server mailbox or into the Postmaster mailbox. To find it, look for the following subdirectories:

```
\tcpip\umail\mailstor\postmstr
\tcpip\umail\server
```

Using Folders to Manage Mail

If you do not use mail intensively, the Mail Cabinet's default Received Mail and Sent Mail folders will probably be sufficient. If you are a heavy user of UltiMail, however, and if you decide to keep much of your correspondence, it's a good idea to create alternative, and more descriptive, containers for mail you send and receive. For example, if you have different projects, you might create distinct folders for each, as shown in Figure 5.7. You can even create subfolders.

FIGURE 5.7.

You can create a hierarchy of folders for organizing your mail.

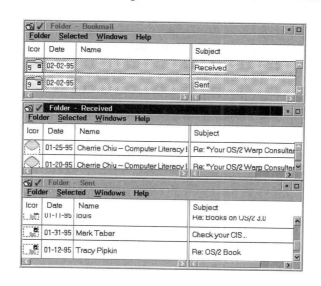

To create a new mail folder in the Mail Cabinet, follow these steps:

1. From the Mail Cabinet menu, choose Cabinet | New Folder (or press Alt+F). The Create New Folder dialog box appears as shown in Figure 5.8.

2. In the Name box, type a descriptive name for the folder (such as `Smith: Received`).

3. You can ignore the Server box unless you are logged on to an actual UltiMail server (as opposed to a POP mail server). If you are logged on to a UltiMail server, choose the server on which you want the new folder created. Otherwise, the default is to create the new folder on your own system (usually displayed as your user ID in parentheses).

4. Click OK.

FIGURE 5.8.

The Create New Folder dialog box.

The folders you create in this way will have actual OS/2 folders associated with them on drive objects. However, UltiMail folders behave differently. For example, UltiMail folders include a count of the number of subfolders and messages contained therein. UltiMail folders also are able to resolve UltiMail directory entries into messages, whereas a normal OS/2 folder cannot. Figure 5.9 contrasts a normal OS/2 view of an UltiMail folder with an UltiMail view.

FIGURE 5.9.

A normal OS/2 folder is much less descriptive than an UltiMail folder.

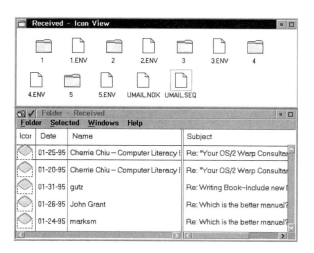

To create a subfolder, open the folder where you want the subfolder to reside. Then press Alt+F and follow the same procedure as shown above to name and create the subfolder.

After the desired folders have been created, you can drag mail to them from the Sent Mail folder and from the In-basket. To do this, open the In-basket. If the target folder is in the Mail Cabinet, you do not need to open the folder to drag mail to it. If the target folder is a subfolder of a folder in the Mail Cabinet, you will need to open the folder in which the subfolder resides. To move mail from the In-basket to its preferred storage location, follow these steps:

1. Position the mouse pointer over the mail item you want to move, and press and hold mouse button 2.

2. While holding the mouse button, move the mouse pointer to the target folder or subfolder; the mail item will move with the pointer as long as the button is held.

3. Release the mouse button when the mail item is over the target folder, as shown in Figure 5.10.

FIGURE 5.10.

To organize your mail, you can drag letters to the folder where you want to keep them.

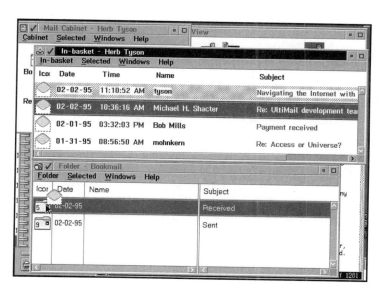

To copy mail rather than move it, hold down the Ctrl key when you drop the mail into the new location. It will be copied rather than moved.

You also can move or copy mail from the In-basket without dragging. Select the items you want to move or copy, then click mouse button 2 on any one of the selected items, and click the Move or Copy option. When the message is displayed, as shown in Figure 5.11, choose the destination folder from the list.

Tip

You also can move a letter from the letter window. After you open a letter, click the dropdown arrow to the right of Folder just under the Date field. Select the folder into which you want the current letter stored. When you close or save the letter, it will be moved to the selected folder.

FIGURE 5.11.

Activate the Move Letter dialog box using the mouse button 2 popup menu.

You also can delete and copy letters from a folder view. Select the letters you want to delete, then use mouse button 2 to display the context menu. Click Delete. Letters can also be dragged from a folder to the Shredder.

Warning

Delete with care! Once letters are deleted, the mail system does not provide a mechanism for undeleting. You sometimes can use OS/2's UNDELETE command (if it's enabled) to recover the deleted mail. However, it's very tedious and uncertain. That's because UltiMail handles mail using files and subdirectories. When you delete a mail message, the underlying files and subdirectories are removed. To use OS/2's UNDELETE command to recover them, you would first have to restore the subdirectories—the names of which you probably don't know and can't determine *ex poste*. Alternatively, some third-party UNDELETE programs sometimes can restore files from subdirectories that no longer exist. Look for filenames that match JW*.* (JW*.TXT for text components, JW*.BIN for binary components, JW*.GIF for GIF files, and so on) for the messages themselves and under *.ENV (where * is a number) for the message headers.

Folder Settings

Mail folders, including the In-basket, can be set to display in a variety of ways. Each folder's settings are stored independently, as are normal OS/2 folders. To change the settings for a folder, choose Folder | Settings from the menu (to change the In-basket's settings, choose In-basket | Settings from the In-basket menu). The Settings notebooks for the In-basket and for other mail folders are identical. Page 1 of a typical Folder – Settings notebook is shown in Figure 5.12.

FIGURE 5.12.

Page 1 of a mail Folder –
Settings notebook.

Why Don't the UltiMail Components Have Settings?

Unlike most OS/2 objects, settings for the UltiMail components (Folders, Mail
Cabinet, In-basket, New Letter, and Names and Addresses) are not available from
mouse button 2 popup menus. To access settings for these, the objects must first be
opened.

You can use the Folder – Settings notebook to change the following:

◆ Which information fields are displayed, and whether or not a separator appears to the
   right of the item
◆ Sort order
◆ Position of individual fields
◆ Text color of individual fields
◆ Width allocated for each individual field
◆ Whether field titles are displayed
◆ Font used to display folder contents (font control affects all fields)
◆ Use and location of the splitbar

Changing folder settings can be confusing. That's because most of the changes you make affect
only one field at a time. Changing the display of fields is a multi-step process. To control the
characteristics of any information field, including whether an information field displays in the
folder, first display the folder you want to change, then choose Folder | Settings from the menu.
Then follow these steps:

1. In the Order list, select the field you want to change.

2. In the Field options, enable Visible if you want the selected field to display in the folder. Optionally, you can cause a separator to appear to the right of the field in the folder.

3. Choose a Size for the field (for uniform fields, choose the smallest possible Size setting that lets the whole field display). For variable-width fields, you can choose 0 to set the width wide enough to accommodate the widest item in the list. You might want not to do that with Name and Subject fields, however, because that sometimes would prevent other information from displaying.

4. Choose a color to change the display of the text for the selected field.

To change the order in which fields appear, do the following:

1. Under Order, make sure the Position option is active.

2. Click on the field whose position you want to change.

3. Using mouse button 2, drag the field to a new position, as shown in Figure 5.13.

FIGURE 5.13.

Drag fields in the Order list to change the position and sort order.

If the desired position is too far away from the current position in the list, you can drag in steps. For example, to drag the Reference item to the top of the list, first drag it as high as it will go in the order window and drop it. Then scroll the order window so that Reference is at the bottom. Repeat the procedure until it's where you want it.

Mail in folders is sorted by multiple fields. The default is to sort by date, time, icon, type, priority, and so on. You can change the sort order in the same way you change the position. First, click the Sort option under the Order window. Then select the field whose sorting priority you want to change. Then drag that field—incrementally, if necessary—to the desired location. Then choose Ascending or Descending to determine what goes first and what goes last in the folder display.

After using UltiMail for a while, I discovered that I had a number of test messages scattered throughout my Sent Mail and Received Mail folders. Using folder settings, I re-sorted the listings so that messages that were both to me and from me all clustered together. Virtually all of them were test messages. This made finding and deleting them much easier.

Throughout, however, I kept the Folder – Settings notebook window open. When I was finished, I clicked Undo in the Folder – Settings notebook to cancel the special sort. That way I didn't have to tediously and incrementally drag those sort fields back to where they were.

Now, of course, I file my test messages in a folder called Test. That makes them even easier to find and delete.

In-Basket

Mail you receive arrives into the In-basket. Mail you receive is not added to the Received Mail (or any other) folder by default. Redirection of received mail—into the Received Mail folder or elsewhere—is a manual operation that you can accomplish in several ways. You can drag received mail from the In-basket into the Received Mail folder, if you like. You can also choose a folder while reading mail, using the Folder dropdown list box. There is no built-in way, however, to cause all mail from a given sender to default to a particular folder. See "Using Folders to Manage Mail" earlier in this chapter for additional information.

To see if you have mail, you must be connected to the Internet. The most efficient way to check new mail, once connected, usually is to double-click on the In-basket in the Ultimedia Mail/2 Lite folder. When you open the In-basket that way, the Mail Cabinet opens first, followed by the In-basket. If the Mail Cabinet is already open, you can open the In-basket from the Mail Cabinet menu. From the menu, choose Window | In-basket.

Each time the In-basket is opened, it is automatically refreshed. Refreshing checks the mail server for any new mail. If the In-basket is already open, you can check for new mail by choosing In-basket, Refresh from the menu. Note that there is no shortcut key to exercise the refresh command, nor is there any built-in setting that will automatically perform the refresh for you. As mail is retrieved, you will see the message `Retrieving message 1 of 3`, or something similar.

Where did all the retrieved mail go? Mail received by UltiMail sometimes arrives in separate pieces, but is put back together by UltiMail. When this happens, you might see a refresh message saying something like `Retrieving message 1 of 5`, then `2 of 5`, and so on. Afterward, however, there's only one thing in your In-basket. What's probably happened is that the mail was split into separate pieces and reassembled by UltiMail. If you think some mail actually was delivered but not displayed, then check in the `\tcpip\umail\server` and `\tcpip\umail\mailstor\postmstr` directories for new entries.

Mail you send can get split, as well. The reason is because some mail handlers can handle message only up to a certain size. Increasingly, however, most mail handlers don't have the kinds of limitations they used to have. This makes UltiMail's default size of about 32KB a little problematic. The more pieces into which your mail is split, the more likely it is that there might be handling problems. The developers of UltiMail recommend that the split size be set at 250KB rather than 32KB—especially if you send people large binary files. That setting will be perfectly acceptable for most of the mail handlers in the modern world. If not, then you will probably get back a message rejecting your mail, with a reason for the rejections. At that point, try a smaller split.

You set the split size in `UMAILSVR.PRO`. See the section titled "Setting Up Ultimedia Mail/2 Lite" at the end of this chapter for a discussion of profile files.

Once the In-basket has been refreshed, you can open any of the letters shown. As shown in Figure 5.14, letters that have never been read are displayed as unopened envelope icons. Note that the back of the envelope is displayed rather than the front. This allows you to see that the envelope is still sealed. After a letter has been opened, the display icon looks like an opened envelope.

FIGURE 5.14.

Letters that have never been read are displayed as unopened envelopes.

Ico	Date	Time	Name	Subject
	02-02-95	11:32:03 AM	tyson	A never-read letter!
	02-02-95	11:10:52 AM	tyson	Navigating the Internet with
	02-02-95	10:36:16 AM	Michael H. Shacter	Re: UltiMail development tea
	02-01-95	03:32:03 PM	Bob Mills	Payment received

In-basket - Herb Tyson
In-basket Selected Windows Help

Contrast the icons of letters you receive with letters you send. The view shown in Figure 5.15 contains four envelope icons: received and opened, received but unopened, sent, and unsent. Once you get accustomed to the icons used by UltiMail, you'll be able to tell at a glance whether mail you see in a folder is mail you created or mail you received. You'll also be able to see if it has been sent or opened. Of course, the latter won't tell you if you've actually *read* the mail—merely whether or not you've opened it.

FIGURE 5.15.

Envelope icons indicate the status of the mail.

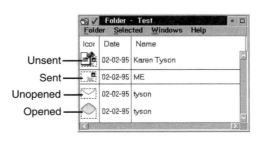

Folder - Test
Folder Selected Windows Help

	Ico	Date	Name
Unsent		02-02-95	Karen Tyson
Sent		02-02-95	ME
Unopened		02-02-95	tyson
Opened		02-02-95	tyson

To read mail you've received, double-click on the envelope icon. The letter is displayed as shown in Figure 5.16.

FIGURE 5.16.
Read incoming mail in a received letter window.

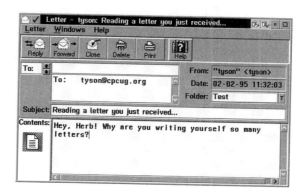

When you receive a letter, you have a number of options, several of which are displayed in the toolbar:

Reply   Compose a reply to the current letter. If you want to quote part of the letter, select the text you want to quote and copy it to the Clipboard before you choose Reply. If you want to quote most or all of the letter, then choose Letter | Forward to Sender from the menu. This might seem like a weird thing to do—after all, why forward Joe Smith's letter back to Joe? It's not so weird, however. It lets you break up the letter into parts, so you can show exactly what your message is responding to, as shown in Figure 5.17.

FIGURE 5.17.
Use selective quoting to show to what your message is responding.

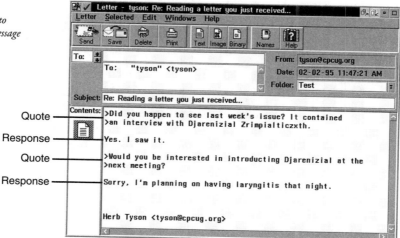

Forward	Use this option to forward the letter to an interested third party.
Close	Close the letter.
Delete	Delete the letter (this is a good option for junk mail and mail whose basic purpose is served by one reading; e-mail can fill up your disk in a hurry if you don't throw out stuff when you're done with it).
Print	Make a paper copy of what you received (that is, if someone sends you directions or instructions that need to be used away from the computer).

Letter Settings

Letter settings can reduce the amount of work and setup you have to perform when you write, reply to, and forward e-mail. To display letter settings, open any letter or start a new one. Then choose Letter | Settings from the menu. The Letter 1 tab of the Letter – Settings notebook is shown in Figure 5.18.

FIGURE 5.18.

Use the Letter 1 tab of the Letter – Settings notebook to customize new letters you create.

This tab affects new letters you create using New Letter or Reply. The components of this page are as follows:

From	This is your return e-mail address. It normally is taken from the profile page of the Mail Cabinet Settings notebook. If you are writing letters for somebody else or a group (for example, the Committee Against Junk Mail), you can put their return address there instead.
Reply to	This is the address to which you want replies sent; it's usually identical to the From address, but it can be different if you want your correspondents to reply to you at a different address, or if you want replies sent to somebody else.

Address   Address style for the To and cc addresses on letters you send: Short (`<tyson@cpcug.org>`), Medium (`"Herb Tyson" <tyson@cpcug.org>`), or Long (`"Herb Tyson 555-555-5555" <tyson@cpcug.org>`).

Signature   Usually your name, e-mail address, and organization (if relevant). This field is inserted in each letter you create, thus saving you the work of having to do it manually.

Create   Use the Create option to specify the default type of mail part that gets created (plain text, binary, graphic, and so on). Most users should leave this set to Text/Plain. The more interesting-looking option, Text/enriched, doesn't work in the lite version of UltiMail unless you specifically set up a handler for enhanced text (using page 5 of UltiMail – Settings, which you activate by choosing Cabinet | Settings from the Mail Cabinet window). Setting up a handler, however, won't do you much good unless your correspondents set up the identical handler (for example, EPM.EXE).

The Letter 2 tab of the Letter – Settings notebook, shown in Figure 5.19, is used to set options for forwarded mail, as well as how letters are viewed and notification about new mail:

Separator   This is the separator that is used to divide a forwarded letter from new text you might write to accompany the forwarded letter.

Annotation   This is the character that is inserted at the beginning of each line of a quoted letter, as shown earlier in Figure 5.17 (lines beginning with > are quoted).

FIGURE 5.19.
The Letter 2 tab of the Letter – Settings notebook.

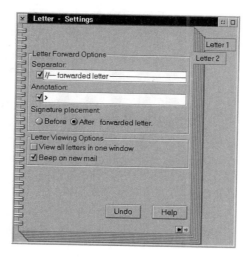

Signature placement   This option controls where your signature is placed in a forwarded letter. Common practice on the Internet is to put it before the text of the forwarded letter so that the reader knows the source of the text before reading it.

View all letters in one window	This option controls whether UltiMail opens a new window each time a different letter is opened. If this option is disabled, you will have multiple letter windows. If this option is enabled, you can use the Ring controls on the letter title bar, just to the left of the minimize (or hide) button to cycle backward or forward among all open letters.
Beep on new mail	This option controls whether or not UltiMail beeps when new mail appears in your In-basket. This option would be a whole lot more useful if UltiMail had a way to automatically refresh the In-basket. But it doesn't, so it's not.

Working in the Letter Window

To read a letter, double-click on an envelope in the In-basket. Note the parts of the letter shown in Figure 5.20. This letter is a fairly complicated one that contains text, an image file, and a binary file. If you're a typical UltiMail user, most of your incoming and outgoing mail will contain just text. However, UltiMail also can be used to send and receive binary files and graphics.

FIGURE 5.20.

The components of the received letter window.

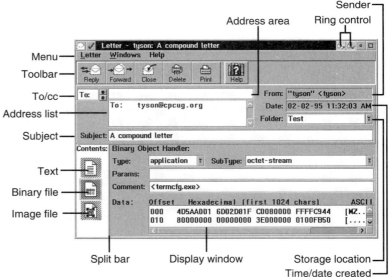

Note that the window menu and toolbar are different for letters you receive and new letters as you are creating them. Let's look for a moment at the parts of the received letter shown in Figure 5.20. The received letter window contains the following areas:

Address area	Shows the address of the main recipient.
Address list	Shows the list of cc recipients.

Date	Shows the time and date that the letter was created (if the time zone is set correctly—see Letter Window Settings).
Folder	Shows the folder where the letter will be stored when you close it.
From	Shows the name of the sender.
Letter Contents or Parts List	Icons indicating the types of letter parts contained in the letter. Letters can contain text, binary, or image parts, icons for which are shown in Figure 5.21. Also shown in the same figure is the popup menu for the letter part icons: Open, Close, and Delete. These options apply just to the part corresponding to the icon the mouse is on when you click mouse button 2.

FIGURE 5.21.

Use the Contents area to control which part of a compound letter is displayed.

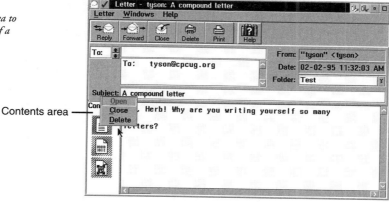

Contents area

Letter display window	Displays the selected letter part: text, a binary display window, or an image.
Menu	The Letter, Windows, and Help menus; use the Letter menu for controlling the current letter, creating a new letter, and for controlling letter settings.
Ring Control	These two icons let you cycle forward or backward among all open letter windows. This option is not available if the View all letters in one window option is disabled (see Letter Settings).
Split Bar	Use the split bar to change the relative display areas for the letter contents list and the letter display window.
Subject	Shows the subject of the letter.
To/cc	Use the To/cc control to set the addressee as the main recipient or a cc recipient (receiver of a carbon copy, even though carbon paper isn't involved).
Toolbar	The letter toolbar contains tools geared to working with received mail.

The window and popup menu change depending on which part of a letter is displayed. To display a different part of a multi-part letter, click on the part type icon in the area to the left of the letter display area. Only one part of a letter can be displayed at a time, although multiple parts can be open at the same time. When viewing multiple graphics in a letter, you can save memory by opening only one part at a time. However, when you open a part that was closed, it will take longer to display.

To open a letter part that is closed, you can click on the letter part icon in the letter contents column at the left of the letter window. To close a letter part, you can choose Close from the display area window or from the corresponding letter part type. Note that a letter part does not have to be displayed in order for you to close it. You also can delete letter parts when you're done with them.

> Note that a letter also can contain multiple parts of the same type. Thus, a letter might contain one text part, three graphics, and a program. You might receive such a letter from someone if they sent some pictures as well as a program to view the pictures, which might be necessary if the pictures are not in BMP or GIF format. Note that this isn't necessarily the most electronically efficient way to send that kind of information. However, it is a way that doesn't require additional software (such as a ZIP archiver). It's also a way that UltiMail can handle without any extra intervention by you. If your Internet connect time is a fixed monthly fee, this might very well be the most efficient way in terms of your own time.

Text Letter Parts

A good way to explore the letter window is to use mouse button 2. If you click mouse button 2 on the letter part display area, for example, UltiMail displays the popup menu shown in Figure 5.22.

FIGURE 5.22.
A text letter part's popup context menu.

Popup menu for text letters

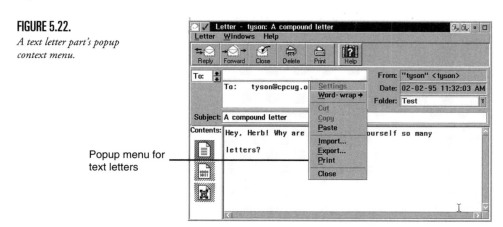

The popup menu for the text part of a letter includes options for working in the text area of a letter. The options are described in Table 5.2.

Table 5.2. Popup menu for the text part of an UltiMail letter.

Popup Option	Description
Word-wrap	When disabled, you must press Enter to break each line so it displays in the current letter window. When enabled, UltiMail automatically wraps the text to fit the window, and inserts two linefeed characters (ASCII 10) and a carriage return (ASCII 13) after each line.
Cut	Delete selected text to the OS/2 Clipboard.
Copy	Copy selected text to the Clipboard without deleting it.
Paste	Insert the contents of the Clipboard.
Import	Replace the current letter part with a file you import. Caution: Many users believe this command will insert an imported file into the current letter at the insertion point. It doesn't; it replaces the whole current letter part. Note also that an Import cannot be undone using Edit | Undo (Alt+Backspace). Undo only undoes editing, and an Import isn't considered an edit.
Export	Save the current letter part to a file, apart from whatever filename UltiMail uses.
Print	Print the current letter part. Note that this works with text and graphics. If you print a graphic image, it will be scaled up to fit on the whole page.
Close	Close the text part of the letter. Note that this does not close the letter window, only the text part. Use the Close tool to close the whole letter.

The Settings option is never available in any of the letter part popup menus in Ultimedia Mail/2 Lite.

Binary Letter Parts

UltiMail displays different popup menus depending on what type of letter part is displayed. When displaying a binary file, for example, the popup menu includes the Run and Process data options, as shown in Figure 5.23.

FIGURE 5.23.
A binary letter part popup menu.

Popup menu for
binary letters

Table 5.3 describes all the options in a binary letter's popup menu.

Table 5.3. Popup menu options for the binary letter part.

Popup Option	Description
Run	Run the selected letter part as a program.
Process data	Specify a program to process the selected letter part.
Import	Replace the current letter part with another file.
Export	Save a copy of the current letter part to your disk.
Close	Close the current letter part (letter parts can be open or closed). This does not close the whole letter, just the current letter part.

Binary letter parts are represented with the icon shown in Figure 5.24. Note that the icon contains 0s and 1s to try to hint to you that it is binary (a misnomer that has resisted redefinition, so I won't fight it here).

FIGURE 5.24.
The binary letter contents icon has little 0s and 1s.

If the displayed letter part is an executable program, you can use the Run option to run the program. For example, suppose someone sends you a letter that contains a program, some spreadsheet files, and a game program of some kind. You can use UltiMail controls to try the game program or to load the spreadsheet files. To run a program from an UltiMail letter window, do the following:

1. Click on the binary part icon that represents the letter part with the executable program.

2. Click mouse button 2 in the data display area (move the mouse pointer so it's in the hexidecimal data), to display the popup menu, as shown in Figure 5.23.

3. Choose the Run option to display the Run/Process data dialog box shown in Figure 5.25. Notice that the Program field is frozen as * current program *. This means that the displayed binary file will be run as a program.

4. Type any necessary parameters and click OK.

FIGURE 5.25.

Use the Run option to run the program stored in a binary letter part.

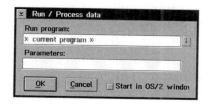

Suppose instead that the binary file is a zipped archive. You can use the Process data option (in the binary letter part popup menu) to unzip it. Use the same procedure as above. This time, however, you will see that the Parameters field is frozen as * current data * (instead of current *program* being frozen in the Run program field). Use the Run program option in the Run / Process data dialog box to type or select the desired program.

If the binary data files you receive are designed to be used with a program you also received, then the entire transaction can't be handled quite so seamlessly. You would need to first export either the data or the program (presumably, whichever you're more likely to keep after reading the letter). Suppose someone sends you data files and a viewer, for example. You might first export the viewer to an .EXE file. You could then use the Process data command and specify the viewer as the program, as follows:

1. Click on the letter part icon for the program you want to export. The program will be displayed in the letter display area, and the name of the program will be displayed in the Comment area of the letter header, such as <VIEWTEST.EXE>.

2. Click mouse button 2 in the hexadecimal or ASCII display area and choose Export.

3. Use the directory controls to navigate to where you want the file to reside, and click OK. (If desired, you can rename the program.)

4. Click on the letter part icon for the data you want to process using the program you just exported.

5. Click mouse button 2 in the letter display area and choose Process data.

6. Use the directory controls to specify the program exported in step 3 and click OK.

One important thing to remember when receiving binary files is that they often consume large amounts of disk space. If someone sends you a multipart letter containing text and binary files, you can preserve the text part (for your records) and delete the binary parts. If you don't delete the binary parts, they will continue to occupy space on your UMAIL subdirectories. If you receive a program and export it to a utilities directory on your hard disk, for example, it doesn't make sense to keep the originally received version around as well. To delete a binary mail part you no longer need, follow these steps:

1. Open the letter that contains the binary part(s) you want to delete.
2. Click mouse button 2 on the letter part icon to display the popup menu.
3. Click Delete.

This action deletes only the binary file in your UltiMail directory. For example, if you created a binary letter part by dragging a .ZIP file onto a letter window (more on this under "New Letter"), a copy of that .ZIP file is created in your UltiMail subdirectory structure. There will be a .ENV header file that tells the original name of the file, but the file will be named something like C:\tcpip\umail\mailstor\tyson\Sent Mail\35\JW512106.BIN. If you choose the Delete option, it's this file that is getting zapped, not the original file. Similarly, if you receive a file and export it to an .EXE or .ZIP or what-have-you, you can then delete the .BIN from your UltiMail directory by choosing the Delete option from the letter part context popup menu.

Image Letter Parts and the Image Editor

The letter window is quite different when displaying an image. It contains a toolbar for creating and editing images, as shown in Figure 5.26. The built-in image-handling capabilities of Ultimedia Mail/2 Lite are limited to just .BMP and .GIF files. Notice that the header for the image window displays the image format (for example, SubType: X-OS2-BMP or GIF). This is an important option when exporting an image.

FIGURE 5.26.

When viewing an image file, the UltiMail window has a vertical toolbar.

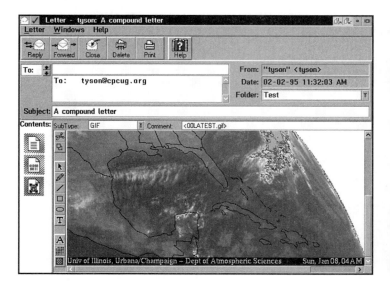

You can edit an image file if you like, changing the way the picture looks, adding annotations or callouts, and so on. The toolbar provides a set of basic tools for working with image files. Note that the image part popup menu has an additional item the other letter part popup menus lacked: Create New. You can—if you like—replace the image with a new one. This option might be more appropriate, however, when working with letters you are creating rather than letters you receive.

The tools provided are very basic, but are useful for performing simple editing and creating graphics. The idea, one supposes, was to provide some basic functionality without trying to provide a full-featured graphics program. If that was the intent, it was successful. Tools provided are as follows:

Cut	Delete selected area to the Clipboard.
Paste	Paste Clipboard contents.
Select	Use mouse button 1 to select an area for a Clipboard cut or copy.
Free Hand	Draw a freehand object.
Line	Draw a straight line.
Rectangle	Draw a rectangle.
Circle	Draw a circle.
Text	Type text.
Fonts	Choose a font for text.
Colors	Choose a fill color for solid objects.
Patterns	Choose a fill pattern.

Most of the tools are intuitive, but using some of them is a little different from what you might expect. When you draw a closed object, for example, like a circle, ellipse, or rectangle, the currently selected color is used and displayed. The next time you select that object, however, the color disappears. This is because you also need to select a fill pattern before drawing the object. The default is no fill at all. Hence, the object effectively uses none of the color you selected. If you select an intermediate or full fill pattern, however, the color will display correctly.

Another difference is how Paste works. When you paste an object, it is placed in the lower-left corner of the drawing area, shown in reverse video. If you then click somewhere in the drawing, the pasted area disappears. That's because you need to *immediately* drag a pasted object to its desired location. Use mouse button 2 to drag the pasted object to where you want it. When you release the mouse button, the object will display in the correct color, and won't disappear with the next mouse click.

Apart from how pasting works, the image-editing tools are not object-oriented. Like Windows Paintbrush, the image you create is all one drawing. If you drop a pasted area in the wrong place, you cannot undo that error. You can either start over, or try to patch it up. Good luck!

Tip

You can use the image window to convert OS/2 .BMP files into .GIF files. Word for Windows, for example, cannot handle OS/2 .BMP files. It can handle .GIF files, however. Someone sent me an OS/2 .BMP file that I wanted to include in a WinWord document. I had two choices:

◆ Select the object in the image window, copy it to the Clipboard, and then paste it directly into WinWord (yes, it does work); or

◆ Use the image window's capabilities to export the file as a .GIF file, which WinWord can handle.

To convert a .BMP file into a .GIF file:

1. Display the .BMP file in an UltiMail letter window (the .BMP file need not have come from an UltiMail letter; you can use the Import option to display any .GIF or OS/2 .BMP file you like).

2. Under SubType, choose GIF (or, if converting the other way, choose OS/2 .BMP).

3. Click mouse button 2 in the image display area, and click Export.

4. Choose the filename and location and click OK.

Customizing the Letter Toolbar

The UltiMail letter window toolbar is customizable. Perhaps this makes up for the fact that it's not drag-and-droppable (that is, you can click on the Print and Delete buttons, but you can't drop a letter part on them for selected printing). In any event, some features, such as Forward to Sender, which quotes a sender's full message, would be handier if they were on the toolbar. Well, you can put them there.

To add an item to a letter toolbar, do the following:

1. Click mouse button 2 on the toolbar and click Create item to display the Customization notebook.

2. Under Position, choose where you want the new tool to appear; under style, choose Regular item, Non-Selectable item, or Spacer item (use the latter to insert gray space between tools). The Non-Selectable item option just creates an option that can't be used. How imaginative!

3. Click the Action tab to display the Action page.

4. Under Function, choose the function you want to assign to the new button (for example, Forward to Sender).

5. Under Parameters, type anything extra you need (that is, you're supposed to be able to set Function to Execute Program and type the name of the program in the Parameters field; however, that's not working at this time).

6. Don't attempt to modify the Function description. The Function description is used by UltiMail to describe what Function does.

7. Click the General tab to display page 3.

8. Type a Title for the button (such as **Reply-Quote**).

9. Choose a Bitmap option (Built-in to use one of UltiMail's ready-made icons; Load file to load a .BMP file of your choosing; or Create to use the OS/2 Icon Editor to create a bitmap). The first time out, just choose Built-in and click on the one you want to use.

10. Close the Customization notebook (Alt+F4 or double-click the title-bar icon), and confirm the tool by clicking Yes to the Add this item prompt.

> At this writing, this feature does not always work. You can add buttons to the menu, but they don't always show up the next time you use UltiMail. Users generally get better results by closing the letter using Letter | Close from the menu (when they close the UltiMail letter window) than when they close by using Close from the title-bar icon. If IBM has updated UltiMail by the time you read this, you might not be reading this.

Once created, you can drag tools to the toolbars of other letter windows, assuming View all letters in one window is not selected. Keep in mind that a tool that makes sense in a window for creating new letters might not make sense in a window for reading mail from someone else. If the customization feature is working properly by the time you read this, you might try disabling the View all letters in one window setting (under Letter | Settings, page 2 of the Settings notebook) to propagate tools to different types of letter windows. You can copy a tool by Ctrl+dragging it where you want it to go. You can move it by just plain dragging it.

If you accidentally drag a customized tool to the Shredder on the letter toolbar, however, it won't be deleted. To delete a tool, you can either drag it to the OS/2 Shredder or choose Delete from the tool button's popup menu.

New Letter

Use the New Letter object to create mail for sending over the Internet. Suppose, for example, you want to send a quick note to an associate with information about a flight you are taking for a meeting. All you need is your associate's Internet address and a connection to the Internet. You can compose letters either online or offline. If you compose mail offline, it is sent the next time you log on to the Internet.

To compose a letter, follow these steps:

1. Open the New Letter object (you can do this either by double-clicking on it in the Ultimedia Mail/2 Lite folder, or by choosing the New Letter option from the Cabinet menu in the Mail Cabinet, or from the Folder menu in any UltiMail folder). UltiMail responds by displaying the new letter window.

2. If an entry exists in your Address Book for your correspondent, click the Names tool in the toolbar. The Addressees list is displayed, as shown in Figure 5.27.

FIGURE 5.27.

Use the Names button to display a list of available addresses.

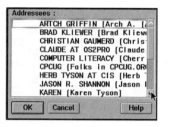

3. Click on the name of the person whose address you want to use. Click once for making this the main recipient (To), click a second time to make this a cc: recipient, and click a third time to deselect the entry. You can choose as many of each type as you like.

4. Under Subject, type an informative description of the message (for example, `Flight arrival information`).

5. The From and Date entries are created by UltiMail using your name and the current time. You cannot change these for the current letter (you can, however, choose Letter | Settings and change your e-mail address; the next letter you create will use the new address in the From field).

6. Under Folder, choose the folder in which you want to store the letter after you're done.

At this point, you have several choices for how the letter is created. You can

◆ Click in the letter display area and type the letter.

◆ Click mouse button 2 in the letter display area and use Import to replace what's there (usually just your signature) with the contents of a text file.

◆ Click the Text tool to add another text part to this letter (letters can contain multiple text parts). Use this option, for example, if you want to append a schedule, a list, or some other distinct document as an enclosure.

◆ Click the Image or Binary tools to import pictures, programs, or data, or (Image only) to create a picture. (The latter might seem silly until you consider that it might be a handy way to draw somebody a simple map!)

◆ If an OS/2 folder is open, drag files to the letter.

Once the letter is finished, or when you're done working on it for now, you can

◆ Click the Send button to queue the letter for sending.

◆ Click the Save button to postpone sending it until later.

◆ Click the Delete button to zap the letter (this is a handy option when you accidentally choose New Letter, or when you change your mind).

◆ Click the Print button to see what your message looks like on paper.

What Happens When You Click Send?

When you click Send, UltiMail runs the `SENDMAIL.EXE` program to post your mail onto the Internet. If you are not logged on to the Internet, the mail goes into the `\TCPIP\ETC\MQUEUE` directory. The next time you log on to the Internet, if you're using the IBM Internet Dialer or the Dial Other Internet Provider dialer, the `MAILQ.EXE` program transmits pending mail from the `MQUEUE` directory. If you don't use IBM Internet Dialer or Dial Other Internet Provider, however, you will need to use `MAILQ` manually. If you're not using the dialers, you probably already knew that, right?

Names and Addresses

The Names and Addresses module (Address Book) is a convenient, integrated storage location for your information about your e-mail correspondents. Names you add to the Address Book become available using the Names tool when you are creating a letter. In addition, you can choose a Folder in which to store all mail that you send to a person listed in the Address Book. Unfortunately, you can't redirect received mail in the same way.

To add a name and address to the Address Book, do the following:

1. Double-click the Names and Addresses object in the Ultimedia Mail/2 Lite folder, or choose Windows|Address Book from any UltiMail window.

2. Click the New Person button at the bottom or on the Person tab at the right.

3. Type a nickname in the Nickname field; this is the name that will be displayed in the Address Book index (with the actual name in parentheses).

4. Put the person's formal name in the Name box (I usually put the same thing in the Nickname and Name fields).

5. Type a telephone number in the Telephone field if desired.

If you use long addresses in creating your mail, each addressee's phone number will appear in mail you send, including for people who get cc'ed. Some of your correspondents might not want others on the list to get their phone numbers; so use discretion if you choose to use the UltiMail Address Book for phone numbers.

Warning

6. In the UserID field, type the first part of the e-mail address (that is, the part before the @ sign, **tyson** as in **tyson**@cpcug.org).

7. In the Domain field, type the part of the e-mail address that follows the @ sign (for example, **cpcug.org** as in tyson@**cpcug.org**).

8. In the Folder field, type the name of the folder where you want to store messages you send to this person. If you leave this field blank, messages default to the Sent Mail folder.

9. Click Create.

After you create an entry in the Address Book, the nickname will now show up when you click the Name tool from an UltiMail letter window. If you need to delete or modify a person's entry, display the index (click the Index tab at the right or the Index button at the bottom) and use the lettered index tabs at the right. To delete the entry, click Delete. To modify an entry, double-click on the nickname in the index. The person's data is displayed, which you now can modify at will. When you close the Address Book, all changes are saved automatically.

Another useful option is to create mailing lists for specific projects and purposes. For example, suppose you have a club, work group, or project. You frequently need to send mail to the entire group. One method would be to add the individuals one at a time using the Name tool. Another option is to create group names. For example, you might have one group name called Users' Group, another called Smith Project, and another called Family Reunion. When you create groups, the names of the groups are also displayed in the Name list when you click the Name tool from the letter window. When you select the name of a group, everyone in that group gets included as an addressee. This can be a big time-saver. It saves mistakes, too, as it might prevent you from accidentally selecting the president of a Fortune 100 company as the recipient of your family newsletter when selecting addressees one-by-one.

Follow these steps to create a mailing list group:

1. Open the UltiMail Address Book.

2. Click New Group.

3. Under Group Nickname, type the name you want to use for the group (for example, Smith Reunion).

4. Under Description, type a short description if you think you might forget what the Smith Reunion group is for.

5. Under Available Nicknames, double-click each entry you want to add (or, you can alternately select entries and click the Add button). If you accidentally add an ex-in-law, you can remove them from the group by clicking the Remove from Group button.

6. When you're done, click Create.

You can create as many groups as you like, and persons can belong to multiple groups. To change group information, display the Address Book index and double-click on the group name. You can then add or remove any names, as needed.

A weird, but sometimes useful, feature of the Address Book is the ability to detach the index. This lets you, among other things, keep only the index displayed when you minimize the rest of the Address Book. You detach the index by clicking and holding either mouse button with the mouse pointer over the index title bar. You then drag it to a convenient location, as shown in Figure 5.28. You can then minimize the rest of the Address Book by clicking the minimize icon in the upper-right corner of the Address Book window.

Okay, but why would you want to do that? The reason is that nicknames in the Index are drag-and-droppable. You can select any or all that you need, and drag the selected name(s) and drop them onto the Address area of an open letter window.

To reattach the index, click the Index tab on the main Address Book and then click the Index button. If the Address Book is minimized or otherwise hidden, you can display it or its icon by double-clicking any entry in the Index. You can then restore the Address Book by double-clicking its icon, if necessary.

Note

FIGURE 5.28.

You can drag the Address Book Index away from the Address Book.

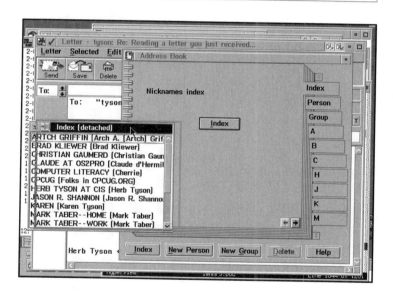

Setting Up Ultimedia Mail/2 Lite

In order to send and receive mail, Ultimedia Mail/2 Lite must be set up correctly. If you are using the IBM Internet Connection through Advantis, your software is correctly configured when you set up your Advantis account. If you are using another Internet provider, however, correct setup must be performed using the Dial Other Internet Providers (SLIPPM) program.

Ideally, once set up properly, Ultimedia Mail/2 Lite obtains the needed information set by SLIPPM in `TCPOS2.INI`. Along the way, UltiMail creates `UMAIL.PRO` and `UMAILSRV.PRO`. After

SLIPPM has been started and you are online, you should check your Mail Cabinet settings to verify that settings were copied properly from SLIPPM. If you encounter problems, the three places to check are in the SLIPPM Settings notebook for your provider (choose Modify Entry from the SLIPPM notebook), and the two UltiMail profile (.PRO) files (on the TCPIP\UMAIL directory). TCPOS2.INI can only be changed by changing the settings through SLIPPM or using an .INI file editor. If you go the latter route, you're on your own! UMAIL.PRO and UMAILSEV.PRO, ideally, should be changed only by manipulating the settings in the UltiMail components— Cabinet settings, In-basket settings, letter settings, and folder settings. However, they can be browsed or changed using any text editor. In any case, you should always make a backup copy before beginning. Under ideal circumstances, these files should never have to be touched by anything other than the UltiMail programs themselves. However, if something goes wrong, you might start with the two .PRO files to see if you can get some clues as to what's going wrong and why.

You might sometimes also hear people talking about SENDMAIL.UML. SENDMAIL.UML is a configuration file used by the SENDMAIL program. When running UltiMail under an Internet session started by SLIPPM, SENDMAIL.UML's default settings should not be touched. If you bypass SLIPPM, or if you start editing UMAIL.PRO and/or UMAILSRV.PRO, there might be some things in SENDMAIL.UML that need to be changed. If you start delving into it at that level, however, you need more documentation than this book can possibly provide. You would do well to try to obtain the documentation that comes with the full IBM TCP/IP package. The only way I know to do that is to buy the IBM TCP/IP program.

UltiMail Error and Log Files

Before you begin troubleshooting a problematic setup, you also should know about UMAIL.ERR and UMAIL.LOG. While the contents of these files are rather cryptic, you might just happen to find a clue about your problems by perusing these files. They are created anew in every UltiMail session. After a session in which something went wrong, examine these files for clues.

For more clues, you can start UMAIL.EXE from the command line with an option that gives lots of information about what UltiMail does and what kinds of problems it encounters. To do this, go to the OS/2 command line and start the UltiMail Mail Cabinet with the following:

```
start umail /loglevel=info
```

Then put UltiMail through the paces to generate whatever errors you're seeing. After you close the Mail Cabinet, take a look at UMAIL.LOG for clues. Mind you, this is not for anyone with a weak stomach, but it can sometimes help pinpoint a problem. Maybe a password was mistyped. Maybe a domain name has a comma instead of a period. Whatever the problem, it's sometimes (not always) easier to find if you have more information. That's what the info option gives you.

As you look through the log and the error file, you should keep in mind that many things that look like errors to you and me are ordinary messages that UltiMail routinely sees in an average session. For example, here's an excerpt from one of my recent full-information logs:

```
01/23-17:51:45 [MAILFLDR.C: 290]  2 E MsomInit: WinLoadPointer, IDI_INOBX0:
err=81003, msg=WIN 1003 E Parameter out of range: 0x0041
01/23-17:51:46 [OBJHNDLR.C: 246]  2 W somClassReady (ObjHndlr): could not locate
➥DLL 'OBJHNDLR', rc=126
01/23-17:51:48 [    ECNR.C: 539]   1 W ECnrQueryCnrWindow: pWindow 0 bad or missing
01/23-17:51:48 [    ECNR.C: 539]   1 W ECnrQueryCnrWindow: pWindow 0 bad or missing
01/23-17:51:48 [    ECNR.C: 539]   1 W ECnrQueryCnrWindow: pWindow 0 bad or missing
01/23-17:51:50 [    FILE.C: 817]   2 W FileGetExePath: DosGetInfoBlocks Method
➥failed, trying to search along EXE path!
```

Looks pretty bad, right? Well, this was from a log named GOOD.LOG. So, apparently, those lines weren't so bad after all. However, the following line turned out to be a real nuisance:

```
01/23-18:00:09 [   SNOTE.C:2329]   2 W NoteExecSendmail: no mail gateway
```

So, if you do much exploring of logs, you'd do well to get a feel for just how bad the *good* ones can look.

Dial Other Internet Providers (SLIPPM)

Information for your Internet e-mail is entered on page 3 of the provider configuration setup. To access this page, start the Dial Other Internet Provider dialer, choose the provider you want to modify, and click on the Modify Provider button. Click the Server Info tab to display page 3. Using information supplied by your Internet provider, carefully enter the information into the appropriate data fields.

POP Mail Server   This is the computer that handles your e-mail. Acceptable entry is either a 32-bit dotted IP address (such as 164.108.312.13) or an Internet name (such as pop02.ny.us.ibm.net). With some providers, your POP mail server and domain might be the same, but not always. Your POP mail server might also be identified as the POP3 server, as well. Note that UltiMail supports only POP (Post Office Protocol) mail—including POP3—and does not automatically work with SMTP (Simple Mail Transfer Protocol) servers.

If you absolutely *must* use UltiMail with SMTP, look for the file umsmtp01.zip in either of the following two FTP sites:

```
ftp.demon.co.uk, in /pub/os2/tcpip/umsmtp01.zip
hobbes.nmsu.edu, in /os2/32bit/network/umsmtp01.zip
```

This file contains a freeware kit that shows you what you have to do to get UltiMail to work with SMTP.

Note

Reply Domain   This is the name of the domain where you receive your e-mail, such as ibm.net or kellogs.com. This field is used to form your e-mail address (*ReplyID.ReplyDomain*). This often is the same as your POP Mail Server, but make sure you put the name into this field rather than a 32-bit dotted IP address.

Reply (Mail) ID   This is the ID you use for sending and receiving e-mail. This and your reply domain, separated with an @ sign, usually form your e-mail address. For example, my e-mail address (at the moment) is `tyson@cpcug.org`. So, my Reply (Mail) ID is `tyson`, and my Reply Domain is `cpcug.org`. Note that when UltiMail and SLIPPM are both working correctly, the Reply (Mail) ID gets carried over to UltiMail (via `TCPOS2.INI`). At present (`UMAIL.EXE` version 2.00), however, the Login ID from the Login Info page (page 1) of SLIPPM's Settings notebook gets used instead. If you have problems retrieving your e-mail, you can try the workaround described in Chapter 4, "Connecting to Other (Non-IBM) Internet Providers," or in the section titled "Bug Alert!" following this list.

POP Login ID   This is the user ID you use to log on to your POP Mail Server (usually not the same ID you use to log on to your SLIP or PPP server). Usually, your Reply (Mail) ID and POP Login ID are identical. If you have a UNIX shell account associated with your SLIP setup, this usually is the same as your shell user ID or login. If your provider gave you a data sheet of some kind, this ID might be called user ID, mail ID, POP mail ID, or something like that. If only one ID and password are provided for a SLIP or PPP account, then it's possible that your SLIP and PPP user IDs and passwords are the same.

POP Password   This is the user ID you use to log on to your POP mail server. If you have a shell account, this password usually is the same as your shell password. If your POP Password and SLIP/PPP Login ID are different, you might get burned by the bug noted above; that is, UltiMail incorrectly uses the Login ID and Password from the Login Info (page 1) of the SLIPPM Settings notebook rather than the mail ID and password from the Server Info (page 3). See the next section, "Bug Alert!" for additional information.

Bug Alert!

When using UltiMail with the Dial Other Internet Provider (SLIPPM), the version of UltiMail available as this book is being written (version 2.00) uses the wrong ID and password fields from SLIPPM's `TCPOS2.INI` file. If you're using the IBM Internet Dialer, you don't suffer from this particular bug.

Ideally, UltiMail should use the POP Login ID and POP Password fields from the Server Info page in SLIPPM. Instead, it uses the Login ID and Password fields from the Login Info page. If your SLIP (or PPP) and POP mail IDs and passwords are the same, you will probably never notice this problem. If they're different, however, you usually will have a problem when you try to refresh your In-basket. Users often get the error message `Authorization Error: Bad user id or password In-basket refresh failed!` Or, you might see the message `Retrieving message 1 of 1` or something like that, but then never see any messages appear in your In-basket!

When using the Dial Other Internet Provider object (SLIPPM), the problem usually is due to the Login ID and Password being used as your POP Mail ID and Password. There probably are a number of ways to fix the problem—assuming that UltiMail and your setup have not been fixed already. One way to fix this problem is as follows:

1. Close all running SLIP client software (except for SLIPPM) and click the Hang-up button in SLIPPM to go offline.
2. Select the provider entry that is in error and click on Modify Entry.
3. On the Login Info page of the Modify Entries notebook, in the Login ID field, put your POP Mail ID; and in the Password field, put your POP password.
4. What you do next depends on what you have in the Login Sequence field. The basic problem is to make sure that your actual login ID and password are sent when the host system requests them.

   If Login Sequence is Blank, try the following script instead of leaving it blank, filling in your actual SLIP login ID for *login_ID* and your actual SLIP password for *password*:

   ```
   \r
   ogin:
   login_ID
   assword:
   password
   ```

   If Login Sequence is an `.RSP` file or a REXX command file, no further editing of the entry is required because your response or REXX file should already be supplying your login ID and password. Press the Esc key and choose the Save option.

After making any necessary changes, click Dial to connect to your provider again. After you're connected, start the UltiMail program by double-clicking the In-basket object. At some point, because your mail ID has changed from UltiMail's point of view, you might be prompted to enter your name, mail ID, and password. Usually, all of the information is present except for your name. Just type your name (for example, I'd type **Herb Tyson**) and press Enter. In most cases, this is all that's necessary to fix the problem.

Using Mail Cabinet Settings to Check Setup

Ideally, most users will not have to modify their Mail Cabinet settings to get UltiMail working properly (although you might want to modify Mail Cabinet settings for other reasons; see "Setup and Advanced Options" later in this chapter). More often, you might instead use the Mail Cabinet settings just to verify that all has been set up properly. **Important:** The following operations should be done while you are online and connected to an Internet SLIP or PPP provider (or using TIA or some other SLIP emulator).

To see if UltiMail is correctly configured, use SLIPPM to connect with your Internet provider. Once connected, open the Mail Cabinet object by double-clicking on it in the Ultimedia Mail/2 Lite folder. Once open, choose Cabinet | Settings from the menu for the Settings notebook shown in Figure 5.29.

FIGURE 5.29.

The Mail Cabinet (UltiMail) Settings notebook.

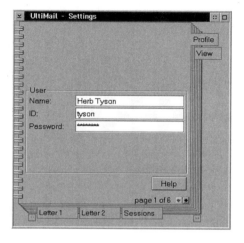

Why do you get prompted for your name, ID, and password sometimes, but not other times? If this is the first time you've opened the Mail Cabinet, or if you open the Mail Cabinet after having changed the Login ID field in the SLIPPM Settings notebook, UltiMail will display the dialog box shown in Figure 5.30. UltiMail wants a real-name entry for each user ID. If a different user ID shows up in the Login ID field in SLIPPM, that will trigger this dialog box. Ideally, this "feature" will be corrected at some point in the future (this presumes a bug fix from IBM and a new release of UltiMail, SLIPPM, and/or related components), when UltiMail becomes properly linked to the Mail ID on page 3 of SLIPPM settings stored in TCPOS2.INI, rather than to the Login ID on page 1. If you're confused, you're not alone. Once you understand the nature of the bug, however, it should become easier to understand how and why it carries over to various UltiMail behaviors.

Much of this discussion becomes irrelevant if the bug gets fixed. However, if the bug hasn't been fixed yet, then see the Warning under "Dial Other Internet Provider" in an earlier section of this chapter.

FIGURE 5.30.

Sometimes UltiMail unexpectedly prompts you for information you thought it already "knew."

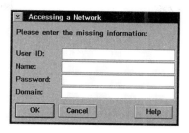

To verify that UltiMail has been configured correctly, check the entries on page 1, shown in Figure 5.30. Your name isn't crucial to the operation of UltiMail, but you probably want it to be correct. You can verify your ID by just looking at it. The ID shown should be the ID used to retrieve mail from your POP mail server. If your ID is wrong, you usually cannot correct it by typing it correctly in this page. Instead, close the Mail Cabinet Settings notebook and then close the Mail Cabinet. Then try the workaround described in the Warning under "Dial Other Internet Provider" earlier in this chapter.

Unlike your ID, you cannot verify your password by just looking at it. That's because it's encrypted, and it is re-encrypted each time the Mail Cabinet is opened. Furthermore, you can't use the Clipboard trick to verify it (that is, copy it to the Clipboard and then paste it into a non-encrypting entry area). You can use the Clipboard trick to verify the source entry (the Password field in the Login Info page of the Modify Entries Settings notebook for this provider, in SLIPPM).

Emergency Repairs

On occasion, you might find that you are unable to refresh the UltiMail In-basket. You choose the Refresh command from the menu, but nothing happens. Moreover, there might not be any folders showing! When this happens, the problem usually is the result of the UMAIL.NDX file getting corrupted or destroyed. If a SYS3175 (access violation) occurs while UMAIL.NDX is being written, it sometimes will end up with a file size of 0. When that happens, the only thing you usually can do is to rebuild the index file using the makeidx program.

The makeidx program rebuilds the mail index (UMAIL.NDX) file based on the current contents of the mail directory. To use this program, enter the following command from the OS/2 command line:

```
makeidx c:\tcpip\umail\mailstor\mailid mailid
```

Replace the disk drive letter with the letter appropriate for your system (that is, if \tcpip is on your D: drive, then replace c: with d:). Replace *mailid* with your actual Internet Mail ID. If you're uncertain what it is, then look at the subdirectories under `\tcpip\umail\mailstor`. There should be a directory name corresponding to your mail ID. In my case, I would enter the following because `tcpip` is located on my F: drive and my mail ID is `tyson`:

```
makeidx f:\tcpip\umail\mailstor\tyson tyson
```

Another occasional problem is that items in your Ultimedia Mail/2 Lite folder might get deleted. If that happens, you can usually recreate them using the `makewps.cmd` program on your `\tcpip\umail` subdirectory. The `makewps.cmd` program can be used to recreate all or part of the Ultimedia Mail/2 Lite folder.

The general syntax for `makewps` is as follows:

```
makewps [?] [components] [/DESTROY]
```

Just using `?` as an argument to the command shows you the command's syntax. If you include the `/DESTROY` switch, then the component is destroyed rather than created. Valid `components` are as follows:

ALL	All components (the default if you omit the component name)
FOLDER	Desktop UltiMail folder
INBASKET	InBasket object
CABINET	Mail cabinet object
NEWLETTR	New Letter object
ADDRBOOK	Address Book object

To recreate the address book, for example, you would enter this command:

makewps ADDRBOOK

Another problem sometimes occurs when using Ultimedia Mail/2 Lite with TIA. Ordinarily, if you're using a real SLIP account, there is no problem determining your host name. Using TIA, however, you don't have a real IP number for the system to use. Although you usually are able to retrieve new mail, letters that you send might go to the `mailq` subdirectory but won't be sent. When this happens, a file called `mailq.log` is created, and it usually will indicate a problem with the `sendmail` program (`TCP/IP not functioning`). This problem usually can be eliminated by including an entry in your `hosts` file that includes the IP number you are using with TIA, along with your mail ID.

For example, many TIA users use the IP number 192.0.2.1. To enable `sendmail`, include the following line in your `hosts` file (in `\tcpip\etc`):

```
192.0.2.1 userid
```

Replace *userid* with your Internet ID. If your e-mail ID is `smith@jones.com`, then your *userid* is `smith`. In my case, I would include the following:

```
192.0.2.1 tyson
```

> The hosts file can also be used to create aliases for any Internet entity. To be able to refer to hobbes.nmsu.edu as just hobbes, include the following in your hosts file:
>
> 128.123.35.151 hobbes
>
> To get the IP number for any given Internet host, use the host command as documented in Chapter 11.

Tip

Using EPM with UltiMail

Covering Ultimedia Mail/2 Lite in its entirety would take a complete book. However, because the built-in editor that comes with UltiMail has some limitations, it probably is appropriate to tell you how you can use something else. As noted in Chapter 6, "Reading News with NewsReader/2," the EPM editor that comes with OS/2 can be enhanced to include spell-checking. If you add the spelling files to EPM, EPM becomes a logical choice to use for UltiMail. Here's how to do it:

1. Open the UltiMail – Settings notebook by choosing Cabinet | Settings from the Mail Cabinet window.
2. Advance to page 5.
3. Under the list of Handler types, choose Text/*.
4. Under the Handler:, click on the Down arrow icon next to OBJMLE.
5. Under Open Filename, type **.exe**.
6. Using the directory controls, navigate to the location of EPM.EXE (usually C:\OS2\APPS).
7. Click on EPM.EXE and then click Select.
8. Close the UltiMail – Settings notebook.

After you do this, UltiMail will default to EPM any time you create or otherwise display a plain-text letter part. Note that UltiMail will display the letter in a binary-type window (just as it displays binary files) and will activate EPM. As slow as UltiMail often is, using EPM will make it even slower. However, you now will have the advantage of spell-checking (assuming the speller is installed), as well as the ability to set your fonts and colors. If you communicate with others who use EPM, you also will be able to include enhanced text in your letters. However, make certain that your correspondent uses EPM before including text enhancements (italics, bolding, and so on). Otherwise, they'll end up viewing your messages using the default UltiMail message window, which displays EPM text enhancements as gibberish.

CHAPTER
SIX READING NEWS WITH
NEWSREADER/2

Using NewsReader/2

Options and Setup

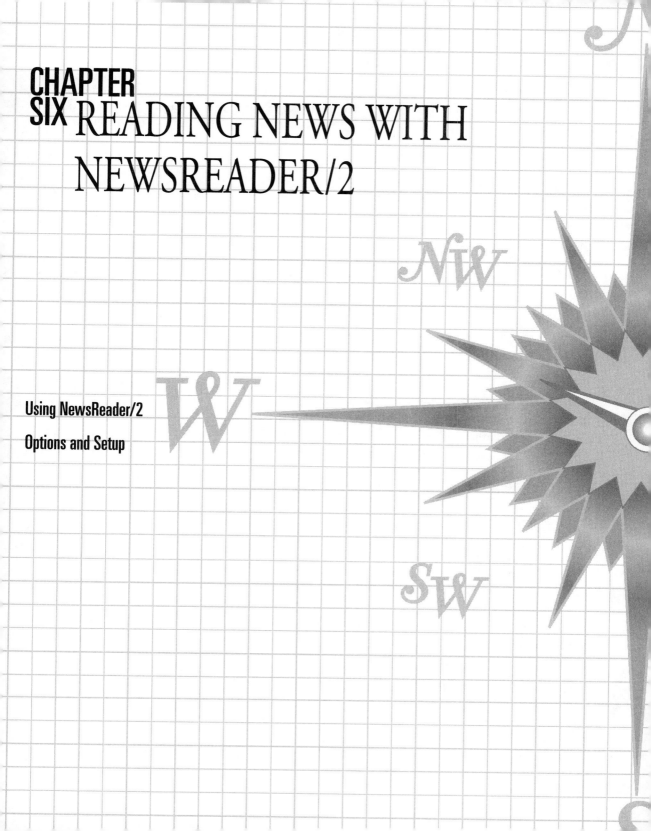

The term *newsgroup* is one of the Internet's many misnomers. Each time I see that term, the imaginary smell of newsprint fills my head. Newsgroups are not groups where you get the news in the AP, New York Times, or UPI sense of the word. Rather, newsgroups are public discussions groups. They are computerized hangouts where interested people can read and participate in discussions relating to every imaginable topic, ranging from abduction by aliens to zyxely, whatever that might be.

Newsgroups might seem a curious and awkward way to refer to discussion groups, especially if you're new to the Internet. For example, on CompuServe, discussions are conducted in messages posted on forums (or fora, if you prefer). On many BBSs, discussion groups might be called Sections, Conferences, or even Discussion groups. On most non-Internet electronic message exchange systems, the basis unit usually is called *message*. On the Internet, however, the basic unit is called an *article*, which is consistent with the term *news*, but often not descriptive of the contents of those articles. Like it or not, however, this is the jargon you're stuck with if you're to be a traveler on the information superhighway.

Usenet

Most newsgroups actually are part of a system called *Usenet*. Usenet is the creation of a couple of grad students at Duke University in North Carolina. They wrote a series of programs that handle message traffic among a number of public users on the Internet. Usenet caught on and now is in use by people numbering in the millions. As time went by, other messaging systems have been added. On any given news server (a system that makes news available), you probably have access not only to Usenet, but to FidoNet, an alternative set of newsgroups called ALT (such as `alt.art.theft.scream.scream.scream`), BIONET, BITNET, RelayNet, and others.

This chapter shows you the ins and outs of using NewsReader/2 (NR/2), which is a part of OS/2 Warp's Internet Access Kit. To really appreciate NR/2, you must have previously read Internet newsgroups using an online newsreader. Many Internet providers have online newsreaders available. While some of them are quite sophisticated, the speed of all operations is limited to the speed of your modem's connection to the service. Most Internet users prefer to use their own newsreader, rather than wrestle with their online counterparts.

Madam, the News Is Served

A *news server* is a computer that maintains and manages newsgroups. Unlike CompuServe, Genie, and America Online, the newsgroups on the Internet are not maintained on one central computer. At any given moment, there are hundreds of news servers in operation, each with an imperfect subset of articles and newsgroups. Not all news servers carry the same newsgroups. Not all news servers maintain messages for the same length of time. Some news servers might remove old messages every week, whereas others might do it every two weeks. Still others use a four-digit queue that recycles every time it reaches 9,999 for any given newsgroup.

When you post an article on your news server, it appears there first. Then, at regularly scheduled intervals, all of your news server's new postings are distributed (uploaded) to other news servers, and new postings from those other servers are collected (downloaded) to your news server. Although items you post show up on your own news server instantly, it might take several days for your article to finally be available to everyone who subscribes to that newsgroup.

Newsreaders act as a go-between between you and your Internet provider's news server. The newsreader obtains lists of newsgroups from the server, and enables you to choose only the newsgroups of interest to you. Once it knows which newsgroups you want to see, it then gets a list of articles, from which you select the ones you want to read. When that is done, it fetches the articles you select. A good newsreader can be a great time saver. Given that tens of thousands of messages are posted every day, you certainly don't have time to read them all. A good newsreader can help you quickly find the newsgroups and articles you want to read, and present them to you in a convenient and legible format.

How Does NewsReader/2 Measure Up?

As good and bad newsreaders go, NR/2 falls somewhere in the middle. It's good, in that the format is convenient and highly customizable. A much-desired feature, however, is the capability to select newsgroups and articles off-line, and then log onto the Internet to retrieve them. You then can peruse and compose response off-line. The next time you log onto the Internet, your postings are uploaded to your news server. This ends up saving you from a *lot* of connect charges, and frees up your telephone line for other uses. There are a number of *off-line* readers designed for the Internet, CompuServe, as well as for a number of electronic bulletin board systems (BBSs). Unfortunately, NR/2 lacks the off-line functionality.

This chapter covers NewsReader/2 version 1.09 (NR/2) and later. Version 1.03 comes on the OS/2 Warp BonusPak Internet Access Kit (IAK). Version 1.09 or later ships with OS/2 Warp version 3 "full pack" edition. You can download and install the latest version using the Retrieve Software Updates object (see Chapter 2, "The OS/2 Warp Internet Access Kit"). Because there are important differences between the way it works and the earlier versions, it's important to have the latest version. Notably, a number of bugs have been fixed. In addition, the location of user information has changed. Because new versions constantly are available over the Internet, it is impossible for this book to cover absolutely every difference. If you see differences between what's written here and what you're using, we'll just have to chalk it up as the price we pay for the technology of instant updates.

> You also can use the WebExplorer to read the news. Just set the URL (uniform resource locator) document to `news:newsgroup name` for a specific newsgroup (such as `news:comp.os.os2.networking.tcp-ip`). Or, you can use * to list all newsgroups. For example, `news:*` lists all newsgroups. See Chapter 8, "Navigating the Web with the WebExplorer," for additional information.

Using NewsReader/2

The best way to learn about NR/2 is to open it up and start playing with it. Much of what you will read here won't make much sense until you actually have had a little hands-on experience with NR/2—so let's get started!

Starting NewsReader/2

To start NR/2, double-click the NewsReader/2 object in the IBM Internet Connection folder (which might be in the IBM Information Superhighway folder, depending on how you installed the IBM Internet Connection), as shown in Figure 6.1. When you start NR/2, it attempts to read the list of newsgroups as well as any newsgroups to which you have subscribed (more on this in a moment).

FIGURE 6.1.

NewsReader/2 is in the IBM Internet Connection folder.

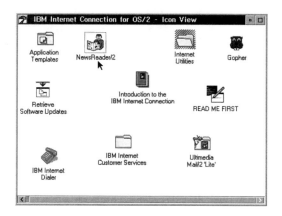

Stopping NewsReader/2

Before you go too far, let me take care of a pet peeve, which is to tell you how to quit NR/2 (for some reason, a lot of texts tell you how to start, but don't tell how to stop). Just in case you don't know how to close NR/2, here's how. You must issue a close command either while in the main NewsReader/2 window or while in the article list. You cannot close NR/2 from an article window, however, except with the F3 key. You can close NR/2 in the following ways:

◆ Double-click the main NewsReader/2 window's title-bar icon (in the upper left-hand corner of the application window).

◆ Activate (click the title bar) either the main NewsReader/2 window or the Article List window and press Alt+F4.

◆ Press F3 from any of the four NR/2 windows.

◆ Choose File|Exit from the NewsReader/2 menu, or choose File|Close from the NewsReader/2 application popup menu (click either mouse button on the title-bar icon).

Overview of How NewsReader/2 Works

NewsReader/2 is designed to let you read articles contained in the Internet's newsgroups. NR/2 displays information in four types of windows, shown in Figure 6.2. The main window is the NewsReader/2 window. Once fully initialized (once the full list of newsgroups is on your system and once you're subscribed to one or more newsgroups), the NR/2 window displays a list of newsgroups to which you have subscribed. When you open one of the newsgroups, a list of articles appears in the Article List window. When you open an article, the article is displayed in an Article window. The list of all newsgroups is displayed in the All Newsgroups window. Getting something into all four windows is your mission. Here's how.

FIGURE 6.2.

NewsReader/2 uses four types of windows to navigate newsgroups.

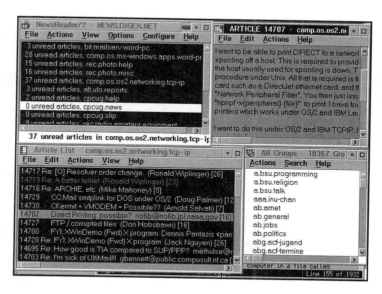

The first step is to obtain a list of newsgroups. When you start NR/2 up for the first time, in fact, it will tell you that such a list isn't available locally (on your own computer, for example), and it will offer to retrieve a list from the Internet (actually, from your news server). Go for it—say "Yes." Once you have a list of newsgroups, choose (subscribe) the ones that interest you. After you've subscribed, a list of articles (messages) appears. Finally, you use NR/2 to read articles of interest. It's really much easier than it sounds!

Getting a List of Newsgroups

The first time you start NR/2, presumably, a list of newsgroups does not yet exist. As shown in Figure 6.3, NR/2 advises you that a list of newsgroups is not available locally (on your computer in a file called \TCPIP\ETC\NEWS.ALL). If you choose Yes, NR/2 will obtain a copy of all available news groups from your news server. Depending on the speed of your computer and the level of activity on your news server, getting this list usually takes somewhere between one and five minutes. For example, as I'm writing this, it took just over two minutes to obtain a list of all available newsgroups from my server. In March 1995, the list from my news server contained more than 10,800 newsgroups!

FIGURE 6.3.

NewsReader/2 prompts before retrieving a complete list of newsgroups available on your news server.

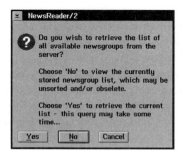

After churning for a few minutes, NR/2 presents a list of newsgroups in the All Groups window, as shown in Figure 6.4.

FIGURE 6.4.

All available newsgroups are displayed in the All Groups window.

It's an extraordinary list that's growing by leaps and bounds, reflecting not only the sheer magnitude of participation on the Internet, but the diversity of human interests as well. Following is just a small sampling of what you'll find:

- ◆ `alt.fan.letterman.top-ten` (all of Dave's top-ten lists, reprinted with permission)
- ◆ `alt.fan.nancy-kerrigan.ouch.ouch.ouch`
- ◆ `alt.ufo.reports`
- ◆ `comp.os.os2.setup`
- ◆ `comp.os.os2.networking.tcp-ip` (likely place to go for help with the IAK)
- ◆ `rec.photo.help` (camera buffs)

Whatever you want to read about or talk about, the Internet probably has a discussion group waiting for you.

> Not all news servers are the same. Some news servers have every conceivable newsgroup, including those from Usenet, FidoNet, Listserv, and others. Other news servers—perhaps due to constrained resources such as disk space—maintain just a subset. What your news server carries is determined by your news-server administrator. If you don't see a newsgroup on your server and you know it exists, you might be able to talk your provider (often the same entity as your news-server administrator) into carrying it. Or, if the newsgroup is vital to you, you might need to shop for a different provider.

Underpinnings for NewsReader/2

NR/2 version 1.09 and later stores its setting in a subdirectory corresponding to the provider name or user ID. The subdirectory is created in `\TCPIP\ETC\RNSPOOL` on your own computer's hard disk. If you have a provider named Digex, for example, NR/2 will create the subdirectory structure shown in Figure 6.5 when you use NR/2 while connected to the Digex provider. Files and directories created by NR/2 are shown in Table 6.1. Note that if you use the Dial Other Internet Providers object, the provider name comes from the Name field on page 1 of the provider settings.

Table 6.1. Files and subdirectories used by NewsReader/2 to maintain your newsgroups.

File or Directory	Purpose
KILL (directory)	Storage location for *killfiles* (a file containing a list of headers and authors whose messages you want blocked; this sometimes is called a *twit filter*). See "Blocking the News," later in this chapter.
LOG (directory)	Location for postings (messages you post) and mailings (messages you mail in response to a newsgroup article).
NEWS.ALL	Listing of all newsgroups.

continues

Table 6.1. continued

File or Directory	Purpose
NEWS.GRP	Listing of newsgroups to which you are subscribed, along with the number of the earliest message and the most recent message you have read.
NEWS.SAV	Backup of NEWS.GRP as of your last newsgroup session.
NEWS.TIM	Date and time you last accessed newsgroups.
NR2.INI	Settings for NR/2.
NR2.INI	Settings used for NR/2 while connected to this provider.
RNSPOOL (directory)	Storage location for the last message you posted to a newsgroup. Ordinarily, you'll see LASTPOST.TMP, POST1.HDR, and POSTx.TMP. The POSTx.TMP file is the text of the message you posted; POSTx.HDR is the message header that was used; and LASTPOST.TMP is the message as it appears in the newsgroup.
SIG (directory)	Storage location for your signature file(s) (files containing your name and e-mail address); this file is appended to messages you post or mail while using NR/2.

FIGURE 6.5.

NR/2 creates a separate subdirectory for each distinct provider name.

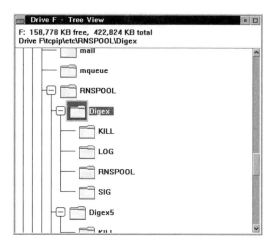

"So what?", you might be asking. Well, remember that NR/2 creates a separate structure for each different provider name you use. In the case of NEWS.ALL, that means a distinct file—200KB or larger—for each provider you use. This is true even if you don't really have different providers, but instead use different provider entries for distinct telephone numbers for accessing a single provider. NR/2 also creates different NR2.INI files. Even if you don't mind the extra disk space, you still might not like having to repeatedly download NEWS.ALL. Instead, however, you could just copy it from the first location in which it's created to other provider subdirectories that are created.

Before you propagate the same copy of NEWS.ALL to all your different provider subdirectories, make sure that is what you want to do. If you really are using different providers, you should be aware that not all newsgroups are available from all news servers. Some news servers are more limited than others. Hence, if you have a limited news server for a local Internet provider, with perhaps only a few thousand newsgroups, then you would want to maintain that version of NEWS.ALL separately from the IBM Advantis news server, which has close to 10,000 newsgroups. Whether copying NEWS.ALL to your other provider subdirectories is a good idea depends on whether they are used for the identical news server.

There also is a clever workaround for the duplication problem. Do you maintain different provider entries (with different names) for accessing the same provider through different phone numbers? If so, then you might be able to trick the Dial Other Internet Provider object into using the same name for multiple entries. Note that any given name—Digex, for example—can be used only once. However, the Dial Other Internet Provider settings for the name field are case specific. Thus, to it, Digex is a different name from DIGEX, or even digex. OS/2, on the other hand, considers Digex, DIGEX, and digex to be identical for directory-naming purposes. Hence, you could call one provider entry Digex and another DIGEX, and OS/2 will put the newsreader files all onto a single directory named Digex (or DIGEX, depending on which name you used first). In theory, this would let you create "different" provider entries for Digex, DIGex, DIGEx, diGEX, and so on. In practice, however, I was unable to get the dialer to accept more than two variations. Even so, that's better than just one.

Similarly, configuring NR/2 can take quite a while. Rather than having to go through the process for each provider directory, you can do the configuration just once, and copy NR2.INI to wherever else you need it. Whether you would want to replicate NEWS.GRP is another matter. The contents of NEWS.GRP changes each time your use NR/2, depending on the groups you read. If you really are using different providers for different purposes, then you might not want the NEWS.GRP files to be identical. You might indeed have distinct groups that you're reading from one provider (for example, one associated with your place of employment, and another set of groups associated with your leisure or civic activities.)

Subscribing and Unsubscribing to Newsgroups

In order to read messages (articles) in a newsgroup, you must *subscribe*. Sure, the terminology might be a bit awkward, but think about it as a new game whose rules you now have to learn in order to play the game. In any event, subscribing is easy, and can be done in several ways. First, you must display the list of all newsgroups by following these steps.

1. From the main NR/2 menu, choose File | List all newsgroups, or simply press Shift+A.
2. Locate the newsgroup(s) to you want to subscribe (more on this in a moment).

3. Click on each desired newsgroup; once selected, the color of the text will change.

4. After you have selected all the newsgroups you want, choose Action, Add groups, or press Ctrl+D.

Jargon Alert!

When some users first encounter the term *subscription* on the Internet, they are concerned that—like all their other subscriptions—subscribing to something via the Internet might incur some extra charge. You can relax. Although reading newsgroups is very addictive and might cost you plenty of time, it won't cost any extra money above and beyond your normal connection charges. Once you're on the Internet, using newsgroups for any given hour doesn't cost any more than reading mail, browsing the Web, or downloading files from an anonymous FTP (file transfer protocol—see Chapter 9, "Sending and Receiving Files with FTP").

NR/2 now adds the groups you selected to the main NR/2 window. Depending on how many articles are contained in the added groups, this process can take a while. NR/2 not only adds the groups, but it counts the unread messages as well, where the newsgroup `comp.os.os2.networking.tcp-ip` was just added (see Figure 6.6). (Note that the count display can be the actual number of unread messages or a percentage unread, as set in NewsReader/2 options; see the section "Show Read Article Statistics as Percentages," later in this chapter.

FIGURE 6.6.

When you add newsgroups, NewsReader/2 displays statistics on unread messages for each added group.

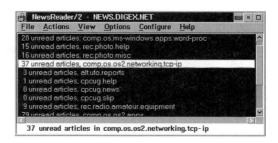

When searching for interesting newsgroups to which to subscribe, just scrolling through a list of 10,000 groups can be a trifle daunting. Rather than pawing your way though the list, it usually is better to search for key words or terms that might be related to the newsgroups you're seeking. Suppose you're interested in newsgroups related to OS/2. Rather than straining your eyes to glimpse os2 embedded in the often-difficult-to-read list of newsgroups, use the built-in search command by following these steps.

1. From the Newsgroup menu, choose Search|Find (or press Ctrl+F).

2. In the Enter search pattern field, type the exact text you want to find (such as os2).

3. Make sure that the Case sensitive option is not selected (this is not essential because all newsgroups are lowercase).

4. Click OK.

5. The newsgroup list now advances to the first match. Double-click the group to add it to the list; or single-click if you want to select a number of groups to add simultaneously.

6. Press Ctrl+N to go to the next match.

7. Repeat steps 5 and 6 until you've found all the groups you want to add, or until the Search pattern not found message box appears.

8. If you single-clicked rather than double-clicked in step 5, press Ctrl+D or choose Actions|Add Groups(s) from the menu.

When you're finished, you can repeat the procedure to locate other patterns. If you're interested in photography, for example, you might search for photo, for numismatics, search for coins, and so on, subscribing to those that look interesting. When you're done, the main NR/2 window will contain a list of all the groups to which you've subscribed.

Get the Local News!

Your Internet provider probably has its own newsgroups. Because the list of newsgroups is so large, users often overlook some very relevant and interesting newsgroups that are a good source of help. Search your newsgroup listing for the name of your provider. If your provider is DIGEX, for example, search for the word DIGEX in your list. Chances are that you'll find a number of newsgroups, such as the following:

```
digex.announce
digex.chat
digex.cnj
digex.general
digex.slip
digex.test
digex.tia
```

Some of these turn out to very useful source of information about your provider and problems you might encounter. For example, do you lose connections frequently? Maybe it's not your fault! Check your provider-related newsgroups to see if there are special tips or advisories that relate to your service.

Removing newsgroups from the main NewsReader/2 listing is very easy. Just select the newsgroup you want to remove (highlight it using the cursor keys or mouse), and press the Delete key (choose Actions|Unsubscribe, from the menu).

When you unsubscribe from a newsgroup, the record of what articles you've read is removed. If you resubscribe later on, NR/2 will retrieve the whole list of articles again. If you resubscribe days or weeks later, it's likely that the list of articles will be quite

Note

different from when you unsubscribed. If you resubscribe five minutes from now, however, you'll be stuck enduring the whole chore anew.

Navigating NewsReader/2 with the Keyboard

You use NR/2 to navigate newsgroups. Navigating NR/2 itself is another matter. There are a few things that will make using NR/2 easier. If you are keyboard oriented, the most important navigation key is the Tab key. When you're in any NR/2 window, pressing the Tab key will cycle you to the next window. Pressing Shift+Tab cycles you in the opposite direction. Of course, you also can use the mouse to click on the desired window, but that works only if part of the window is showing. When it's not, pressing Tab a few times sometimes is easier than pressing Ctrl+Esc (to display the OS/2 Window list) and searching for the window name you want.

Another important key is the Enter key. When the main NR/2 window is active and a newsgroup is selected, pressing Enter obtains a list of articles for that newsgroup, and moves the focus to the Article List window. Double-clicking on the newsgroup will accomplish the same thing. When the Article List window is active, pressing Enter (or double-clicking on the desired article) opens the selected article.

In the Article window, the Enter key performs a different action—one that can be defined by the user. By default, pressing Enter causes the next unread article to be displayed in the current window. If there are no more unread articles, pressing Enter just beeps. Alternatively, you can define Enter to be any of six actions. To choose an alternative action for Enter, follow these steps:

1. Activate the main NewReader/2 window, as shown in Figure 6.7, and choose Options|Article, and click the Define Enter Key button.

2. Choose the desired action for Enter (see Table 6.2).

3. Click OK to close the Define Enter Key dialog box, and then click OK to close the article Options dialog box.

FIGURE 6.7.

Define the use of the Enter key from the main NewsReader/2 window.

Table 6.2. Alternative actions for the spacebar and Enter key when viewing articles.

Action	Meaning
Next Article	Displays the next unread article.
Next Reference	Displays next unread article with the same subject.
Nothing	Doesn't do anything.
Page Down	Scrolls down the window one page.
Page Down, Next Article	Displays the next page. If the last page is displayed, then it displays the next article.
Page Down, Next Reference	Displays the next page. If the last page is displayed, then it displays the next article with the same subject.

The spacebar can be defined identically. Follow the same procedure, choosing Define Spacebar. The default assignments usually work out quite well, letting you use the spacebar as a "next page" key and using the Enter key to skip to the next article. If you don't sort articles by subject, however, and want to follow a given thread, it often is useful to modify the definitions of Spacebar and Enter so that the go to the next reference (article with the same subject) rather than the next article.

Keyboard shortcuts for the main NewsReader/2 window, the Article List window, and the Article window are shown in Tables 6.3, 6.4, and 6.5.

Table 6.3. Main NewsReader/2 window keyboard shortcuts.

Purpose	Keystroke(s)
Article List window options.	Ctrl+Shift+H
Article window options.	Ctrl+Shift+A
Close NewsReader/2.	F3 or Alt+F4
Color options.	Ctrl+C
Custom editor selection.	Ctrl+Shift+D
Edit the blockfile for all newsgroups (ALLGROUP.KIL).	Ctrl+Shift+E
Edit the blockfile for the currently selected newsgroup.	Ctrl+E
Font options.	Ctrl+F
Main NewsReader/2 options.	Ctrl+Shift+O
Move to bottom of window.	End
Move to top of window.	Home
Open the All Groups dialog box.	Shift+A
Post an article to the currently selected newsgroup.	F5

continues

Table 6.3. continued

Purpose	Keystroke(s)
Posting configuration.	Ctrl+Shift+P
Printer selection.	Ctrl+Shift+T
Refresh all newsgroups.	Ctrl+Shift+R
Refresh the currently selected newsgroup.	Ctrl+R
Refreshing options.	Ctrl+Shift+G
Save window positions.	Ctrl+W
Scroll down the list of newsgroups.	PgDn or F8
Scroll up the list of newsgroups.	PgUp or F7
Signature file selection and creation options.	Ctrl+Shift+S
Subscribe to the currently selected newsgroup.	Ctrl+O
Unsubscribe from currently selected newsgroup.	Del

Table 6.4. Article List keyboard shortcuts.

Purpose	Keystroke(s)
Block the author of the current article (add to killfile).	Shift+K
Block the subject of the current article (add to killfile).	Ctrl+K
Delete the selected article from the list (note that this does not delete the actual article).	Del
Display all subjects in the article list (opposite of Ctrl+S).	Ctrl+A
Display only the current subject in the article list (see Ctrl+A).	Ctrl+S
Display the Mark by Subject dialog box.	Ctrl+T
Display the Unmark by Subject dialog box.	Shift+T
Edit the blockfile/killfile for all newsgroups.	Ctrl+Shift+E
Edit the blockfile/killfile for the current newsgroup.	Ctrl+E
Exit Same subject mode (same as Ctrl+A).	Esc
Load the next newsgroup with unread articles.	n
Load the previous newsgroup with unread articles.	p
Mark all articles as read.	Ctrl+L
Mark all articles as unread.	Shift+L
Mark all articles with current subject as read.	Ctrl+J
Mark all articles with the current subject as unread.	Shift+J
Mark current article and all below it as read.	Ctrl+D

Purpose	*Keystroke(s)*
Mark the current article and all above it as read.	Ctrl+U
Mark the current article and all above it as unread.	Shift+U
Mark the current article and all below it as unread.	Shift+D
Mark the current article as read.	Ctrl+C
Mark the current article as unread.	Shift+C
Move to bottom of window.	End
Move to top of window.	Home
Page Down.	F8
Page Up.	F7
Post a new article in the current newsgroup.	F5
Refresh all newsgroups.	Ctrl+Shift+R
Refresh the current newsgroup.	Ctrl+R
Repeat the last search.	Ctrl+N
Search article headers and text for text string.	Shift+F7
Search article headers for text string.	Ctrl+F
Sort the Article List window by ascending number.	Ctrl+I
Sort the Article List window by author.	Ctrl+H
Sort the Article List window by descending number.	Ctrl+G
Sort the Article List window by subject.	Ctrl+B

Table 6.5. Article keyboard shortcuts.

Purpose	*Keystroke(s)*
Append the article to USEFUL.NEW in the LOG subdirectory.	F2
Block the author of the current article.	Shift+K
Block the subject of the current article.	Ctrl+K
Cancel a post (only posts you create, see the section titled "Deleting Articles you Post").	F9
Close the current Article window.	Alt+F4 or Esc
Convert the current article from ATOI-8 to ASCII (Note that you can't undo this; you'll need to reload the article if ATOI-8 isn't appropriate).	Shift+R
Copy selected text to the Clipboard.	Ctrl+Ins

continues

Table 6.5. continued

Purpose	Keystroke(s)
Deselect all article text.	Ctrl+\
Edit the blockfile/killfile for all newsgroups.	Ctrl+Shift+E
Edit the blockfile/killfile for the current newsgroup.	Ctrl+E
Forward a copy of current article via e-mail.	Ctrl+M
Load the next article (as modified by the Skip read option; press Ctrl+Shift+O).	n
Load the next article of the same subject (as modified by Skip read).	Alt+N
Load the previous article (as modified by Skip read).	p
Load the previous article of the same subject (as modified by Skip read).	Alt+P
Mail a reply to the author of the current article.	F6
Move to bottom of window.	Ctrl+End
Move to top of window.	Ctrl+Home
Post a reply to the current article.	F5
Print the article to the default printer.	Ctrl+P
Repeat the search.	Ctrl+N
Save or append the article to a file of your choice.	F4
Search the article for a string.	Ctrl+F
Select all article text.	Ctrl+/
Toggle ROT13 encryption.	Ctrl+Shift+U

What To Do If You Get Disconnected

If you get disconnected during a session, you usually do not need to close NR/2 and restart. Instead, use the dialer to reconnect. Once reconnected, you can resume using NR/2, usually just where you left off. If the reason for the disconnection is that your provider went down, however, then you're out of luck—for now at least. Or, sometimes your news server goes down, in which case you're also out of luck for the time being.

If you are in the process of posting a message and you lose your connection to your provider, or if your news server goes down, you might be able to save the post as a file and use it later. To do this, simply open the file using an editor that allows use of the Clipboard. Then copy the contents of the article to the Clipboard. Then choose the appropriate Post action (Actions, Post from the Article List to post a new article, or choose Post Reply to post a reply to an existing article).

Navigating Newsgroups

Once you've subscribed to newsgroups, a window is displayed with a list of articles headers, as shown in Figure 6.8. Depending on your settings, NR/2 also can download new article headers each time you start the news reader (see Options and Setup, later in this chapter).

FIGURE 6.8.

The Article List window displays a list of article headers.

The next step is to read the article headers to see which of the messages you want to read. An *article header* is a block of information that tells you about each article. The default header information displayed in the article list includes the following:

◆ Article number

◆ Article subject

◆ Author

◆ Number of lines

Article Number

Articles are numbered sequentially, as they are received, on your news server. NR/2 uses these numbers to keep track of what you have read during the current session. *Article numbers* do not necessarily reflect when the messages were written however. Rather, they reflect when the message was received by your news server. Article numbers are not absolute, either. News servers periodically reset the count to 1.

Moreover, the article numbers that appear in NR/2 are not useful for referring to messages when you write to someone else. For example, if you see an interesting message about the mating habits of frogs, numbered 5423, you should not use that number in a message you post. The article numbered 5423 on your news server will have entirely different number on other people's news servers. What you see as 5423 might appear as 12333 to someone on one service, 123 on another, or 9254 on yet another. Don't rely on these numbers.

Deja Vu!

Another thing you'll discover is that sometimes the same article is posted more than once. You might be asking yourself "Haven't I read this before?" This doesn't occur all the time, but it's not unusual either. When it happens, it usually is because of a glitch in one or more of the systems that routes news to various news servers. The Internet—you might recall—was designed to create redundant systems so that information always can get through, even if several computers are not working properly. When a large bundle of articles is not delivered through one system, it might be rerouted. Sometimes, however, a temporary glitch is fixed, and information ends up getting routed through the main system as well as through a backup system. The end result is duplicate messages you've already seen. In extreme cases, a newsgroup will get a flood of duplicate messages for an extended period of time. When that happens, it often is best to unsubscribe until the problem is resolved.

Article Subject

The *article subject* is a one-line descriptive title of the article. Each time you post a new article on the Internet, it is your responsibility (see the section titled "Netiquette—Newsgroup Etiquette and Customs" later in this chapter) to title your articles in such a way that other busy people—much like yourself—can make a quick determination about whether or not the article will be of interest. For example, suppose you're interested in articles about video problems running OS/2 3.1. If the article subject is merely "OS/2 3 problem," that won't tell you much. If it's "OS/2 3.1 video problem," then that's a little better. Better still is an article title "Diamond SpeedStar Pro problem using OS/2 3.1." That lets you tell at a glance whether or not the article is what you're looking for.

Depending on the newsgroup size, in any give day, there might be hundreds of new messages. If you're regularly reading a dozen newsgroups each day, you might have to sift through thousands of messages. Although NR/2 has tools to help you locate what you're looking for, they're not perfect. Using appropriate and descriptive article subjects can help you and others make the best use of their time on the Internet. To see the difference between useful and useless article subjects, take a look at the article list in Figure 6.9. Clearly, some users *get it*, while others do not. Some article subjects, in fact, are so utterly useless that you might want to block them from view. See "Blocking the News" later in this chapter.

FIGURE 6.9.

Thoughtful choices of subject help Internet users decide what to read.

Author

The *author* part of the header tells the reader who wrote the article. This is useful information for a number of reasons. First, if you're looking for a reply about an earlier article from the original poster, the author line will tell you at a glance whether the article at hand is from that person.

A sometimes necessary, although unfortunate, use for author information is to provide you a mechanism for preventing messages from that author from showing up in NR/2 while you are using it. A sad but true fact about the Internet is that it contains its share of people with a lot of spare time on their hands. After you become a regular reader of some newsgroups, you quickly will begin to realize which participants have useful information to convey, and which do not. NR/2 allows you block messages from certain authors. See "Blocking the News," later in this chapter.

Number of Lines

Although it might not seem so important at first glance, the *number of lines* is a crucial piece of information in helping you decide whether to read an article. Some people don't like to wait for articles that contain hundreds of lines. In some newsgroups, some articles contain encoded binary data that's not readable at all. These articles often are used to send programs and pictures. If you're not looking for programs and pictures, you definitely should bypass such messages. They usually are too long to "read" onto your system—sometimes several minutes.

By looking at the line count and article title, you usually can make a determination about whether an article contains information or an encoded file of some kind. If the article has the subject LOVELACE.GIF and contains 6,000 lines, you can bet that it probably is not a treatise written by somebody who loves to tat (make lace). If, on the other hand, you *are* interested in receiving an encoded file, see "Articles Containing Encoded Binary Data," later in this chapter.

Blocking the News (Twit Filters)

NR/2 enables you to *block* news articles that contain a given subject or that were written by a specific author. In a perfect world, there would be no twits. On the other hand, maybe that wouldn't be such a perfect world after all. One person's twit might well be another's mentor. *Chacun à son goût!* Even without twits, you still might have need to use the blocking feature. Occasionally, a newsgroup might get *spammed* with many messages having the same author or subject. If the spam has a common author or subject, you can filter it out, sometimes making an otherwise useless newsgroup useful again.

Spam?

There seems to be some disagreement as to exactly what *spamming* is. All Internet denizens, however, do appear to agree that *spam* refers to worthless articles. Sometimes, spam refers to any posting by a detested individual. Other times, spam seems to be used

---

to refer to an onslaught of unwanted articles, usually posted by accident. In any event, if you don't want it there, it's spam to you. Spamming is posting unwanted junk into newsgroups.

Articles can be blocked based on author or on subject. You also can make such blockages specific to any individual newsgroup(s), or you can make it apply to all newsgroups to which you subscribe. To block articles by subject, with either the article list or the article window on-screen, choose Action, Block subject, and choose either Current group or All groups (see Figure 6.10).

FIGURE 6.10.

NR/2 enables you block further messages of the same subject or author.

If you choose Current group, the subject will be blocked only in the currently selected newsgroup, as identified in the article or article list title bar. To block articles by author, with either the article list or the article window on-screen, choose Action, Block author, and choose either Current group or All groups.

> To block the *subject* for the current newsgroup, press Ctrl+K. To block the *author* for the current newsgroup, press Shift+A.

Once you've blocked a subject or an author, the blocking doesn't take effect right away. Instead, the *blockfiles* (also called *killfiles*) are read into memory each time NR/2 is initialized. Thus, if you block a particularly annoying author or subject and want to see the effect right away, you will need to end and restart the NR/2 session.

Getting a List of Read and Unread Articles

One thing that sometimes frustrates users of NR/2 is that there is no obvious way to get a complete list of all articles on the news server—both read and unread. Each time you connect to the news server, you get a new list of articles you haven't read yet. There should to be a way to get a list of all articles in the newsgroup—old and new. There are, in fact, two ways.

The brute force way is to simply delete the newsgroup and resubscribe. Simple, eh? There's another way, albeit not terribly intuitive. If you double-click a newsgroup in the main NewsReader/2 window when the count of unread message is 0, NR/2 will retrieve a complete list of all articles from the news server. To be sure you get the full list, first refresh the article list

(Ctrl+R) and mark any new articles as *read*. Then, when you double-click the completely-read newsgroup, NR/2 retrieves the full list of articles. If you don't like using the mouse, you also can highlight the newsgroup in the main NewsReader/2 window and press Enter.

For really old news—that is, news that's no longer on the news server at all—try `ftp.uu.net` using FTP-PM. This is the location where old news is archived. See Chapter 9, "Sending and Receiving Files with FTP," for information on using FTP-PM.

Managing the Article List—Sorting, Marking, and Other Tidbits

NR/2 provides several tools for viewing articles listed in the Article List window. These tools enable you to sort articles and mark articles as read (or unread). In addition, sorting options can be saved for future sessions. For the latter, see "Options and Setup," later in this chapter.

Depending on what you're trying to accomplish, the sorting and marking facilities can make life easier. If you want to group articles by content, for example, you should sort them by subject. If you are interested in article from a single source, sort by author. If you want to see articles in the order in which they were received by your news server, then sort by number. You should know, however, that sorting by number is not identical to sorting by date. The number reflects when articles were received by the server, not when they were posted. Given the amount of time it takes for news to travel, it's likely articles posted by you on your local news server will show up much sooner (therefore having a lower number) than articles posted by someone in Russia.

One option some users wish they had in NR/2 is the capability to sort by thread. A *thread* is a chain of articles that shows the original post, all replies, and all offshoots (or sequels). About the closest you'll come using NR/2 is to sort by number, and then use the Next Reference option for moving from article to article (see Navigating NR/2 with the Keyboard). This approach by no means gives you actual threads, but it's close enough for most.

To sort articles, follow these steps:

1. From the Article List window menu, choose View, Sort.
2. To sort by subject or author, click the corresponding choice; to sort by number, click number and choose Ascending or Descending.

You can use the following shortcut keys:

Crl+B	Sort by subject.
Crl+H	Sort by author.
Crl+I	Sort by increasing article number.
Crl+G	Sort by decreasing article number.

When viewing articles, note that as you read them, the color of the header in the Article List window changes to show that you have read them. Under some circumstances, blocked messages also will show up as marked in the Article List window (see "Setup and Options"). After all articles are marked as read, they won't show up the next time you open NR/2. You also might want to selectively mark articles as read and unread to help with navigation, or selecting just the messages you want to read. To mark articles as read, follow these steps:

1. From the Article List window menu, choose Action, Mark as read.

2. Click to mark any of the following (see Figure 6.11):

Current	Mark current article as read.
Current subject	Mark all articles with the same subject as read.
Current and up	Mark all articles from the top to the current as read.
Current and down	Mark all articles from the current to the bottom as read.
All	Mark all articles as read.

FIGURE 6.11.

Selectively mark messages as read to manage to manage the Article List.

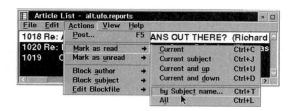

3. To specify a subject to mark as read, choose by Subject name, as shown in Figure 6.12.

FIGURE 6.12.

NewsReader/2 lets you mark messages based on a word or phrase in the subject.

4. To match an exact subject, type the text into the Enter pattern to match by textbox to match. Leave the Start from beginning of subject option enabled.

5. To match text anywhere in the subject, type the text (often just a word or phrase) into the Enter pattern to match textbox, and deselect the Start from beginning of subject option.

6. Click OK to complete the operation.

You can use the following keyboard shortcuts:

Ctrl+C	Current.
Ctrl+J	Current subject.
Ctrl+U	Current and up.
Ctrl+D	Current and down.
Ctrl+T	Specify subject containing matching text.
Ctrl+L	All.

If you want to go through the list in a different way, you sometimes might want to unmark all or part of the messages. To mark articles as unread, follow these steps:

1. From the Article List window menu, choose Action, Mark as unread.

2. Click to mark any of the following:

Current	Mark current article as unread.
Current subject	Mark all articles with the same subject as unread.
Current and up	Mark all articles from the top to the current as unread.
Current and down	Mark all articles from the current to the bottom as unread.
All	Mark all articles as unread.

3. To specify a subject to mark, choose by Subject name.

4. To match an exact subject, type the text into the Enter pattern to match by textbox to match. Leave the Start from beginning of subject option enabled.

5. To match text anywhere in the subject, type the text (often just a word or phrase) into the Enter pattern to match textbox, and deselect the Start from beginning of subject option.

6. Click OK to complete the operation.

You can use the following keyboard shortcuts:

Shift+C	Current.
Shift+J	Current subject.
Shift+U	Current and up.
Shift+D	Current and down.
Shift+T	Specify subject containing matching text.
Shift+L	All.

Tip

> Two of the most useful options for marking articles are Ctrl+L (mark all as read) and Shift+T (mark as unread all containing selected text). First, press Ctrl+L to mark all articles as read. Then use Shift+T to mark as unread only those articles you want to read. If you want to see all articles whose subjects mention PPP, then press Shift+T, type **PPP**, and deselect the Start at beginning of subject option. Then, with Enter defined as Next Article (from the main NR/2 menu; Options|Article|Define Enter Key), you can easily step through all PPP articles.

Searching Articles and Headers

In trying to find a way to deal efficiently with the great volume of information in newsgroups, the capability to search through headers can really help. While it takes a bit longer, NR/2 also enables you to search through articles, without having to read them one-by-one. Suppose that you searched for PPP but still didn't find an article with the information you wanted. You can tell NR/2 to search through the articles themselves—not just the headers—to match any mention of the search text. To search messages for text, follow these steps:

1. Display the Article List window.
2. Press Shift+F7 (or choose Edit|Search).
3. Type the search text into the Enter String to Search for Field, as shown in Figure 6.13.

FIGURE 6.13.

NewsReader/2 enables you to search through articles without actually displaying them.

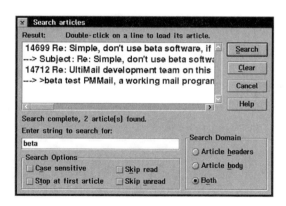

4. Choose the options you want (Case sensitive, Stop at first article, Skip read, and Skip Unread).
5. Choose the part of the article you want searched: headers, body, or both.
6. Click Search.

If you choose the Stop at first article option, the search will stop on the first match, listing only that article. If you don't choose the Stop at first article option, the search fills the Result list box with matching articles. To read an article on the list, double-click it. To read the next matching article, press Esc to get back to the Search window, and then double-click the next article.

> Drag the Search articles window off to the side so that it still can be seen when the Article window is on-screen. That way, you can bypass the Esc key and click directly on the next article you want to read.

Tip

Netiquette—Newsgroup Etiquette and Customs

Considering some of the abusive, ignorant, bigoted, X-rated, and bizarre things I read in newsgroups, I was startled at the inclusion of a *netiquette* (etiquette on the Internet) advisory in the NR/2 the first time I posted an article. Nonetheless, there is a certain netiquette that you should observe. Namely, when in Rome, do as the Romans. The best advice you'll see anywhere about using newsgroups is to spend at least several hours reading existing articles to learn the flavor and content. Although newsgroup titles usually indicate what they're about, that might not always be true. If you annoy others, they will *twit* you, by filtering out messages from you. If you're in search of help, you won't get it if people have instructed their software to ignore you.

The first concrete rule about newsgroups is that they're not for private conversations. If you want to send messages to individuals, use Ultimedia Mail/2 Lite. Newsgroups are fully public. You cannot send a newsgroup posting to any individual. You might be tempted to try to broadcast messages to specific individuals. However, they usually succeed only in making other newsgroup users angry.

Another important thing to know about newsgroups is their anarchical nature. There is a sense of complete freedom of (written) speech everywhere, and everywhere everybody resists being told what to say and how to say it. If you're easily offended, then choose your newsgroups carefully.

Despite the anarchy, there are some rigid rules of use. If a newsgroup has a stated purpose (such as for reporting UFO sighting, posting pictures, advanced programming, and so on), then don't use it for a contrary purpose. The only things that seem to rankle longtime Internet users are people using newsgroups for purposes other than that stated in their charter (see the newsgroup news.announce.newusers, and people who try to impose political correctness in a virtual society that is the very antithesis of polite society. Miss Manners rules need not apply.

Please don't take this as an invitation to be as rude and raw as others you might observe on the Internet. The rule for others' behavior is *be tolerant.* The rule for your own behavior is to never write anything on the Internet that you wouldn't want read by your employer, employees, clients, spouse, children, pastor, psychiatrist, auditor, or deity. In other words, behave as if every word you write could be used against you. It could.

One more thing—use normal mixed case when typing messages for the Internet. Scientific studies confirm that mixed case is much easier to read than all uppercase or all lowercase. Moreover, laboratory rats, when exposed to all uppercase text were measurably more aggressive and had higher blood pressure. Some even started smoking and drinking! Using just lowercase for your messages is considered lazy. Using just uppercase is considered YELLING. Neither is considered appropriate on the Internet, but laziness is tolerated more often than YELLING. Use mixed case unless you want to have a lot of angry rats *flaming* you (writing angry messages to you and about you).

Posting Replies

Now that I've scared you off from wanting to post any articles, it's time to learn how easy it is. Suppose that you see a question to which you know the answer, and it's unlikely that others will know the correct answer. Such an occasion might be a good time to post a public message. Keep in mind that sometimes users request mail answers, such as when a number of replies are anticipated and the poster of a question intends to collect the replies and post a summary for the Net. Other times, however, public replies are more useful, and might prevent someone from making a mistake. This often is the case when you are attempting to refute or correct a mistake already in the public record.

To post a reply to an existing article, follow these steps:

1. Use NR/2 to display the article to which you want to post a reply.

2. From the Article window, choose Action | Post reply (or press F5). Unless you have configured NR/2 to use a different editor, the reply window appears as shown in Figure 6.14, with a quoted copy of the message to which you are replying.

FIGURE 6.14.

NewsReader/2 defaults to a multiline editing window for posting replies to articles.

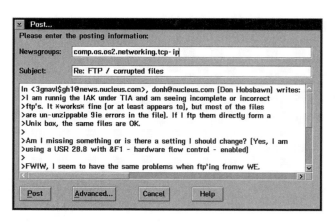

3. Using normal OS/2 cut, copy, and paste operations, trim away excess parts of the original article so that enough remains to show the relationship between it an your reply, but not so much as to make your reply look like a rehash of the existing

message. Then compose your reply. Try to be succinct. Experience shows that unduly long articles are not read.

4. Click Post to send the complete reply.

If you want to modify any of your default article header settings, choose the Advanced option instead of Post. Use the advanced options as follows:

Distribution	The largest geographical location where your article should appear (for example, `world`—the whole world, `na`—North America, `us`—United States, `eu`—Europe, and so on)
Followup-to	The newsgroup in which replies to your articles should be posted
Keywords	Descriptive terms that those might be looking for if they are trying to track down articles similar to yours
Organization	The relevant organization, if any, with which you are associated
Reply	The Internet address to which interested readers can e-mail a reply
Summary	An optional summary that would appear in the whole article header, which would let others locate your message if they were just scanning whole headers

The advanced options often are more valuable in more formal and scientific newsgroups than in informal discussion newsgroups. For example, if medical researchers studying AIDS post articles on the Internet, they might want to include keywords such as AIDS, HIV, AZT, or other elements related to their research. Similarly, a very short synopsis of your article might be appropriate for the summary (such as "AIDS delayed by use of megadoses of vitamin C"). For most articles, you do not need to use the advanced options. When and if they are appropriate, however, they are available. Several advanced options settings also can be made on a more permanent basis using the main NR/2's Configure | Posting command. See "Options and Setup," later in this chapter for more information.

Mailing Replies

It sometimes is more appropriate to e-mail an article reply directly to a user, rather than publicly posting a reply. Sometimes, the original poster requests e-mail answers, so he or she can tabulate and summarize information for the benefit of the Net. This often is better than having useful information scattered over the Net for a period of days or weeks. Other times you might see someone you know and just want to say "Hello." In such cases, it's more appropriate to mail a reply. To mail a reply to a NR/2 article, follow these steps:

1. Display the article using NR/2, and then choose Actions | Mail reply from the menu, or press F6.

2. Enter the Internet address of the recipient; NR/2 usually will correctly distill the address from the article header.

3. Change the subject, if appropriate.

4. If you'll be sending a copy of the same reply to other people, include their names and Internet addresses in the CC: box (note that this will not direct e-mail to those addresses; instead, this simply is a courtesy to your primary addressee).

5. Compose your reply.

6. Click Send.

From an e-mail standpoint, this is equivalent to sending a mail message using Ultimedia Mail/2 Lite. Given the context of the operation, however, using the Mail reply option directly from NR/2 is more ergonomic.

Posting New Articles

You also can post new articles. This is appropriate when you want to start a new thread or pose a question you haven't seen answered. To post a new article, follow these steps:

1. Display the article list for the newsgroup in which you want to post the article.

2. From the menu, choose Actions|Post, or press the F5 key.

3. Ensure that the newsgroup is correct, and type a descriptive subject: if you're writing a question about a keyboard problem with Windows 3.11, for example, then a subject such as *Keyboard problem in Windows 3.11* would be a much better choice than *Windows 3.11 problem.*

4. Compose your message, and click Post.

Tip

> If your article relates to another article, even though you're using a new subject, you still can include bits and pieces from relevant articles. The OS/2 Clipboard works not only in the Post window in which articles are composed, but in the article window as well. Display the article that contains information you want to include, select the text you want to include and press Ctrl+Insert (or Edit|Copy from the menu) to copy it to the Clipboard. Then switch back to the Post window, click the mouse where you want the insert to appear, and then press Shift+Insert to copy the contents of the Clipboard.

As when posting replies, you can use the Advanced option to add information to your message header.

Printing Articles

You sometimes might want or need a paper copy of an article. NR/2 enables you to print articles from the article window. To print, just press Ctrl+P. If you forget that keystroke, you also can choose File|Print from the menu.

> In some setups, NR/2 printing doesn't work until you explicitly set a printer using Configure|Printer (from the main NewsReader/2 menu), as shown in the section "Setting the Default Printer" (later in this chapter).

Deleting Articles You Post

Often, if you're quick about it, you can remove article you post. If the article has not been transferred from your news server to others, you can delete your post from your own news server before it is transferred. Why might you want to do this?

Well, sometimes you might pose a question, and subsequently discover the answer. Rather than glob up the Net with the question and possibly dozens of answers, it is a courtesy to other Internet users to remove the now-unnecessary query. Other times, you might have posted incorrect information and later realize your mistake. To spare yourself embarrassment, it's a good idea to remove the erroneous post just a soon as you realize your error. Other times—heaven forbid—you might regret a post. Perhaps it's too angry or off-color. Perhaps it's just plain stupid. There have been a number of times—I'm afraid to say—that I've awoken in a cold sweat realizing that something I had posted two hours earlier was just plain dumb. I race to my computer and turn it on (I guess that's a good argument for leaving your system on all the time, eh?), and quickly try to expunge evidence of my mistake before it's too late.

If you suffer similar sweats, sometimes it's not too late. To cancel an article you posted, follow these steps:

1. Display the article in an Article window.
2. From the menu, choose Actions|Cancel your post... (or press F9 if you're *really* in a hurry).
3. NR/2 will prompt `Are you sure you wish to remove your post?`. Click Yes.
4. If NR/2 is capable of removing your post from the news server, you will receive a `Cancel successful` message.

Now, for the bad news. Even if you get a `Cancel successful` message, it might be too late. The message might already have appeared on other servers. All you can do is remove the message from your own server. If your server does cancel your post, then the cancel request also is forwarded to other servers. Even if they comply with the request, however, it's possible that your message has already been posted and picked up by thousands of Internet users. If you posted a message several days ago, canceling it now would be like going through your neighbors' recycling bins and destroying yesterday's newspaper. In the School of Technosarcasm, this is known as a "nice try."

Articles Containing Encrypted (Rotated) Text

Earlier, I alluded to the fact that the Internet often contains raw, coarse, or even offensive language (offensive to some, that is). When language is especially offensive, users sometimes will encrypt the text using something called ROT13. *ROT13* is a simple encryption that rotates the alphabet by 13 characters; only letters are rotated. For example, *a* becomes *n*, *b* becomes *o*, and so on. The phrase *Suddenly, she became Sheena, queen of the jungle, and was sitting athwart the Congressman* in ROT13 becomes *Fhqqrayl, fur orpnzr Furran, dhrra bs gur whatyr, naq jnf fvggvat ngujneg gur Pbaterffzna.*

If you come across text that looks like it might be rotated, press Ctrl+Shift+U (or choose File | Unrot13 from the menu) to unrotate it. If it's rotated, it will make sense after you unrotate it. By the same token, if an unrotated message looks like something you don't want to read, or if prying eyes have suddenly approached from behind you, you can quickly encrypt the article on-screen by pressing Ctrl+Shift+U. It's handy to have if you don't want others to know what you're reading.

The Help system for NR/2 also seems to suggest not only that you can rotate and unrotate articles you read on the Net, but that you can rotate text in messages you post as well. Unfortunately, that capability is not present in NR/2's Post window. If you replace the Post editor with EPM, however, you could use an EPM macro to do the rotation for you. We'll leave that as an exercise for the student!

Spoiler Alert

Sometimes an article you read will contain the text *Spoiler Alert* in the title. Your computer also might beep when you display the article. Spoiler-alert messages are used to signal readers that the message might in some way spoil something. For example, if someone is writing about movies, books, or the outcome of a tennis match and thinks that the message will spoil it for someone, the polite thing to do is to include a Spoiler Alert.

You can include a Spoiler Alert in your messages. First, use the words *Spoiler Alert* in the article subject. Second, in the article—preferably at the very beginning—include a Ctrl+L (formfeed) character. You can insert this character by turning on NumLock and pressing Alt+1,2 on the number pad (that is, hold down the Alt key and press 1 followed by 2). Depending upon your code page, the scientific symbol for female (♀) is inserted. When NewsReader/2 and other news programs encounter this symbol in an article, they usually cause the reader's computer to beep, signaling the presence of a Spoiler Alert.

Articles Containing Encoded Binary Data

If you spend a large amount of time on the Internet, you eventually are going to see articles similar to the one shown in Figure 6.15. This message does not contain a letter from Aunt Sarah, nor does it contain encrypted text. Rather, it contains a file (often a picture—`.GIF`, `.BMP`, `.JPG`, and so on—or other binary file) that has been encoded using uuencode. `Uuencode` is a

UNIX program that converts binary files (files containing 8-bit characters) into ASCII files (files that contain just 7-bit characters). The two *u*'s stand for *UNIX* to *UNIX* encoding. Although IBM-PCs can handle most 8-bit characters just fine, some other computers cannot. Even the IBM-PC, however, would have trouble with a number of characters below ASCII 32. Hence, to transfer binary data in a message normally intended only for ASCII text, the data must be converted into something that's universally (more or less) readable by a wide range of computers.

FIGURE 6.15.

Articles encoded with uuencode *contain binary files.*

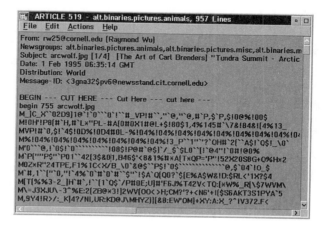

If you want to send binary files over the Internet, the preferred method is *FTP* (file transfer protocol, see Chapter 9). When FTP isn't always an option for you, uuencode provides another method. The uuencode method is used not only for NR/2, but for Ultimedia Mail/2 Lite as well, whenever you want to transfer binary files. Fortunately, when used under Ultimedia Mail/2 Lite, handling of binary files is handled much more elegantly than under NR/2 (see Chapter 5, "Handling E-mail with Ultimedia Mail/2 Lite"). However, I'll see if I can impose a little elegance on NewsReader/2.

Why Are UUE Files Larger than the Originals?

Unlike ZIP and ARC archiving, with which most OS/2 users are more familiar, uuencoding a file does not compress data. Instead, it expands it. The reason is that you have to somehow use only 64 ASCII characters—33 through 96—to represent the standard 256 characters (bytes) used on most computers. Fortunately, this does not make the files four times larger, due to a clever encoding scheme. However, make no mistake, the resulting files are larger, often as much as 50 percent larger.

If you want to post files in a public location, however, FTP isn't always an option. While some users might have the resources to set up anonymous FTP sites (a public location in which anyone can obtain files), not all users do. In any event, and for a variety of reasons, someone somewhere standardized a method for converting binary files—such as pictures and executable files—into ASCII files that can be posted in newsgroups.

Do I Need a Secret Decoder Ring?

No, but in order to decode these files, you will need `uudecode`. There are versions of `uudecode` that have been ported (converted) from UNIX to work under OS/2. In order to create such files yourself, you'll need a working version of `uuencode`. You can find several OS/2 versions of these at an anonymous FTP site called HOBBES. To set up FTP with HOBBES, specify the host as `ftp-os2.nmsu.edu`.

The best UU decoder I have found is in a file called `\os2\32bit\archiver\uudoall.zip`. This marvelous program handles multipart uuencoded files that have been copied or appended together, without any need for cutting or trimming. For general-purpose encoding and decoding, I have found `\os2\32bit\archiver\ucode101.zip`, which has long filename and wildcard support.

Translating binary files can be a little tricky. The most important thing is to make sure that you get all the parts. Often, as shown in Figure 6.16, different articles are labeled as 1/7, 2/7, 3/7, through 7/7. They often are divided into multiple parts when the whole uuencoded file is too large to fit into a single article. Often there is a 0/7 article as well, which contains a description of the whole binary, above and beyond the subject information in the header.

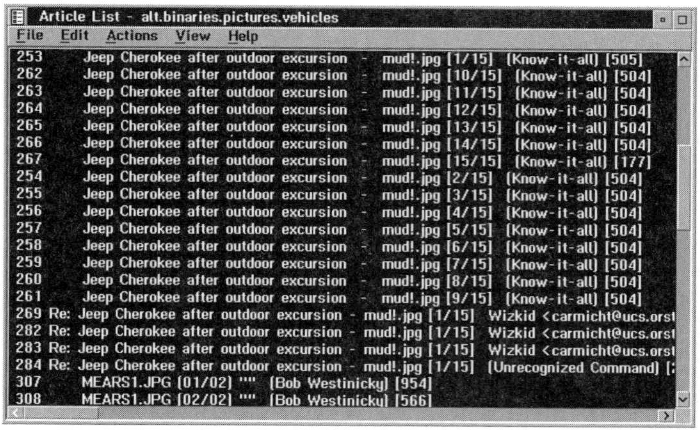

FIGURE 6.16.

Uuencoded files often span multiple articles. Make sure you get all the parts!

There probably are many ways to go about it, but here is a way that I find effective, which I use in conjunction with `uudoall` (see the sidebar titled "Do I Need a Secret Decoder Ring?"). To decode one or more articles containing a uuencoded binary file (for use with `uudoall`), follow these steps:

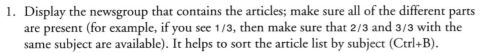

1. Display the newsgroup that contains the articles; make sure all of the different parts are present (for example, if you see 1/3, then make sure that 2/3 and 3/3 with the same subject are available). It helps to sort the article list by subject (Ctrl+B).

2. Display the first article.

3. From the menu, choose File|Save as (F4).

4. Navigate to the disk and directory in which you want to save the resulting .uue file.

5. Type a filename, and include the .uue extension (such as canyon.uue; the use of the .uue extension isn't always required, but later it will help you identify the type of file it is).

6. Don't select the Append to file option. You will later, when appending the other parts.

7. Click OK.

8. Display the next article. (The order is crucial—make sure you append part 2, part 3, and so on.)

9. Press F4 (Save as), choose Append to file, leaving the filename the same as in step 5, and then click OK.

10. Repeat steps 8 and 9 until all the article parts have been appended to the whole.

In step 8, due to a bug in the way NewsReader/2 1.09's Article window works, you must close each article (which you can do by pressing the Esc key while the Article window is active) before retrieving the next one. If you retrieve successive articles in the same window, the subsequent pieces might contain corrupted data. In fact, when retrieving independent multiple uuencoded files (as opposed to multipart uue files), you still would need to close the Article window before retrieving the next article. Often, the uudecode program won't complain, and the only hint that it didn't work is an error message from whatever program you use to handle the resulting file (for example, a graphics viewer might return the error message Unexpected end of file).

Next, if you have uudoall, you use uudoall to unencode the .uue file. You can do this via the command line, or using drag-and-drop. If you create a program reference object for uudoall.exe, you can drag the resulting .uue file onto the uudoall object, and it will be undecoded into the binary file (often an .exe, .jpg, or .gif file). Or, you can use uudoall from the OS/2 command line, as in the following:

```
uudoall filename.uue
```

The original filename is encoded into the .uue file. Once decoded, you can use the file in a way that's appropriate for the file type.

If you don't have `uudoall` or the equivalent, you probably will need to do some editing to the .uue file before you can run your uudecoder. Edit the file with a text editor, taking care to trim the file where indicated. Do not insert any extraneous carriage returns or other data into the file. When done correctly, a .uue file begins something like the following:

```
begin 644 bg000755.jpg
M_]C_X_"X"02D9)1@`"`0$`8`!@``#_VP!#``T)"@L*"`T+"@L.#@T/$R`5$Ar
M_____
```

and ends with this:

```
M\7_HQ:GT;_D#V7_7!/\'T$?5$$=HH"3(>+,N*!2Kr[:XFY!4FH!N_/??J$W(UIQ
M******_____************RO$]'T2;)^Q\\?_?'_*#Yq+/xG.~~L
#0__9
'
end
sum -r/size 28583/14768 section (from first encoded line to "end")
sum -r/size 13233/32763 entire input file
```

Depending on how many parts there are, make sure you edit each of the boundaries correctly. If you have `uudoall`, then none of this is necessary because it detects correctly the boundaries when it decodes the .uue file.

Drag It!

If you set up a program reference object for your uudecode program, you won't even have to save an article before converting it. The uuencode programs are designed either to work with a file, or with a piped stream of ASCII data. Thus, you will be able to drag an article directly from the article window, and drop it onto your uuencode object for decoding. To do this, follow these steps:

1. Create a program reference object for your uuencode program. Click mouse button 2 on an existing Gopher object and click Create Another. Fill in the title as **uudecode** and then click Create. This creates a new program object and open its Settings notebook.

2. Fill in the program field with the location and name of your uudecode program.

3. If your uudecode program needs any special parameters, enter them into the Parameters field.

4. Fill in the Working directory with the location in which you want to store the decoded files.

5. Close the Settings notebook.

After this is done, you can drag an article from the Article window to your uudecode object for decoding. Move the mouse so that the pointer is over the Article window icon, in the upper-left corner of the Article window, as shown in Figure 6.17. Press and hold down mouse button 2 and drag the icon over the uudecode object. Release the mouse button to drop the article. At this point, the uudecode program decodes the article into its binary packet, and writes the packet to the location set in the Working directory field (refer to step 5).

I need to caution you, however. There are text mode uudecoders and PM (GUI) uudecoders. Paradoxically, this trick works only with the text mode uudecoders. None of the PM based uudecoders I have seen work with drag-and-drop.

FIGURE 6.17.

If you set up a uudecode object, you can drag an article directly from the Article window to the uudecoder.

Drag the article icon to a uudecode object

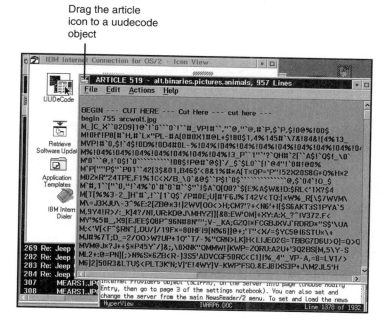

Options and Setup

NR/2 contains a number of options that enable you to make its use more convenient. Options are set in several places. You define most settings using the Options and Configure choices on the main NewsReader/2 menu. If you're looking for a conceptual difference between Configure and Options, good luck. The general consensus is that IBM simply ran out of room under Options. Why, for example, isn't Printer under the File menu, as in most other OS/2 and Windows program? Why isn't the option to load a different news server on the Configure menu? The answer is: Because they're somewhere else. And, now you know where!

Choosing a News Server

Ordinarily, your news server is chosen based on the news server entry in the Dialer. If you use the IBM Internet Connection, the news server is xxxx. If you use another provider, the news server is set in the Dial Other Internet Providers object (SLIPPM), on the Server Info page (choose Modify Entry, and then go to page 3 of the Settings notebook). You also can set and change the server from the main NewsReader/2 menu. To set and load the news server, follow these steps:

1. From the main NewsReader/2 menu, choose Actions | Choose news server... (this option is not available if you are already connected; to start NR/2 without a connection, enter **nr2** **/nc** at the OS/2 command line).

2. Type the exact name or IP address of the news server to which you want to connect (such as **news1.digex.net** or **164.109.13.10**), and click OK.

3. From the menu, choose Action | Load newsgroups.

Note

> Most providers limit you to a single news server. Where this capability most often comes in handy is when you start NR/2 with the /NC switch (no connection; this switch tells NR/2 to start up without connecting to a news server). Although there is very little you can do from NR/2 without a connection, there is one thing you can do *only if you are not connected*: import a NEWS.GRP file from a UNIX .newsrc file. See "Importing Newsgroups (.newsrc) from UNIX" later in this chapter for additional information.

NewsReader/2 Options

Most NR/2 options are set using the NewsReader/2 options window shown in Figure 6.18. Display the NewsReader/2 options window by choosing Options, NewsReader/2 from the main NewsReader/2 window, or press Ctrl+Shift+O.

Inform About Creation of New Groups

Each time you start NR/2, it checks to see if new newsgroups have been added since your last login to the news server. If new newsgroups have been added, NR/2 displays the new groups in a window. If you want, you can subscribe to the new groups to see what they look like. Often, when a new newsgroup is created, it will not have any messages in it at first. So, it might take a few days for the newsgroup to develop enough of a following for you to see what it really is for.

FIGURE 6.18.

Press Ctrl+Shift+O to access the main NewsReader/2 options window.

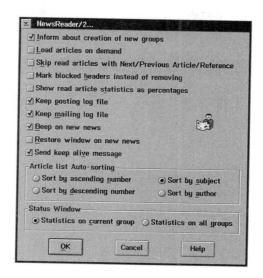

Where Do They Come From?

Users cannot create new newsgroups at will. How new newsgroups are created varies by type. For Usenet newsgroups, the primary type of newsgroup you see on the Internet, users post an *RFD* (Request For Discussion) article in news.announce.newgroups, suggesting the creation of a new newsgroup, along with the proposed purpose. After a month of discussion, a call for votes is issued. If the YES votes outnumber the NO votes by at least 100, the new newsgroup gets created. If you're really interested in this stuff, see the articles *How to Create a New Usenet Newsgroup* and *Usenet Newsgroup Creation Companion* in news.announce.newusers, news.answers, and news.groups. As for how groups such as alt.barney.dinosaur.die.die.die are created, your guess is as good as mine.

Load Articles on Demand

When you first start NR/2, it does not load article lists until you request them—this is what's meant by *Load articles on demand*. This option is selected by default. With this option enabled, you will not get a list of articles until you request it (by double-clicking on the desired newsgroup, or by selecting the newsgroup and pressing Enter). Depending on your needs, this option might not be ideal for you.

Optionally, you can configure NR/2 to load the complete lists of articles each time NR/2 goes online. If you subscribe to many active newsgroups, the latter might not be a very good idea. If, for example, you want to go online to check the articles in a single newsgroup, you might not like the idea of having to wait five or ten minutes while NR/2 loads in all of the new article headers.

On the other hand, if you have a manageable number of newsgroups, and perhaps have a few other chores to perform while NR/2 collects the article titles for your subscribed newsgroups, collecting them all at once can save you connect time.

Skip Read Articles with Next/Previous Article/References

Use this option to skip articles that have been marked as already read when using Next and Previous keystrokes. For example, when using the article window, n and p display the **n**ext or **p**revious article, respectively. When the Skip read articles option is enabled, n and p display the next or previous unread article. Similarly, Alt+N and Alt+P (also called next or previous *reference*) display the next or previous article having the same subject as the one currently displayed. If Skip read articles is enabled, Alt+N and Alt+P take you to the next or previous unread reference. When the Skip read articles option is not enabled, the n, p, Alt+N, and Alt+P commands display both read and unread articles.

Mark Blocked Headers Instead of Removing

If you have set up a blockfile (also called a a killfile, see the "Blocking the News" section of this chapter), NR/2 provides the option of screening out blocked authors or subjects entirely, or just marking them as read. This enables you to see what you might be missing. Suppose that you have the subject *Santa Claus isn't real* blocked, because you know it simply is not true. However, if a message in that subject appears one day and the author is Santa Claus... well, you would like to know that, right? If blocked messages screened out entirely, you would miss Santa's message. If messages are marked, however, then you could see at a glance that one of the messages is worth reading.

Show Read Article Statistics as Percentages

The main NewsReader/2 window displays to the left of each newsgroup as well as in the bottom of the window the number of percentages of unread messages remaining (See Figure 6.19). Use this option to display that statistic as a percentage rather than a number. Use this option in conjunction with the Status Window options discussed in the following section.

FIGURE 6.19.

The Article List window displays the percentage unread or a count of unread messages.

Keep Posting Log File

The *Keep posting log file* option instructs NR/2 to keep a copy of everything you post to newsgroups. If you need to keep track of what you say and where, this is how you do it. If you enable this option, a file called NR2POST.LOG is created in the LOG directory for your provider. See the "Underpinning" section for additional information on the NR/2 directory structure.

Keep Mailing Log File

The *Keep mailing log file* option is similar to the posting log file option, except that this file retains a copy of all messages you mail from NR/2. The name of the file is NR2MAIL.LOG. Note that Ultimedia Mail/2 Lite is in no way integrated with NR/2, so any messages you send in this way are kept separately.

Beep on New News

If you start NR/2 up and then go onto other things, or if you have NR/2 set up to check periodically for new news, this option tells NR/2 to beep if and when it finds new articles. Use this option in conjunction with the Options|Refreshing setting.

Restore Window on New News

If the preceding option isn't distracting and annoying enough for you, you also can tell NR/2 to surge to the foreground whenever new news shows up. This especially can be useful if there are a variety of reasons why your system might beep at any given moment, and you've learned to ignore them (as I have). With this handy little option enabled, you might not get *any* work done. Seriously, however, if you have an important question pending, and your work depends on receiving an answer just as soon as it appears, you can enable this option so that you get the word as soon as possible (but no more often than every 10 minutes).

Send Keep Alive Message

A couple of weeks after I signed on with my current service, I started getting disconnected while reading messages and composing replies. It turned out—due to increased demand for service—that the administrators of my Internet provider had the inactivity timer set at 5 minutes. Previously, it was set to every 60 minutes. Use the Send keep alive message option to thwart your provider's attempts to boot you. Often, you can read a message in a few seconds. However, posting articles and reading longer and more informative articles often takes longer than 5 minutes. And, unfortunately, the current version of NR/2 does not support off-line reading and composition of messages. So, until that capability is provided, you can use the keep alive message to stay online.

> You also can use the keep alive message to stay online even when you're not particularly interested in the news. While NR/2 does use memory, the system load really isn't all that heavy. I find that keeping up NR/2 during sessions in which I have to maintain a connection keeps me from getting cut off.

Article List Auto-Sorting

NR/2 provides the capability to sort messages on demand, as well as to set a default. Depending on how you like to read articles and your own strategy, NR/2 enables you to set the default sort to any of the following options:

- ◆ Sort by ascending number
- ◆ Sort by descending number
- ◆ Sort by subject
- ◆ Sort by author

Unfortunately, NR/2 does not offer the posting date as a sorting option at this time. Until they do offer it, sorting by article number may be about the best you can do.

Status Window

The *status window* is the display at the bottom of the main NewsReader/2 window. This window can display statistics for unread messages for all subscribed groups or just the currently selected group. See also "Show Read Article Statistics as Percentages," earlier in this chapter.

Article List Options

Use the *Article List* options to control how the Article List is presented. To display Article List options, choose Options, Article List from the main NewsReader/2 window, or press Ctrl+Shift+H. Using the Article List option, you can select the header items you want to display in the Article List window, as well as the order in which you want them to appear.

Use the mouse to check the box next to each header item you want to display. Next, use the Field ordering controls to manipulate the Sample Header display so that it looks the way you want. For example, if the article subject is of paramount importance to you, then select Article Subject and click the Move Left button until the article subject in the Sample Header is at the left. To move an item to the right, select it and click the Move Right button. (Note that unlike some NR/2 options, the article list option takes effect immediately).

If—later on—you wonder what the article list looked like before you changed it, use the Default button to restore the factory settings. Very often, you might find that you ended up selecting the same article list options IBM selected as the defaults—and for the same reason.

Article Options

Use *Article options* to set the way the Article window itself appears on-screen. Did you ever want to display two or more articles at the same time? Well, you can. Would you like to see what the myriad news servers messages go through to get to you? Well, you can do that too. Have you ever gotten an article on-screen that extended too far to the right to read? Well, you can fix that as well. And, have you ever been infuriated with the fact that the NR/2 post editor doesn't automatically wrap text you type? Well, that one you can forget about, because the Article option won't help you one bit!

Multiple Windows

This option causes NR/2 to open a new article window each time you display an article using the Article List (for example, by double-clicking or by selecting an article and pressing Enter). If you use the Next and Previous options (n, p, Alt+N, Alt+P, spacebar, and Enter) from within an Article window, however, only the current window is used.

Highlight Subject

This option causes NR/2 to highlight the subject each time the Article window is displayed. If you're navigating using keystrokes rather than by selecting subjects through the Article List, this feature can be quite useful. Even in terse viewing mode (see the following section), article headers can be rather difficult to sort.

Terse Viewing Mode

Believe it or not, the header information you normally see in articles could be even more cluttered than it is currently. By default, NewsReader/2 sets articles to display in *terse viewing mode*. Header routing and cross-reference information—not normally of use to most Internet users—is removed for display purposes. With terse viewing mode turned off, however, headers display considerably more information. Figure 6.20 shows the identical message header in its full form and in the terse form.

FIGURE 6.20.

Sometimes, terse is better, not worse!

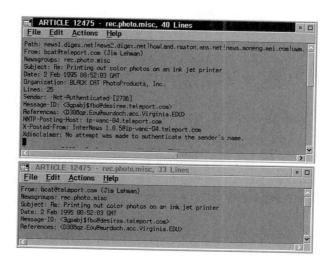

Word Wrap Long Lines

Internet customs call for users to press Enter at the end of each line, just like when you're at an old-fashioned typewriter. Sometimes, however, if the poster uses a word processor as an editor (or even using OS/2's E.EXE System Editor), intraparagraph lines automatically are wrapped. Everything looks fine to the user while they are composing the article. Once it's posted, however, the article is posted in its true form, which means that each paragraph might look like one long line that scrolls to the right.

The politically correct thing to do on the Internet is to make sure that articles you post have a real carriage return at the end of each line, and two at the end of each paragraph. When you encounter articles written by folks who aren't politically correct, however, NR/2's Word wrap long lines option will tame those lines that scroll way off to the right. It's a good idea to enable this option, just in case.

On the other hand, some users mistakenly think this option affects outgoing posts as well; however, it does not. You will need to press Enter at the end of each line if you post articles using NR/2's built-in Post editor. You can—if you prefer—designate an alternative editor, such as EPM. See the section "Setting the Posting editor" later in this chapter for additional information.

In addition to the display option, you also can change the way the Enter and spacebar keys advance the article window. See the section "Navigating NewsReader/2 with the Keyboard" earlier in this chapter for a description of the available options.

Posting Options

The *Posting options* enable you to set information that will become part of the header for any articles you post. This information often is of use for others who might need to contact you. This information also is used to define the scope of your articles. If your articles have no use outside a certain area, then you can specify the default distribution. Posting options also enables you to get rid of the posting etiquette reminder you see each time you post an article, as well as the postability warnings you sometimes get.

From

The *From* field should be your e-mail address and name. For example, my From field is

```
tyson@cpcug.org (Herb Tyson)
```

As you'll see if you become active in using newsgroups, the from field will be used by your correspondents' software in addressing replies and cross-references. A From setting is required for all articles you post.

Reply To

The *Reply To* field is optional, and tells readers where to send e-mail replies. Usually, the Reply To field is unnecessary because it's the same as the From field. You might use it, however, if you want replies sent to a different address.

Organization

The *Organization* field is optional and can be used to tell your correspondents the name of your employer or other relevant organization. While this field is optional, if you don't include one, your Internet provider sometimes provides a default of its own. It often is more useful to have an organization of your own choosing appear in this header field.

Default Distribution

Use *Default Distribution* to expand or limit where your articles go. If you never want your article read outside your own country, then include your country code in this field. In the U.S., the code is us, of all things. The codes for North America and the whole worlds are na and world.

> When posting an article, you can override Reply-to, Organization, and Distribution by choosing the Advanced button in the Post dialog box.

Tip

Check Group Postability

Select *Check group postability* if you want NR/2 to see if the selected newsgroup accepts post. It's pretty aggravating to spend a half-hour composing an article, only to later discover that it didn't go through. Keep in mind, however, that even if NR/2 *thinks* your post might go through, that's no guarantee. However, NR/2 usually *is* correct.

> NR/2 tries to determine the newsgroup from the header, but it sometimes gets it wrong. If you get a postability warning, check the newsgroup listed in the header against the one listed in the article to which you are replying ensure that it was transcribed by NR/2 correctly.

Note

Warning About Etiquette

The etiquette warning is enabled by default, just to make sure new Internet users are aware that etiquette *is* an issue. While you can turn it off once you know the score, it's often a good idea to enable this option when setting up new users (if you're a system administrator, for example). For one thing, it makes new Internet users think twice about posting articles. For another, it slows them down, and might keep them from spending too much work time cruising Usenet. Finally, by they time they figure out how to suppress the warning, they will be experienced enough Internet users that the warning won't be necessary.

Setting the Posting Editor

NR/2 enables you to choose a different editor for writing articles. By default, NR/2 uses the Post window, shown in Figure 6.21. Many users find the capabilities of the built-in editor too limiting, requiring them to press Enter at the end of each line.

FIGURE 6.21.

Unless you specify your own editor, NewsReader/2 uses the Post window for composing articles.

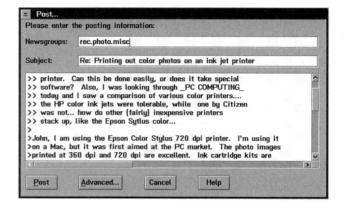

An intermediate update of NR/2 allowed only the use of an OS/2 PM editor. A later revision (version 1.09 and later), however, corrects that problem and allows any type editor that runs under OS/2—text mode OS/2, OS/2 PM, DOS, or Windows.

To choose an editor rather than NR/2's built-in editing window, follow these steps:

1. Choose Configure | Editor from the main NewsReader/2 window, or press Ctrl+Shift+D.

2. Deselect the Use NewsReader/2 editor option.

3. Type the path and name of the editor (such as `C:\OS2\APPS\EPM.EXE`), as shown in Figure 6.22.

FIGURE 6.22.

Press Ctrl+Shift+D to specify a custom editor for composing articles.

4. Type any needed command line arguments into the Arguments field.

5. If you want, enable the Auto-close upon task completion option (more on this in a moment).

6. Click OK.

> NR/2 uses the custom editor for creating signature files (see "Setting your Signature Lines," later in this chapter). If you don't specify a custom editor, NR/2 will use EPM by default, even if you have selected the Use NewsReader/2 editor option in step 2.

When using an editor that you specify, the sequence for posting an article changes a little. When you choose the Post action, NR/2 first displays an abbreviated Post dialog box, where you verify the name of the newsgroup and type the subject (if necessary), as shown in Figure 6.23. Next, the editor you specify, such as EPM, is opened. If you're replying to an article, the original article is reproduced in your editor, with standard Internet quoting characters (> for first author, >> for second author, and so on). The question of how to proceed now arises because you don't necessarily know what NR/2 is looking for.

FIGURE 6.23.

When using a custom editor, NR/2 first prompts you for the subject and newsgroup.

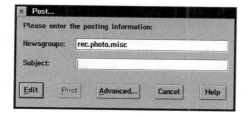

Spelling in EPM

Although the necessary files don't ship with Warp, the EPM editor is capable of performing spell checking on messages you compose. To perform this miracle, you'll need to obtain a file called `os2/32bit/editors/epm_spel.zip`. It is available from `hobbes.nmsu.edu via FTP`.

NR/2 is looking for a saved copy of `POSTn.TMP` to appear in the `rnspool` subdirectory of your provider directory. The n is a sequential number corresponding to how many posts you have made during this session. If you're using EPM as your editor, you can cause a saved copy of `POSTn.TMP` to appear by pressing F2 (File | Save). You also can cause it to appear by pressing F3 (File | Exit), and confirming the save, or pressing F4 (Save and Close). Control then passes back to NR/2.

Some users like to keep EPM open so that the startup time is reduced for the next post. They then disable the Auto-close option in step 5 of the procedure. In order to prevent EPM from closing, however, you not only need to deselect the Auto-close option, but you need to use F2 (Save). Unfortunately, however, that also still leaves the same POSTn.TMP open. The next time you post an article, the exiting POSTn.TMP window isn't used. Instead, a new one is created. To do this, NR/2 doesn't need to open a new copy of EPM—it just opens another window. Unfortunately, if you now consistently use F2 to close your posts, you'll leave a long trail of windows still open: POST1.TMP, POST2.TMP, and so on.

Actually, the Auto-close option is designed for editors like DeScribe and IBM Works, wherein you have a Close Window (Ctrl+F4) command that is distinct from the Close Application (Alt+F4) command. When using those editors, which involve a lot of startup time, you likely would *not* want to use Auto-close. Once the editor is opened, you want to leave the editor open until you finish all posts.

With EPM, a different strategy works best. One way is to open an untitled EPM session, independent of NR/2. Then, when you want to compose a post, a new EPM window is opened, using the existing copy of EPM that's already running. When you close the session using F4 (Save and Close), that window closes, but the first copy of EPM stays open. This method does not depend on having Auto-close deselected.

Alternatively, you could disable Auto-close. When you create your first post, use F2 to save it. That will trigger a return to NR/2, leaving EPM open (with the now no-longer-needed POSTn.TMP window). That EPM session now serves the same purpose as the untitled session. Because it was opened from NR/2, however, you need to disable the Auto-close option. Otherwise, even though F2 is not EPM's signal to close, NR/2 itself will close EPM once it sees a saved version of POSTn.TMP. For the next post, you need to save and close with F4. The first POSTn.TMP remains, but the current post does not. By using F4 rather than F2 from then on, you avoid leaving many POSTn.TMP windows open.

All in all, it could be handled better. Ideally, for example, the Post editor should automatically wrap and insert carriage returns at the appropriate locations. It doesn't, however, as neither do word processors such as IBM Works and DeScribe. Moreover, to get EPM to do what you want, you might have to change its setting, as shown in the following sidebar.

Configuring EPM for Posting Usenet Articles

Articles you post into newsgroups are supposed to have lines no longer than 75 characters in length. Many readers actually prefer them to be 65 characters or shorter. By default, EPM is set up to produce 254 character lines. That's not what you want for Usenet. To cause EPM to create shorter lines, with a carriage return between each line, follow these steps:

1. Choose Options|Preferences|Settings from the EPM menu.
2. Click Margins in the EPM Settings notebook.

3. Set Left to 1 and Right to something between 60 and 75 (such as 64). Set paragraph to 1 for no indentation, or to 5 if you want paragraphs to look indented.

4. Click Set.

5. From the menu, choose Options|Save Options to save the new EPM settings.

Using EPM can take a little getting used to. Like most things, however, it can be done.

Reformatting EPM Paragraphs

A tip that might save you some aggravation is how to reformat a paragraph after you add or delete text from it. In a normal word processor, text automatically is reflowed when you add or delete text. Because EPM breaks your lines into physical lines, however, reflowing an EPM paragraph is not automatic. The trick is Alt+P. If you want to reflow the current paragraph, just press Alt+P.

Saving Window Positions

One of the more tedious tasks of using NR/2 is getting the windows set up exactly right. Unless you know about the Save window positions option, you might find NR/2 rather tedious to use. To use this option, it's best to display all of the windows—Article, Article List window, NewsReader/2, and the All newsgroups window—and arrange them so that their setup is optimal for you. Then choose Options|Save window positions (Ctrl+W) from the main NewsReader/2 menu. Thereafter, any time you tweak your positions, make sure you save them by pressing Ctrl+W.

Setting NR/2 Colors and Fonts

There's good news and bad news. The good news is that you can use drag-and-drop from OS/2's color and font palettes to change the colors and fonts displayed in the NR/2 windows. The bad news, however, is that they won't remain that way. The next time you close and reopen them, they revert to their previous setting.

To make the changes in colors and fonts stick, you'll have to use NR/2's menu options. To set NewsReader/2 colors, follow these steps:

1. Choose Options|Color from the menu (or press Ctrl+C).

2. Choose the Field you want to change.

3. Select the attribute you want to change (Foreground or Background, where foreground is the color of the text, and background is the color behind the text).

4. Select the color you want to apply.

5. Repeat steps 2 through 5 for each of the fields whose colors you want to change.

6. Click Apply to apply the changes to the current session only. Click Save to save the changes for the current and future sessions.

> It's a good idea to choose the Apply option when making extensive or radical changes. This preserves your option to revert to the set of colors that set previously, simply by closing and reopening NR/2. If you like the colors you apply, however, you can reselect the color options and choose Save. Save now will save the last colors you applied during the current session. If you choose the Default option, however, NR/2's colors will revert to their original factory defaults.

You also can set the fonts to display in the NR/2 windows. Like colors, the font palette can't be used to change NR/2's stored settings. The font settings enable you to set only one font for all NR/2 windows. To set fonts, follow these steps:

1. Choose Options|Fonts from the main NewsReader/2 menu.

2. Choose the desired name, size, style, and emphasis. Keep in mind that the fonts you set here will not affect the size of fonts in your posts.

3. Click OK.

> You cannot permanently change the display fonts in the built-in post editor. You can change them temporarily using the OS/2 system Font Palette. However, when the post editor is closed and reopened, the font will be back to the default System Proportional.

Setting the Default Printer

NR/2 enables you to choose the default printer for printing articles you come across. To set the printer:

1. Choose Configure|Printer from the main NewsReader/2 window, or press Ctrl+Shift+T.

2. Click on the printer you want to set for the default.

3. Click OK.

Setting Your Signature Lines

Many users like to include a signature, in addition to the information in their article headers. NR/2 enables you to create and use signature files for messages mailed and posted from within NR/2. To create a signature file, follow these steps:

1. Choose Options|Signature from the main NewsReader/2 menu, as shown in Figure 6.24, or press Ctrl+Shift+S.

FIGURE 6.24.

*Press Ctrl+Shift+S to
control how your articles
get "signed."*

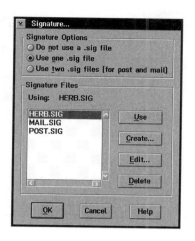

2. Choose the desired Signature option (no signature file, one signature file for both mail and posts, or separate mail and post signature files).

3. Click Create.

4. Type a name for the signature file you want to create and click OK (if you're using one signature file, the name can be anything you want; if you're using two signature files, they must be named MAIL.SIG and POST.SIG).

5. NR/2 now opens your custom editor (the default is EPM). Type your signature file as you want it to appear at the end of articles you mail or post from within NR/2. Close the editor (Alt+F4) when done. If you choose to use two signature files, repeat steps 4 and 5 for the other file (to create POST.SIG and MAIL.SIG).

6. If you are using two signature files, click OK to close the Signature dialog box. If you're using one signature file, click it, click Use, and then click OK.

Refresh Options

NR/2 provides a number of refreshing options. To see them, choose Options|Refreshing (Ctrl+Shift+G) from the main NewsReader/2 menu, as shown in Figure 6.25. The available options are discussed in the following sections.

FIGURE 6.25.

Press Ctrl+Shift+G to control what happens when newsgroup get refreshed.

Remove Read Headers

Use this option to cause NR/2 to remove articles marked as read anytime that the Article List is refreshed. The Article List can be refreshed automatically, or by pressing Ctrl+R (for a single newsgroup) or Ctrl+Shift+R (for all newsgroups).

Remove Canceled Headers

Use this option to cause NewsReader/2 to remove article you have canceled when the Article List is refreshed. In addition to cleaning up clutter, this also provides some reassurance that your articles really were canceled. Of course, that reassurance may be empty, but that's another matter (refer to "Deleting Articles You Post," earlier in this chapter).

Auto-Refresh Only When Idle

It sometimes is distracting to have what you're doing interrupted with a beep. Or, perhaps you're working carefully with your Article List, and don't want it refreshed while you're working. Use the *Auto-Refresh only when idle* option to cause NR/2 not to refresh when any of the NR/2 windows are active.

Auto-Refresh

Use the *Auto-Refresh* option to enable automatic refreshing of Article Lists. Use the Time Interval slider control to set the Auto-Refresh frequency. You cannot set the frequency any more often than every 10 minutes. If you want to refresh the Article List more often than that, then display the Article List window or main NewsReader/2 window and press Ctrl+R (current newsgroup) or Ctrl+Shift+R (all newsgroups).

Importing Newsgroups (*newsrc*) from UNIX

Many Internet users who are switching to SLIP or PPP accounts already have been using the host newsreading facilities built into their provider systems. If you fall into this category, you probably have a .newsrc file on your provider system. NewsReader/2 enables you to import that file for use in NR/2. You also can export your NEWS.GRP file for use on your UNIX host system.

To import a .newsrc file for use by NewsReader/2, follow these steps:

1. Use FTP or some other file transfer method to download .newsrc to your own system (the file usually is called .newsrc, in lowercase letters). Rename it as NEWSRC, if necessary, and copy it to the provider subdirectory (such as TCPIP\ETC\RNSPOOL\DIGEX).

2. Start NR/2 without a news server. To do this, you can start NR/2 up while you are not online to your provider, or start it from the OS/2 command line with the following /NC (no connection) switch:

   nr2 /nc

3. From the main NewsReader/2 menu, choose File, Import NEWS.GRP from NEWSRC.

To go the other way—to export a NEWS.GRP file to NEWSRC format—you must be online to your news server, and then follow these steps:

1. Connect to your provider and start NR/2.

2. Once the connection is established, choose File | Export NEWS.GRP to NEWSRC.

The completed NEWSRC is placed onto your news server provider subdirectory (such as TCPIP\ETC\RNSPOOL\DIGEX). You now need to rename it so that it matches the name needed by your provider (often .newsrc), and then delete or rename the existing version in your directory on your provider's computer. Either FTP or otherwise upload your version of .newsrc to your provider.

CHAPTER SEVEN
NAVIGATING WITH OS/2 GOPHER

Getting Started with OS/2 Gopher

The OS/2 Gopher Command Bar (Menu)

Raw Internet is hard for most folks to take. A while back, some enterprising people decided to find ways to make navigating the Internet a bit easier. A number of tools were developed, including FTP, the World Wide Web, and Gopher. Why is it called Gopher? Well, perhaps because Minnesota—where Gopher began—is known as the Gopher State. Maybe because the University of Minnesota's mascot is a Gopher, and the University of Minnesota is the premier Gopher server for the world. You get the picture. According to the University of Minnesota's Gopher server, Gopher is "software following a simple protocol for tunneling through a TCP/IP internet [*sic*]."

And, indeed, the user interface is quite simple. Press Enter to dig deeper, and press Esc to back out. Or, if you're into rodents, double-click an OS/2 Gopher object to dig in; and double-click the title bar icon to dig out. Personally, however, I much prefer the *enter* and *escape* metaphors.

In its heyday, Gopher was warmly received and widely implemented. It provides a fast and flexible way to ferret out (or, should that be *go fer*?) information and files to which computer systems might provide access. Nowadays, Gopher seems to be falling into disuse, as many users trend toward the World Wide Web (WWW). Even so, because the WWW is so resource-intensive, many users still prefer to dig in with Gopher, finding it somewhat faster at modem connect speeds.

Gopher—like FTP and the World Wide Web—is a way to present resources—files and information—on the Internet. It is a way to make resources publicly available in a way that is useful to the Internet community, while at the same time secure for the Gopher site. Resources available via Gopher include information and files. Some information is available by telnet (a limited communications program that enables you to communicate directly with a remote computer host). If you open a search item, OS/2 Gopher opens a dialog box in which you can specify the search data. When you retrieve a file using Gopher, the OS/2 Gopher client tries to use or display that file immediately. If you open a text file, for example, OS/2 Gopher displays it for you. If you open a program file, OS/2 Gopher downloads it, and then—if so configured—it will try to run it. You can even set up OS/2 Gopher to decompress archive files (such as .ZIP, .ARC, .LZH, .ZOO, and so on).

Getting Started with OS/2 Gopher

As is the case with most of the Internet client applications that come with OS/2 Warp, the easiest way to get up to speed with OS/2 Gopher is to start it and start using it. OS/2 Gopher perhaps is the easiest IAK application to learn and use. It is powerful, elegantly simple, and intuitive.

When talking about Gopher, there is a problem with terminology because Gopher can refer to the GOPHER.EXE program that comes with OS/2, or it can refer to the general term Gopher in the Internet community. There also is a problem because each Gopher window is a Gopher menu, and the OS/2 Gopher program itself has a menu. To avoid confusion, in this chapter I refer to the OS/2 Gopher program as OS/2 Gopher, and the Internet Gopher as just plain Gopher. I refer to GOPHER.EXE's menu as the command bar, and the Internet Gopher window menu either as the Gopher window or the Gopher menu, depending on which aspect is being discussed.

Note

To start OS/2 Gopher, double-click on the OS/2 Gopher object in the IBM Internet Connection folder (see Figure 7.1). What you see when you start OS/2 Gopher for the first time depends on how you access the Internet. If you access the Internet using the IBM Internet Connection, or if you did not specify a Gopher server in the Server Info page of the provider settings in the Dial Other Internet Provider object, then OS/2 Gopher defaults to an IBM Gopher server. If you specified a different Gopher server in the Dial Other Internet Provider object, then OS/2 Gopher will use that server.

FIGURE 7.1.
The OS/2 Gopher object is located in the IBM Internet Connection folder.

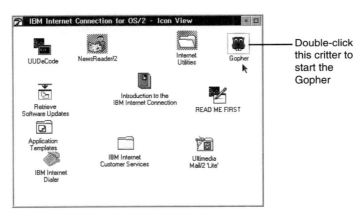

Double-click this critter to start the Gopher

The OS/2 Gopher Window

Based on the assumption that you are using the IBM Gopher server (os2info.gopher.ibm.com), you will see something similar to Figure 7.2. Note that the default view displays icons for Gopher items.

FIGURE 7.2.

The IBM Almaden Gopher server.

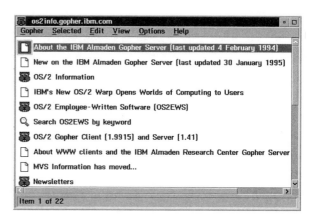

Items in an OS/2 Gopher window fall into the following four general categories:

◆ Gopher links (a cross-reference to another Gopher menu); represented by a picture of a Gopher.

◆ Files, represented by various file icons. File types include text, archived files (.ARC, .ZIP, .ZOO, and so on), pictures (.IMB, .GIF, and so on), sound (.AU, .WAV, .SND, and so on), and others.

◆ Telnet or telnet 3270 sessions that usually provide direct access to a remote host for running a specific program (such as information searches, games, and so on).

◆ Searchable links; a dialog box provides a way for you to specify for what you are searching.

Note

The OS/2 Gopher client has 19 built-in icons for displaying Gopher item types (see Figure 7.3). Different types are set in the OS/2 Gopher Configuration options (see "Options" later in this chapter).

The OS/2 Gopher window in some respects is similar to a normal OS/2 folder-type window. A notable exception is the command bar at the top of the window. To a certain extent, the OS/2 Gopher window is object-oriented. Although you cannot drag the objects in a Gopher window, they do have context-sensitive popup menus you can activate with mouse button 2 (see Figure 7.4).

FIGURE 7.3.

OS/2 Gopher has 19 built-in Gopher icons.

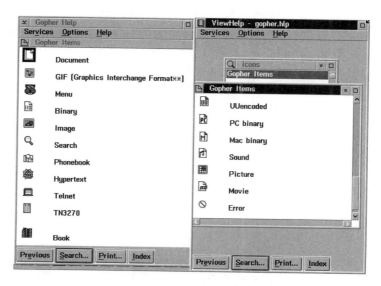

FIGURE 7.4.

Click mouse button 2 to display a popup menu for the selected Gopher item.

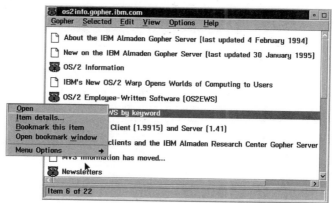

What Is a Port?

In many of the Internet clients, a *port* address is called for. Most of us are used to thinking of ports as COM ports for communications or LPT ports for printing. In TCP/IP parlance, courtesy of IBM (from the *TCP/IP for OS/2 User's Guide*):

"A port is an end point for communication between applications, generally referring to a logical connection. A port provides queues for sending and receiving data. Each port has a port number for identification. When the port number is combined with an Internet address, a socket address results."

In plain English, ports might be considered channels that TCP/IP uses for sending different types of information. Gopher uses port 70, telnet uses port 23, FTP uses port 21, POP mail uses port 109, and so on. By using ports, TCP/IP knows exactly what type of service is being performed and how to perform it.

OS/2 Gopher Navigation

Most basic OS/2 Gopher navigation can be accomplished using the cursor-pad keys (Up, Down, PageUp, PageDown, Home, and End), Enter, and Esc keys. Use the cursor-pad keys to move up and down in the OS/2 Gopher window. Home takes you to the first Gopher item, and End takes you to the last Gopher item. The PageUp and PageDown keys scroll the OS/2 Gopher window up and down, as does the vertical scroll bar. When an item in the OS/2 Gopher window is selected, it is highlighted (see Figure 7.5).

FIGURE 7.5.

Selected Gopher items are highlighted in reverse video.

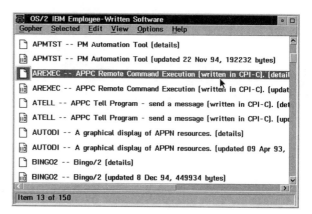

Pressing Enter causes one of the following actions, depending on the selected item:

◆ Opens the selected Gopher

◆ Displays the selected item

◆ Downloads the selected file

If the selected item is a Gopher (as represented by the Gopher icon), pressing Enter opens that Gopher and displays another OS/2 Gopher window. If the selected item is a text file or other displayable file with a corresponding viewer (as set in Options|Configure), pressing Enter causes OS/2 Gopher to download the file and then start the associated viewer (see "Viewers and Viewing Gopher Items" later in this chapter).

Pressing Enter opens a Gopher menu in the same window space. Unless you explicitly separate the new window, it remains attached to the previous window, with the previous window not visible. If you need to see two Gopher menus at the same time, you can choose Selected | Open in another window. Or, you can drag the current Gopher window away from its current location, press Ctrl+Esc, and then choose the other window from the Window List. To drag the current Gopher window, move the mouse pointer so that it is over the window's title bar; press and hold either mouse button; move the mouse, which then *drags* the window to a new location; and then release the mouse button when you're finished.

Note

Pressing Esc closes the current Gopher window. If the current item is displayed in an external viewer (such as MMPM.EXE, AB.EXE, IB.EXE, and so on), then normal controls of the viewer are used (the Enter and Esc keys cease working in the viewer, unless they're part of the viewer's own setup). In other words, while in an external viewer, OS/2 Gopher no longer is in control of that process. When you exit from the viewer and return to OS/2 Gopher, control returns to OS/2 Gopher. If only one Gopher window is open, then pressing Esc displays a prompt that asks if you want to close the OS/2 Gopher application.

Pressing Enter on successive Gopher items takes you deeper and deeper, loading additional windows. Pressing Esc closes windows. As shown in the Window List in Figure 7.6, it is possible to open many OS/2 Gopher windows as you traverse Gopherspace (a collective term often used to describe the universe of Gopher servers). The OS/2 Gopher client (GOPHER.EXE) uses about 992KB of memory to run, and each additional window uses about 20KB to 40KB. Keep this in mind if your computer has limited memory.

FIGURE 7.6.

OS/2 Gopher uses a single window to display many Gopher menus.

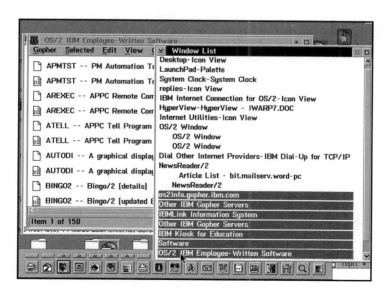

Tip

When you open a new OS/2 Gopher window, you do not need to keep its *parent* window open. Consider, for example, which windows open if you navigate a series of Gophers:

Animal Gophers

    Bird Gophers

        Tree Clinging Gophers

           Woodpecker Gophers

Even though the last item began at Animal Gophers, you do not need to keep Animal, Bird, or Tree Clinging open for Woodpecker to remain open. In fact, even if you have 50 OS/2 Gopher windows open, you can close all but the most recently opened. If you have that many windows open, you will get back about 1MB to 2MB of memory by closing them!

Viewers and Viewing Gopher Items

Each of the different types of items that you see in a Gopher window has a default viewer associated with it. When you open a text file in a Gopher window, for example, unless you have specified otherwise, the file is displayed using OS/2 Gopher's default document viewer. If you open a .GIF (graphics interchange format) image file, OS/2 Gopher attempts to display it using the IB.EXE program. If you open a sound file (such as .WAV, .AU, or .SND), then OS/2 Gopher attempts to use the MMPM.EXE program.

Your Sound-Handling Program Could Not Be Found!

When you attempt to display sound files, image files, video files, book files, or other types of files, you might get messages from the OS/2 Gopher program that it cannot find the default viewing programs: IB.EXE, VB.EXE, GOBOOK.CMD, MMPM.EXE, and so on. The problem usually is because OS/2 Gopher assumes that certain features have been installed, even though they have not. The IB.EXE and VB.EXE programs, for example, are installed with the MultiMedia Viewer on the Warp BonusPak. If you did not install the MultiMedia Viewer, those programs won't be anywhere in evidence. The MMPM.EXE program is part of the OS/2 base multimedia and sound support. Multimedia support is part of OS/2 Warp itself, and not on the BonusPak. If you didn't install it, however, then MMPM.EXE won't be present. The GOBOOK.CMD program is a REXX program that accesses the READIBM.EXE program. The READIBM.EXE program is part of something called the IBM BookManager (TM) READ/2 program for reading .BOO files. Parts of the BookManager program are included with a variety of IBM products, but not with OS/2 itself.

A viewer or handler also might be missing due to a specification error on the part of the user, or because a file or directory was deleted or moved. Using Options | Configure, you can tell OS/2 Gopher which viewer to use for each file type. If you moved or delete IB.EXE, for example, then OS/2 Gopher will not be able to find the image-handling program. Similarly, if the viewer was specified as c:\viewers\ib.exe rather than c:\viewer\ib.exe, then the extra s will haunt you later.

Or, perhaps a path in CONFIG.SYS is not specified correctly. If the program is specified merely as ib.exe, for example, and if ib.exe really is on your disk, then it is possible that the path statement in your CONFIG.SYS file is wrong. When the MultiMedia Viewer is installed, your CONFIG.SYS file is modified to include the necessary path for the MultiMedia Viewer. A number of users, however, install the MultiMedia Viewer and then decide that they don't want it adding to their system memory use. So, they revert to a version of CONFIG.SYS that precedes the MultiMedia Viewer installation. Even if they didn't delete ib.exe, it no longer is in their path. Hence, OS/2 Gopher will gripe about its not being present.

Whatever the cause, the solution is to modify OS/2 Gopher settings so that an appropriate handler is referenced. It need not be the defaults carried by OS/2 Gopher. For .GIF files, for example, there are a number of alternative programs that will work. Similarly, sound and movies can be viewed by different programs. If you have other programs installed, feel free to specify them rather than OS/2 Gopher's defaults. See the section titled "Configure" later in this chapter for additional information.

The different types of Gopher items are shown in Table 7.1. When using Gopher, each item in a Gopher server's menu includes the *type* indicator and a descriptive name for the item, as shown in the Type field and the Name field, respectively, of Figure 7.7. In OS/2 Gopher's default *Name* view, types are displayed as icons. In reality, however, the underlying menu at the Gopher server site uses a one-character (except /i) indicator for each type. Type 0, for example, is an ASCII text document; type 1 is a Gopher menu, and type g is a .GIF file. Unlike in other programs, the types are not determined by file extensions. Instead, the type indicator tells whatever Gopher browser you are using (GOPHER.EXE, for example) the type of each item. The type indicators are standardized across Gopher sites. Hence, /i always means a Gopher heading item, 0 always means text document, and 1 always means Gopher menu item.

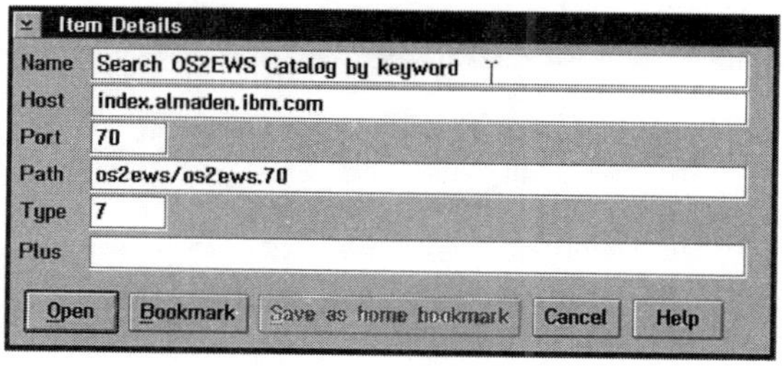

FIGURE 7.7.

Each item in a Gopher menu is determined by the Gopher type.

Table 7.1. Gopher items and default viewers.

Type	Name	Description
/i		Topical heading dividers in Gopher menus—this type cannot be modified by the user.
0	Document	Internal: Gopher text window.
1	Menu	Internal: Gopher window.
2	Phonebook	Internal: Dialog interface to search a Gopher phonebook.
3	Error	Internal: Error display of problem with item.
4	Mac binary	External: Program specified by the user to handle HQX files.
5	PC binary	External: Program specified by the user to handle ZIP files.
6	Uuencoded	External: Program specified by the user to handle UUE files.
7	Search	Internal: Dialog interface to search a Gopher database.
8	Telnet	External: Telnet to a customized server (telnetpm.exe).
9	Binary	External: Program specified by the user to handle BIN files.
b	Book	External: BookReader (READIBM.EXE).
g	GIF	External: GIF (Graphics Interchange Format) viewer (IB.EXE).
h	HTML	External: HTML (WWW hypertext) viewer (no default; however, I suggest EXPLORE.EXE).
I	Image	External: GIF viewer (IB.EXE).
s	sound	External: Sound file player (MMPM.EXE).
T	TN3270	External: 3270 telnet to a customized server (PMANT.EXE).
>	Sound	External: Sound file player (MMPM.EXE).
:	Picture	External: IMG viewer (IB.EXE).
;	Movie	External: Digital video player (VB.EXE).

Why Are There Two Types for `.GIF` Files?

Gopher, although standardized, isn't 100 percent standardized. At one point during its development, one group of Gopher server managers decided to use type I (image) for `.GIF` files, while another later decided to use type g (`.GIF`). You also might find other types of picture formats hiding under type I, such as `.JPG`, `.PCX`, or `.TIF`. When, and if, that happens, and if an entire filename (complete with the appropriate extension) isn't provided in the Gopher item's description, you might need to modify the OS/2 Gopher configuration so that the correct extension is appended to files that are downloaded. See the "Configure" section later in this chapter.

To see what's really going on, display a Gopher menu, and choose View | Details (see Figure 7.8). Notice that most items are type 0, text files that contain information. Many others are type 1, which correspond to Gopher menus. Other types shown here are 7 (a search Gopher) and 5 (binary files for downloading). Icons should be intuitive and informative. In using a program such as OS/2 Gopher, which has a number of unfamiliar icons, you might not find most of them very self-revealing. If you want to find out why a particular file is being processed the way it is, then you might need to take a look at the type by changing to details or text view.

FIGURE 7.8.

Details view shows you what really is in the Gopher menu.

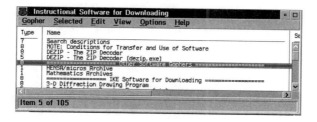

You also can see the type of the currently selected Gopher item by choosing Options | Configure. This shows you the default program, directory, and any other available information. Doing this can be useful when trying to determine whether displaying a given item will succeed, or why a display did not succeed.

Tip

> *Note*
>
> If you frequently use the OS/2 Gopher, you might—on very rare occasions—encounter Gopher item types that are not defined in the OS/2 version of Gopher. You can use Options | Configure to define new types. See the "Configure" section later in this chapter.

When you press Enter or double-click to display a Gopher item that involves a file, the OS/2 Gopher program first downloads the file, and then uses any associated program to process or view that file. If the Gopher type is g (for .GIF), for example, the OS/2 Gopher's default behavior is to download the .GIF file to the same directory as gopher.exe (tcpip\bin). Because the file must be downloaded, some Gopher displays can take a long time. Unfortunately, there is no built-in mechanism in Gopher for knowing the size of the files before you download them. Some sites, as shown in Figure 7.9, include the file size in the listing; however, most (except for Gopher Plus sites) do not. This probably stems from earlier days on the Internet when virtually everyone was connected directly, with high-speed lines and very large university-sized disks. With so many people now connecting by much slower telephone connections, the size of files—and hence, the amount of time it takes to download them—is a more important factor.

FIGURE 7.9.

Some Gopher items show you the file size.

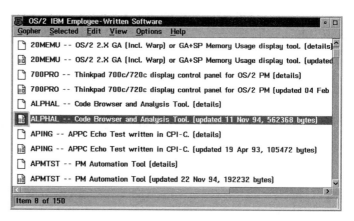

Another hazard is that the file you are downloading might be too large to fit on the target disk. Unfortunately, OS/2 Gopher does not attempt to ensure that the file will fit before beginning a download. All in all, this type of uninformed file activity sometimes makes using Gopher like working in the dark. You could, I suppose, try to find the same files using FTP to see how large they are. Once you've done that, however, you might as well use FTP for the transfer.

Why Is My Disk Filling Up?

After downloading files for viewing, be sure to delete what you no longer need. Otherwise, you soon might find that your hard disk is filled with .GIFs. If you routinely download many images, you probably should create a special directory to receive those files. That not only helps you ensure that there's enough disk space (because you get to choose the location), but it makes it easier to manage. Performing a DEL *.GIF in a subdirectory that contains *only* disposable .GIF files probably is safer than trying to find and delete .GIF files that are scattered through other directories. This especially is true because you might not know up front whether there were any nondisposable .GIFs on that directory.

Aside from incidentally downloading files, you can do so deliberately, as well. Select the item you want to download, and click mouse button 2 on it. Then click the Get option, and set the Save As information to store the file where and how you want. You also can do this from the menu by choosing Selected | Get.

OS/2 Gopher Views: Name, Text, and Details

The OS/2 Gopher window has three views. The default view is the *name* view along with *text* view (see Figure 7.10). Depending on how you use OS/2 Gopher, you occasionally might have a need to use a view other than the default. Text view essentially is the same as name view, except that in text view, the OS/2 Gopher type icon is replaced by text. If your screen display is especially slow or if you find OS/2 Gopher's icons not terribly intuitive, you might prefer text view.

FIGURE 7.10.

In name view, all you see is an icon and a description.

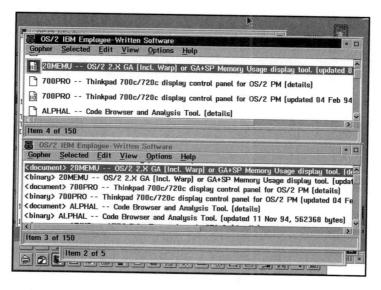

OS/2 Gopher's other view is the *details* view (see Figure 7.11). For true Gopher devotees, as well as for exploring and troubleshooting, this perhaps is the best view. It shows at a glance exactly what and where each Gopher item is. If you're attempting to locate a specific file or Gopher site, the details view probably is what you need.

FIGURE 7.11.

Details view shows you the specifics of each Gopher item.

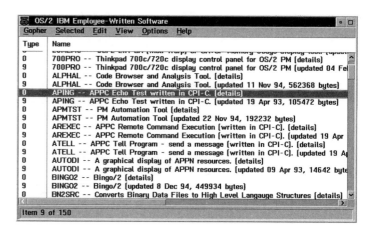

One thing to keep in mind is that Gophers are not perfect. They are set up and maintained by humans. It is entirely possible that they aren't being kept up to date, or that mistakes were made when the server Gopher menu was set up. A typo or an out-of-date reference can stand between you and what you seek. Often, just seeing the item's specification can reveal a problem.

Tip

> You can—even without going into details view—see at any time the detail specification of any Gopher item. Just select the item and choose Selected | Item details from the command bar. The OS/2 Gopher then shows you the details in a dialog box (see Figure 7.12). If you see an error, or a likely change in specification that might make an errant item work, you can change it. Then click Open to see if your specification is correct.
>
> To see the details of the entire current Gopher menu (rather than just the selected item), choose Gopher | Menu details from the OS/2 command bar. The dialog box is identical to the one that appears when you display the Item details, but shows information for the whole menu. This is identical to what would appear if you were to select Item details in the parent menu.

FIGURE 7.12.

You can modify the details in the Item Details dialog box and reopen the menu item.

Backtracking: Getting Back to Where You Began

On occasion, you might find yourself in a Gopher menu without having the parent or root menu immediately available. This can happen if the previous menu launched you to a location inside another Gopher server's menu so that you never saw the root menu to begin with (at least not for the current menu). It might happen if you use a bookmark to bypass a series of Gopher menus. It might also happen if you open a series of Gopher menus, and then close all but the current window.

When you find yourself without a clear path to the parent or root menu, there are two ways in which you can get back without recalling what you did. The easiest way is to choose Gopher | Open this server's root menu from the command bar. When you do that, the OS/2 Gopher uses information in the current Gopher item to return to the root. To do this, it just strips away the Path information in the current menu details, and then tries to reopen that location. Consider the Art and Images Gopher window and menu item details shown in Figure 7.13. To return to the root for this Gopher's menu, you could display the menu details, delete the Path information, and then click Open. Or, you could do it the easy way by choosing Gopher | Open this server's root menu (Ctrl+T) from the OS/2 Gopher command bar.

FIGURE 7.13.

The Art and Images Gopher menu.

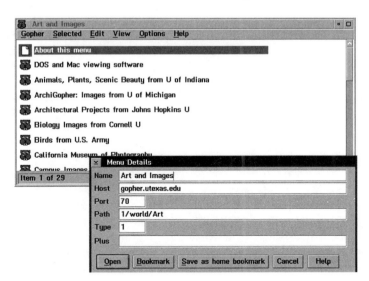

The latter method has an added benefit, in that it gives the window a different title, which can keep you from getting confused when you navigate using the OS/2 Window List. If you navigate manually, you might tend to forget (or just not bother) to type a new name into the Name field for the menu item details. When you click Open, OS/2 Gopher opens the new window with the same name it had previously, even though it now contains different information. If you use this approach, you might become confused when you press Ctrl+Esc to display the Window List.

Another approach to returning to the root of your current Gopher menu requires you to have been there previously, by way of the Gopher History List window. As you navigate through Gopherspace, the OS/2 Gopher program keeps track of each Gopher site you visit. If you get lost or need to renavigate to a place you visited earlier, you can use that list. It often is easier to use the history list than to use the OS/2 Window List. To display a list of all the Gopher sites you've visited during the current session, choose Gopher | Open history window (or press Ctrl+H) from the OS/2 Gopher command bar.

As shown in Figure 7.14, the OS/2 Gopher History List window is similar to the regular Gopher menu window, with only a few differences. One important difference is that any currently opened Gopher menus are displayed with diagonal hash marks—the same way that open objects usually are displayed in OS/2 folders. Another difference is that the command-bar choices are fewer because the history list is a local list rather than an online Gopher menu. For example, the history list window command bar wouldn't contain a Gopher | Menu item details entry, although it does contain a Selected | Item details command-bar item for each entry.

FIGURE 7.14.

The OS/2 Gopher History List window.

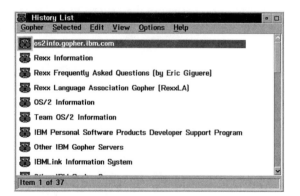

The OS/2 Gopher Command Bar (Menu)

One problem in talking about menus when discussing Gopher is confusion about which menu is being discussed. After all, each Gopher window is a menu. Gopher, however, has an application menu at the top of the Gopher window, just below the title bar. In this chapter, however, that menu is called the *command bar*. The Gopher command bar consists of six main items:

◆ Gopher
◆ Selected
◆ Edit
◆ View
◆ Options
◆ Help

This section discusses Gopher's application command bar (menu) and the purpose of each menu item (except for Help, the purpose of which seems rather obvious).

Gopher

The OS/2 Gopher command bar contains items relating to the current Gopher window (menu) as a whole, as well as command-bar items for navigating.

Well-Known Gopher Servers

To get you started, the OS/2 Gopher lists three major Gopher servers:

◆ IBM Almaden Gopher Server (os2info.gopher.ibm.com)

◆ University of Minnesota (gopher.micro.umn.edu)

◆ University of Illinois Weather Machine (wx.atmos.uiuc.edu)

Unless you change it, the OS/2 Gopher program uses the IBM Almaden Gopher Server as the *home* bookmark. This is the default Gopher server that OS/2 Gopher uses when started. See the section titled "Make this Item the Home Bookmark" later in this chapter for information on how to change the home bookmark.

Menu Details (Ctrl+M)

The *Menu Details* item displays information about the menu displayed in the active Gopher window. Following is the information that appears:

Name	Name used in the OS/2 Gopher window's title bar
Host	The Internet address of the Gopher server (this item can be text or an IP address)
Port	The TCP/IP port instruction number for processing Gopher requests and responses by the OS/2 Gopher application
Path	The location of the current Gopher menu on the host computer
Type	1, for Gopher menu
Plus	Blank or + indicates whether the server is a GopherPlus site (enhanced Gopher sites, some of which have multimedia offerings, and most of which provide file size information when you begin a file download)

Bookmark This Menu

Use the *Bookmark this menu* command to add the current menu (not the selected item) to the list of bookmarks. Bookmark information is stored in the GOPHER.INI file. This feature is especially handy for bookmarking Gopher menus that you have to specify yourself (see "Specify Gopher Item" later in this chapter).

Reload This Menu (Ctrl+R)

Use the *Reload this menu* item to reload the current Gopher menu. Although this might seem redundant, it is not. If you modified the specification and opened a variation of the "official" menu, using the Reload option will open the original, unmodified Gopher menu.

Reload This Server's Root Menu (Ctrl+T)

Use the *Reload this server's root menu* item to go to the root directory of the current Gopher server. Often, a Gopher item will take you to a specific directory or file. Use the Reload root option to burrow up to the top level directory on the current Gopher server. Technically, the name of this command is a misnomer, because you need not have loaded the root at all to get to where you are currently.

Specify Gopher Item (Ctrl+S)

Use *Specify Gopher item* to open a Gopher server directly. As shown in Figure 7.15, pressing Ctrl+S opens a blank Gopher specification dialog box in which you can type the server information. You sometimes might need to use this option if the name of a server has changed to something other than what's listed in a Gopher menu you're using. If you're not sure of the exact path, it often is better to leave that blank and navigate to it after the server is connected. Note that if you include the name for the Gopher item, it will help navigation during the current session because the name you specify will appear in the OS/2 Window List.

FIGURE 7.15.

Press Ctrl+S to specify a Gopher server directly.

> If you come across an incorrectly specified item in a Gopher menu, and you can find what you want anyway, you can save that information. You can't save it in the Gopher server's menu—that's up to the host administrator. You can, however, add the modified Gopher item to your own list of bookmarks. After you do that, you will be able to navigate back to the same location without having to hunt and peck. See the section, "Bookmark This Menu," earlier in this chapter.

When specifying the Gopher item directly, you're usually best off to leave the default port set to 70. If you try different port numbers, however, you might sometimes get an interesting surprise. For example, the Retrieve Software Updates Gopher item uses the Gopher item `updates.gopher.ibm.com`. If you specify that Gopher item, however, you get a plain IBM

Gopher menu that does *not* lead you to the same Gopher selections you get when you run the Retrieve Software Updates object. However, if you specify the port as 77 instead of 70, you now *will* get the same Gopher selections that you get from the Retrieve Software Updates object.

Open Bookmark Window (Ctrl+B)

Use the *Open bookmark window* command to display the Bookmark List window (see Figure 7.16). The Bookmark List window is very similar to other Gopher windows, with just a few differences in the window command-bar choices. Important to managing your Bookmark List, for example, is the capability to remove bookmarks that are no longer needed. To remove a bookmark you no longer want, select the item and choose Selected | Delete this item, or just press the Delete key.

FIGURE 7.16.

The OS/2 Gopher Bookmark List.

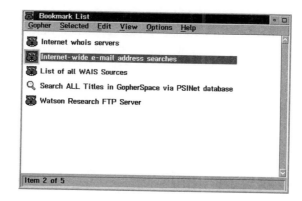

Other than command-bar differences, the Bookmark List window works the same as other Gopher windows. Press Enter to dig in; press Esc to dig out.

Open History Window (Ctrl+H)

The Open history window item enables you to retrace your footsteps. Unlike the Bookmark List window, however, the history list is good only for the current session. You cannot save an OS/2 Gopher history window between Gopher sessions. When you close and restart OS/2 Gopher, the history list is, well, history!

Home Bookmark Details

The *Home bookmark details* item displays the Gopher details of the home bookmark. You can use this setting to modify the home bookmark. This item is available only when a home bookmark has been set. To change the home bookmark manually, choose Gopher | Home bookmark details. Then make any modifications you want and choose Save as home bookmark.

Clear Home Bookmark

Use the *Clear home bookmark* item to clear the current home bookmark. If you close OS/2 Gopher without setting a new home bookmark, it defaults to the IBM Almaden server the next time OS/2 Gopher is started.

Previous Menu (Esc)

As you may recall, the Enter key digs you in, and Esc digs you out. The *Previous menu* command is the equivalent of pressing Esc. Pressing Esc closes the current Gopher window and returns you to the previous one.

Exit program (F3)

The *Exit program* item closes all Gopher windows. Recall that Alt+F4 is the usual system key for closing an application, while Ctrl+F4 usually closes only a window within an application. In OS/2 Gopher, the individual windows are more or less independent; so Alt+F4 closes individual windows. To close all Gopher menus at once, press F3, or choose Gopher | Exit from the command bar.

Selected

The *Selected* menu is used to control individual Gopher items within a Gopher menu. In lieu of using the Selected command-bar item, you also can click mouse button 2 on an item for a popup menu (see Figure 7.17). The one you use depends on your working style.

FIGURE 7.17.

Click mouse button 2 to display an item's popup menu.

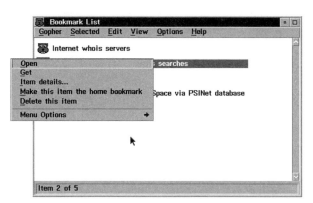

Open (Enter)

One potentially confusing aspect of OS/2 Gopher is the way in which windows are opened. When you press Enter in a Gopher menu, it is the equivalent of choosing Selected | Open from the Gopher command bar. When you do that, OS/2 Gopher opens the selected item in the same window. If you move that window, you will not see the previous window underneath.

For example, suppose that the IBM OS/2 Gopher server is displayed in a window. If you select the Newsletter Gopher item, it is displayed in the same window space as the IBM OS/2 Gopher. For all intents and purposes, it appears that the Newsletter Gopher menu has now replaced the IBM OS/2 Gopher server menu. If you move the Newsletter window by dragging its title bar, you will not see the IBM OS/2 Gopher window underneath.

If you press Ctrl+Esc and select the IBM OS/2 Gopher window after having moved the Newsletter window, however, you now will be able to see both windows. Unless you make such an effort to display two (or more) windows separately, however, each successive window you open will use the same space as the previous one—as in this example. This results in far less screen clutter. Keep in mind, however, that previous Gopher windows are still in fact open, and you can see by pressing Ctrl+Esc to display the Window List.

Open in Another Window

As described in the previous section, each new Gopher menu you open appears in the same window space, unless you explicitly separate them by moving one and then accessing the other from the Window List. If you want a new window created for a Gopher you open, you can do so, however. Rather than pressing Enter, choose Selected | Open in another window. Unfortunately, there is no keyboard shortcut for this (except for Alt+S, A).

Get

Use the *Get* command to save the selected item to a file. Note that Get is the default behavior when you press Enter while a nonviewable file is highlighted. Hence, if a file named XYZ.ZIP is selected, pressing Get and Enter are equivalent.

What if a viewable file is selected, but you don't really want to view it? What if you just want to download it and tend to its contents later? Pressing Enter might download the file, but it usually invokes a viewer of some kind as well. What you need is the Get command. In addition to not displaying the file, the Get option always prompts for you to confirm the filename and target directory. This gives you more control than simply pressing Enter.

The Get option downloads a file, even if it is displayable. Even if the selected item is a Gopher menu and can be resolved successfully, the menu itself will be saved as a file. OS/2 Gopher attempts to use the name from the item's Path field (choose Selected | Item details to see the pathname).

Item Details

Use the *Item details* option to display information about the host and path associated with the selected Gopher item. When working in OS/2 Gopher, it often is useful to know exactly what you're going to get when you press Enter. Knowing the item details also can help in problem resolution, as well as modifying a Gopher item whose specification is slightly wrong, and whose correct specification you either know, or can guess correctly.

Bookmark This Item

Use the *Bookmark this item* option to add the select item to the index. Contrast the Selected | Bookmark this item option with the Gopher | Bookmark this menu option. The former bookmarks just the selected item, whereas the latter bookmarks the entire current Gopher menu. Make sure which one you want before adding the item.

Make This Item the Home Bookmark

Use the *Make this item the home bookmark* selection to make the selected item your home bookmark—the default Gopher server that is displayed when OS/2 Gopher is opened.

Edit

You use the Edit command-bar items to search within a Gopher menu and move directly to a numbered Gopher item.

Find (Ctrl+F)

Use the *Find* option to locate text within a Gopher menu. This can be helpful when browsing long menus that won't fit on-screen. Unfortunately, the Edit | Find option is missing from the default text window that OS/2 Gopher uses to display text files.

Find Next (Ctrl+N)

Use the *Find next* option to find the next match, after having used Ctrl+F to first specify the search text.

Go to Item

The items in each Gopher menu are numbered. Use the Edit | Go to item to go directly to an item by number.

View

Use the *view* command-bar options to control the way in which the Gopher menu windows are displayed and sorted. The default view is name view. You can change the default view, but the method isn't obvious. To change the default view, follow these steps:

1. Open a single Gopher window.
2. Set the view and window size to the desired defaults. (You cannot save default fonts and colors this way; see the section titled "Options" later in this chapter.)
3. Close OS/2 Gopher.

Thereafter, each time you open OS/2 Gopher, it will use the view and window size set in step 2.

Name

The *Name* option is the default view. It shows a Gopher type icon at the left and the descriptive name of the Gopher item at the right.

Text

The *Text* option is identical to the Name option, except that the Gopher type is displayed as text rather than as an icon.

Details

The *Details* option gives you the same information you get by choosing Selected | Item details from the command bar. Note that the item usually identified as Path in the Item Details dialog box is called Selector in the details view (see Figure 7.18).

FIGURE 7.18.

The Selector in details view corresponds to the Path entry in the Item Details dialog box.

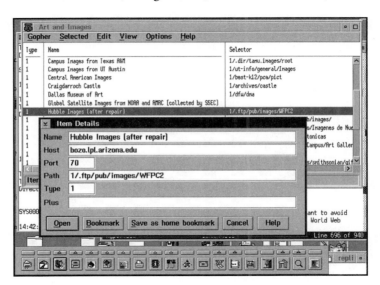

Sort

Use the *Sort* option to control the way in which items are sorted in a Gopher menu window. Note that the options that make sense in details view might not make sense in other views because the sorting attribute might not be visible. Following are the sorting options:

Name	Sorts items by the descriptive name.
Type	Sorts items by Gopher type (this is useful if you like to keep files and menus separate).
Port	Sorts items by port (this is useful if you want to avoid accidentally launching non-OS/2 Gopher processes such as Wide World Web items).

Host	Sorts items by the host computer. This option is useful if some hosts within a Gopher menu aren't responding. By sorting by hosts, you can more easily isolate the problem host.
Path	Sorts items by path (this option is useful when you're looking in a large list for a specific path and/or filename).
Restore original order	Returns items to their original order. Many Gopher menus have a "natural" or deliberate order that helps the entire menu make more sense. If you sort it in a different order to find a pattern of some kind, you can use this option to put things back as they were. Note that you also can get back to the native order by choosing Gopher	Reload menu from the OS/2 Gopher command bar.

> You can sort a Gopher menu as many times as you want. You cannot, however, change the default sort order. Gopher menus always are initially displayed in the order determined by the Gopher server.

Options

Use Options to set the font and colors, as well as to set up individual Gopher type defaults. All options are saved in GOPHER.INI, which is maintained in the TCPIP/ETC directory.

Font

Depending on your display resolution, as well as on the view you use for OS/2 Gopher, the default font might not be appropriate. Use the *Font* control to choose the display font you want (see Figure 7.19). To make a font the default, you first must change the font, save the scheme, and then choose the Save as default option.

FIGURE 7.19.

Choose Options | Font from the command bar to change OS/2 Gopher fonts.

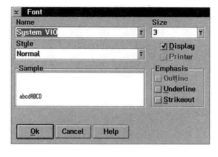

Don't Be Fooled!

You can use the OS/2 font and color Palettes to change the fonts and colors in OS/2 Gopher. When you close and reopen Gopher, however, the colors revert to their previous settings. The only way to save color and font changes in OS/2 Gopher is to use the Options | Font and Color choices in the command bar, and then save the new scheme as the default.

Color

Use the *Color* option to set the background color. At this writing, foreground color (color of the text) is frozen so that you cannot change it (see Figure 7.20). Both colors and fonts preferences can be saved as the default only by first saving a scheme, and the using the Save as default option.

FIGURE 7.20.

Choose Options | Colors from the command bar to set OS/2 Gopher colors.

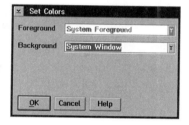

To change the text color temporarily, you can use Ctrl+drag to drag a new color to an OS/2 Gopher window from an OS/2 Color Palette. The change cannot be saved, however.

Save Scheme

Use the *Save scheme* option to save your font and/or color preference as a named scheme (see Figure 7.21). Because different display views take up different amounts of room on-screen, you might find that a smaller font works better for details view, while a large font works fine for name or text view. You might consider giving the scheme a particular name. You also might have special colors or fonts you like to use for specific Gophers. Whatever the reason, use Options | Save scheme to save your fonts and colors. Note that the Save scheme option is not available until you change fonts or colors during a session, or until you load a named scheme.

FIGURE 7.21.

Use Options | Save scheme to save color and font sets for future use; click Save as default to make the current scheme the default.

Load Scheme

Use the *Load scheme* option to load a named scheme. This option is not available until you save a scheme.

Delete Scheme

Use the *Delete scheme* option to delete a named scheme. Note that it is possible for a scheme to remain the default even after it has been deleted. To restore the original defaults, you need to set the colors and fonts to the defaults, and save that as the default scheme.

Configure

Use the *Configure* options to set the default OS/2 Gopher type file handlers, as well as the default code page for displaying Gopher menus.

Types

Following are the three distinct categories of Gopher item types:

Internal	Set by the system and cannot be changed by the user (except for the type names, such as `error`, `menu`, `phonebk`). Internal types are: `type i`, `error`, `menu`, `phonebk`, and `search`.
File handlers	These are user-configurable and used to set the default location for a downloaded file, as well as default handling programs. File handler types are: `binary`, `Book`, `document`, `gif`, `html`, `image`, `Mac binary`, `Movie`, `PC binary`, `Picture`, `sound`, `Sound`, and `Uuencoded`.
Telnet	These options are somewhat user-configurable telnet and telnet 3270 terminal connections for connecting directly with non-Gopher telnet links.

Internal

The first group of Gopher item types—Internal—cannot be changed by the user, except for their names. If you find the current names bothersome or limiting, you can change them. To change `phonebk` to `phone`, for example, follow these steps:

1. Choose Options | Configure from the command bar.
2. Select the `phonebk` entry by clicking it with mouse button 1.

3. Click the Rename button.

4. Type a new name for phonebk (such as **Phone Book**).

5. Click OK.

Some of the Internal types, such as phonebk and search, have a dialog box interface for you to enter a query that is submitted to the Gopher server. When the Gopher server receives the query, it then runs a program to search for the information you seek. The Search item, for example, usually connects to a WAIS (wide area information server). When you search, a number of *hits* (or *matches*) are displayed, with an opportunity for you to display more information.

File Handlers

The second group of Gopher item types enables you to set the following options:

Drive and directory	Physical location in which downloaded files are stored.
File extension	Default extension used for file naming when the selected item does not have a file extension.
Run after receiving Program	The path and name of a program to run against a file (that is, using the file as a source file of some kind) after it is received. In the case of sound and video files, this would be a player or viewer program of some type. In the case of .ZIP or .UUE files, you might specify an unarchiver program.
Parameter	Optional parameters to use in the startup command line for the program named in the previous item.

Suppose that you want all incoming sound files to be placed in the c:\mmos2\sounds directory, and played by PLAY.CMD, rather than by MMPM.EXE. PLAY.CMD is a REXX program that is installed in your MMOS2 directory. Although it doesn't give you any control over a sound that is played, it loads much more quickly than the default MMPM.EXE. To use PLAY.CMD, follow these steps:

1. Choose Options | Configure.

2. Choose Sound or sound, depending on the exact Gopher item type.

3. In the Receive to file Drive and directory text box, type the location in which you want the files to go (such as **c:\mmos2\sounds**).

4. In the File extension box, type the default extension you want to use when an extension is missing from the incoming file reference (**.AU**, for example).

5. In the Run after receiving Program text box, type **c:\mmos2\play.cmd**. (Use the appropriate drive letter to indicate where mmos2 is installed on your system.)

6. In the Parameters text box, type **file=**. This is essential when using the PLAY.CMD program. The parameter you type will be placed immediately before the incoming filename (file=xxxxx.au, for example, not xxxxx.au file=).

7. Close the Configure Settings notebook.

Now, when you open a sound file corresponding to this Gopher type, the file will download to the directory you specified, and it will be played using PLAY.CMD.

Telnet

The third group of Gopher types launch telnet and telnet 3270 sessions. These sessions usually are used to run specific programs at a Gopher site. Often, there are specific passwords or user names that you must use to access the telnet servers.

By default, before the telnet client window appears, the OS/2 Gopher displays a message box that shows any special instructions you need (such as a special user name, program name, account name, or password); see Figure 7.22.

FIGURE 7.22.

Telnet displays special login instructions in a dialog box, as well as in the telnet title bar.

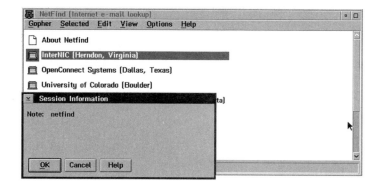

In addition, the notes are displayed in the telnet title bar. If those notes annoy you, you can disable them by clicking to turn off the Message Box and Title Bar options (either or both) in the Configure settings for telnet or telnet 3270 (see Figure 7.23).

FIGURE 7.23.

Use Options | Configure to tell telnet if and how to display special login instructions.

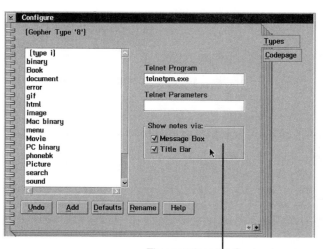

These options tell Gopher how to display special messages

In addition, you can change the telnet programs. By default, the OS/2 Gopher program uses `telnetpm.exe` for telnet and `pmant.exe` to start a 3270 telnet session. You also can specify telnet parameters. For `telnetpm.exe`, for example, you can use `-h 50` as a parameter to start telnet in 50-line mode. For additional telnet settings, see Chapter 10, "Connecting to Other Systems Using Telnet."

Resetting Defaults and Deleting Gopher Types

You can only delete Gopher items that you create. The built-in Gopher items can be modified, but you cannot change the type character. Note, as shown in Figure 7.24, that the Delete button is replaced with a Default button. When you click the Delete button, a user-defined Gopher type is removed. When you click the Default button, the built-in defaults for the current item are restored.

FIGURE 7.24.

When you delete a Gopher type, there is no Undo!

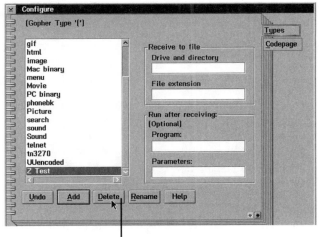

After you click Delete, the Undo button won't be available

When you choose the Delete button to remove a Gopher type, it is deleted without a confirmation. Furthermore, the Undo option will not put it back, so be careful using this option.

Warning

Adding a New Gopher Type

As you make your way around Gopherspace, you eventually might encounter a Gopher type that is not already defined in the OS/2 Gopher client. If that happens, you can add the new type to the OS/2 Gopher's vocabulary. First, open the Gopher window to display the unknown type. Switch to Details view to see the character used to indicate the type. Also note any clues you have about the type's handling. Suppose that the type is shown as `w`, and the selector (path) shows the item to have a `.WAV` extension. If you are familiar with OS/2 MultiMedia, you know that you usually can play files with .WAV extensions using MMPM.EXE or AB.EXE. Follow these steps to create a new Gopher type that uses AB.EXE as a viewer:

1. From the command bar, choose Options | Configure.
2. On the Types page, click Add to display the dialog box shown in Figure 7.25.

FIGURE 7.25.

Define a new Gopher type.

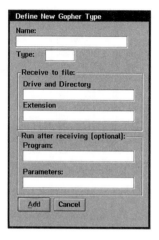

3. In the Name field, type a short descriptive name (such as **wave**).
4. In the Type field, enter the one-character type indicator from the OS/2 Gopher window Details view (such as **w**).
5. In the Receive to file field, type the directory in which you want incoming files of this type to be copied (such as **c:\mmos2\sounds**).
6. In the Extension field, type the extension you want to be used when the incoming reference doesn't provide an extension (such as **.wav**). (See the Note box at the end of these instructions.)
7. In the Run after receiving field, enter the name of the program you want to run after receiving the file (such as **c:\viewer\bin\ab.exe**).
8. In the Parameters field, type any needed parameters (none generally are needed for AB.EXE).
9. Click Add. After you click Add, the type is added to the list of types.

If you later want to change the type character, you cannot edit the wave (as named in step 3) definition you created. Instead, you need to delete the wave type (using the Delete button) and add a new type.

Also, the extension you enter is not always used. Usually, in fact, the selector (path) reference in the Gopher menu shows a full filename that already includes an extension. The extension in the Gopher type definition is used only when no extension is provided.

Code Page

The Code page selection determines how characters appear on-screen. Chances are, if you *should* be using something different from the specified default (usually 1004, for ISO8859 Latin-1), you already are. Code page 1004 accommodates most of the European languages, including English. For other code pages, changes to settings in your OS/2 CONFIG.SYS may be needed to the CODEPAGE, DEVINFO, and COUNTRY lines. See the online information that comes with your version of OS/2 for information.

CHAPTER EIGHT NAVIGATING THE WEB WITH THE WEBEXPLORER

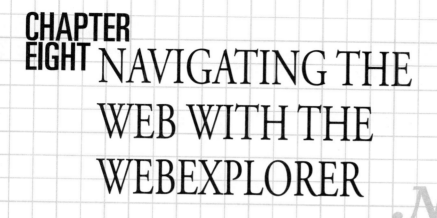

For some Net surfers, the World Wide Web is at the center of all the excitement about the Internet and the so-called Information Superhighway. Some long-time Internet users, however, see the World Wide Web and heavy dependence on slow, graphical software, and say, "There goes the neighborhood." However you look at it, it's here to stay—at least until something *sexier* comes along.

What exactly is the World Wide Web? Beats me. However, it appears to be zillions of *HTML* (*hypertext markup language*) documents all ultimately linked together by numerous World Wide Web servers. More than that, however, it also appears to be a relatively new way to look at a variety of resources on the Internet. Not only are HTML documents involved, but Gopher documents, FTP sites, and newsgroups as well. WWW browsers seem to be expanding almost weekly in what they can do, in an apparent effort to make as much of the Internet as possible available from a single compact tool.

HTML?

HTML, or *hypertext markup language*, is a word and data processing and presentation format. Who knows, it might even be the universal OpenDoc format of the future. Basically, HTML is a way of presenting words, references to files, and references to Internet resources. HTML documents contain a combination of regular text and links. Links contain the necessary information for viewing additional HTML documents or data. For a *short* course in putting together your own Home page, see the "HTML 101—Designing Your Own Home Page" section at the end of this chapter.

Navigating Using the WebExplorer

Some things defy description. The WWW is one of them. Your best bet is to start up the WebExplorer and take a look for yourself. The WebExplorer (WE) is installed in your IBM Internet Connection for OS/2 folder (see Figure 8.1). Unlike most other OS/2 Warp Internet clients, the WebExplorer is designed to be used both on and off the Internet. As you soon will learn, you can use the WebExplorer to create impressive presentations. You can view those presentations without logging onto the Internet. Because connect time is fairly expensive to many users, I'll start by touring as much of the WebExplorer as I can without actually being logged onto the Internet. So, without getting onto the Internet, go ahead and start the WebExplorer by double-clicking on its icon in the IBM Internet Connection for OS/2 folder.

Viewer Not Found!

Did you install the Multimedia Viewer? If you jump ahead, you might encounter, or already have encountered, files, such as .AU and .SND, embedded in documents you encounter on the Web. There are other files, too, that the WebExplorer seems willing—almost eager—to let you download. If you click on such a file, you might see many minutes pass by as the file fills your disk. When it finally arrives, you're all set to listen to a sound file or watch a video, and then watch, unamused, as the WebExplorer tells you it can't find the viewer for the file (see Figure 8.2). A typical reason for this is that the WebExplorer, by default, expects that the files AB.EXE (audio browser), IB.EXE (image browser), and VB.EXE (video browser) already have been installed.

Those viewers are part of the Multimedia Viewer that comes in the OS/2 BonusPak. See the OS/2 installation instructions for information on how to install the BonusPak components. If you didn't install Multimedia, then you need to install it, or you need to modify the viewer settings for the corresponding files. See "Viewers" later in this chapter for additional information.

If you click on a file for which no viewer type has been set, the WebExplorer's default behavior is to tell you there is no viewer for that type of file (see Figure 8.2). It then asks if you want to save the file to disk. In the case of files for which viewers *are* defined, it downloads the file to a temporary file and directory before informing you that you've just wasted your download time. If this happens to you, check in the \TCPIP\TMP directory file for recently created files with the corresponding extension. If you have been downloading an .AU file, for example, look for something in the \TCPIP\TMP directory that has an .AU extension. Rather than downloading it again, you can copy it to another location to preserve it, and look at it later, once the proper viewer has been installed. Or, if you have a correct viewer (for example, the Digital Audio object in the Multimedia folder will play an .AU file), you can use it at this time to play the file right where it is.

FIGURE 8.1.

Once installed, the WebExplorer is placed in your IBM Internet Connection for OS/2 folder.

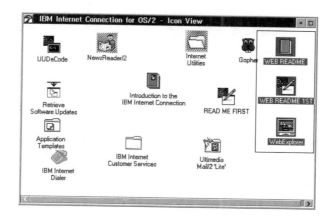

FIGURE 8.2.

The WebExplorer expects you to install the Multimedia Viewer, which is in the BonusPak!

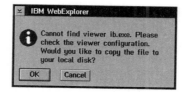

The first time you start the WebExplorer, you'll see a potentially upsetting message that EXPLORE.INI is missing. Relax—it's not there until you use the WebExplorer at least once, so, click on the OK button to proceed (see Figure 8.3).

FIGURE 8.3.

The first time you run the WebExplorer, EXPLORE.INI *has not yet been created.*

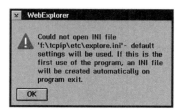

EXPLORE.INI Is Missing!

Depending on how you installed the WebExplorer, the first time you start it, you might see a warning dialog box like the one shown in Figure 8.3. Don't be concerned. This little warning is simply saying that the WebExplorer is making a fresh start, without an EXPLORE.INI file. On the other hand, if this *isn't* your first time to run the WebExplorer, and if you used to have a well-chiseled setup, it would appear to be gone. The only way this file usually disappears, however, is if you accidentally or deliberately delete it. If so, then you might be able to retrieve it using Undelete or another undelete utility.

A Tour of the WebExplorer

When you first start the WebExplorer, you see the rather bland view shown in Figure 8.4 (unless you have logos enabled—see the following tip). By default, the WebExplorer does not load a home page. And, because you're not logged onto the Internet right now, that's just as well, unless you happen to have a few stray HTML documents lying around on your disk, just waiting to be loaded.

Tip

Do logos and *Do you really want to quit* messages bug you? If so, and if you haven't already discovered it, you can turn both off in the WebExplorer. First, many OS/2 programs—by default—display a logo when they're first started. Most of these use an OS/2 system command to display the logos. You can control both how long the logos display and whether or not they display at all. Follow these steps to turn logos off:

1. Click mouse button 2 on the Desktop, and then click on System setup.

2. Open the System object.

3. Click the Logo tab.

---

4. Click None.

5. Close the System – Settings notebook.

You also can turn off the Do you really want to exit the WebExplorer message. To do this, open the Settings notebook for the WebExplorer, and put **-q** into the Parameters text box (if you have a URL or other parameter already, then put a space followed by **-q** at the end of the parameters already there).

FIGURE 8.4.

By default, the WebExplorer comes up blank.

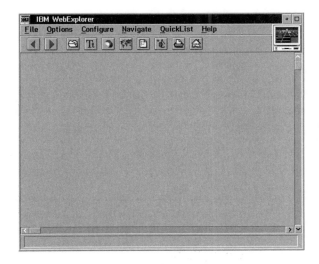

As a GUI application, the WebExplorer is designed to be navigated with a mouse. You learn all the keyboard shortcuts in a while, but for now, you can explore with the mouse. Move the mouse so that the pointer is over the strange looking square in the upper-left corner of the WebExplorer window—just under the Maximize/Minimize/Restore buttons. Notice that the international Do Not Enter sign appears. Under no circumstances should you ever try to crawl through that square! Just remember what happened to Alice!

Seriously, however, as you move the pointer over the square, look at the status area at the bottom of the WebExplorer window. It says Select the animation button to HALT loading. If you were logged onto the Internet right now and WebExplorer was loading a document of some kind, you could halt loading the document by clicking on the animation button. While a document is loading, the animation button appears to be moving, as if it were coming towards you. This is supposed to be an animation of the Information Superhighway. If you use your imagination, it will look as if you're traveling forward, whizzing past various little squares and other shapes. You also can press the Escape key to halt loading a document—just in case the animation button is too cute to click.

Move the mouse so that the pointer is over the icons that are under the main menu bar—make sure to watch the status area. As you move the mouse, the purpose of the objects under the pointer are displayed on the status bar, so that those intuitive icons aren't so darned cryptic. Shown in Figure 8.4, from left to right, the tools are described in Table 8.1.

Table 8.1. The WebExplorer toolbar.

Tool	Explanation
Back (Ctrl+B)	Moves backward in the WebMap
Forward (Ctrl+F)	Moves forward in the WebMap
Open URL (Ctrl+D)	Opens a text window for you specify a URL directly
Fonts (Alt+C,F)	Selects fonts
Colors (Alt+C,C)	Selects text colors and background color
WebMap (Ctrl+W)	Displays the WebMap
QuickList (Ctrl+Q)	Displays full QuickList for selection and editing
Add to QuickList (Ctrl+A)	Adds the current URL to the QuickList
Print (F7)	Prints the currently displayed URL
Load Home Document (Ctrl+H)	Loads the home document

What's the WebMap?

As you proceed through the Web, the Explorer keeps a log of your travels, called the WebMap. It's a list of every URL you display. You move backwards in the WebMap by clicking on the Left arrow. It displays the previous Web page. If the Back arrow is gray, then there is no Back relative to where you are right now. That might happen because you're already at the beginning, or because you are at your original point of entry. When you surf the Net, your journey isn't always a smooth path! When you click on the Right arrow, you move forward along your WebMap. Note that you can't move forward until you've moved backwards. Heavy, dude!

Now that you're familiar with the basic equipment, it might be a good time to actually go on-line. If the WebExplorer already is running, you don't have to shut it down. Log onto the Internet using IBM Internet Dialer or the Dial Other Internet Provider dialer. If the WebExplorer isn't running, you can double-click on the WebExplorer icon. Don't be worried if the appearance of the WebExplorer doesn't change from what you saw off-line. Unless you've changed the startup options in the Configure|Servers menu, you're still looking at a blank gray page.

To see something more interesting, choose Navigate|Load home page from the menu, or press Ctrl+H. If you have an average speed computer system (that is, not especially fast), you'll see text appear as shown in Figure 8.5. After a few more seconds, the rectangle at the top of the display area becomes filled with some rather cute-looking graphics.

FIGURE 8.5.

When starting the WebExplorer, text appears before the graphics.

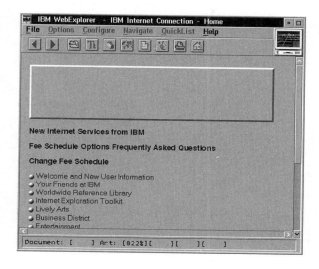

This is the IBM Internet Connection home page. By default, the WebExplorer is set up to use this as your home page. You can change it, if you want—and most users do, just as soon as they discover a Web page they like better.

Congratulations! You've taken your first step into the Web.

> The World Wide Web is addictive. If you're using an Internet provider that charges by the hour, it's easy to rack up the charges in a hurry. Keep this in mind as you begin entangling yourself in the Web.

Warning

Web Basics

The basic unit of measurement on the WWW is the Web page. To see Web pages on the Internet, you must first connect to a Web server. A WWW server is a computer that's set up to be accessed by a Web browser (or client), just as Gopher, FTP, or telnet servers are set up to be accessed by those respective clients. Web servers dispense their service in the form of what are called Web pages. No, I'm not talking about spiders or ducks that work at the theater. A Web page is an HTML document that is accessible over the Internet.

Now that you're logged in and connected to a Web site, see where you are. Move the mouse so that the pointer is over the gray area to the right of the fancy graphical rectangle (see Figure 8.6). As you move the mouse, look at the status area at the bottom of the WebExplorer. If you move the mouse pointer over any blank area below the command bar, the current URL will be displayed. Here, it says `Current URL: http://www.ibm.net/`, which means that you're looking at the top-level directory on a Web site named `www.ibm.net`.

FIGURE 8.6.

The status area tells you the underlying URL for each item on the page.

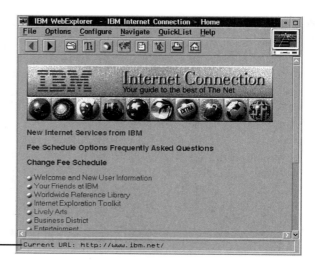

Status area ——

URL stands for *uniform resource locator*. Simply put, a URL is a Web-ese address for anything you can access using a Web browser, such as the WebExplorer. The WebExplorer supports the following types of URLs:

HTTP servers	`http://host[/ path][/document]`; for example, `http://www.ibm.net/`
FTP servers	`ftp://host/path/filespec`; for example, `ftp://ftp.ibm.net/pub/games/TRICKLE.ZIP` (Note: You can use `file:` rather than `ftp:`)
Gopher servers	`gopher://host[/ path][file]`; for example, `gopher://os2info.gopher.ibm.com`
News servers	`news://newsgroup`; for example, `news:comp.os.os2.apps`
Telnet servers	`telnet://host`; for example, `telnet://vnet.ibm.com`

Take a look at the screen for a moment. You should see three different kinds of areas in the WebExplorer display: plain black text, highlighted blue text, and graphic areas. The black text might be considered the body of the Web page document. The graphical rectangles are where incoming pictures are displayed. The highlighted blue areas are the hypertext *links* that lead to other documents, pictures, and Web pages.

Move the cursor over the blue text items under the graphic rectangle. What types of names do you see in the status area? I see names such as `ibmnet.html`, `support/feefaq.html`, `http://regsvr01.fl.us.ibm.net/svcplan.html`, `menux1.html`, `menux2.html`, and so on. You might see different names than I do. In fact, the IBM Internet Connection home page might look rather different by the time you read this. That's because it frequently is updated. Some aspects of the information contained in it, in fact, probably change daily or weekly. Unless I put this book into a home page on the Web, there's no way in the world that I can guarantee the paragraph you see here describes the current state of the Web.

Each time you move the mouse pointer over a highlighted (blue, by default) area, the text in the status area tells you the name of the underlying *link*. A link is a hypertext point of departure for another document. If you click on the Lively Arts link, for example (assuming that your IBM Internet Connection home page still has a Lively Arts item), the WebExplorer displays a document called `menu85.html`.

When you click, watch the status area carefully. Unless your computer is a *lot* faster than mine, you'll see a description of what's happening. First, the Text part of `menu85.html` is downloaded from the Web server. The WebExplorer displays `Document: [WAIT]`, and then the word `WAIT` is replaced by an increasing percentage. Next, you see `Art: [WAIT]`, and `WAIT` is replaced by an increasing percentage, the word `DRAW`, and finally by nothing, as the graphics part of the Web page springs into view.

As you use the WebExplorer, at times, you probably will notice multiple `[ ]` items after `Art:`. The WebExplorer uses one `[ ]` item for each graphic in the Web page. Although the WebExplorer does not tell you in advance how large graphics or document files are, you can get an idea by watching the percentage in the `[ ]` box. If it says `001%` and takes 10 seconds to go to `002%`, you have a long wait ahead of you. If it's not something you really want to see, you can press Esc or click the Halt button.

Bypassing Graphics

After using the WebExplorer for a while, you're bound to notice that it takes a long time (unless you have a very fast connection to the Internet) for heavy-duty graphics to load and display. Even if you *do* have a fast connection, displaying some of the pictures and other files (such as audio files) can take a long time. At some point, you'll need to ask yourself whether you really want to see and hear all that stuff. Sure, a little here and there makes it more interesting; however, when you're trying to find something in particular, wading through megabytes of pretty junk gets old in a hurry.

You can do two things. After the text part of the page is loaded, the vertical scroll bar appears to the right of display area. At that point, you can click the Halt icon (or press Esc) to stop loading the page. You will get the message `All of the URL information for links have been loaded` so that you can continue on your journey by clicking on the next link.

If you prefer not to navigate by slamming on the brakes, you can turn off graphics all the time, so that all you see is the text. From the WebExplorer menu, choose Options, and click to remove the check next to Load graphics. Now, when you read in a Web

> page, only the document will be loaded. This can make using the WebExplorer a lot more efficient. If you find a Web page that you want to see more of, just choose Options | Load graphics again to re-enable graphics, and then choose Navigate | Reload document, or press F5. This then will reload the document from the source.
>
> Note that after you re-enable the Load graphics option, Web pages that are cached on your system (either in memory or on-disk) will not yet contain graphics that were bypassed. Thus, if you use the WebMap or the Backward (Ctrl+B) and Forward (Ctrl+F) commands to navigate, you won't see graphics until you explicitly reload the URL from the source (F5).

You also might notice that some files—such as. AU sound files, for example—are loaded as Document: rather than Art:. There's nothing insidious about this. Just don't get upset that the WebExplorer's vocabulary for describing incoming files consists entirely of the words Document: and Art:.

The WebExplorer leave a visible trail as you surf through. By now, you probably have noticed that some of the links (the highlighted blue text) have been turning purple. After you viewed a link during a session, the WebExplorer changes its color so that you can tell that you've already "been there, done that." At any time while using the WebExplorer, you can take a look at where you've been during that session. Click the WebMap icon, or press Ctrl+W. The WebMap shows you the contents of the QuickList, if any, plus all hypertext links you've displayed during the current session. If you saw something earlier that you liked, but can't seem to get back there by backing up (Ctrl+B, or clicking the blue Backward arrow in the toolbar), display the WebMap. If you've been there and done that during the current session, the WebMap will have it on record!

As implied in Table 8.1, you also can use the WebExplorer to navigate more than just Web sites. It works for Gopher, newsgroups, and FTP sites, as well. It is limited, however, —except for form links—to begin read-only. Notice, for example, the Reply to link for the displayed news article (see Figure 8.7). If you click on it, you see a dialog box that tells you that the Mailto protocol isn't yet supported. If you try to upload files using FTP, you'll discover quickly that FTP is a read-only affair as well.

One other thing you might note is that the WebExplorer works differently from some other SLIP programs. When you use FTP-PM to connect to a site, you remain connected all the while. When you use the WebExplorer, however, you don't remain connected the whole time. Technically, you're connected only while a hyperlink is loading (and the animation icon is moving). Once a page and graphics have been downloaded, the connection is closed until you click on another hyperlink. Ordinarily, this is a good thing, because it frees up resources for other users to connect to them.

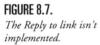

FIGURE 8.7.

The Reply to link isn't implemented.

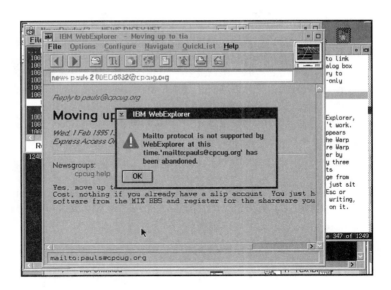

For FTP-PM, however, it's a problem. It's not uncommon to connect to an FTP site just fine but discover that the connection has been broken only moments later when you try to change directories. This can be especially frustrating if you're trying to download a file from a popular FTP site that has a limited number of connections available.

FTP from the WebExplorer Not Working?

Using version 1.0 of the WebExplorer, a number of Warp users find that FTP transfers of binary files don't work. The exact cause and reason isn't known at this time; however, it appears that users who had the full IBM TCP/IP package and then installed the Warp IAK over it are able to perform FTP from the WebExplorer, while pure Warp IAK users are not. The specific symptom is that you start a transfer by clicking on a file, and it appears to start downloading. After three or four seconds, however, the download stalls, with just little bits dripping in after that. After a few minutes, you might get a message from the WebExplorer that the transfer has been abandoned. Or, it might just sit there with the clock icon for a long time. When you finally press Esc or click on Halt, you get the dialog box shown in Figure 8.8. At this writing, this problem has not been resolved; however, IBM reportedly is working on it.

The good news is that there is a workaround. If you replace your inet.sys file with the version of inet.sys from the TCP/IP 2.0 CSD (corrective services diskettes), you will be able to perform FTP transfers from the WebExplorer. The necessary file is contained in tcp20c4.exe, which you can get from ftp.cdrom.com in the 32bit/tcpip directory. Once you have tcp20c4.exe, place it into an empty directory and enter **tcp20c4**. It will expand into several files, including BASEOC1.ZIP. Unzip BASEOC1.ZIP—it contains inet.sys version 2.04.

If you don't know what unzip is, then you'll also need to obtain the file unz512x2.exe, which is on ftp.cdrom.com in the 32bit/archiver subdirectory. Once you get that file, place it into an empty directory and enter **unz512x2**. It will create several files, including a documentation file that explains how to use it. Basically, however, you will get a file called UNZIP.EXE (among others). Place that file into your path, change to the location of BASEOC1.ZIP, and enter the following command:

unzip -j baseoc1 *inet.sys

This will unzip inet.sys version 2.04. Although this file is older than the version that comes with the Internet Access Kit, it will allow FTP transfers to work from the WebExplorer. Rename the current inet.sys as inetwarp.sys, and copy the replacement version into the tcpip\bin directory. The next time you boot OS/2, the new version will be used.

FIGURE 8.8.

FTP doesn't work for some WebExplorer users.

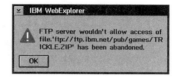

Using and Setting Up the WebExplorer

The WebExplorer might look pretty simple at first glance, but it has a lot of hidden power under the hood. There are limits to what it can do and how it does it, but all in all, it's a remarkable piece of programming. If you want to see how it was created and who created, check out the following URL:

http://www.ibm.com/Features/4guys.html

Check It Out—How?

As you surf the Net, and as you read about the Net—even in the daily newspaper—you will start to notice people saying things like "Hey, check out this URL!" or "Hey, go take a look at this Web page!" If you're like most people who are new to the Internet, you probably will thank your lucky stars that you're not in the same room with people who talk like that. However, when you get the urge to "check it out," here's how. For this example, check out http://www.ibm.com/Features/4guys.html.

1. Go online to the Internet using either the Dial Other Internet Provider dialer or the IBM Internet Dialer.

2. Start the WebExplorer.

3. From the menu, choose Options | Show current URL (unless it's already enabled).

   Notice, as shown in Figure 8.9, that when you tell the WebExplorer to show the current URL, the current location on the Web is displayed in a text box at the top of the WebExplorer display area. This is very handy for manual navigation. If you load a URL or home page by default, then its URL is displayed in the text box. Otherwise, the text box is empty.

4. Replace whatever is in the text box with the following:

   `http://www.ibm.com/Features/4guys.html`

   If it already says `http://www.ibm.com`, however, then you can simply add `/Features/4guys.html`. Once you correctly enter that into the text box, press Enter. In this instance, you'll get a description of the efforts of the programming team that created the WebExplorer.

FIGURE 8.9.

Choose Options | Show current URL to activate a URL list box.

This text box shows the current location on the Web

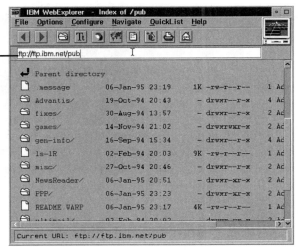

Case Counts!

As elsewhere on the Internet, everything you type in the URL specification potentially is case-specific. Use lowercase unless you see or hear otherwise. If, in the preceding example, you type `features` rather than `Features`, you will get a `404 Not Found` error (see Figure 8.10). More often than not, that means that you incorrectly typed the URL. If you typed the URL *exactly*, but suspect that the specification might have been printed or published incorrectly in your source, then try specifying just the server name, such as `http://www.ibm.com`. Very often, once on the server, you will be able to locate the URL you want and see the error. It's always possible, however, that the URL has been changed or deleted.

Keep the case issue in mind when you write messages telling others where to find items of interest on the Web. Your best bet usually is to display the URL using WebExplorer, and then copy it to the OS/2 Clipboard. That way you can paste an exact reference rather than having to retype it. If, for whatever reason, that approach isn't convenient or possible, then take a look at "View File (HTML)" section later later in this chapter.

To use the OS/2 Clipboard, select the URL you want to copy (drag with the mouse or use Shift+Arrow keys). Press Ctrl+Insert to copy the selected text to the Clipboard. Press Shift+Insert to paste the contents of the Clipboard to a new location.

FIGURE 8.10.

URLs are case specific—
Features is not the same
as features.

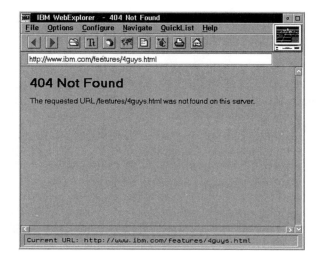

The WebExplorer Command Line

An interesting consideration when setting up the WebExplorer is the WebExplorer's Settings notebook. To display the WebExplorer's Settings notebook, press Alt and double-click on the WebExplorer icon.

You also can open the Settings notebook for an object by selecting it and then pressing Alt+Enter.

By default, as shown in Figure 8.11, there is nothing in the WebExplorer's Parameters box and Working directory fields. This means that WebExplorer will not load anything in particular when you start it (unless you change a setting from within the WebExplorer) and that any file operations you perform will default to the main root directory on you your OS/2 boot drive.

FIGURE 8.11.
You can customize what the WebExplorer loads and a working directory.

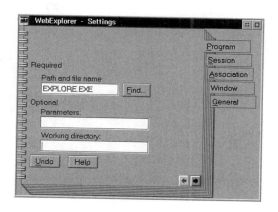

For the Parameters option, you might consider this an opportunity to set up a number of different WebExplorer objects that you use for different purposes. In the Configure | Servers dialog box, there is an option that enables you to load the home document URL at startup. If you have another file or URL reference in the Parameters setting, however, it overrides the Load at startup option. This allows you to have your cake and eat it too. You could create one WebExplorer object that loads your normal home page, another object that loads a listing of art-related URLs, another that loads an OS/2-related HTML document or saved WebMap, and so on. If you're paying for your own Internet time by the hour, having the WebExplorer set up for distinct and topical starting points can help you minimize wasted time on the clock.

The Working directory option also is one you should exercise. Leaving it blank means that any time you want to save or load a file, you will need to navigate to a more acceptable location. For example, I save all of my miscellaneous webbings to a directory called \TCPIP\WEB. That way, they aren't scattered all over kingdom come. Another likely spot might be \TCPIP\ETC because that is the location in which the WebExplorer expects to find linked files in any local HTML documents you open. If you create special purpose WebExplorer objects, you can choose the working directory in accordance with the purpose of the object.

The WebExplorer Menu

This section looks at the WebExplorer menu and its options. If you use the resources provided, the WebExplorer can become a powerful and flexible tool for exploring the Internet as well as for storing and presenting information.

File

Use the WebExplorer's *File* menu to access the options shown in Figure 8.12. Use these options to open URLs, save displayed Web pages to your hard disk, print, and so on.

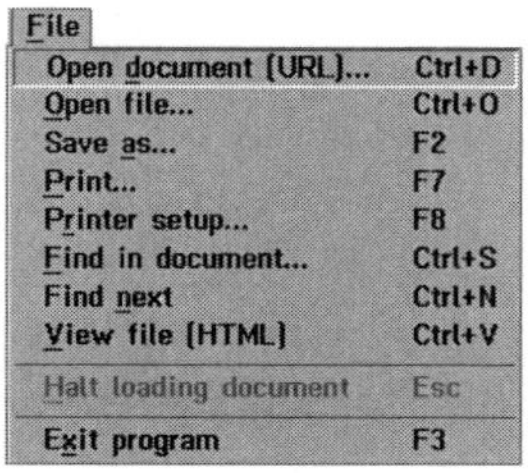

FIGURE 8.12.

The WebExplorer File menu.

File	
Open document (URL)...	Ctrl+D
Open file...	Ctrl+O
Save as...	F2
Print...	F7
Printer setup...	F8
Find in document...	Ctrl+S
Find next	Ctrl+N
View file (HTML)	Ctrl+V
Halt loading document	Esc
Exit program	F3

Open Document (URL) (Ctrl+D)

Use the *Open document* option to specify a URL you want the WebExplorer to open online. If you have the Show current URL option enabled (see "Options"), using Ctrl+D is equivalent to typing the URL into the URL text box at the top of the WebExplorer display window, and pressing Enter. You sometimes might prefer the Ctrl+D approach, such as when you want to display on-screen as much of the document as possible, or when using the WebExplorer in Presentation mode.

Open File (Ctrl+O)

Use the *Open File* option to open a local file. By local, I mean a file that's available through your directories (or over a LAN), rather than a file that's available only over the Internet. The file can be a regular text file or an HTML document. If the file contains HTML formatting, it will be interpreted as an HTML document.

The Open File option is a handy way to test HTML document you create. It also is a way to load saved Web pages or WebMaps.

To load a local file into the WebExplorer display area, follow these steps:

1. Press Ctrl+O.
2. Use the directory controls to navigate to the file you want to open.
3. Click OK.

See the section "Save As (F2)" for some neat things you can do to make finding interesting Web trails easier.

Drag-and-Drop Loading

You can drag files from an OS/2 folder and drop them directly on the WebExplorer to display them (see Figure 8.13). If you drop an HTML file, for example, it will appear as a Web page. If you drop a .GIF or .JPG file on the WebExplorer, what it does depends on whether the Use internal viewer option is enabled. If so, then .GIF and .JPG (as well as a number of other formats) will appear in the WebExplorer window. If the Use internal viewer option is not enabled, then it will display the pictures using the viewer set in the Configure|Viewers menu (assuming that it's installed).

FIGURE 8.13.

You can drop files onto the WebExplorer.

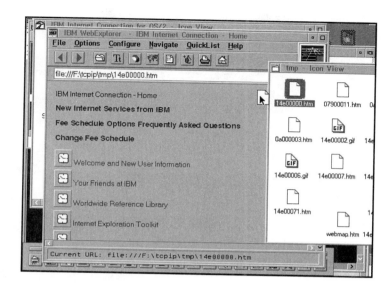

Save As (F2)

Use the *Save as* option to save the Web page or document that's displayed in the WebExplorer. Assuming that you don't already have an HTML editor, this is a great way to learn HTML composition.

Suppose that you come across a very interesting Web page with numerous URL references you want to save. Display the Web page, and then follow these steps:

1. Chose File | Save as from the menu (or press F2).
2. Navigate to the place in which you want the file to reside. (Make sure there's enough room.)
3. Adjust the filename, if you want. (It's a good idea to use .HTM as the extension for HTML documents.)
4. Click OK.

Suppose that you just stumbled onto a GIF (picture) that you want to save. If the GIF is already displayed in the WebExplorer, then you can follow the identical procedure to save the GIF onto your system.

Make Sure You Get the Pieces!

When you save a Web page to an HTML file, you're not necessarily saving everything you see. The Web page shown in Figure 8.14, for example, has several pictures in it. If you save the current document, you won't be saving the pictures. Instead, you'll just be saving the references to those pictures. Most often, when .GIFs are referenced in a Web page, they are not URL links. Instead, they are references to local files. Hence, if you want your HTML document to look identical to the one you're saving, you would need to save each of the graphic elements as well. Moreover, when you display your own HTML file using WebExplorer, it expects to see the hyperlinked files in the SET ETC directory (usually \TCPIP\ETC). You can specify the directory, however. See section "HTML 101—Designing Your Own Home Page" at the end of this chapter.

You can make all this easier. Any time you want to capture an entire URL document— including the underlying graphics—choose Options | Save to disk mode. This way, the WebExplorer will prompt you to save to disk each element you display. Just waltz through the Web page and click on each link you want to save.

FIGURE 8.14.

Saving a Web page doesn't save its components.

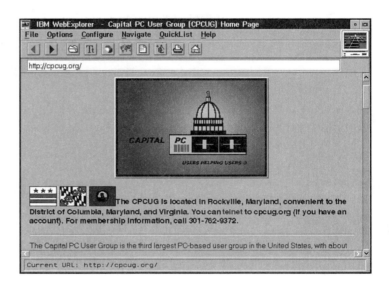

Another interesting thing you can do using the capability to save files as HTML documents is to save specific WebMaps. Suppose that you've been on a particularly interesting surfing safari, but you haven't been saving URLs to your QuickList. You know that everything is being saved to your WebMap, however. So, why not load the WebMap and then save *it*. If it contains too much information, you can always trim it down (see "HTML 101—Designing Your Own Home Page," later in this chapter). To save the current WebMap as a file, follow these steps:

1. Click the WebMap tool or press Ctrl+W to display the WebMap.

2. Press F2 (or choose File | Save as from the menu).

3. Navigate to the desired location to save the file, and type a useful name. Note that the default name of WebMap.HTM might not prove terribly informative later on.

4. Click OK.

Now, whenever you want to go back over that route, just load the saved WebMap. Or, edit it to trim away the parts that aren't so interesting. That way, if you want to resume your safari, you can skip the cab ride to airport, the flight, and the lost luggage, and head right for the elephant caravan. (Stop me if you think I'm taking this navigation/safari metaphor too far!).

Drag-and-Drop Saving

When displaying some types of URL documents, you can use drag-and-drop to copy elements to disk. Note that drag-and-drop saving works from a regular URL, but not when displaying an FTP or Gopher directory.

When a displayed document contains a .GIF, for example, you can copy it your disk by dragging it to the folder in which you want it copied. To do this, follow these steps:

1. Display the .GIF picture and the destination folder on-screen.

2. Move the mouse so that the pointer is over any part of the displayed graphic; confirm the location by observing the URL in the status area (it should display the name of the file).

3. Press and hold mouse button 2 and move the pointer away from the picture to the destination folder.

4. To begin the Save to disk operation, release the mouse button when the picture icon is over the destination folder.

5. Notice that the file name is unacceptable, so you should immediately rename it. Hold down the Ctrl key and click mouse button 1 on the icon title for the copied file.

6. Replace the filename with an acceptable name (leaving the extension, however, for graphic files such as .GIF).

7. Click on the icon to close the editing field (if you changed the extension's name, you might be prompted twice to prove to OS/2 that you know what you're doing).

Print (F7)

The WebExplorer will print the formatted Web page that currently is displayed—including any graphics. To print the currently displayed document, follow these steps:

1. Click the Print icon or press F7.

2. In the dialog box shown in Figure 8.15, change the options you want, such as adjusting the priority up or down, depending on how long the document is and how soon you need the printed version.

3. Click OK.

FIGURE 8.15.

The WebExplorer will print a formatted WYSIWYG Web page.

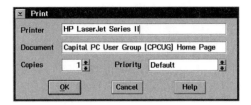

> To print text only, temporarily turn off the Load graphics option (in the Options menu), reload the URL (F5) to exclude the graphics, and then choose Print (F7).

Printer Setup (F8)

Use the *Printer setup* option to change printer objects or printer properties. From the menu, choose File|Printer setup or press F8 to display the dialog box shown in Figure 8.16. If you want to use a different printer than the one highlighted, then click to select it. To change printer properties, click the Printer Properties button. The dialog box you see for printer properties varies by printer; click OK to return to the WebExplorer Printer Setup dialog box. After you select the correct printer and properties you want, click OK. Note that this option does not print anything—it merely changes the printer setup.

FIGURE 8.16.

Use File|Printer setup to change printers or printer settings.

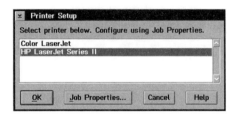

Find in Document (Ctrl+S) and Find Next (Ctrl+N)

Some Web documents can be quite long. When you're looking for a needle in a haystack, even a small haystack can seem gigantic. If you're looking for something in particular, choose File|Find in document, or press Ctrl+S to display the dialog box shown in Figure 8.17. Type in the text box the text you want to find, and click OK. Press Ctrl+N to find successive matches.

FIGURE 8.17.

Press Ctrl+S to search for text in the current URL document.

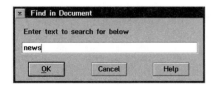

> The search in the WebExplorer is case-specific. If you want to match IBM, for example, you'll have to type **IBM**; ibm won't work.

Note

View File (HTML) (Ctrl+V)

This misnamed command doesn't really view the HTML. By default, this command uses the OS/2 System Editor (E.EXE) to open the current HTML for editing, as shown in Figure 8.18. Loading the current HTML into an editor is a perfectly okay thing to want to do; but calling it View seems a little strange. That notwithstanding, press Ctrl+V to load the current HTML into the E.EXE editor.

FIGURE 8.18.

Without the benefit of the WebExplorer, you can see how HTML documents area created.

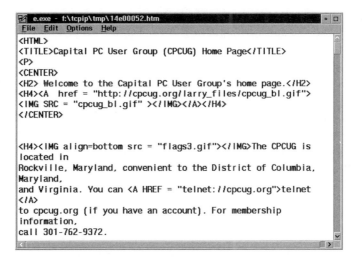

If you have an HTML editor you would rather use, then choose Configure | Viewers, and change the Editor for HTML Source option to use your HTML editor.

> If you can't get to the URL you want to copy to the Clipboard, then press Ctrl+V. This opens the current document for editing and enables you to go directly to the URL tags so that you can copy anything you want to the Clipboard.

Tip

Halt Loading Document (Esc)

Press Esc or click the Halt button to abort the current load. If you're loading something that turns out to be larger or more time-consuming than you thought, or if you accidentally clicked on the wrong link, you can use the Halt option to nip it in the bud.

Turning off the Load graphics option is one way to speed up the WebExplorer. Another way is to selectively Halt loading a URL once the link or other information you want has already appeared on-screen. If the text already is loaded, but the graphic is taking too long, press Esc or click Halt to abort downloading the picture. You then can use the partially-loaded document.

Exit Program (F3)

Press F3 (or Alt+F4) to close the WebExplorer. Back in the days of OS/2 version 1.*x*, F3 was a popular keystroke for closing PM applications. Somewhere along the way, it seems to have been changed to Alt+F4. Thankfully (for people who don't like having to press Alt+F4), the F3 tradition is being preserved in the hallowed halls of IBM. Most of the IAK PM applications, in fact, can be closed by pressing F3. You can tell which OS/2 applications were written by old hands—they use F3 to close (PMComm, DeScribe, Golden CommPass, a number of the IBM Employee Written Software applications, and many others).

Options

The *Options* menu toggles a number of display and behavior states. User options are stored in \tcpip\etc\explore.ini. The explore.ini file is a text file you can edit using a normal text editor, such as E.EXE. It also can be ruined by careless editing. As a general rule, you should make your changes from the WebExplorer menu to avoid messing up your settings. At the very least, make a backup copy before changing anything. To reset the WebExplorer to the factory defaults, rename explore.ini or just delete it. Unlike other OS/2 applications, the WebExplorer won't croak if explore.ini is deleted.

Underline Links

Use the *Underline links* option to control whether the WebExplorer displays links as underlined. This can be a useful option on monochrome monitors on which links are otherwise difficult or impossible to discern.

Load Graphics

Use the *Load graphics* option to control whether the WebExplorer loads graphics when displaying a URL document. With this option enabled, only the text part of the URL is loaded, which speeds up considerably the operation of the WebExplorer. Selectively using this option (such as turning on graphics only for those pages on which there's something you want to see) is a good strategy for reducing on-line connect charges.

Use Internal Viewer

Use the *Use internal viewer* option to control how the WebExplorer displays graphics. With Use internal viewer enabled, the WebExplorer uses its own internal viewers to display all graphics. With this option turned off, the WebExplorer still displays as part of the document (inline) graphics that are part of a Web page. Other graphics, however, are displayed using the external viewers specified in the Configure | Viewers settings.

On the positive side, the internal viewer for the WebExplorer is faster than most other viewers. When you want to get an idea of what pictures look like, the internal viewer provides an acceptable (to me, anyway) display without unnecessarily lengthening your on-line time. On the other hand, the quality provided by the internal viewer is not optimal. Some users regard the display as somewhat fuzzy and ill-suited for viewing items such as on-line works of art. Getting a 500KB image over a 9,600-baud modem connection, however, isn't exactly optimal either. If you want optimum quality, then you probably would do well to save the graphic to disk, log off the Internet, and then view the graphics at your leisure.

Presentation Mode (Ctrl+P)

The *Presentation mode* option is designed for those times when you're using the WebExplorer to present documents and graphics, rather than to navigate the Internet. In Presentation mode, the menu, title bar, toolbar, scroll bars, and status area are removed so that the entire display area can be used (see Figure 8.19). Presentation mode is only available for full-screen display. When viewing in Presentation mode, use Ctrl+P to toggle back to non-Presentation mode.

FIGURE 8.19.

Press Ctrl+P to toggle Presentation mode on and off.

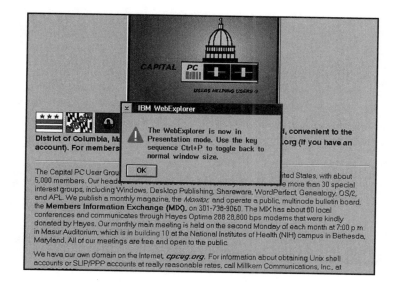

Customized Animations

The cute little graphics in the upper right corner of the screen is used to show data being loaded. Some Web servers have their own versions of that graphic. Use the *Customized animations* option to control whether the WebExplorer always displays its own, or displays the Web server's customized loading animation. The latter requires more memory and takes longer, but is worth trying just to see some of your fellow Internetters' creativity at work.

Show Current URL

The *Show current URL* option displays all the time the current URL in an editable text box at the top of the display area (see Figure 8.20). If you must edit URLs, this option can be a real time saver.

FIGURE 8.20.

Choose Options | Show current URL to show the source of the current URL document in a text box.

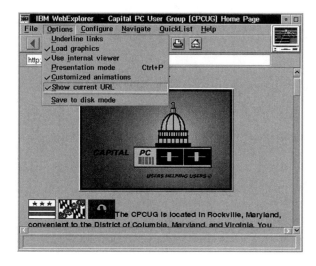

Save to Disk Mode

Enable the *Save to disk mode* option to save all subsequent URLs to disk, locally. If you're trying to copy an entire HTML document, this option can make the procedure somewhat more automatic. It prompts you for a file location and name each time you load a different element for display (see Figure 8.21).

FIGURE 8.21.

When using Save to disk mode, the WebExplorer prompts for each file.

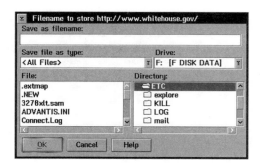

Configure

Use the *Configure* menu to change the configuration. The Configure settings, like the Options and the QuickList, are stored in EXPLORE.INI.

Servers

Use the *Servers* options to instruct the WebExplorer where to look for a particular item on the Internet. These options also specify who you are.

Home Document URL	Use this option to set your default home page. By default, the WebExplorer uses `http://www.ibm.com`. Choose the Load at startup option to do this. If you specify in the Parameters field of the WebExplorer object Settings notebook a different URL or document, then the Load at startup option is ignored. Some people find it useful to make a simple HTML document with their favorite Web sites listed by category and then define this as their home page. Just enter your home page document as `file:///drive:\directory\mypage.htm`, and select Load at startup. See "HTML 101—Designing Your Own Home Page," later in this chapter, for additional information.
Email Address	This is your e-mail address (for example, mine is `tyson@cpcug.org`).
News Server	This specifies the computer you use to connect to usenet newsgroups. (It might look something like `news.acynquw.net`.)
Proxy Gateway	Some Internet systems use what is referred to as a *proxy gateway* or *firewall* to prevent unwanted intrusion by Internet surfers. If you must use a proxy gateway, then put its name in this space. Check with your Internet provider for details.
Socks Server	If relevant, put the name or 32-bit address of your socks server. Check with your Internet provider to find out if this applies to you.

Putting anything in the Proxy Gateway field when you don't have a proxy gateway can prevent the WebExplorer from loading any more URLs during that session. To recover, you must clear the Proxy Gateway field, close WebExplorer, and then restart. Also note that some users report having to specify a complete HTTP URL for the proxy server name to work, such as `http://myproxy.net:8080/`.

Warning

Fonts

Use *Fonts* to control the fonts used by the WebExplorer. You basically can choose the typeface (Times Roman, Helvetica, or Courier) and the size (Small, Normal, Large, and Extra Large). To set the font and size, follow these steps:

1. Choose Configure|Font from the menu.
2. Choose the typeface you want—Courier, Times Roman, or Helvetica (see Figure 8.22).
3. Choose the size you want—Small, Normal, Large, or Extra Large. Observe the sample to see what the result look like.
4. Click OK. Note that you can click Default to return the WebExplorer fonts to the internal defaults.

FIGURE 8.22.

Use Configure | Fonts to change fonts.

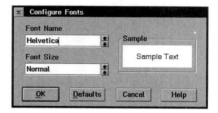

From the "Don't waste your time trying" school of philosophy, you can drag fonts from the OS/2 palette to the WebExplorer display area, but it won't work.

Colors

Use the *Colors* control, as shown in Figure 8.23, to set the display of the following:

Text	Normal text
Links	Hypertext URL links
Visited links	Linked URLs that you've already displayed
Background	The background for the entire WebExplorer display area

FIGURE 8.23.

Use Configure | Colors to set the display colors in the WebExplorer.

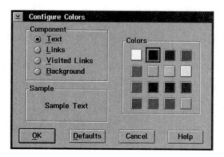

To set the colors for the WebExplorer display area, follow these steps:

1. Choose Configure|Colors.

2. Click on the type of color you want to change (Text, Links, Visited links, or Background).

3. Click on the color you want to assign.

4. Repeat steps 2 and 3 until you have made the changes you want.

5. Click OK.

Invisible Ink?

Make sure you don't inadvertently set the background and text colors the same. If you want to de-clutter the Web page as you explore, however, you can cause visited links to disappear. "Find the missing link" also makes a great party game. Set the background and link text to the same color. When you find a link, it will appear to show that you've found it.

Viewers

Use the *Viewers* options to choose external programs to process files you read using the WebExplorer. For inline graphics—pictures that are part of HTML Web page documents—the internal WebExplorer viewer will continue to be used. External viewers are used for links that are standalone files.

Viewers you can set are shown in Table 8.2. Note that the IB.EXE, AB.EXE, and VB.EXE programs are part of the Multimedia Viewer that comes on the OS/2 Warp BonusPak. (Refer to the "Viewer Not Found!" sidebar in the beginning of this chapter.) If you prefer to use different viewers for these file, this is your opportunity to do so.

Table 8.2. Default viewer settings for the WebExplorer.

Viewer	*Default*	*Viewer*	*Default*
Editor for HTML Source	E.EXE	.ETX Enhanced Text	None
AIF/AIFF/AIFC Audio	ab.exe	.GIF images	IB.EXE
.AU and .SND sound	ab.exe	.GNU tar file	None
.AVI video format	vb.exe	HDF NCSA HDF Data	None
.AVS video format	vb.exe	.HLP help file format	None
.BIN binary file	None	.IEF images	None
.BMP bitmap images	IB.EXE	.INF help file format	view.exe
BOOK BookMaster format	None	JPEG images	IB.EXE
.CSH C-Shell script	None	LATEX source files	None
.DOC MS Word format	None	MAN UNIX Man Pages	None
.DVI TeX formatting	None	MOVIE SGI movie	None

continues

Table 8.2. continued

Viewer	Default	Viewer	Default
MPEG video format	vb.exe	.SRC WAIS source	None
NC/CDF Unidata netCDF	None	SVR4 CPIO	None
Old Binary CPIO	None	SVR4 CPIO with CRC	None
.PBM Portable Bitmap	None	TAR 4.3BSD tar file	None
.PGM Portable Graymap	None	.TCL script files	None
.PGM Portable Pixmap	None	.TEX TeX source files	None
Plain Text files	None	TEXI TeX info files	None
.PNM Portable Anymap	None	.TIFF images	IB.EXE
Posix CPIO	None	TROFF source files	None
Posix tar file	None	TROFF with ME macros	None
PS/EPS/AI Postscript	None	TROFF with MS macros	None
QT/MOV QuickTime video	vb.exe	.TSV Tab-Separated Text	None
.RAS raster images	None	.WAV audio	ab.exe
.RGB Image	None	X-Bitmap Image	ib.exe
.RTF format	None	X-Pixmap image	None
.RTX Rich Text format	None	X-Window Dump	None
.SH Shell script	None	Z Compressed file	None
SHAR Shell archive	None	.ZIP PkZip format	None

Suppose that you prefer to use PMMPEG.EXE rather than VB.EXE for your MPEG video browser. PMMPEG.EXE is an excellent shareware MPEG player from SES Computing, that many OS/2 users prefer to use rather than VB.EXE. To configure the WebExplorer to use PMMPEG.EXE rather than VB.EXE, follow these steps:

1. From the menu, choose Configure | Viewers.

2. Click in the Types list and press **M** to accelerate to the M items. The MPEG video format item should pop into view, as shown in Figure 8.24.

3. In the Program text box, type the full specification for PMMPEG.EXE, or whatever alternative program you want to use (**d:\utils\pmmpeg.exe**, for example). Alternatively, you can click the Browse button to navigate to the location of the program on your disk; if you aren't sure where it is or the name of the directory, this can be handy. It also keeps you from having to type—and possibly muff—the specification.

4. Click OK.

FIGURE 8.24.

You can configure the default viewers used by the WebExplorer.

Caching

Use the *Caching* option to control how the WebExplorer handles documents and graphics. When you read a document or an image using the WebExplorer, it downloads a copy on the local disk (in the directory set as TMP in your CONFIG.SYS file, usually \TCPIP\TMP). That way, if you need to see the file again soon, it is available locally so that you don't have to download it again. By default, the WebExplorer saves the last 32 document and 16 graphics files before recycling files in the TMP directory. If you have enough disk space, you can improve the WebExplorer's "memory" of your WebMap by setting these as high as you can. If the default TMP location isn't large enough, you can move it. Also, if the default TMP location isn't fast enough, you can move it to a faster disk by changing the SET TMP statement in your CONFIG.SYS file.

As shown in Figure 8.25, the WebExplorer has two related options. The first—turned on by default—is Keep cached images in memory. With this option enabled, the images are stored in memory as well as on-disk. This makes switching between previously loaded displays much faster. On the other hand, if you have limited memory on your system, the images and text might end up being swapped to disk, anyway. Even if you don't have limited memory, if the graphics images downloaded by WebExplorer are large, you still might experience a memory crunch when using the WebExplorer. Experiment with the Keep cached images in memory setting to see if the extra delay is noticeable. If it's not, you can specify more memory to your other applications by turning off this option.

FIGURE 8.25.

Use the cache settings to choose among speed, disk usage, and memory usage.

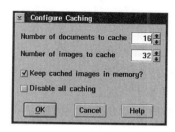

The other option is Disable all caching. This option prevents the WebExplorer from saving documents on-disk or in memory. If you don't switch among previously loaded Web pages, this setting will not noticeably affect WebExplorer performance, *per se*. It will, however, increase available memory for applications (including the WebExplorer itself) and reduce the amount of disk activity and clutter on your system.

When doing presentations with the WebExplorer, you will want to have a system with as much free memory as possible, and you'll want to make the cache large enough to keep all of your images in memory. Thus, when doing presentations, you probably should minimize the number of other programs you are running.

Navigate

Earlier, I mentioned the WebMap. The WebMap is a record of the places you've been during a session. By session, I mean from the time you start the WebExplorer until you close it. Each time you start the WebExplorer, a new map is created. Initially, it contains your QuickList. As you explore, each URL you visit is added to the map. As mentioned previously, even though the WebExplorer does not save and restore prior WebMaps when you close and restart the WebExplorer, you can do so manually. One strategy, for example, might be to explicitly save the WebMap before closing the WebExplorer, and then explicitly loading the file WEBMAP.HTM on the next venture. You can do that by designating WEBMAP.HTM as your home page, or by putting it into the Parameters field in your WebExplorer's Settings notebook.

Backward (Ctrl+B)

The *Backward* option corresponds to the Backward tool (the large blue left arrow) on the toolbar. Use this option to move backwards in the WebMap. You also can use the Backward tool on the toolbar. If the Backward tool is dimmed as unavailable, then there is no logical Backward from where you are.

Forward (Ctrl+F)

The *Forward* option corresponds to the Forward tool (large blue right arrow) on the toolbar. When you click on the Right arrow, you move forward along your WebMap. You can't move forward until you've moved backwards.

Home Document (Ctrl+H)

Use the *Home document* option to explicitly load your Home page (set in Configure | Servers).

Reload Document (URL) (F5)

Use the *Reload document* option to explicitly reload the current URL document. If you enable the Load graphics option or make a change to an HTML file you are editing, you will need to explicitly reload the page to see the changes take effect in the WebExplorer display area.

WebMap (Ctrl+W)

Use the *WebMap* option to display the WebMap. The WebMap is a chart, in addition to your QuickList, of all the places you've been during the current session.

QuickList

The QuickList might be considered a sort of selected WebMap. Anytime you visit a site on the Web that you think you'd like to visit again, you can add it to your QuickList, an example of which is shown in Figure 8.26. The QuickList is automatically included in your WebMap each time you start the WebExplorer. Unlike the WebMap, the QuickList *is* saved from session to session. It is kept in your EXPLORE.INI file, which is in the SET ETC location (usually \TCPIP\ETC).

FIGURE 8.26.

You can save your favorite WWW sites in the QuickList.

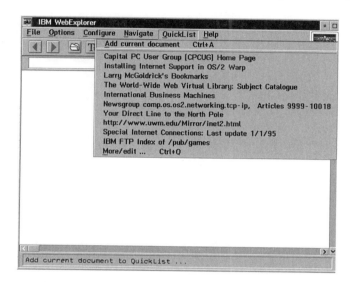

Add Current Document to QuickList (Ctrl+A)

Use the *Add current document to QuickList* option to add the current URL to your QuickList.

More/Edit (Ctrl+Q)

Use the *More/edit* option to display the entire QuickList for selection, editing, and other management. If the QuickList becomes too large to fit in the main QuickList, you can display the entire list by pressing Ctrl+Q (see in Figure 8.27). Following are the options found in this dialog box:

Load	Loads the selected URL (click on the listed URL you want to load and then click Load)
Close	Closes the QuickList dialog box
Add	Adds the currently displayed URL to the QuickList
Delete	Deletes the selected URL from the QuickList (click on the listed URL you want to delete and then click Delete)
Edit	Edits the selected URL's title. To edit the URL itself, you need to edit your EXPLORE.INI file.

List as Titles/URLs Displays URL items as titles or as URLs. This option affects only the Ctrl+Q QuickList dialog box; it does not affect the Alt+Q QuickList you see from the main menu.

FIGURE 8.27.

Press Ctrl+Q to display a scrollable, editable QuickList.

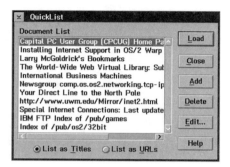

HTML 101—Designing Your Own Home Page

I want to show you how incredibly easy it is to write your own Web pages. It's a piece of cake. Just take a text file and put HTML tags into it. That's it!

What's an HTML tag? It's an HTML keyword and/or instruction placed between two angle brackets (< >). Look at Figures 8.28 and 8.29. Figure 8.28 is the source for the HTML document shown in Figure 8.29. Easy, right? To design your own Web page, that's all you need.

FIGURE 8.28.

HTML source documents use HTML tags.

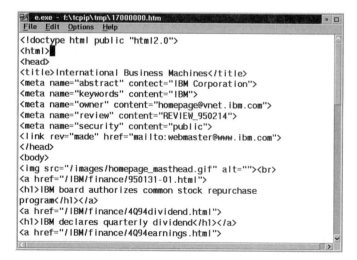

FIGURE 8.29.
The WebExplorer can be used as an HTML viewer.

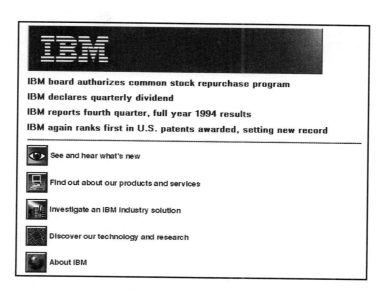

Let's set up a simple Web page right now. Open the OS/2 System Editor (E.EXE), and type the following, replacing *your Name* with your name.

```
<TITLE>The your name Homemade Home Page</TITLE>

<H1>Here is a list of a Few Useful OS/2 URLs</H1><P><P>

<a href="gopher://www01.ny.us.ibm.net/">
IBM Gopher
</a><p><p>
<a href="gopher://www01.ny.us.ibm.net/">
IBM Watson Research Center
</a><p><p>
<a href="gopher://ctc.ctc.edu/1ftp%3asoftware.watson.ibm.com%40/pub/os2/ews/">
IBM Employee Written Software (Free!)
</a><p><p>
```

Tag, You're It!

HTML (hypertext markup language, just in case you've forgotten since the beginning of this chapter), consists of text and tags. A *tag* is a set of angle brackets that contain an HTML keyword of some kind. The <TITLE>, for example, is the title of the dialog box when the resulting file is displayed. The <H1> tag is the tag for a top-level header. This means that the text will be dark and big.

You use an opening tag to turn something on, and a closing tag to turn something off, as in the following:

```
<TITLE>This is the title</TITLE>This is not the title
```

The <TITLE> tag turns on the title attribute, and the </TITLE> turns it off.

For creating links in an HTML file, you use the <A> tag. The URL is enclosed in the opening tag, followed by the Link text, followed by the </A> tag. If I wanted to create a tag to the main IBM WWW server, which is `http://www.ibm.com/`, for example, I would enclose that text in an <A> tag as follows:

```
<a href="http://www.ibm.com/">
Main IBM WWW Server
</a>
```

Notice that in this example, I used lowercase characters (<a> instead of <A>). Unlike most everything else in Internetdom, HTML tags are not case-specific (Hallelujah!). Also notice, however, proving that UNIX still holds a powerful spell, that forward slashes are used for directories rather than backslashes.

> When referring to OS/2 files, you can use backslashes.

The other popular thing to do in HTML files is include graphics. To work with the WebExplorer, the graphic files you include must be in the SET ETC directory (usually \TCPIP\ETC), or you need to specify the URL directory in UNIX style. First, to load an image into an HTML page, include a reference to it in an image tag. To include a file called `giraffe.gif`, for example, include the following reference:

```
<img src="giraffe.gif">
```

If that file is located in a directory other than the ETC directory, such as `g:\pictures\`, then include the directory reference in one of the following two ways:

```
<img src="file:///g:/pictures/giraffe.gif">
```

```
<img src="file:///g:\pictures\giraffe.gif">
```

Note that you can specify the OS/2 file with / or \, but the initial slashes must be ///.

> If you're not into tag—and who could blame you—then Web or FTP your way to the Macmillan FTP site and pick up HTML Generator for OS/2. See Chapter 12, "Additional Internet Applications and Related Utilities," for additional information.

How Do You Make Your Web Pages Available?

Well, that's the 64-dollar question. The answer is—it varies. The easiest way—unless you want to install a full-time Internet link—is to put your Web page onto a public access location. If you have a full-service Internet provider, then there most likely is a public area in which users such as yourself can install your own Web home page that others can access. The best way to find out is by asking. On the system I use, for example, I logged into my shell account and entered `help`. One of the options listed was something called `your-web-page`. I entered `help your-web-page`, and got complete information on how to set up my own Web page.

Once *you* find out, there usually are some administrative chores to perform at the UNIX shell. The following are very generic steps, the details of which will vary by provider:

1. Create a directory for your .HTML files and any supporting text or graphics files. Do this according to the directions supplied by your Internet provider. Take care not to exceed any limits on the amount of disk space you can consume, keeping in mind, as well, the possibility that having those files on the system might incur a storage charge.

2. If your HTML documents were created and tested on a FAT system, change any internal .HTM references to .HTML so that they can be found once the HTML documents have been properly installed on the UNIX system.

3. Use FTP or some other means to upload the files to the UNIX system.

4. If you created the files on a FAT system, then rename the .HTM files to .HTML (in congruence with step 2).

5. Use the UNIX command CHMOD (or whatever else might be appropriate for that system) to set the access levels on the directory and files so that they are publicly available.

6. Use the WebExplorer to inspect your HTML page to see if it's working properly.

Web Resources for OS/2

The number of Internet WWW sites of interest to OS/2 users is growing almost daily. Following is a list of URLs that are of current interest as this book is being written. Keep in mind that the Internet is like a growing, living being. Expecting all the cells in your body to be in exactly the same place two weeks from now is unrealistic. Similarly, it's nearly impossible to guarantee at this moment that all the following URLs will still work by the time you get this book. Let's give it a shot anyway.

GoHTTP Home Page
> http://w3.ag.uiuc.edu/DLM/GoHTTP/GoHTTP.html

HTTPD systems for OS/2
> http://w3.ag.uiuc.edu/DLM/HTTPDforOS2.html

IBM FTP Index of /pub/
> ftp://ftp.ibm.net/pub/

IBM introduces OS/2 Warp!
> http://www.austin.ibm.com/pspinfo/warp.html

IBM OS/2 Warp Home Page
> http://www.austin.ibm.com/pspinfo/os2.html

Index of /pub/os2/32bit
> ftp://ftp.cdrom.com/pub/os2/32bit

International Business Machines
> http://www.ibm.com/

KnowledgeBase for OS/2

http://www.cen.uiuc.edu/~jt11635/os2/Docs/KnowledgeBase.html

Newsgroup

comp.os.os2.networking.tcp-ipnews:comp.os.os2.networking.tcp-ip

OS/2 Information Page

http://www.cen.uiuc.edu/~jt11635/os2/os2.html

Raj's OS/2 Urbana-Champaign AREA HOME PAGE

file:///F:\tcpip\etc\rajpage.htm

The OS/2 WWW Home Page at MIT

http://www.mit.edu:8001/activities/os2/os2world.html

Your Direct Line to the North Pole

http://north.pole.org/santa/talk_to_santa.html

The REXX Language Page

http://rexx.hursley.ibm.com/rexx

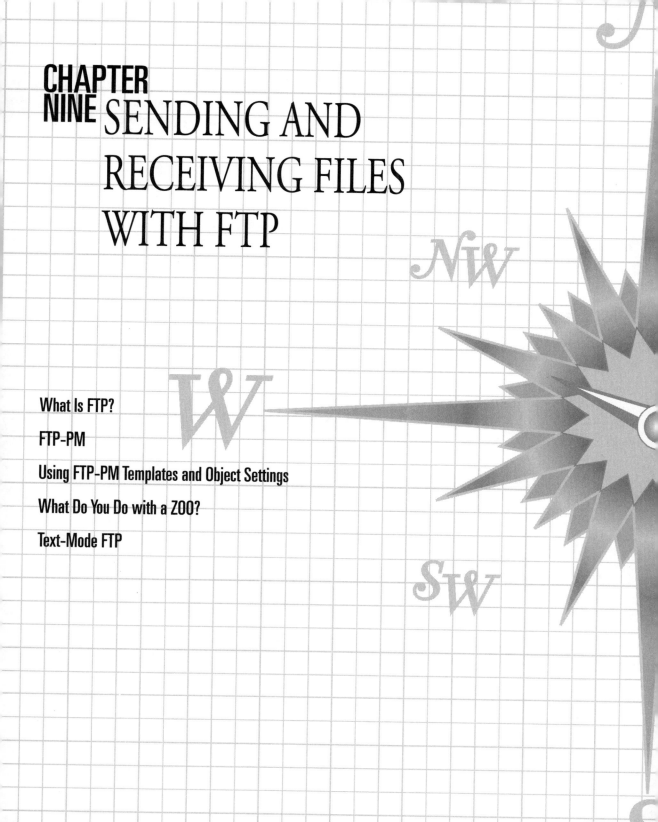

CHAPTER NINE
SENDING AND RECEIVING FILES WITH FTP

To many Internet users, anonymous file transfer protocol (FTP) is one of the most attractive aspects of the Internet. If you download a .ZOO, .ZIP, .ARC, or .LZH file and don't know how to make heads or tails out of it, however, FTP won't do you much good. You also need to know about FTP sites, where to find them, and how to use them. New users also need to know about the hazards of uploading copyrighted files or offensive materials, and the potential consequences.

What Is FTP?

FTP stands for *file transfer protocol*. While it is a mouthful, it is really just a way to copy (transfer) files from one computer to another. Transferring files most often is called *uploading* and *downloading*. *Uploading* is copying a file from your computer to another computer. *Downloading* is copying a file from another computer to yours.

FTP sounds a bit formidable. If you've had any experience with modems and electronic bulletin board services (BBSs), however, then you've probably downloaded files to your system from a BBS, CompuServe, America Online, GEnie, or perhaps even between your home and your workplace. If so, then you probably used a communications program that can transfer files using Xmodem, Ymodem, Zmodem, Kermit, or perhaps some other method.

Surprise! Each of those methods is a file transfer protocol: that is, a specific way to transfer a file between two computers. If you think about it, even something like the COPY, XCOPY, and REPLACE commands are file transfer protocols. They are specific ways to transfer (copy) files from one place to another.

On the Internet, using UNIX, FTP is a universally accepted way to transfer files. It is not the only way, mind you, but it is a way that's available on virtually every UNIX system on the Internet. If you have a UNIX shell account, and if you choose the download command while online with your host system, you very likely will be given a choice of other protocols, including Xmodem, ASCII, and Zmodem. Those methods often are still available. Even so, once you know a little more about FTP, you probably will want to use it because of the simplicity it provides.

While the Internet's FTP and other file transfer protocols are similar in concept, the approach to FTP probably is different from what you're used to. The primary reason is that Xmodem, ASCII, Kermit, Ymodem, and Zmodem usually are part of a larger communications program, such as Procomm, Qmodem, PMComm, Telix, and so on, whereas FTP itself is a communications program. You have a copy of FTP that is installed on your computer when you install Warp's IAK. In fact, you have two different versions: FTP and FTP-PM.

FTP (FTP.EXE) is a text-mode OS/2 program, with an interface and command set that is similar to the UNIX version of FTP that runs on your Internet provider's computer. FTP-PM (FTPPM.EXE) is a graphical version of the FTP program. The one you use is largely up to you.

Most users, however, seem to find that FTP-PM's capability to use point-and-shoot and drag-and-drop for transferring files gives it a decided edge. You also can perform FTP from the WebExplorer. See Chapter 8, "Navigating the Web with the WebExplorer," for additional information.

FTP Sites

Many new Internet users most often encounter the term FTP in conjunction with the word anonymous: *anonymous FTP* (see "Anonymous FTP" following this section). That notwithstanding, not all FTP is anonymous. In fact, most FTP is *not* anonymous. Almost every computer connected to the Internet potentially is an FTP site. If you've only experienced using anonymous FTP, for example, you might be surprised to know that you very likely can log—*un*anonymously—onto your own domain computer using FTP, just as you can using telnet. The difference between FTP and telnet is that using FTP connects you in a specific way that is set up for file transfer.

If you've ever tried to download a file from your domain's computer using telnet, then you will immediately appreciate having FTP. Using telnet, there is no way to download files. If you have ever used telnet to connect to your domain and wanted to download a file—such as .newsrc—but didn't find a way, then FTP is what you need.

To connect to your own domain using FTP, you use the name of your domain as the Hostname, and your normal user or mail ID and password (such as the ID and password you would use to connect to your UNIX shell account). These often are different from your SLIP or PPP ID and password.

Anonymous FTP

Anonymous often sounds clandestine or bad to some people. You hear about anonymous threats, anonymous telephone calls, and anonymous terrorists. Of course, you also hear about anonymous benefactors, so maybe the word anonymous isn't completely stigmatized. In any event, anonymous FTP simply means that you don't have to have an account in your name. Anonymous FTP sites are set up so that anyone who has FTP software and access to the Internet can log on, usually using the word anonymous as the user ID.

Organizations set up anonymous FTP sites for a variety of reasons, often for product support. Companies such as IBM, 3COM, and Microsoft, for example, have anonymous FTP sites to support their product lines. If users can obtain product updates and fixes directly from an anonymous FTP site, it reduces the amount of direct customer support the organization needs to provide. Speaking of benefactors, a number of organizations set up anonymous FTP sites simply because they're a good idea. In addition to finding OS/2-related files on ftp.ibm.net, for example, you also will find anonymous FTP sites at a number of public universities, such as New Mexico State University (hobbes.nmsu.edu).

> ### How Anonymous Is Anonymous?
>
> Although it is called anonymous, it usually isn't. Anytime you connect with another computer on the Internet, your host and domain names are known to that other computer. Data could not flow unless both computerized locations are known. If you have a SLIP or PPP connection, then your computerized identity is completely known. If you are using another method, such as TIA, your domain is known. Anonymity exists not to keep who you are a secret, but rather as a way to provide you access that you would not have otherwise.

Different anonymous FTP sites have different procedures for logging in. Many require just a user ID of anonymous and no password at all. Some use the word anonymous as the user ID, and guest as the password. An emerging standard is to use anonymous as the user ID and your Internet address as the password. If you're concerned about being anonymous, then the latter should allay any guilt.

In some cases, it might take some experimentation to get the combination of user ID and password correct. It always helps, however, if whoever tells you about the anonymous FTP site also tells you any about any unusual procedures for logging on. If you have any doubts, especially if you want to set up a dedicated FTP-PM object, it sometimes is useful to try the text-mode (command-line) version of FTP so that you can see any special prompts that indicate a different procedure for anonymous FTP. For more information, read on.

FTP-PM

The FTP-PM object corresponds to an executable program called `ftppm.exe` in your `tcpip\bin` directory. The FTP-PM object, however, is a special class of object that cannot be created using a normal program template. Contrast the unique object Settings notebook used for FTP-PM with the popup menu for a regular program object (see Figure 9.1). Rather than the usual Program, Session, and Association pages in the Settings notebook, the FTP-PM object has pages for Host, Authentication, and Options. You can use these pages to customize the FTP-PM object for particular FTP sites. At the very least, you might want to create a dedicated FTP-PM object for your own domain, for downloading and uploading files.

Note

> Even though the FTP-PM objects created as part of the OS/2 Internet Access Kit are of a special class, you still can create ordinary program reference objects for running FTP-PM. However, you will not be able to set the logon ID, password, and directories in the object settings. Instead, you will need to create a `netrc` file on the `\tcpip\etc` directory. See "Using a `netrc` File and FTP Macros" later in this chapter. The advantage of using a `netrc` file is that you can bypass the `linkup.exe` program in running FTP-PM. Many users find that FTP-PM starts up much more quickly without `linkup.exe`.

FIGURE 9.1.

FTP-PM objects are a unique class of object and have a special type of Settings notebook.

Starting FTP-PM

To use FTP-PM, you must already be connected to your Internet provider. Use either the IBM Internet Dialer or the Dial Other Internet Providers object to establish an Internet connection. Once connected to the Internet, to run FTP-PM, double-click the FTP-PM object, which is in the Internet Utilities folder in your IBM Internet Connection folder.

If you're using the general FTP-PM object that doesn't have the host and authentication settings already entered, you are presented with the window shown in Figure 9.2. Type the name of the host system to which you want to connect in the Host box. This corresponds to the Hostname field in the FTP-PM Settings notebook. To connect to IBM, for example, type the host name as **ftp01.ny.us.ibm.net**. To connect via FTP to your own domain, if your Internet e-mail address is jsmith@jonesdog.org, type your domain host name as **jonesdog.org**.

FIGURE 9.2.

FTP-PM prompts for the host name and login information.

If you're connecting to your own domain, type your user ID and password in the User and Password fields. Your User ID most likely is the portion of your e-mail address before the @ sign. If you are jsmith@jonesdog.org, for example, then your User name probably is jsmith. The password would be the same one you used to log on to your shell account. This usually is the same as your mail password. The account field often is left blank for individual SLIP accounts. If you need an account name, you very likely have been given one by your Internet provider.

If you are using a `netrc` file, you can skip the user and password sections because they are supplied by the `netrc` file. For more information, see "Using a `netrc` File and FTP Macros" later in this chapter.

If you are connecting via anonymous FTP to IBM, type the user ID as **anonymous**, and the password as your complete Internet e-mail address, such as `jsmith@jonesdog.org`. Leave the Account field blank.

Once you've entered the necessary logon data, click the OK button. If you are not successful in establishing a connection, FTP-PM will display an error message. Sometimes the error message is useful and informative, other times it is not. If the Host name is incorrect, for example, FTP-PM will display the `Unknown Host` error shown in Figure 9.3.

FIGURE 9.3.
If the host name is wrong or doesn't exist, FTP-PM displays an error message.

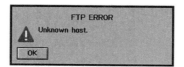

If the host exists, but the connection still fails, then you will get the `Login or relogin failed` error message (see Figure 9.4). This error usually is displayed for one of the following reasons:

◆ User ID, Password, and/or Account is incorrect.

◆ The site is closed or full.

FIGURE 9.4.
FTP-PM displays the Login or relogin failed error if login is rejected from a valid host.

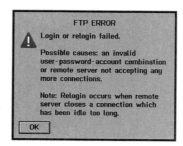

Tip

If you're using TIA and can't get FTP-PM to connect or if connection takes a long time, there usually is a solution. The problem is that FTP-PM uses the `icmp` message protocol (the same protocol used by Ping) to verify the host before establishing a connection. For `icmp` to work, you must be using a valid IP number. Because it doesn't work under TIA, FTP-PM can't proceed until the Ping attempt times out.

A work-around is to disable `icmp`. You do this by putting a remark (#) character at the beginning of the `icmp` line in the `\tcpip\etc\protocol` file. Because the current editions of TIA don't support `icmp` anyway, you won't be losing anything. To disable `icmp`, add a # at the beginning of the `icmp` line, as follows:

```
# icmp    1       ICMP    # internet control message protocol
```

If you later switch to real SLIP, don't forget to put the protocol back the way it was. Otherwise, Ping won't work.

If you are trying to connect to a site to which you have connected in the past, then the site might be closed or full. It is not uncommon for some FTP sites to close down for periodic maintenance, or—heaven forbid—a crash of some kind. More likely, however, many FTP sites do not allow an unlimited number of simultaneous connections. When you use the text-mode FTP program to connect to an FTP site, you often will get a message that tells you the number of connections allowed, and which one you are, as shown in Figure 9.5. If the connection is not successful, you usually will get much more information about why not.

FIGURE 9.5.

The text-mode FTP program often displays more site information than does the FTP-PM program.

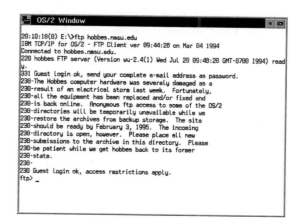

The FTP-PM Window

Once you successfully connect FTP-PM to a remote site, the window shown in Figure 9.6 appears on-screen. The top half of the screen shows your local directory (files on your own computer), and the bottom half displays files and directories on the remote system. Obtaining files via FTP-PM is a three-step process.

1. Locate and select the file(s) you want on the remote system.
2. Set your local directory to the place in which to copy the downloaded files.
3. Drag the files to your local directory.

FIGURE 9.6.

The results of a successful connection with an FTP server.

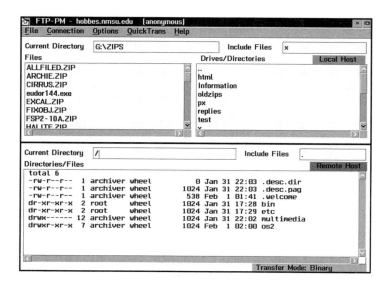

Navigating a Remote FTP Site with FTP-PM

The structure of UNIX directory and file listings is different from that of OS/2 and DOS. Note the entries shown in Figure 9.7. Some begin with -rw and others begin with drwx. The -rw entries are files. The drwx entries are directories. The d stands for directory. To change to a lower subdirectory, move the mouse over the name of the subdirectory and double-click on the name. To move to the directory named mail, for example, you would double-click on the word mail.

FIGURE 9.7.

UNIX directories are somewhat different from DOS and OS/2 directories.

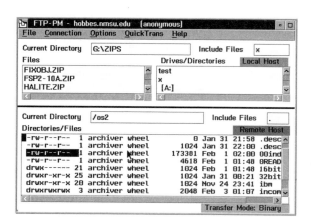

> Some directories contain thousands of files. To list them all would take tons of time and system resources. FTP-PM's remote directory window is limited to showing about 1,024 items. Not only will trying to display the whole list not get you the whole list, but it will take an extremely long time. Often, FTP sites will include a warning in the parent directory if a subdirectory contains zillions of files. This warning usually isn't visible from FTP-PM, however, but it is visible from text-mode FTP and from the WebExplorer.

To move to a parent (higher) directory, there is no simple GUI method. You have several non-GUI choices, however. One way is to simply delete the subdirectory portion of the displayed directory in the Current Directory field so that the desired directory is displayed in the field. To move from /homeb/tyson/mail back to /homeb/tyson, for example, select mail, press Delete, and then press Enter. Or, delete all of /homeb/tyson/mail, type .., and press Enter. If you're fond of menus, choose Connection|Quote Command, type **cdup**, and press Enter. Another way is to add /.. to the end of whatever directory is showing.

If you know the exact location and name of a file, you can skip navigation, *per se*. Just enter (or paste, if the information is on the OS/2 Clipboard) the path and filename into the remote host's Current Directory text box, and then press Enter. If the file exists in that location, it will be displayed in a short file listing.

> Navigating FTP site directories is a bit easier and more direct using the WebExplorer. Files and directories are displayed as icons, and navigating to a parent directory is a simple double-click away. Unfortunately, however, when using the WebExplorer, you are limited to downloading only, and downloading files can be a little tricky. See Chapter 8, "Navigating the Web with the WebExplorer," for additional information.

To move to a specific directory—if you know the name of the subdirectory—you can type the name of the directory in the Current Directory field and press Enter. If you always want the same directory for a specific FTP site, you can use the Options page in the FTP-PM Settings notebook to set the starting directory of both the local and remote sites. See "Using FTP-PM Templates and Object Settings" for additional information.

> **Caveat Case!**
>
> Unlike DOS and OS/2, UNIX file and directory names are case-specific. Directories named Mail, MAIL, and mail are three different directories. Files named time.zip, Time.Zip, and TIME.ZIP would be three different files. If you type a filename or directory and receive an error message that the target was not found, check your specification carefully to make sure the case was typed correctly.

Navigating the Local Directory

Navigating local directories is somewhat easier than remote directories using FTP-PM. Local directories are displayed using an ordinary file, directory, and disk dialog list box. To change to a subdirectory, double-click on the displayed subdirectory in the Drives/Directories list. To change to a parent directory, double-click on .. at the top of the list. To change to a specific disk, double-click on the corresponding drive letter.

If you prefer keyboard navigation, you also can navigate using the Tab key, space bar, cursor pad keys, and Enter key. Use Tab and Shift+Tab to move among the areas (text boxes and list boxes); use cursor keys to move within areas; use the spacebar to toggle the selection of directory items; and use the Enter key to carry out directory changes.

Downloading a File from a Remote Site to Your System

FTP-PM enables you to download one or more files from a remote system to your local system. After you navigate to the location of the remote files, as well as to the location on your system in which you want to place the files, click once on each remote filename to select it. Selecting files in FTP-PM is different from selecting files in an OS/2 window. When you double-click to select a file, you do not automatically deselect other files.

To download one or more files from a remote site to your own computer, follow these steps:

1. Navigate both local and remote directories, as necessary, to the desired source file and the desired target location.

2. Click once on just the filename(s) to select each file (see Figure 9.8). Note that unlike normal OS/2 selection, you do not need to hold the Ctrl key to select multiple filenames. To deselect a filename, just click again.

3. Move the mouse pointer so that it is over any of the selected files, and press and hold mouse button 2.

FIGURE 9.8.

Click once on each file you want to select.

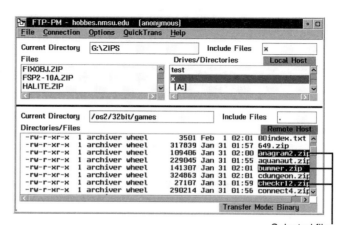

Selected files

4. Drag the files by moving the mouse pointer over the directory shown in the local file listing; release the mouse button to drop the files there. (In lieu of steps 3 and 4, you also can press Ctrl+G or choose File|Get remote files, from the menu.) Note that the target subdirectory must be displayed; you cannot drop a file on an unopened subdirectory.

5. Depending on your settings, FTP-PM now will prompt you to confirm the name and the transfer (see Figure 9.9). If you want, you can modify the name—you might want to do this when transferring some UNIX files to an OS/2 FAT partition that does not accept long filenames.

Before you say yes to a transfer, check the transfer type indicator in the lower-right corner of the FTP-PM window. Does it say Binary or ASCII? If you're transferring a multimegabyte .ZIP file, it better say Binary! Failure to correctly set the transfer type leads to getting error messages from your unarchive program. In ASCII transfer mode, the 8th bit of each data byte is removed. This is fine for ASCII files, but it makes binary files rather useless. If the mode is wrong, then choose Options|Transfer mode, and change it!

FIGURE 9.9.

FTP-PM prompts you to confirm the transfer.

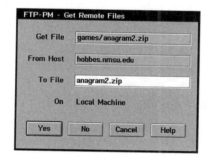

6. Click Yes to confirm each transfer. If you're FTPing more than one file, you can click No to cancel any individual file. Clicking Cancel cancels all files.

In some situations, when you are connected to multiple remote hosts at the same time, FTP-PM will incorrectly interpret the drag operation. This is a bug. As a work-around, press Ctrl+G (or choose File|Get remote files, from the menu) rather than attempting to drag the files. Using Ctrl+G usually corrects the incorrect drag fault.

As the transfer proceeds, FTP-PM displays the number of bytes transferred. It does not display a transfer rate or estimated time. Unless the host system especially is loaded down, FTP-PM provides transfer rates roughly equivalent to Zmodem when using the same modem connect speed.

Selecting All Files in a Subdirectory

You can select all files in a subdirectory by selecting the subdirectory rather than individually selecting each file. If you want to transfer all of the files in the `.tin` subdirectory to your own system, for example, just click on `.tin` in your remote host directory and press Ctrl+G (or drag the file to the local directory window). FTP-PM now will *get* all of the files in that subdirectory. It will not, however, transfer files in any subdirectories in that directory. If `.tin` contains 70 files and three additional subdirectories, for example, only the 70 files will be downloaded. Even so, being able to select a whole subdirectory can improve the efficiency of working with FTP-PM. When doing a wholesale transfer, you might want to make sure you turn off confirmation—at least for transferring that subdirectory (see "Setting Options"). Otherwise, you will have to endure one confirmation for each file in the subdirectory.

Uploading a File from Your System to a Remote System

Uploading files is the reverse of downloading. Rather than selecting remote files and dragging them to your local directory, you do the reverse. When putting files onto a remote system, make sure the remote system has enough storage space, and that you are authorized to make the transfer.

To upload one or more files to a remote system, follow these steps:

1. Navigate both local and remote directories, as necessary, to the desired source files and the desired target location.

2. In the local directory, select each of the files you want to transfer.

3. Move the mouse pointer so that it is over any one of the selected files, and press and hold mouse button 2.

4. Drag the files by moving the mouse pointer over the directory shown in the remote file listing; release the mouse button to drop the files there. (In lieu of steps 3 and 4, you also can press Ctrl+P or choose File | Put local files from the menu.)

5. Depending on your settings, FTP-PM now will prompt you to confirm the name and the transfer. If transferring a file to become a `.newsrc` file, for example, you want to make sure it is named `.newsrc`, as required by the NewsReader software on your UNIX host.

6. Click Yes to confirm each transfer. If you're FTPing more than one file, you can click No to cancel any individual file. Clicking Cancel cancels all files.

Just as when uploading, you can select a local subdirectory rather than selecting files individually. However, when using that approach, you will not be able to drag the subdirectory to the remote directory listing. Using File | Put local files or pressing Ctrl+P, however, does work.

> **Why Don't Files Go Where You Drop Them?**
>
> When dragging and dropping files in OS/2 directory folders, you can point directly to a closed subdirectory folder to drop a file there. You cannot do this when using FTP. To drag a file to specify subdirectory, that subdirectory must already be open and displayed in FTP-PM's remote host window.

QuickTrans: Downloading and Uploading with One Command

Sometimes you want to move files in two directions: from the local system to a remote site, and vice versa. To use QuickTrans, select the files you want to *put* (upload) using the local directory. Select the files you want to *get* (download) using the remote directory, then choose QuickTrans from the menu.

Transferring a File Between Two Remote Systems

You also can transfer a file between two remote systems. Why would you want to do this? Well, depending on your connection speed and the size of the file you want to transfer, you might not want to occupy the remote location that has the file for a long transfer. Although your connection to your provider is limited to your modem speed, your provider's computer is connected to the Internet at a much higher data rate. Although it might take 5 or 10 minutes (or even longer) to transfer a 2MB file from a remote system to your own system, it might take just a few seconds to transfer the same file from one remote system to another. Once the file is on your own provider's system, you then can log off the other remote system and perform a guiltless download from your provider's system to your local system. As an added bonus, the transfer from your own provider's system to your local computer often will be faster than the transfer from another remote FTP site. That's because your connection is through your modem only, rather than through other system hardware. For particularly large files, the total transfer rate is much faster when you first transfer the file(s) to your own provider, and then download them to your system.

Another reason you might want to do remote-to-remote transfers is to make particular files available to a different remote system. If you find a particularly useful piece of shareware or a software fix or upgrade on a lesser known FTP site, you might want to copy that file to one of the better known sites. Rather than FTP it to your own system and then FTP it to another remote system, you can FTP it directly from one remote system to the other.

Tip

> When transferring a number of files to the system where your own Internet account exists, it often is a good idea to create a new subdirectory for the transfers. That prevents you from overwriting any existing files with the same names (assuming that's *not* what you want to do). It keeps you from getting confused about what came from where. It also makes it easier to locate and remove the files once the need to have them

on your provider's system has passed. See "Creating a Subdirectory Using FTP-PM." Also note, as mentioned previously, that you can select whole subdirectories to transfer all the files contained in those subdirectories (but not any sub-subdirectories contained therein). When doing mass transfers, consider turning off the confirmation prompt (Options|Confirmation).

When might you need remote-to-remote transfer capabilities? When I was testing Lantastic for OS/2, I discovered that I needed new NDIS drivers for my Etherlink III network adapter. I found the necessary file on 3COM's FTP site (`ftp.3com.com`). Because many OS/2 users have a need for that file, I then checked Hobbes (considered by many OS/2 users as a library for all files that are useful for OS/2) to see if the file already existed there. An older version of the file did exist, but the current one did not. So, I transferred the file from 3COM's anonymous FTP site to Hobbes' incoming OS/2 files. That transfer took only a few seconds. After doing that, I then transferred the file to my own system, which took several minutes.

Before doing remote-to-remote transfers, make sure you're authorized to do so, and/or that there will not be any adverse consequences. In most cases, if you're not authorized to transfer a file to a system, the attempt will fail. In transferring files to your local provider, however, make sure that you are not exceeding your allotted storage space. And, by all means, if you're using your provider as an intermediary, make sure you delete the file(s) from your local provider's system once the need for having them there has passed. For more information, see "Deleting Files and Subdirectories Using FTP-PM."

To perform an FTP-PM transfer from one remote site to another, follow these steps:

1. Use an FTP-PM object to open a connection to the target sites in which you want the transferred files to reside.

2. Navigate to the subdirectory where you want the files to be placed.

3. From the menu, choose Connection|Open remote host (or press Ctrl+O, and open a connection to the source remote site, the location where the files currently reside).

4. Navigate to the subdirectory in which the files are located, and select the files you want to transfer.

5. From the menu, choose File|Transfer between remote hosts.

6. Click on the host you want to receive the file, and click OK.

Don't Panic!

While the transfer proceeds, FTP-PM displays the Transferring File progress indicator. The number of bytes, however, remains at 0. That's because the transfer is proceeding between the two hosts, and FTP-PM has no real way to monitor the progress. Relax! The transfer is taking place nonetheless, and is taking place much more quickly (usually) than between a host and a local computer connected with a modem.

Creating a Subdirectory Using FTP-PM

It sometimes is convenient to create new subdirectories while you're using FTP-PM. Rather than having to switch to another process to do it, you can do it directly from FTP-PM. To create a subdirectory, follow these steps:

1. Navigate to the parent directory in which you want the subdirectory to be.

2. From the menu, choose File | Make directory, and choose either Local or Remote, according to your need.

3. Type the name for the subdirectory. (You can specify an entire path if you want, but each of the parent subdirectories must already exist; that is, you can create `\user\bin\test\my\dir` only if `\user\bin\test\my` already exists.)

4. Click OK.

Renaming Files and Subdirectories Using FTP-PM

Sometimes, especially when performing complicated file transfers, it is necessary to rename files. For example, when replacing `.newsrc`, you might want to rename the existing one as something such as `old.newsrc`. FTP-PM enables you to rename files and directories. To rename a file or directory, follow these steps:

1. Click to select the file or directory you want to rename.

2. From the menu, choose File | Rename directory/file, and then choose Local or Remote.

3. Type the new name in the Rename Local Directory/File dialog box and click OK (see Figure 9.10).

FIGURE 9.10.

FTP-PM enables you to rename local and remote files.

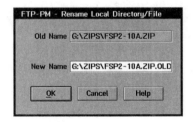

Deleting Files and Subdirectories Using FTP-PM

As noted previously, when you use your provider's system as an intermediary location for FTP, you should delete the files once the need to have them on your provider's system has passed. Fortunately, FTP-PM enables you to perform deletions, from your local disk as well as from authorized remote directories. You also might have created a temporary subdirectory for a complex file transfer. Again, FTP-PM enables you to create and remove subdirectories.

Warning

> Be extremely careful, especially when removing files from your provider's system. You often have read and write access to files that you don't want to remove. If you delete the wrong file, something on the Internet might no longer work correctly. If you *do* inadvertently delete a vital file, check with your provider's technical support as soon as possible. It is likely that they maintain a backup and can restore the deleted files; however, you want to make sure that you get the restoration done before another backup occurs. Depending on how system maintenance is performed, if you wait beyond a backup cycle, it might be too late!

To remove local or remote files or directories, follow these steps:

1. Select the files or directories you want to remove.
2. From the menu, choose File | Delete directory/file, and choose either Local or Remote (or press Ctrl+R for Delete Remote or Ctrl+L for Delete Local).
3. Choose Yes to confirm the deletion of this file or directory; choose No to cancel deletion of a specific file or directory; or choose Cancel to abort the entire delete operation.

> **You Can't Delete a Directory that Contains Files**
>
> Just as in normal OS/2 file operations, FTP-PM does not allow you remove a directory that contains files. You first must navigate to that directory, remove any files, and then navigate back to the parent subdirectory to remove the now-empty subdirectory.

Executing Site and Quote Commands

Sometimes what you want to do exceeds the built-in capabilities of FTP-PM; for example, you might need to execute a command that exists only on the remote server while FTP-PM is running. Other times, you might need to use an FTP command that exists on the host system, but for which there is no corresponding command in your local version of FTP-PM or FTP. In such situations, you can send a site command or a quote command for execution by the remote system.

A quote command is an instruction to the remote system's version of FTP. A quote `mput` command, for example, is an instruction for the remote system to upload files to you, whereas `mput` usually is an instruction to upload a file from your system to the remote site. In some situations, however, as might be the case when a file specification from the remote host is more efficient than individually marking files, an `mput` quote command might be exactly what you need. To send a quote command to a remote host, follow these steps:

1. Choose Connection│Quote command from the menu.
2. Type the exact FTP command that you want the remote site to execute, including any parameters.
3. Click OK.

> The Connection│Quote command option is identical to the `quote` command in the text-mode FTP program.

On occasion, you also might need to use non-FTP capabilities of a remote system when running FTP-PM. In those cases, you can use the Site command option. The Site command option is equivalent to `site` command in the text-mode FTP program. To run a site command, follow these steps:

1. Choose Connection│Site command from the menu.
2. Type the exact system command that you want the remote site to execute, including any parameters.
3. Click OK.

> Many commands that are otherwise usable are not available through FTP-PM. If you receive a response that the command isn't recognized, it usually is because the command isn't supported in the context of FTP.

Setting Options

Use the *Options* settings to configure FTP-PM for the type of file transfer you want to make. If you choose settings from the object popup menu, many settings options are available from the FTP-PM object itself.

Transfer Mode

Files can be transferred in ASCII or binary mode. Most text files call for ASCII transfer, while programs, pictures, and compressed files require binary transfer. As a general rule, you will benefit by setting the default transfer mode to binary. (For more information, see "Using FTP-PM Templates and Object Settings.")

Confirmation

Use the *Confirmation* setting to instruct FTP-PM to prompt you to confirm file and directory operations. When transferring many files—especially if you are certain of what you're doing—you can speed up the operation considerably by turning off confirmation. When deleting files and removing directories, however, it usually is a good idea to keep confirmation turned on.

Assign Unique

The *Assign unique* option corresponds to the runique and sunique options in text-mode FTP. When a transferred file would otherwise overwrite an existing file, the Assign unique option instructs FTP-PM to create unique names for the files.

Mark Remote

Use the *Mark remote* option to instruct FTP-PM to automatically select all parts of multipart filenames. Without this option, you might inadvertently select only part of a filename, resulting in erroneous File not found reports. On the other hand, if you want to be apprised of any multipart filenames, then keep the Mark remote option set to free form.

Trace Commands/Replies

Use the *Trace commands/replies* option to log the communications session. Ordinarily, the "dialog" that takes place between FTP-PM and the remote FTP site is invisible to you. If you enable the Trace option, FTP-PM creates a file called \tcpip\etc\ftppm.trc that contains a log of the commands and replies.

Checking the Connection with *ping*

The ping command provides a way to verify that a host currently is on the Internet. This is useful for those occasions when attempts to log on to a remote host fail. By using ping, you can at least determine whether the remote system is online.

In order to ping another computer on the Internet, you must be able to control a computer that's connected to the Internet. If you use a SLIP or PPP account, your computer is connected directly to the Internet, and you will be able to use ping directly from your computer. If your connection is via TIA (a program that simulates a SLIP connection, thus enabling you to use SLIP client software), however, your host system is on the Internet, but your computer is not. So, if you're using TIA , you will not be able to use ping from your computer.

How To ping When You Don't Have a SLIP or PPP Account

If you're connected to the Internet using TIA or some other system that doesn't provide you with your own IP address, you still can use ping, but not the one that's on your OS/2 system. Instead, you need to use telnet to sign onto your SHELL account and then use your host's version of ping. The UNIX version of ping has similar syntax to the OS/2 version but with a few differences. The default behavior for the OS/2 version of ping connects with the remote system and tells you how long it takes for data to be sent from your system to it, and back again. The UNIX version, however, defaults to report-ing only whether the remote system is *alive* (online) (see Figure 9.11). To see the additional information on timing, add the -s switch when using the ping command at the UNIX command line:

```
ping -s ftp.ibm.net
```

Consult your online UNIX help system for additional options (options can vary depend-ing upon which version of UNIX is installed).

FIGURE 9.11.

The default behavior of the UNIX version of ping just reports whether the host is alive.

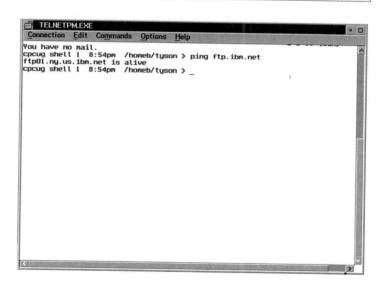

If you are using a SLIP or PPP account, and if you have an FTP object set up for the site you want to check, you can use the object's popup menu to ping the site. Follow these steps:

1. Click mouse button 2 once on the FTP-PM object to access its popup menu (see Figure 9.12).

2. Choose Ping from the menu.

FIGURE 9.12.

Use a customized FTP-PM object to ping *the host.*

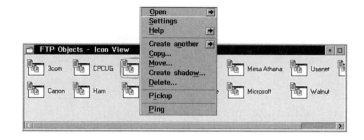

OS/2 runs the text-mode ping command in an OS/2 command window. You will need to watch very closely. If ping fails to detect the FTP site, you will get a message similar to that shown in Figure 9.13.

FIGURE 9.13.

Watch carefully—the unsuccessful ping *message is easy to miss!*

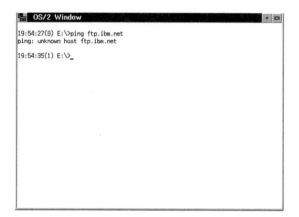

On very fast computers, however, the message can be displayed too quickly for you to see unless you're watching carefully. If the FTP host is online, you will see a window like the one shown in Figure 9.14. Once you're satisfied that the site is online, you can press Ctrl+C to end ping.

FIGURE 9.14.

The OS/2 version of ping *provides information on the quality of the connection.*

If you do not have an FTP-PM object set up for the site you want to check, then you will need to run `ping` from the OS/2 command line. To do this, open an OS/2 command line session and enter either **ping ip address** or **host name**.

You can use either the IP address or the site's name. For example, to `ping hobbes.nmsu.edu` (also known as `ftp-os2.nmsu.edu`), whose IP address is `128.123.35.151`, use any of the following commands:

```
ping 128.123.35.151
ping hobbes.nmsu.edu
ping gftp-os2.nmsu.edu
```

In addition to telling you whether a particular computer is online, the OS/2 version of `ping` also tells you the quality of the connection. If you run `ping` from an FTP-PM object's popup menu, you might miss the output because the output isn't frozen when `ping` is interrupted. If you run `ping` from the OS/2 command line, however, then you can see the additional information.

In this example, `ping` computes statistics for the operation. Fifteen packets were sent and 14 were received, providing a 6 percent packet loss. The `ping` statistics also show the average, minimum, and maximum lengths of time to send and receive packets. This is the amount of time it takes for data to go from your system to the remote system and back again to you.

If you do not specify a number of packets for the `ping`, and if you close it by pressing Ctrl+C, the final packet often is truncated. In a case such as the one shown here, the 6 percent data loss is entirely explained by the fact that you pressed Ctrl+C. If, on the other hand, you were to see substantial packet loss in the absence of a reasonable explanation, then it probably is not a good time to try to perform an FTP transfer with that site. Because of data loss, FTP will need to resend packets during a data transfer, making the transfer much slower than need be.

Difficulty Connecting with FTP Hosts

If `ping` indicates that the remote FTP site is online, that still is no guarantee that you will be able to connect to it. FTP sites do not have an unlimited number of connections. If the FTP server already is at its limit, then you might get a message similar to the one shown in Figure 9.15.

FIGURE 9.15.

*FTP servers don't have
infinite capacity.*

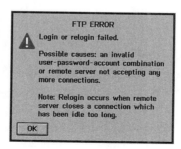

Unfortunately, this message is ambiguous. The only surefire way to determine whether the problem is on your end or on the remote host's end is to try the text-mode version of FTP. It usually will tell you the reason the connection isn't being allowed, and often provides additional information that enables you to connect. Some anonymous FTP sites, for example, have additional password or ID requirements. Once you determine what those are, you usually can adjust the settings for the FTP-PM object to work around any problems.

Using FTP-PM Templates and Object Settings

When you start FTP-PM, you are prompted for the name of the host, your user ID, your password, and the account (see Figure 9.16). Using FTP-PM templates, you can create unique FTP-PM objects for FTP sites that you frequent. In these FTP-PM objects, you can specify the host name, user ID, password, and account information. You also can specify the default type of file transfer (ASCII or binary), the local directory where FTPed files are to be placed on your system, as well as the default directory on the remote system. This can save you a lot of time and maneuvering. It saves the FTP site time as well, as it reduces the amount of online navigation you have to perform, shortening your entire session.

FIGURE 9.16.

An uncustomized FTP-PM object prompts for host and login information.

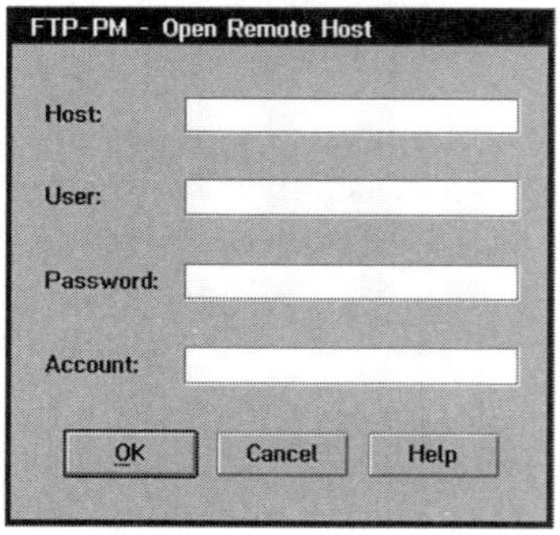

To create a new FTP-PM object, follow these steps:

1. Open the Application Templates object in the IBM Internet Connection for OS/2 folder.

2. Move the mouse pointer over the FTP-PM template and press and hold mouse button 2.

3. Drag the template image to the IBM Internet Connection for OS/2 folder, and release the mouse button.

4. The Settings notebook for the new FTP-PM object now opens; type the name of the host in the Host box (for example, **hobbes.nmsu.edu**, **ftp.ibm.net**, and so on).

5. Click on the Authentication tab (see Figure 9.17). Type the user ID, password, and account into the respective fields; for an anonymous FTP site, type **anonymous** as the password, type your Internet e-mail address (such as **jsmith@jamestown.org**) as the password, and leave the Account field blank.

FIGURE 9.17.

Use the Authentication page to customize an FTP-PM object.

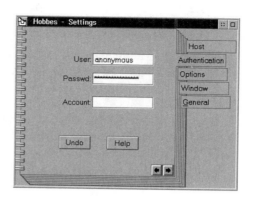

6. Click the Options tab. In the Local directory field, type the path you want to appear in the FTP-PM window (this would be the location in which you want incoming files placed, or from which you want to upload files). In the Remote directory field, type the desired directory on the FTP host. Under File Mask, type the system default for showing either all files (* for OS/2 and . for a UNIX FTP server) or just the files of interest. Set the transfer type to Binary. If you don't want to automatically overwrite existing files, then enable Store Unique and Get Unique. If you don't want to be prompted to confirm individual file actions, then disable the Prompt option. If applicable, type the name of the code page you want to use into the appropriate field and click the Code Page option. If you want the FTP-PM object to automatically select two-part filenames, enable the Two-Part File Name option.

7. Close the Settings notebook (press Alt+F4 or double-click the Settings notebook control icon in the upper-left corner of the Settings notebook window).

Now, each time you use the new FTP-PM object, the session will be configured for that FTP site. This saves you setup time each time you use that FTP site. Setting up unique FTP-PM objects has another advantage as well. Using the FTP-PM object popup menu, you will be able to ping the FTP location without starting FTP-PM. If the FTP site is not working at the moment, this can save you time.

What If ping Doesn't Work?

To use ping, you must have a direct connection to the Internet. If you have a SLIP or PPP connection, ping works fine from the OS/2 command line. If you are using TIA (The Internet Adapter), however, you do not have a direct connection. To ping a remote location, you instead would have to use telnet to access your Internet host, and then use the UNIX version of ping from the UNIX command line.

What Do You Do with a ZOO?

ZOO, ZIP, ARC, and LZH are popular archive compression formats that simplify file transfers. Archive compression collects a number of related files into a single file with an extension such as .ZOO, .ZIP, .ARC, and .LZH. This means that you only have to download one file rather than several. Archive compression also stores data in a compressed format so that files take up a lot less disk space. This means that file sites can store many more files than would otherwise be possible. A 600KB .PCX file, for example, might only require 60KB or so to store once it has been compressed.

In order to deal with such files, you will need a collection of archive tools. There are dozens of archivers—some free, some not—for you to choose from. A number of popular OS/2 versions of archivers are shown in Table 9.1, all available at this writing from hobbes.nmsu.edu.

Table 9.1. Archivers available from hobbes.nmsu.edu.

Filename	Size in KB	Directory	Description
pmuue11.zip	45351	/os2/32bit/archiver	PM UNIX-to-UNIX encoder/decoder (UUENCODE/UUDECODE)
pmzip01.zip	97363	/os2/32bit/archiver	Zipmeister v0.1, graphical zip/unzip utility
ucode101.zip	42370	/os2/32bit/archiver	UUdecode/UUencode with long filename and wildcard support
unarj241.zip	84237	/os2/32bit/archiver	UNARJ 2.41 ARJ-extractor
unarj32.zip	110035	/os2/32bit/archiver	UNARJ with wildcard and extract path support
unz512x2.exe	176000	/os2/32bit/archiver	Info-ZIP UNZIP version 5.2—32-bit executables
uu_codes.zip	25211	/os2/32bit/archiver	Extract/create ASCII versions of binary files
uudoall.zip	81536	/os2/32bit/archiver	Decode multipart UUENCODED files from one large file
zip201x2.zip	119552	/os2/32bit/archiver	Info-ZIP ZIP version 2.01—32-bit executables
zoo21_2.zip	299000	/os2/32bit/archiver	ZOO 2.1 (HPFS/FAT aware)—32-bit version
lh2_222.zip	114258	/os2/16bit/archiver	LHARC version 2.22 (16- and 32-bit versions)

Text-Mode FTP

In addition to FTP-PM, OS/2 Warp's Internet tools also include a text-mode FTP client—
FTP.EXE (which I'll call FTP). If you like GUI applications, you might not like the text-mode
FTP program very much. On the other hand, there are things you can do with text-mode FTP
that you cannot do with FTP-PM, including resolving login problems and automating file
transfers.

Running FTP

To run the FTP program, you open an OS/2 command-line session and enter **ftp *hostname***,
where *hostname* is the name of the FTP site. FTP host names can be any valid alias listed in
your nameserver (such as hobbes.nmsu.edu, ftp-os2.nmsu.edu, ftp.ibm.net, and so on), or it
can be a plain IP address (128.123.35.151, for example, is the IP address for Hobbes, and
165.87.194.246 is the IP address for ftp.ibm.net).

When you start FTP, the response you get depends on the site to which you have connected,
as well as whether you specified a site when you gave the FTP command. Following is a typical
FTP session:

```
C:\TCPIP\BIN>ftp ftp.ibm.net
IBM TCP/IP for OS/2 - FTP Client ver 09:44:28 on Mar 04 1994
Connected to ftp01.ny.us.ibm.net.
220 ftp01.ny.us.ibm.net FTP server (Version wu-2.4(1) Fri Aug 12 13:18:44 CDT 19
94) ready.
331 Guest login ok, send your complete e-mail address as password.
230 Guest login ok, access restrictions apply.
ftp> lcd g:\zips
Local directory now G:\zips
ftp> cd pub
250 CWD command successful.
ftp> dir
200 PORT command successful.
150 Opening ASCII mode data connection for /bin/ls.
total 80
drwxr--r-x   4 Advantis ftp-adm     512 Oct 19 20:43 Advantis
drwxr-xr-x   2 Advantis ftp-adm     512 Dec 22 00:19 NewsReader
drwxr-xr-x   2 Advantis ftp-adm     512 Dec 21 16:08 WebExplorer
drwxr--r-x   2 Advantis ftp-adm     512 Aug 30 13:57 fixes
drwxrwxr-x   2 Advantis ftp-adm     512 Nov 14 21:02 games
drwxr--r-x   4 Advantis ftp-adm    2048 Sep 16 15:34 gen-info
-rw-r--r--   1 Advantis ftp-adm    7995 Dec 22 00:22 ls-lR
drwxr--r-x   2 Advantis ftp-adm     512 Oct 27 20:46 misc
drwxr-xr-x   2 Advantis ftp-adm     512 Dec 19 20:54 warpcom
226 Transfer complete.
577 bytes received in 0.41 seconds (1 Kbytes/s)
ftp> cd games
250-
250-WARNING: File names are case sensitive when trying to download!
```

```
250-
250 CWD command successful.
ftp> dir
200 PORT command successful.
150 Opening ASCII mode data connection for /bin/ls.
total 1952
-rw-r--r--   1 Advantis ftp-adm        65 Nov 14 21:00 .message
-rw-r--r--   1 Advantis ftp-adm    941360 Nov 14 21:02 SIMDEMO.ZIP
-r--r--r--   1 Advantis ftp-adm     53248 Nov 14 21:03 TRICKLE.ZIP
226 Transfer complete.
210 bytes received in 0.093 seconds (2 Kbytes/s)
ftp> binary
200 Type set to I.
ftp> hash
Hash mark printing on.
ftp> bell
Bell mode on.
ftp> verbose
Verbose mode off.
ftp> verbose
Verbose mode on.
ftp> mget *.ZIP
mget SIMDEMO.ZIP (yes¦no¦quit)?y
200 PORT command successful.
150 Opening BINARY mode data connection for SIMDEMO.ZIP (941360 bytes).
##########################################################################
##########################################################################
##########################################################################
##########################################################################
##########################################################################
##########################################################################
##########################################################################
##########################################################################
##########################################################################
##########################################################################
##########################################################################
##########################################################################
##########################################################################
##########################################################################
##########################################################################
##########################################################################
##########################################################################
##########################################################################
#####################################################################
226 Transfer complete.
local: simdemo.zip remote: SIMDEMO.ZIP
941360 bytes received in 7.2e+002 seconds (1 Kbytes/s)
mget TRICKLE.ZIP (yes¦no¦quit)? n
ftp> quit
221 Goodbye.

C:\TCPIP\bin>
```

The best way to become familiar with FTP is to start a session. See the "FTP Commands" section later in this chapter as a guide for what you can do. Also, note that if you do a large amount of FTPing—either from the text-mode FTP program or from FTP-PM—you might benefit from setting up a `netrc` file, which is explained in the following section.

Using a *netrc* File and FTP Macros

If you spend a lot of time using FTP, you probably can benefit by creating a `netrc` file. The `netrc` file contains information that can help automate your FTP sessions. It contains the names of FTP sites, user IDs, passwords, and macros. The `netrc` file goes into your \tcpip\etc subdirectory. It is a text file that you can create using the E or TEDIT editors. At the least, the `netrc` file will contain just login information.

In addition to helping automate logins in FTP, the `netrc` file's user ID and password information also is used by FTP-PM. Although setting up dedicated FTP-PM objects is fine, they don't help when you try to open a different host from an object other than the one explicitly set up for that host. If you have a `netrc` file, however, each time you open a connection from the menu, the `netrc` file settings are used, saving you the trouble of manually entering your ID and password.

The following is a simple `netrc` file set up for logging on to the Walnut Creek FTP server (`ftp.cdrom.com`), a major IBM FTP server (`ftp.ibm.net`), and Hobbes (`hobbes.nmsu.edu`):

```
machine ftp.cdrom.com login anonymous password jones@provider.org
machine ftp.ibm.net login anonymous password jones@provider.org
machine hobbes.nmsu.edu login anonymous password jones@provider.org
```

Rather than entering `jones@provider.org`, however, you would include your own e-mail ID. Many anonymous FTP sites require the sequence of anonymous for the login ID and your Internet e-mail address as your password.

You also can include macros in the `netrc` file. An FTP macro is a list of FTP commands that are performed when a macro name is issued with the $ command. Macros are useful for automating repetitive procedures. Suppose that you must perform an FTP transfer daily or weekly to update data files. You can use a macro to automate the process. Shown here is a `netrc` file that defines a macro for the IBM FTP site. This macro turns on the beep when files are downloaded, sets the transfer mode to binary, enables hashing, changes to an appropriate local subdirectory, changes to an appropriate remote subdirectory, and then downloads a file. The file in this case is `ls-1R`, which is a listing of all public files on the `ftp.ibm.net` server. Following is the `netrc` file:

```
machine ftp.ibm.net login anonymous password jones@provider.org macdef getlist
bell
binary
hash
```

```
lcd g:\filelist
cd /pub
get ls-lR
```

```
machine hobbes.nmsu.edu login anonymous password jones@provider.org
```

Note the blank line after the last line of the macro. This tells FTP that this is the end of the macro. To use the macro, you start FTP (enter **ftp ftp.ibm.net**, for example), then enter the command **$getlist**, which runs the getlist macro. For a description of the commands used in the macro, see the "FTP Commands" section later in this chapter.

Tip

> To completely automate running a macro, create a file containing the $*macroname* command. For example, create a plain text file called getlist, which has the following contents:
>
> ```
> $getlist
> quit
> ```
>
> Then, invoke FTP with the following command, which starts FTP and opens a connection to ftp.ibm.net:
>
> **ftp ftp.ibm.net <getlist**
>
> It then looks to the getlist file for additional input. Because getlist contains $getlist, that macro is run, and FTP exits. Actually, the quit command in getlist isn't necessary. For even more thorough automation, you could put the entire ftp ftp.ibm.net <getlist into a .CMD file.
>
> By the way, once you discover that redirection (using < and >) works with FTP, it should be clear that you can create your own *de facto* macros, without using macdef. Just put the entire set of instructions into a script file and feed it to the FTP command from the OS/2 command line.
>
> Another way to automate macros is with the init macro. If you have a sequence of actions that you want run each time an FTP site is accessed, you can name the macro init. When FTP starts, if init is defined, that macro is run just after connection.

Another useful shortcut source is the hosts file. You can use the hosts file to create aliases for Internet sites. This is especially handy for FTP sites, because remembering names can be quite tedious and error prone. What's easier: ftp01.ny.us.ibm.net or ftpibm? If you include the following line in your hosts file, you can refer to ftp01.ny.us.ibm.net as ftpibm:

```
165.87.194.246 ftpibm
```

This method along with automatic login information from the netrc file makes using FTP-PM (as well as the FTP text-mode program and WebExplorer) quite a bit simpler (in WebExplorer, you'd specify it as ftp://ftpibm). See the description of the hosts file in the section titled "host" in Chapter 11, "Other Warp Internet Tools and Programs," for additional information.

FTP Commands

In a way, FTP is like a mini-operating system. It has a complete command set that you can use while working at the FTP command prompt. While FTP-PM is very useful for some types of tasks, it is very difficult to automate tasks using FTP-PM's GUI interface. If you need automation, FTP is your best bet.

Each of the FTP commands is discussed below, with a few exceptions. Some FTP commands— namely `struct`, `tenex`, and `form`—do not appear to have any use in the current implementation of FTP. Thus, they are omitted from the following discussion.

! *command parm*

Use the `!` *command parm* command to shell to the OS/2 prompt, or issue a single OS/2 command (for example, type `!` to go to the command prompt; type `!time 23:00` to set the system time to 11 p.m.).

$ *macname parm*

Use the `$` *macname parm* command to run a `macdef` macro (`macdef mymac 123`, for example, runs a macro called `mymac`, using the parameter 123). For more information, see `macdef`.

account *accountname*

The `account` *accountname* command sends account information to the host (`account pickles`, for example, tells the host that you have an unusual account name).

append *source target*

The `append` *source target* command appends the *source* file to the *target* file.

ascii

The `ascii` command sets the transfer mode to ASCII (text files, for example).

bell

The `bell` command toggles a download beep signal off and on. (With `bell` on, FTP issues a beep each time a file transfer is complete). The default is on.

binary

The `binary` command sets the transfer mode to binary (such as for program files, graphics, and other files with embedded codes).

bye

The `bye` command terminates the FTP connection and closes FTP.

cd dir

The `cd dir` command changes directories to *dir*.

cdup

The `cdup` command changes to the parent directory of the current directory.

close

The `close` command closes the current connection without closing FTP.

cr

The `cr` command toggles carriage return stripping off and on for ASCII files. The default is off.

delete *filename*

The `delete filename` command deletes the indicated file.

debug

The `debug` command toggles debug mode on and off.

dir *spec*

The `dir spec` command displays a directory listing of *spec*.

disconnect

The `disconnect` command performs the same tasks as `close`.

get *file*

The `get file` command downloads the specified file from the host to the local system.

glob

The `glob` command toggles the use of wildcards (also called *filename expansion*) for the `mdelete`, `mget`, and `mput` commands. The default is on. With `globbing` enabled, you can use patterns such as `*.zip` and `d??.txt` to match files ending in `.zip`, or `.txt` files beginning with `d` followed by any two characters, respectively. With `globbing` off, the `*` and `?` characters are used literally; that is, `*.zip` would match a file actually named `*.zip`, and `d??.txt` would match a file actually named `d??.txt`.

hash

Use the `hash` command to toggle the display of `#` characters to indicate the progress of file transfers.

help *command*

The `help` command displays help for *command*. The command `help mget`, for example, displays the following: `mget   get multiple files`.

image

The `image` command sets the transfer mode to `image`. This command performs the same function as `binary`.

lcd *spec*

The `lcd spec` command sets or displays the current local directory (for example, `lcd e:\os2` changes to `e:\os2`). Note that `lcd` can change drive and directory at the same time.

ls *spec*

The `ls spec` command displays just filenames matching `spec`. Contrast this with `DIR`, which displays file statistics as well.

macdef *macname*

The `macdef macname` command defines a macro name and begins macro input mode. Macros remain defined for as long as the current connection is open. You can have up to 16 macros at the same time, but all macros cannot exceed a total of 4,096 characters.

mdelete *spec*

The `mdelete spec` command deletes multiple files matching `spec`. Note that `glob` must be enabled.

mget *spec*

The `mget spec` command downloads multiple files matching `spec`. Note that `glob` must be enabled.

mkdir *dir*

The `mkdir dir` command creates a subdirectory called `dir`.

mode *type*

The `mode type` command sets the transfer mode; `type` can be `ascii`, `binary`, or `image` (`binary` and `image` are synonyms).

mput *spec*

The `mput spec` command uploads multiple files matching `spec`. Note that `glob` must be enabled.

nmap *remote local*

The nmap *remote local* command toggles filename mapping. The default is off (type **nmap** without any parameters to turn off nmap). Filename mapping is used when the put, mput, get, and mget commands are issued without a local filename. The nmap setting is useful when the local file system doesn't support UNIX filenames. Use the tokens $1, $2, $3, and so on, to specify distinct file parts separated by periods. The following command, for example:

```
nmap $1.$2.$3 $1.$2
```

truncates the end part of a three-part filename, so that file.zip.old becomes file.zip. If ntrans is active, character translation is performed before any name mapping.

ntrans *remote local*

The ntrans *remote local* command enables translation of characters when using get, mget, put, and mput. This is useful when the local file system doesn't support UNIX file characters, such as :, ;, and ,. The following command:

```
ntrans :;,< $_-
```

translates characters as follows:

Character	Translation
:	$
;	_
,	-
<	Deletes (because there is no corresponding character in the fourth position)

open *host*

The open *host* command opens the specified *host* FTP site.

prompt

The prompt command toggles interactive prompting between files during a multifile mget, mput, or mdelete. If prompt is turned off, then all files are transferred or deleted without any prompting. If prompt is turned on, you are prompted to confirm each transfer or deletion.

proxy *command*

Use proxy *command* to substitute a secondary host connection as the destination for commands rather than the local system. If you use FTP to connect to Hobbes and to your own Internet provider at the same time, for example, then you could use proxy to transfer files from Hobbes to your provider. Once you've logged in to the appropriate directories, you can transfer the file PPP.ZIP from Hobbes to your provider using the following command while the Hobbes connection is active (primary):

```
proxy mput ppp.zip
```

Ordinarily, mput ppp.zip would transfer a file to your system. Prefaced by proxy, however, the transfer instead is directed to a secondary FTP connection.

To initiate a proxy site, you first must open the site by proxy. If you already have FTP open to your Internet provider, for example, you can open an additional FTP server, such as Hobbes, by using the proxy command:

```
proxy open hobbes.nmsu.edu
```

Thereafter, all commands you issue are relative to the proxy site—Hobbes. Hence, any files you see are considered "local" when you use the proxy command. Use proxy dir, proxy cd, and proxy cdup to navigate. Use proxy put to transfer a file.

All resulting transfers go to the intermediate FTP site rather than to your own local system. As noted previously, this is a useful strategy when downloading large files from a site that is in heavy demand.

put *file*

The put *file* command uploads a file to the host FTP site.

pwd *password*

The pwd *password* command sends your password to the host FTP site.

quit

The quit command terminates any connections and ends the FTP session.

quote

The quote command sends an exact command to the remote system.

recv *file*

The recv *file* command performs the same functions as get.

remotehelp *item*

The remotehelp *item* command displays help on *item* on the remote FTP site. Use this command to obtain help on site-specific commands and features.

rename *old new*

The rename *old new* command renames a file on the remote system.

reset

Use the reset command to clear out any pending commands and replies. The local and remote FTP programs must be synchronized in order to work properly. Sometimes, due to an error at the local or remote sites, the command and reply sequence is disturbed. When this happens, you likely will receive error messages for commands you type. Use the reset command to put the local and remote FTPs back into synch.

rmdir *dir*

Use the rmdir *dir* command to remove the remote directory named *dir*. To work, the directory must be empty.

runique

Use the runique command to toggle the unique naming of files downloaded when using get and mget. If runique is off, then downloading a file named file.dat will overwrite any existing file.dat on the local system. If runique is on, then FTP will create unique names so that existing files are not overwritten.

send *file*

The send *file* command performs the same functions as the put command.

sendport

Use the sendport command to toggle the use of FTP port instructions for file transfers.

site

Use the site command to send a site-specific command or instruction to the remote FTP host.

status

Use the status command to display the status of all connections, settings, and toggles, as shown in Figure 9.18.

sunique

Use the sunique command to toggle unique naming of files uploaded using put and mput. For more information, see runique.

FIGURE 9.18.

The status command reports all current settings.

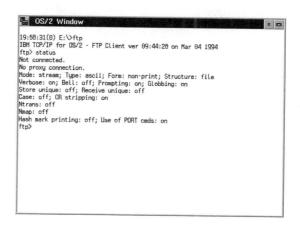

```
    OS/2 Window

19:58:31(8) E:\>ftp
IBM TCP/IP for OS/2 - FTP Client ver 09:44:28 on Mar 04 1994
ftp> status
Not connected.
No proxy connection.
Mode: stream; Type: ascii; Form: non-print; Structure: file
Verbose: on; Bell: off; Prompting: on; Globbing: on
Store unique: off; Receive unique: off
Case: off; CR stripping: on
Ntrans: off
Nmap: off
Hash mark printing: off; Use of PORT cmds: on
ftp>
```

trace

Use the `trace` command to toggle the tracing of transmitted packets. If you're having trouble downloading or uploading files, you sometimes can use `trace` to determine where the problem is. With `trace` enabled, FTP reports the route of packets transferred, as well as the time it takes for the transfer.

type

Use the `type` command to set the transfer type to ASCII or binary—for example, `type ascii`. Note that `type ascii` and `type binary` are synonymous with the plain `ascii` and `binary` commands.

user *id password*

Use the `user` *id password* command to tell the remote FTP host who you are. Normally, this command isn't necessary. However, if you mistype your ID or password, or if the remote system for some reason fails to prompt you for logon information, use the `user` command to supply the information.

verbose

Use the `verbose` command to toggle information from the server. With `verbose` on, you will get information such as the efficiency of file transfers.

? *command*

Enter **?** to obtain a list of FTP commands. Use **?** *command* to find help for a specific command. For example, **? verbose** provides help for the `verbose` command.

CHAPTER TEN CONNECTING TO OTHER SYSTEMS USING TELNET

Why Telnet?

Using TelnetPM on Your Shell Account

The Other Telnet (Text Mode)

3270 Telnet (PM and Text Mode)

What is telnet? Although it sounds tautological, telnet is a communications program that uses the telnet protocol, which is part of TCP/IP. Telnet is to UNIX what communications programs such as Procomm are to BBSs—but only sort of, so stand by. The OS/2 Warp Internet Access Kit (IAK) comes with four different versions of telnet:

`telnet.exe`	A traditional text-mode version of telnet.
`telnetpm.exe`	A PM version of telnet.
`tn3270.exe`	A text-mode version of telnet that emulates an IBM 3270 terminal.
`pmant.exe`	A PM version of telnet 3270.

When you're online to the Internet and want to connect to another host system to retrieve data or information, you often have several alternatives that you can use. These alternatives include Gopher, the WebExplorer, FTP, and telnet.

Like Gopher, the WebExplorer, and FTP, telnet uses a special protocol to connect to other computers. Unlike the others, however, telnet doesn't simplify the process. Rather, telnet provides you with terminal access to a remote system. Thus, when using telnet, you must navigate directly on the UNIX command line using native UNIX commands and whatever programs might be installed on the remote system.

Note

> When do you use 3270 versus regular telnet? You can used 3270 only when the host supports it. A few hosts support the use of 3270 terminals, whereas most support the more typical VT100 and VT220 terminals. Use telnet or 3270 telnet, whichever is appropriate for the system and programs being used. If you don't know which terminal type to use, plain telnet is probably appropriate. Use of 3270 is uncommon in public access hosts available via telnet. You might find 3270 emulation needed for some systems to which you have password access, but you generally will already know what's needed before you log in. Typical home and small office users of the IAK almost never encounter a need to use the 3270 versions of telnet.

Why Telnet?

Most OS/2 users' first encounters with telnet are not knowingly. Instead, they choose an option from Gopher or the WebExplorer that leads to a telnet session. For example, the Gopher menu shown in Figure 10.1 contains one icon that looks like a computer terminal (okay, so use your imagination). That icon connects you to a telnet session. Usually, when you connect to a telnet session via Gopher, it's to run a specific program such as whois, netfind, or WAIS (Wide Area Information Search). Although telnet is capable of putting you directly onto the command line of a host system, when you telnet into a special program via Gopher or the WebExplorer, you are limited to using just that program on the host system. Telnet, however, gives you a way to access those programs.

FIGURE 10.1.

*Telnet access points often
are found while Gophering.*

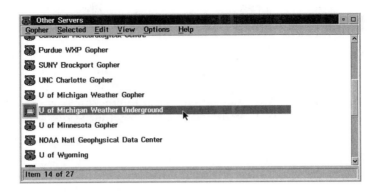

There is, however, another common use of telnet that should be of interest to OS/2 users: logging onto your Internet provider's host system. "Huh?" you ask. "I'm already logged in once I connect with my SLIP account, right?"

Yes and no. If you connect via SLIP or PPP, your session is routed directly to the Internet. Although your provider's system does provide a gateway to the Internet, you are in fact directly on the Internet and not really logged on to your provider system—at least not in the same way as when you're using a UNIX shell account. During a SLIP or PPP session, programs such as Ultimedia Mail/2 Lite briefly log on to your system to fetch or send mail (unless a different system is used as a mail server). For the most part, however, you are on the Internet itself, not on your host system.

If you're using TIA, however, it's a different matter. You first log on to your host system and start the SLIP emulator software (such as TIA). The SLIP emulator software then emulates a SLIP session, which makes your SLIP client software—such as FTP, Gopher, the WebExplorer, and telnet—*think* you are on the Internet. Even though you are logged on to your shell account the whole time, however, it's still not the same as when you're working at the UNIX command line (fortunately, for most of us who aren't fluent in UNIX).

> If you need telnet access to hosts with any frequency, do yourself a favor. Obtain and register Ray Gwinn's SIO replacement communications drivers. With them comes Vmodem. Vmodem is a virtual modem program that enables your ordinary communications program for telnet. If you have PMComm, Zap-o-Com, or some other communications program, you'll be happy to discover that you can use them instead of telnet. If your communications program supports scripting and scrollback, you'll be able to use those as well. In fact, with SIO and Vmodem, you even can access CompuServe from the Internet using the CompuServe Information Manager for OS/2! See Chapter 12, "Additional Internet Applications and Related Utilities," for additional information.

Using TelnetPM on Your Shell Account

While connected via SLIP, PPP, or even TIA, you often can log on to your Internet provider system using FTP-PM, Gopher, or one of the other SLIP clients. Have you ever, for example, used FTP-PM to download a copy of .newsrc, or to FTP a program from another computer to your Internet provider system? Does your Internet provider have its own Gopher server or its own home page on the Web? If so, you've been using SLIP clients to access your own provider's system.

Telnet gives you another way, assuming your account is set up for it. As a general rule, if you have access to a UNIX shell account, you can access the same shell account using Telnet while connected via SLIP. Many Internet providers, in fact, set up both shell and SLIP (or PPP) accounts even though you might have requested only the latter. The SLIP or PPP connections get you onto the Internet. However, your shell account provides a place for your mail to go when you're not logged in.

Note

> If you're using the IBM Internet Connection (also known as The IBM Global Network or Advantis) to access the Internet, you don't have a shell account to which you can telnet. Or, if you do, nobody at Advantis or IBM seems to know about it or how to specify the Internet name or address. If you find out otherwise, please let me know at tyson@cpcug.org.

Why might you want to access your shell account using telnet? One reason is that there are some things you can do from the UNIX command line that you can't do otherwise. For example, suppose you want to change your password. If you're using the IBM Internet Connection, changing your password is straightforward. You just click that button. If you're using the Dial Other Internet Provider dialer, however, there is no method built into the IAK tools that come with OS/2 Warp.

Most UNIX shell accounts, however, have some kind of built-in way to change your password and other account information, short of your having to call the system administrator. On the provider system that I use, for example, there is a menu I can use that helps perform the chore. Let's take a look at a typical telnet session to a UNIX provider.

To start a telnet session, double-click on the Telnet object in the Internet Utilities folder (located in the IBM Internet Connection for OS/2 folder), and the TelnetPM window opens, as shown in Figure 10.2.

FIGURE 10.2.

The TelnetPM window.

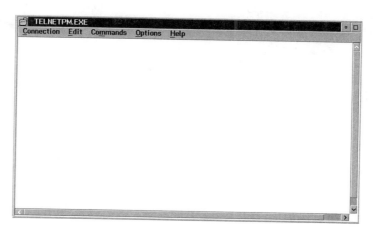

Perform the following steps:

1. Choose Connection|Open Session from the menu.

2. In the Open Session dialog box (shown in Figure 10.3), type the name of your host system in the Host name box (such as **amalgum.com**). Note that you also can type a 32-bit dotted IP address such as 555.55.55.555, but typing a name usually is easier and less error prone. See the sidebar titled "Creating a Customized Telnet Object" following this procedure.

FIGURE 10.3.

Choose Connection | Open session to log on to a host using telnet.

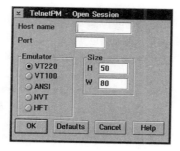

3. Under Emulator, VT100 or VT200 usually work fine; select a different emulator if appropriate.

4. Under Size, specify the desired height (H) and width (W) to use for the telnet session. Then click OK. Here's a tip: telnet does not have a scrollback facility, so make the height as tall as the host will allow (usually 50).

5. After a few seconds (usually), the telnet session will sputter to life with your host system identifying itself and prompting for your login name (see Figure 10.4). Type your name and password, and you're logged on.

FIGURE 10.4.

When logging on to a host via telnet, you sometimes must use a login ID and password.

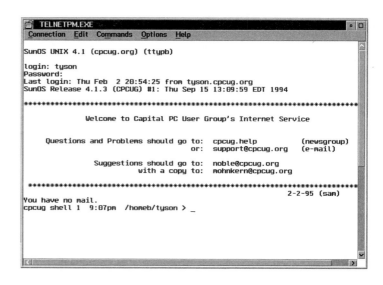

Creating a Customized Telnet Object

If you plan to be a regular Telnet user for any given Telnet site, you can set up a customized Telnet object for each host:

1. Open the Application Template folder in the IBM Internet Connection for OS/2 folder.

2. Using mouse button 2, drag a copy of the Telnet template and drop it where you want the customized Telnet object to reside. This creates the new object and opens the Telnet – Settings notebook, as shown in Figure 10.5.

FIGURE 10.5.

The TelnetPM Settings notebook.

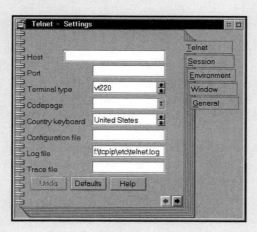

3. Fill out the host name (for example, `host.name.edu`). If you want to keep a log (capture the session to disk) while connected to this host, type a name for a file.

Note that the other fields can be used as well; however, the defaults generally work best when first getting started.

4. Click the Session tab for the view shown in Figure 10.6. Here, choose the desired Session type. If you choose OS/2 Window or Full Screen, TELNET.EXE will be used. If you choose Presentation Manager, TELNETPM.EXE will be used.

FIGURE 10.6.

The Telnet Session settings page.

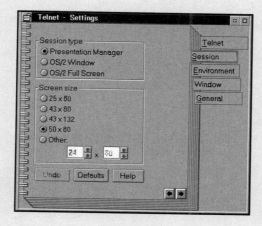

5. Choose the desired screen size (the maximum height is 50, and the maximum width is 132).

6. Click the Environment tab. In the space provided, you can type any environment settings you want exported when the host session is opened (see Figure 10.7). Type them as *envvar=setting*, as in path=/usr/mypath. Note that not all hosts support exporting environment settings from a telnet client. Environment variables are set from the UNIX command line using the setenv command.

FIGURE 10.7.

You can export environment settings to the host.

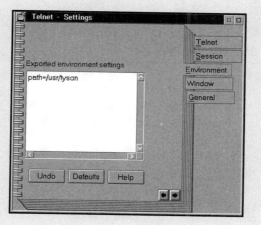

7. Click the General tab. In the Title field, type the name that you want to identify this Telnet object on the Desktop (such as **MyHost Telnet**).

To create a customized 3270 Telnet object, do the following:

1. Using mouse button 2, drag a copy of the 3270 Telnet template and drop it where you want the customized object to reside. This creates the new object and opens the 3270 Telnet Settings notebook, as shown in Figure 10.8.

2. Fill out the host name (such as **host.name.edu**). Note that the host must be a 3270 system, or the 3270 Telnet object won't work. Under Translation, you can enter the name of a file that contains an ASCII to EBCDIC translation table.

3. Set the following options as you desire: Enable extended data stream (allow colors, blinking text, program screen changes, and so on); Disable the bell (prevent programs from beeping); Enable square brackets (cause brackets and backslashes to appear onscreen as they do on the keyboard); and Maintain screen size (prevent the program from changing the screen size; this option doesn't apply to the text mode TN3270.EXE program). The defaults generally work best when first getting started.

4. Click the Session tab, which is identical to the TelnetPM Session tab. Here, choose the desired Session type. If you choose OS/2 Window or Full Screen, TN3270.EXE will be used. If you choose Presentation Manager, PMANT.EXE will be used. Choose the desired screen size (the maximum height is 50 and the maximum width is 132).

FIGURE 10.8.

The 3270 Telnet – Settings notebook.

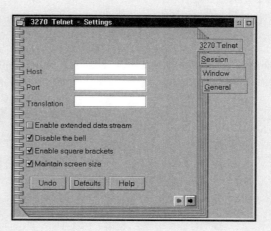

Note that the 3270 Telnet – Settings notebook does not have an Environment tab. After you've created a customized Telnet object, you can start a session with that host by double-clicking the new object. If you do a lot of telnetting, you might consider creating a Telnet folder for keeping your Telnet objects. This can cut clutter from the IBM Internet Connection for OS/2 folder.

After you're logged on, what you do is largely up to you. You can (if you don't already know how) take the opportunity to learn to use your host's Internet tools from the shell account. If nothing else, it usually gives users a better appreciation for the OS/2 client versions of Gopher, FTP, and so on, which come with the Warp IAK.

Many UNIX shell systems provide a menu to access major features, such as the menu shown in Figure 10.9. Note that the menu lists online UNIX versions of the same capabilities that are provided by OS/2 Warp Internet clients (see Table 10.1).

FIGURE 10.9.
Many UNIX shell systems are bolstered by menus.

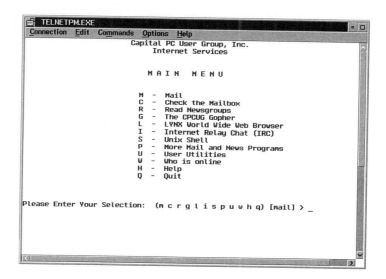

Table 10.1. Online UNIX equivalents to OS/2 Internet programs.

Online UNIX Program	OS/2 Version
Mail	Mail cabinet (in Ultimedia Mail/2 Lite folder)
Check the Mailbox	In-basket (in Ultimedia Mail/2 Lite folder)
Read Newsgroups	NewsReader/2
Gopher	Gopher
LYNX World Wide Web Browser	WebExplorer
FTP	FTP-PM and FTP Text mode (not shown in Figure 10.9)
Telnet to another computer	Telnet and TelnetPM (and the 3270 versions) (not shown in Figure 10.9)

If you type **u** as a response to the menu shown in Figure 10.9, you'll see a few more UNIX-based versions of programs similar to some in the IAK, such as FTP and Telnet. Hence, they are shown in Table 10.1, but not in Figure 10.9.

If you abandon the menu, you'll get to the UNIX shell command line. In some ways, it's similar to the DOS command line. Some systems set up a number of DOS-like synonyms for UNIX commands to accommodate users who are more familiar with DOS (basically, most of us, right?). Later on, I show a log of a telnet session to a UNIX host system. On the system shown in the log, commands such as dir, type, and cd work just as they do in DOS. One of the most useful commands you'll find, though, is help.

In the session log shown, text entered by the user is shown in bold. In this session, I logged on and started by entering the **who** command. The who command tells you who is currently using the system. Your host might not have a who command. Or, you might use the w command, which is kind of a who-and-what program. It shows not only who is logged on but what program they're running as well.

Next, I entered **menu** to start the host's menu system. Your system probably has a menu, as well. Next, I used the menu to navigate to the Utilities menu and to the Change Password menu. Then, I changed my password.

> Many UNIX shell accounts have simple menu systems that start up by default. My system's menu starts up by default, but I disabled it by editing my .cshrc file. If you are similarly inclined, the file that you edit might be different on your system. Consult your local Help system, and always make a backup copy of any files you edit before editing the original. On most UNIX systems, you'll find that the copy command works just the same as on the OS/2 command line, as in the following example:
>
> ```
> copy .cshrc .cshrc.old
> ```

After that, I navigated back to the MAIN MENU and quit the menu. I then entered **dir** to get a list of files and directories. Notice that, just like at the OS/2 or DOS command line, the UNIX command line shows the current directory. However, notice that forward slashes are used instead of backslashes. As you cruise around the Internet, keep this in mind if filenames you specify don't seem to work. Also keep in mind that in the UNIX world, everything is case-specific. You could have different files named mail, Mail, and MAIL all in the same directory. Finally, I entered **exit** to close the session.

```
SunOS UNIX 4.1 (cpcug.org) (ttyp7)

login:tyson
Password:<suppressed>
Last login: Tue Jan 24 15:11:47 from tyson.cpcug.org
SunOS Release 4.1.3 (CPCUG) #1: Thu Sep 15 13:09:59 EDT 1994
*************************************************************************
             Welcome to Capital PC User Group's Internet Service

     Questions and Problems should go to:   cpcug.help          (newsgroup)
                                      or:   support@cpcug.org   (e-mail)
```

```
                  Suggestions should go to:  noble@cpcug.org
                         with a copy to:  mohnkern@cpcug.org
*****************************************************************************
                                                          1-24-95 (sam)
You have no mail.
cpcug shell 1  11:47am  /homeb/tyson > who
oj3        ttyp2    Jan 25 10:48
fmancino   ttyp3    Jan 25 11:40
signell    ttyp4    Jan 25 10:43
buskirk    ttyp5    Jan 25 11:38
dbkirby    ttyp6    Jan 25 10:49
noble      ttyp7    Jan 25 11:39
jmcn       ttyp8    Jan 25 11:43
finucane   ttyp9    Jan 25 10:34
patmark    ttypa    Jan 25 11:30
tyson      ttypb    Jan 25 11:47       (tyson.cpcug.org)
jelks      ttypc    Jan 25 11:17
jsussman   ttypd    Jan 25 11:33
ramster    ttype    Jan 25 11:09
erskine    ttypf    Jan 25 11:34
harryr     ttyq0    Jan 25 11:43
sspuler    ttyq1    Jan 25 11:46
aborden    ttyq4    Jan 25 11:00
cpcug shell 1  11:47am  /homeb/tyson > menu
                        Capital PC User Group, Inc.
                           Internet Services

                      M A I N   M E N U

                 M  -  Mail
                 C  -  Check the Mailbox
                 R  -  Read Newsgroups
                 G  -  The CPCUG Gopher
                 L  -  LYNX World Wide Web Browser
                 I  -  Internet Relay Chat (IRC)
                 S  -  Unix Shell
                 P  -  More Mail and News Programs
                 U  -  User Utilities
                 W  -  Who is online
                 H  -  Help
                 Q  -  Quit

Please Enter Your Selection:  (m c r g l i s p u w h q) [mail] > u

                 U T I L I T I E S

                 C  -  Change your Password
                 L  -  List the files in your Home Directory
                 U  -  Upload a File to your Home directory
                 D  -  Download a file from your Home directory
                 F  -  FTP (Internet file transfer)
                 N  -  NcFTP (Advanced FTP)
                 T  -  Telnet to another computer
                 E  -  Edit an ASCII file using Pico
```

```
                       V  -  View the "Message of the Day"
                       M  -  Main Menu

Please Enter Your Selection:  (c l u d n f t e v m) > c
Changing password for tyson on cpcug.org.
Old password:<suppressed>
New password:<suppressed>
Retype new password:<suppressed>

                    U T I L I T I E S

                 C  -  Change your Password
                 L  -  List the files in your Home Directory
                 U  -  Upload a File to your Home directory
                 D  -  Download a file from your Home directory
                 F  -  FTP (Internet file transfer)
                 N  -  NcFTP (Advanced FTP)
                 T  -  Telnet to another computer
                 E  -  Edit an ASCII file using Pico
                 V  -  View the "Message of the Day"
                 M  -  Main Menu

Please Enter Your Selection:  (c l u d n f t e v m) > m
                 Capital PC User Group, Inc.
                      Internet Services

                    M A I N   M E N U

                 M  -  Mail
                 C  -  Check the Mailbox
                 R  -  Read Newsgroups
                 G  -  The CPCUG Gopher
                 L  -  LYNX World Wide Web Browser
                 I  -  Internet Relay Chat (IRC)
                 S  -  Unix Shell
                 P  -  More Mail and News Programs
                 U  -  User Utilities
                 W  -  Who is online
                 H  -  Help
                 Q  -  Quit

Please Enter Your Selection:  (m c r g l i s p u w h q) [mail] > q

Type "menu" to return to the Main Menu

cpcug shell 1  11:49am  /homeb/tyson > dir
total 238
drwx--x--x  7 tyson          512 Jan 24 15:31 .
dr-xr-xr-x534 root          9728 Jan 24 16:56 ..
-rw-------  1 tyson            0 Nov 17 23:50 .addressbook
-rw-------  1 tyson         1257 Nov 17 23:50 .addressbook.lu
-rw-------  1 tyson            6 Nov 11 12:23 .bash_logout
-rw-------  1 tyson           47 Nov 11 12:23 .bash_profile
-rw-------  1 tyson          227 Nov 11 12:23 .bashrc
-rw-------  1 tyson         4141 Jan 12 16:35 .cshrc
-rw-------  1 tyson         4140 Jan 12 16:34 .cshrc.before
-rw-------  1 tyson          391 Nov 11 12:23 .emacs
-rw-------  1 tyson            0 Jan  6 07:28 .gopherrc
```

```
-rw-------  1 tyson          525 Nov 11 12:23 .login
-rw-------  1 tyson            6 Nov 11 12:23 .logout
-rw-------  1 tyson          680 Nov 11 12:23 .mailrc
-rw-------  1 tyson           11 Nov 20 17:53 .mh_profile
-rw-------  1 tyson       183412 Jan  8 21:06 .newsrc
-rw-------  1 tyson         5434 Jan 12 16:10 .pinerc
-rw-rw-rw-  1 tyson          287 Jan 24 15:46 .plan
-rw-------  1 tyson          109 Nov 11 12:23 .profile
drwx------  4 tyson          512 Jan  8 21:06 .tin
-rw-------  1 tyson          639 Nov 11 12:23 .zlogin
-rw-------  1 tyson          441 Nov 11 12:23 .zshrc
drwx------  2 tyson          512 Nov 20 17:53 Mail
drwx------  2 tyson          512 Dec 11 16:32 News
drwx------  2 tyson          512 Nov 11 12:23 bin
drwx------  2 tyson          512 Nov 17 23:50 mail
cpcug shell 1  11:50am  /homeb/tyson > exit
logout
```

Using Telnet: Quirks and Limitations

If you spend much time using telnet at the UNIX command line, you quickly notice that Telnet, TelnetPM, and TN3270 do not have a built-in scrollback buffer. That means that if information scrolls off the screen, you can't scroll back up to see it again. Some commands that you enter might invoke a UNIX facility to the DOS and OS/2 more command. Using more, you can cause the OS/2 or DOS command line to pause after each screenful of data.

Tip

Use a log. Because telnet does not have scrollback capability, and because it might be your only means of connecting with a remote host, you probably want to get into the habit of using the log feature. When you enable a telnet log, the entire session is captured to a disk file. To create a default log, open the Settings notebook for the Telnet object to the Telnet page. In the log field, type the full specification for where you want the log kept, and what you want it to be called (for instance, **c:\tcpip\etc\telnet.log**). If you set up customized Telnet objects, you might want to create distinctly named logs for each object.

When you're online in a TelnetPM session without the log turned on, you can turn it on for only that session. From the menu, choose Options | Log file for the dialog box shown in Figure 10.10. Navigate to the desired directory and type a name for the log file. Or, if you don't like navigating, you can type the full specification directly, as shown in the preceding paragraph. Although having a log file doesn't entirely make up for the lack of having scrollback, it can make using telnet a little more friendly. If necessary, you can use a browser such as HyperView to look at the log while it's still open. See Chapter 11, "Other Warp Internet Tools and Programs," for information on HyperView and other useful tools that don't come with the IAK.

FIGURE 10.10.

Use Options | Log file to capture the telnet session to a log file.

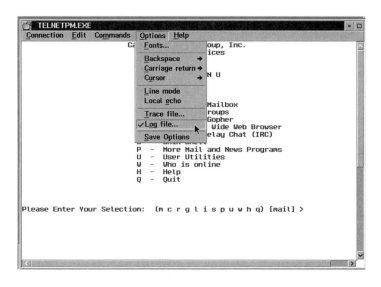

The lack of a scrollback buffer is softened somewhat by the fact that many UNIX host systems automatically implement a feature similar to more, as shown in Figure 10.11. Note that the word More and a percentage appear in the lower left corner of the screen. Unlike the OS/2 and DOS more command, however, the UNIX version will not advance a full screen if you press Enter. Instead it advances just a single line. To get it to advance a full screen, press the spacebar. Or, if you want it to advance a certain number of lines, type that number. If you just want the listing to stop, you usually can press Ctrl+C.

FIGURE 10.11.

Many UNIX shell commands are automatically set up to pause data between screens.

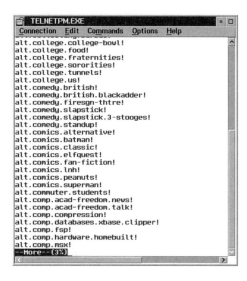

> Use Line mode. As described later under "TelnetPM Options," using Line mode can make using TelnetPM bearable. This mode gives you a text window for composing commands on your system before they get sent to the remote host. Choose Options|Line mode, and then choose Options|Save options.

Tip

Unfortunately, the UNIX more command isn't always used. When it's not, you'll see tons of output cascade off the screen. When that happens, you sometimes can stop and start screen output by using Ctrl+S (Stop) and Ctrl+Q (Start). However, that method doesn't always produce satisfactory results. You also can try the menu for Commands|Suspend. By the time you do that, however, whatever it was you wanted to see has usually already scrolled out of sight. Another alternative is to enter **help** for your UNIX system to see how to explicitly use your system's version of more (note that it might not even be called more because some system administrators set up DOS-like command synonyms, and some don't).

You'll also notice that telnet does not have any built-in capabilities for uploading or downloading files. In the case of my host, the system itself can upload and download using ASCII, Xmodem, Ymodem, Zmodem, and Kermit protocols. Telnet, however, can't do any of that. In order to get files to or from my host system, I would have to call in using a regular communications program such as PMComm or HyperAccess Lite. Or, I could use the telnet-enabled TE/2. Or, using Ray Gwinn's SIO drivers and Vmodem, almost any communications program can be enabled for telnet (see Chapter 12, "Additional Internet Applications and Related Utilities"). If I didn't want to leave the pure Warp IAK environment, I could use FTP or FTP-PM. However, I could not use telnet to do the data transfer.

> Try using the Up and Down arrows at the UNIX command line. Very often, the local host has set up a scrollable command buffer, just as you get when using the OS/2 command line with KEYS ON or using the DOS command line with DOSKEYS enabled. When you press the Up and Down arrow keys, it displays commands you've previously entered. That way, you often can edit a command you entered, rather than having to retype the entire command.

Tip

The TelnetPM Menu

When you use TelnetPM, the menu provides access to commonly needed telnet commands. If you use the text-mode version of telnet, you'll need to learn its command, but you'll have a bit more control and power. One of the biggest problems with TelnetPM is the lack of keyboard shortcuts. Don't waste a lot of time looking for them—they simply are not there.

In addition to Help, which all menus seem to have, the TelnetPM menu bar includes the following main menu items. It's a good idea to acquaint yourself with the menu so you'll know what's available when the need arises.

> Connections
> Edit
> Commands
> Options
> Help

Connections

Use the Connections menu to open and close connections, as well as to terminate the TelnetPM session. At any moment, only the Open session or Close session command will be available. Unlike FTP-PM, a single instance of TelnetPM can be connected to only one host at a time. If no session is open, you can open a session as follows:

1. Choose Connections | Open session from the menu.
2. Type the name of the host to which you wish to connect.
3. Choose the terminal, screen size, and port. (From a practical standpoint, the only option that usually makes any sense to change is the screen size; setting it to 50 lines rather than 24 often makes TelnetPM sessions more manageable.)
4. Click OK.

To close a TelnetPM session, just choose Connections | Close session from the menu. To close TelnetPM altogether, choose Connections | Exit.

Note

> Before you choose the TelnetPM application, it's considered polite to use the `exit` command on the UNIX system to which you are connected. Entering `exit` logs you off.

Edit

Unfortunately, if you want to use the Clipboard from TelnetPM, you must do it through the menu. The normal OS/2 system Clipboard keys do not work, making using the TelnetPM Clipboard much more cumbersome than in other PM applications. To copy text from the TelnetPM window to the Clipboard, perform the following steps:

1. Position the mouse pointer so it's at the upper-left edge of whatever you want to select.
2. Press and hold mouse button 1, and drag the mouse down and to the right. Notice that a box is drawn as you move the mouse. Positioning can be clumsy, and it might take several tries to get exactly what you want selected.
3. When the text that you want is in the selection box (as shown in Figure 10.12), release the mouse button.
4. Choose Edit | Copy from the menu.

FIGURE 10.12.

Selecting text in the Telnet window is different from in other PM programs and VIO (virtual input/output) windows.

Pasting text is easier, but the inability to use Shift+Insert is crippling to some users. To insert text that's in the Clipboard, choose Edit|Paste from the menu. You might want to do this, for example, if you need to enter a complicated filename that you copied from elsewhere.

Commands

Use the Commands menu to send commands to the remote host. Some of these might not work on some systems. To find out what works, it's largely a matter of trial and error, but it helps if the terminal type is matched. You usually can discover the terminal type on UNIX systems by entering **set**. As shown in Figure 10.13, the set command has a variety of settings.

FIGURE 10.13.

You usually can enter set to see your current settings in a UNIX session.

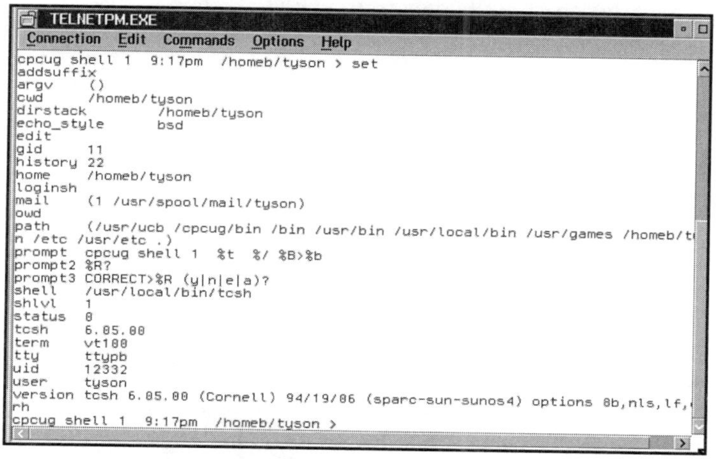

Options on the Commands menu are as follows:

Abort output (Alt+M,A)	Aborts the flow of data to the terminal from the remote system. If you enter a command that generates too much data, you sometimes can abort the output by choosing Commands| Abort. Optimally, this command stops the flow of data while letting the underlying program continue to comple tion.
Are you there? (Alt+M,Y)	Sends a query to the remote system to see whether it's still online. If it is, it usually responds [Yes]. Break (Alt+M,B) For systems that support this command, it sends a break command to the remote system. It's similar to pressing Ctrl+C but often not nearly as useful.
Interrupt process (Alt+M,I)	For systems that support this command, it sends a command to *abend* (halt) the current problem. It's similar to Ctrl+C but often doesn't work as well as Ctrl+C.
Suspend(Alt+M,S)	For systems that support it, this command temporarily stops the output of data to the terminal. This is similar to pressing Ctrl+S on many systems.
Synch (Alt+M,N)	For systems that support it, this is the antonym of Suspend. It restarts the output of data to the terminal. It's similar to pressing Ctrl+Q on many systems.

TelnetPM Options

Use the Options menu to control local behavior of the TelnetPM session. Options you save apply to all future TelnetPM sessions. Options you save in the settings for specific TelnetPM objects, however, apply only to that object. Options you can control from within TelnetPM are as follows:

Fonts	Provides a limited selection of fonts, as shown in Figure 10.14.
Backspace	Controls the meaning of the backspace key. Normally, the backspace key in OS/2 is destructive. On some UNIX systems, the default is a destructive backspace; on others, it does the same thing as pressing the left cursor arrow. You might have to experiment with the backspace option to determine which setting gives you the desired behavior.

FIGURE 10.14.

TelnetPM provides a limited selection of fonts.

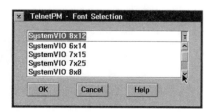

Carriage return

Determines what kind of carriage return TelnetPM sends: carriage return only (ASCII 13), or a combined carriage return and linefeed (ASCII 13 followed by ASCII 10).

Cursor

Determines the cursor characteristics, as shown in Figure 10.15.

FIGURE 10.15.

Choose a cursor that shows up well on the screeen.

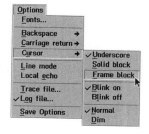

Line mode

Arranges the screen as shown in Figure 10.16, giving you a local entry window for commands you enter and a dropdown list of the last 10 commands. I recommend using this option on systems with slow response, especially those that take forever to echo every character you type.

FIGURE 10.16.

Line mode can make slow-response systems more usable.

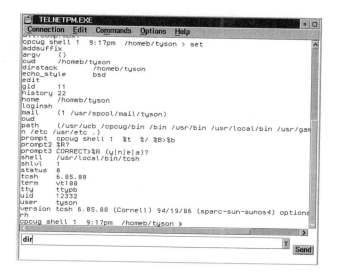

Note

Slow system response can make typing almost painful. Also, some systems don't support command-line editing, making it very difficult to correct errors as you type. In Line mode, you have a local text box for composing your command before sending it to the remote system. It makes using many remote telnet connections tolerable.

When using this mode, you can use the Up and Down arrows to retrieve the command history (such as the last 10 command lines you've entered during this session), as well as a dropdown arrow next to the send button that shows a list of the last 10 commands. A problem with Line mode, however, is something called *automatic command completion*. If you enter the command **dir WebExplorer**, the next dir command you type will match the full dir WebExplorer command. This makes it difficult to enter a shorter, but different, command. In the case of dir, you can get around it by typing **dir .**, instead, which explicitly requests a list of files on the current (.) subdirectory.

When in Line mode, any excess lines that don't fit into the current window are made scrollable. Unfortunately, if you choose 50 lines for display, this doesn't suddenly give you more than 50. However, at least you don't lose any of those lines by choosing Line mode.

Warning

One of the convenient things about Line mode is the fact that it lets you compose your password without having to peck carefully at the keyboard. You actually can see what you're typing. This is nice, but it might not be so nice if you work in a large office and don't want others to know your password. If you type your password while in Line mode, it will be available in the local command buffer by pressing the up and down arrow keys. If you use the IAK from a small office or your home, however, you probably don't need to be concerned as much about security. *Hey, I think my goldfish just saw my password!*

Local echo	Causes characters you type to be displayed. This option some times is necessary for systems that don't echo commands you type.
Trace file	Gives a detailed log of all characters sent and received from the host system. For complex streams of data, it provides a hex dump, as shown in Figure 10.17.
Log file	Gives a complete capture of all characters sent by the remote host. Characters that are not echoed (such as passwords) are not included in the log.
Save options	Saves the options currently set. This is useful if you find a collection of Options that work well for you. Options are saved in TELNETPM.INI in the \TCPIP\ETC directory.

FIGURE 10.17.

The trace file shows a hex display of data transmitted.

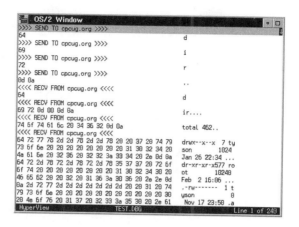

Netfind: An Exercise in Frustration

I have to laugh when people tell me that the Internet is the information superhighway. Sometimes, it's more like trying to navigate a cobblestone road on a thin-tired bicycle: It's an exercise in frustration. Take Netfind, for example. I had planned to show a successful Netfind session. In trying to find my acquisitions editor, however, I met with utter failure. In fact, I was only able to find myself and somebody named Lee Gates (at Microsoft). The results of my desperate searches are shown next. Let this be a lesson to you: Very often, you can find out only what you already know.

```
========================================================
Welcome to the University of Colorado Netfind server.
========================================================
I think that your terminal can display 24 lines.  If this is wrong,
please enter the "Options" menu and set the correct number of lines.
Top level choices:
        1. Help
        2. Search
        3. Seed database lookup
        4. Options
        5. Quit (exit server)
—> 2
Enter person and keys (blank to exit) —> taber macmillan
Netfind: No seed information is available for keys 'macmillan'.
Please try a different search.  Note: You might try specifying fewer keys.
Enter person and keys (blank to exit) —> taber sams
Netfind: No seed information is available for keys 'sams'.
Please try a different search.  Note: You might try specifying fewer keys.
Enter person and keys (blank to exit) —> gates microsoft
Please select at most 3 of the following domains to search:
        0. hkmsug.org (hong kong microsoft user group, central, hong kong)
        1. microsoft.com (microsoft corporation, redmond, washington)
        2. microsoft.net (microcomputing concepts, inc, brooklyn, new york)
        3. msn.net (microsoft network, redmond, washington)
        4. windycity.com (microsoft, inc, redmond, washington)
```

```
          5. research.microsoft.com (research laboratory, microsoft corporation,
             redmond, washington)
          6. rhino.microsoft.com (microsoft corporation, redmond, washington)
Enter selection (e.g., 2 0 1) —> 1 5 6
( 3) SMTP_Finger_Search: checking domain rhino.microsoft.com
( 2) SMTP_Finger_Search: checking domain research.microsoft.com
( 3) do_connect: Mail service not available on host rhino.microsoft.com ->
               cannot do mail forwarding lookup
( 3) ask_smtp: Failed to connect to SMTP daemon
( 2) do_connect: Mail service not available on host research.microsoft.com ->
               cannot do mail forwarding lookup
( 2) ask_smtp: Failed to connect to SMTP daemon
( 1) got nameserver atbd.microsoft.com
( 1) SMTP_Finger_Search: checking domain microsoft.com
( 2) do_connect: Finger service not available on host research.microsoft.com ->
               cannot do user lookup
( 3) do_connect: Finger service not available on host rhino.microsoft.com ->
               cannot do user lookup
( 1) do_connect: Finger service not available on host microsoft.com -> cannot
               do user lookup
- - - - - -
Domain search completed.  Proceeding to host search.
- - - - - -
( 1) SMTP_Finger_Search: checking host ingate.microsoft.com
( 4) SMTP_Finger_Search: checking host netmail.microsoft.com
( 5) SMTP_Finger_Search: checking host siamsrvr.microsoft.com
( 2) SMTP_Finger_Search: checking host gymflkd.microsoft.com
( 3) SMTP_Finger_Search: checking host netmail2.microsoft.com
( 3) do_connect: Finger service not available on host netmail2.microsoft.com ->
               cannot do user lookup
( 3) SMTP_Finger_Search: checking host atbd.microsoft.com
( 4) do_connect: Finger service not available on host netmail.microsoft.com ->
               cannot do user lookup
( 4) SMTP_Finger_Search: checking host www.microsoft.com
( 5) do_connect: Finger service not available on host siamsrvr.microsoft.com ->
               cannot do user lookup
( 5) SMTP_Finger_Search: checking host ftp.microsoft.com
( 5) do_connect: Finger service not available on host ftp.microsoft.com ->
               cannot do user lookup
( 5) SMTP_Finger_Search: checking host chopin.microsoft.com
( 4) do_connect: Finger service not available on host www.microsoft.com ->
               cannot do user lookup
( 4) SMTP_Finger_Search: checking host gopher.microsoft.com
( 3) do_connect: Finger service not available on host atbd.microsoft.com ->
               cannot do user lookup
( 3) SMTP_Finger_Search: checking host bartok.microsoft.com
( 5) do_connect: Finger service not available on host chopin.microsoft.com ->
               cannot do user lookup
( 5) SMTP_Finger_Search: checking host mahler.microsoft.com
( 4) do_connect: Finger service not available on host gopher.microsoft.com ->
               cannot do user lookup
( 4) SMTP_Finger_Search: checking host www.research.microsoft.com
( 3) do_connect: Finger service not available on host bartok.microsoft.com ->
               cannot do user lookup
( 5) do_connect: Finger service not available on host mahler.microsoft.com ->
               cannot do user lookup
( 4) do_connect: Finger service not available on host www.research.microsoft.com
               cannot do user lookup
```

```
SYSTEM: ingate.microsoft.com
        Login name: leeg                        In real life: Lee Gates
        Directory: /usr/l/leeg                  Shell: /bin/csh
        Last login Mon Jan 16 14:45
        No Plan.
( 2) connect timed out
FINGER SUMMARY:
- Remote mail forwarding information queries (SMTP EXPN) were not
  supported on host(s) searched in the domain 'research.microsoft.com'.
- Remote user queries (finger) were not supported on host(s) searched in
  the domain 'research.microsoft.com'.
- Remote mail forwarding information queries (SMTP EXPN) were not
  supported on host(s) searched in the domain 'rhino.microsoft.com'.
- Remote user queries (finger) were not supported on host(s) searched in
  the domain 'rhino.microsoft.com'.
- The most promising email address for "gates"
  based on the above finger search is
  leeg@ingate.microsoft.com.
Continue the search ([n]/y) ? --> n
Enter person and keys (blank to exit) --> tyson cpcug
Searching cpcug.org
( 1) SMTP_Finger_Search: checking domain cpcug.org
Mail for Herbert Tyson is forwarded to tyson@cpcug.org
NOTE:   this is a domain mail forwarding arrangement - so mail intended
        for "tyson" should be addressed to "tyson@cpcug.org".
SYSTEM: cpcug.org
        Login name: tyson                       In real life: Herbert Tyson
        Directory: /homeb/tyson                 Shell: /usr/local/bin/tcsh
        On since Jan 26 11:26:59 on ttypd from tyson.cpcug.org
        1 minute 3 seconds Idle Time
        Plan:
        Herb Tyson

        Current books:

        Your OS/2 Warp Consultant, ISBN 0-672-30484-8
        Word 6 for Windows Super Book ISBN 0-672-30384-1
        Navigating the Internet with OS/2 Warp, ISBN 0-672-30719-7
( 1) SMTP_Finger_Search: cpcug.org leads us to 1 other machines
( 2) SMTP_Finger_Search: checking host tyson.cpcug.org
( 2) do_connect: Finger service not available on host tyson.cpcug.org ->
               cannot do user lookup
FINGER SUMMARY:
- The most promising email address for "tyson"
  based on the above finger search is
  tyson@cpcug.org.
Continue the search ([n]/y) ? --> n
```

As I said, sometimes you can find out only what you already know. One thing that frustrates any attempt to use the OS/2 Telnet clients is the lack of a scrollback buffer. Notice the listing for all the possible sites for *gates*—there are more than 24. Moreover, efforts to pause the screen using Ctrl+S and using Command|Suspend from the menu were fruitless. If you need to find somebody, you can try Netfind at any of the following locations (the list of which usually is displayed when the Nefind server you try is too busy):

```
nsh: Too many Netfind sessions are active.  Please try again later.
Or, please try one of the Alternate Netfind servers:
        archie.au (AARNet, Melbourne, Australia)
        bruno.cs.colorado.edu (University of Colorado, Boulder, USA)
        dino.conicit.ve (Nat. Council for Techn. & Scien. Research, Venezuela)
        ds.internic.net (InterNIC Dir & DB Services, S. Plainfield, NJ, USA)
        eis.calstate.edu (California State University, Fullerton, CA, USA)
        krnic.net (Korea Network Information Center, Taejon, Korea)
        lincoln.technet.sg (Technet Unit, Singapore)
        malloco.ing.puc.cl (Catholic University of Chile, Santiago)
        monolith.cc.ic.ac.uk (Imperial College, London, England)
        mudhoney.micro.umn.edu (University of Minnesota, Minneapolis, USA)
        netfind.ee.mcgill.ca (McGill University, Montreal, Quebec, Canada)
        netfind.elte.hu (Eotvos Lorand University, Budapest, Hungary)
        netfind.fnet.fr (Association FNET, Le Kremlin-Bicetre, France)
        netfind.icm.edu.pl (Warsaw University, Warsaw, Poland)
        netfind.if.usp.br (University of Sao Paulo, Sao Paulo, Brazil)
        netfind.mgt.ncu.edu.tw (National Central University, Taiwan)
        netfind.sjsu.edu (San Jose State University, San Jose, CA, USA)
        netfind.vslib.cz (Liberec University of Technology, Czech Republic)
        nic.uakom.sk (Academy of Sciences, Banska Bystrica, Slovakia)
        redmont.cis.uab.edu (University of Alabama at Birmingham, USA)
```

Note well the first line, however. That's the response I got on each and every Netfind server I tried when I just created this listing. The server was kind enough to point me to a list of other, equally busy Netfind servers. Good luck!

The Other Telnet (Text Mode)

OS/2 also provides a text-mode version of telnet: `telnet.exe`. It works from the command line, as you might expect. A typical session looks very much like a typical TelnetPM session, except that you don't have a menu to help issue commands and save settings.

Note

> In fact, you can't save your settings at all, unless you have `setterm` and `termcfg.exe`, which are utilities that comes with the full IBM TCP/IP for OS/2 package. Without these utilities, using the text mode version can be a fairly frustrating experience. These programs are used for setting options for the text-mode telnet. Those options get saved into a file that can then be loaded using the `-f` command line option (discussed later). Unfortunately, `setterm` and `termcfg` don't come with the Warp IAK.

To start the text-mode telnet, enter **telnet** at the OS/2 command line. After you start telnet, the > prompt appears, as shown in Figure 10.18.

FIGURE 10.18.

The text-mode version of telnet prompts with > to show you are in command mode.

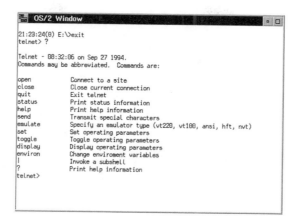

```
OS/2 Window

21:23:24(8) E:\>exit
telnet> ?

Telnet - 08:32:06 on Sep 27 1994.
Commands may be abbreviated.  Commands are:

open          Connect to a site
close         Close current connection
quit          Exit telnet
status        Print status information
help          Print help information
send          Transmit special characters
emulate       Specify an emulator type (vt220, vt100, ansi, hft, nvt)
set           Set operating parameters
toggle        Toggle operating parameters
display       Display operating parameters
environ       Change enviroment variables
!             Invoke a subshell
?             Print help information
telnet>
```

One of the first and most frequent things you'll probably enter is **?**. It will present a list of the telnet commands. These commands are listed in Table 10.2.

Table 10.2. Text-mode telnet commands.

Command	Meaning
open	Connect to a site.
close	Close current connection.
quit	Exit telnet.
status	Print status information.
help	Print help information.
send	Transmit special characters.
emulate	Specify an emulator type (VT220, VT100, ANSI, HFT, NVT).
set	Set operating parameters.
toggle	Toggle operating parameters.
display	Display operating parameters.
environ	Change environment variables.
!	Invoke a subshell.
?	Print help information.

Telnet works in two modes: online and command mode. After you're connected to a host, you get the command line of your host, rather than the telnet command line. Use the *escape sequence* to enter command mode if desired. By default, the escape sequence is Ctrl+] (that is, when you're online, you can get back into command mode by pressing Ctrl+]). When in command mode, you can get back to the online screen by pressing Enter at the > prompt.

Most of the telnet commands have subcommands. You can get a list of subcommands by typing **?**, the command name, and pressing Enter. For example, the following command shows a list of toggles:

```
telnet> ? toggle
Toggle operating parameters
autoflush      Toggle flushing of output when sending interrupt characters
crlf           Toggle sending carriage returns as telnet <CR><LF>
crmod          Toggle mapping of received carriage returns
localchars     Toggle local recognition of certain control characters
echo           Toggle local echo characters
bs             Toggle backspace key from ascii backspace to ascii delete
wrap           Toggle wrapping of long output lines
log            Toggle logging
debug          Toggle debugging
```

For instance, suppose you press the backspace key to delete a letter you typed, and you see a ^H instead of getting the character deleted. To toggle using the backspace for your intended purpose, do the following:

1. Press Ctrl+] to enter command mode.
2. Type **toggle bs** and press Enter.
3. Press Enter again.

To turn on logging, enter **toggle log** while in command mode. Telnet then prompts you for the name of the log file to create. Only the online session is logged. If you enter command mode, that part of the session is not included in the log.

Another useful thing to know about telnet is the **!** command. If—while connected via telnet—you need to perform other tasks outside of telnet, you can of course open another OS/2 command window. If you don't want to do that, however, you can enter command mode, type **!** and press Enter. This temporarily suspends telnet and puts you at the OS/2 command line. When you're done doing whatever needed to be done (talk about tautological!), type **exit** and press Enter to return to telnet.

You also can include various options and switches when you start telnet from the OS/2 command line. To see what's available, enter **telnet -?** at the OS/2 command line:

```
F:\TCPIP\etc>telnet -?
Telnet - 08:32:06 on Sep 27 1994.
Usage: telnet [-c codepage] [-d filename] [-e envlist]
              [-f config]   [-h height]   [-k keyboard]
              [-l filename] [-o printer]  [-p port]
              [-t termtype] [-u color]    [-w width]    [hostname]
Option:
       -?              display this help message
       -c codepage     specify code page translation table
       -d filename     specify debugging filename
       -e envlist      specify environment variables
```

```
-f config     specify configuration filename in <ETC> directory
-h height     specify screen height
-k keyboard   specify keyboard type
-l filename   specify logging filename
-o printer    specify local printer port name
-p port       specify remote port number
-t termtype   specify terminal emulator type
-u color      specify color for underline
-w width      specify screen width
```

From this, you can see that you can open a telnet session to a specific host, specifying a variety of information. If you prefer the text-mode version of telnet over TelnetPM, you could set up .CMD files to start your telnet sessions or Telnet program objects for specific sessions. To create a text-mode Telnet object to log on to your provider, for example, you could do the following:

1. Drag a template from the OS/2 Template folder to create a new object in any folder.

2. In the File/Program field (shown in Figure 10.19), type **c:\tcpip\bin\telnet.exe** (replace c as needed for your disk setup).

FIGURE 10.19.

Setting up a program object for TELNET.EXE.

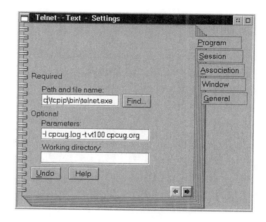

3. In the Parameters field, type any desired options, followed by the name of the host. For example, I might type **-l cpcug.log -t vt100 cpcug.org**. This says to create a log file called cpcug.log, to set the terminal emulation to vt100, and to log on to a host named cpcug.org.

4. In the Working directory field, type the location where you want the log file and any other files to be created during the telnet session.

5. Click on the Session tab to display the Session settings shown in Figure 10.20. Choose OS/2 Full Screen or OS/2 Window. Note that because TELNET.ICO is contained in the same directory as TELNET.EXE, the default Telnet icon automatically is assigned to the object the moment you click the Session tab.

6. Click the General tab. Replace the default name, Program, with something more useful.

7. Close the Settings notebook.

FIGURE 10.20.

Choose OS/2 Full Screen or OS/2 Window for the text-mode Telnet program reference object.

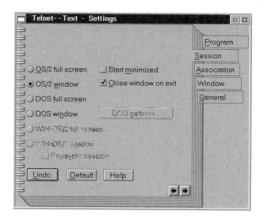

3270 Telnet (PM and Text Mode)

If you connect to a VM system or some other system that uses 3270 terminals, you can use the 3270 versions of telnet: PMANT.EXE (the PM version) or TN3270.EXE (the text-mode version). Using these versions, operation usually is full screen, whereas the non-3270 version usually is line oriented. I say *usually* because there are exceptions.

PMANT (3270 Telnet for PM)

Finding 3270 systems to log on to can be difficult. When you do find one, a PMANT session looks something like Figure 10.21. Using PMANT, you'll find that you can use the Tab key and cursor keys to move to the part of the screen you want.

FIGURE 10.21.

The PM version of 3270 Telnet.

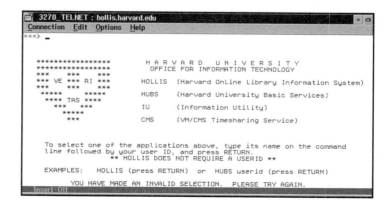

You also will be able to use the mouse. Mouse options are shown in Figure 10.22. You can bind mouse actions to any function key or to the Enter key. The default (Def) for mouse button 1, for example, is to move the text cursor to the location of the mouse click. If you instead wanted a single mouse button 1 click to press the F1 key, click Up/Down controls until F1 is displayed. Click on Apply to change the setting for this session only. Click on Save to change the setting now and save it for future settings.

Keyboard mappings are stored in `pmant.key`, which is located in the `set etc` directory (usually `tcpip\etc`, as set in your `CONFIG.SYS` file). `pmant.key` can be edited using an ordinary text editor such as TEDIT or the OS/2 System Editor. By default, only two keys are defined in the sample `pmant.key` that is provided with the Internet Access Kit. The format is as follows:

```
OS2_Key<space>3270_Function
```

For example, the following maps the Escape key to the 3270 `clear` function, and the Enter key to the 3270 `enter` function:

```
escape          clear    ; Esc key performs the Clear function
enter           enter    ; Enter key performs the Enter function
```

The word at the left is the key you press, and the word at the right is the function that `PMANT` performs. Available `os2_key` names are as follows:

F1 through F12
Control+F1 through Control+F12
Alt+F1 through Alt+F12
Shift+F1 through Shift+F12
Control+'*unshifted*_key'
Alt+'*unshifted*_key'

> The syntax for `pmant.key` requires that `Control` be spelled out. When I talk about the keys in general, I'll use normal OS/2 terminology, for example, Ctrl+S. When I specify the syntax needed in `pmant.key`, I'll use what's required, for example, `Control+S`.

Note

Note that you can redefine Ctrl+*unshifted_key* or Alt+*unshifted_key* so that the Shift key is not pressed. For example, you can map Ctrl+1 through Ctrl+0, but not Ctrl+! through Ctrl+) because the latter would really be Ctrl+Shift+1 and Ctrl+Shift+0, which aren't allowed.

The following are additional OS/2 key names:

Backspace	Esc
BackTab (same as Shift+Tab)	Home
Delete	Insert
Down	Left
End	Left-Alt
Enter	Left-Control

Newline	Right
PgUp	Right-Alt
PgDn	Right-Control
Pause	ScrLock
PrtScr	SpaceTab

The following are available 3270 functions that you can map to OS/2 keys:

Attn	Forward-Word
Backspace	Home
BackTab	Insert
Backward-Word	Kill-Word
Backward-Kill-Word	Left
Cent	Newline
Cursor-Move	PA1
Clear	PA2
Delete	PA3
Down	PF1–PF24
Dumpfields	Reset
Dup	Right
End	String
Enter	Sysreq
Erase-EOF	Tab
Erase-Input	Unlock
Field-Mark	Up

The system keys cannot be remapped; otherwise, they wouldn't be of any use to you in controlling the application from OS/2. These are the system keys:

System Key	Function
Alt+F4	Close application
Alt+F5	Restore from minimized or maximized state
Alt+F7	Move window
Alt+F8	Resize window
Alt+F9	Minimize window
Alt+F10	Maximize window
Shift+Escape	Menu
Ctrl+Escape	Window list

TN3270 (Text-Mode 3270 Telnet)

The text-mode version of 3270 Telnet works in a very similar way to the PM version. Three notable exceptions are as follows:

Key mappings	Identical to PMANT's, but stored in TN3270.KEY.
Mouse	Not available.
Menu	Activate using Ctrl+]; the menu is vertical, as shown in Figure 10.22.

FIGURE 10.22.

Activate text-mode 3270 Telnet's menu by pressing Ctrl+].

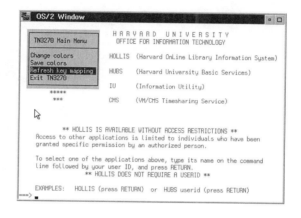

CHAPTER ELEVEN
OTHER WARP INTERNET TOOLS AND PROGRAMS

arp and assist

finger

host and hostname

ifconfig, ifolder, inetcfg, inetver, ipformat, and iptrace

linkup

makeidx

netstat and nslookup

ping and ppp

route

sendmail, slattach, slcfg, slip, sliphold, slipkill, slipmsg, and slipterm

tracerte

update

The OS/2 IAK is so well integrated and woven together that most users won't realize there are more than 60 different programs hard at work to keep it all together. Many of these components can be used directly by the user for exploration and problem solving. In this chapter, I describe some of these programs. Some of them are only marginally useful, but they might be of interest to curious minds.

Most of the OS/2 commands described in this section feature self-help. At the OS/2 command line, just enter the name of the command followed by -?. For example:

`E:\>ping -?`

When you do that, the ping command prints the syntax and options at the command line.

In this chapter, I show the syntax and explain what the command is used for, as well as provide some examples. The syntax usually is illustrated by showing you how to obtain the syntax online. Many of the commands have additional uses far beyond the examples shown here. For a complete reference for most of these, you should obtain the full IBM TCP/IP for OS/2 package. Note, however, that some of the commands described here are available only in Warp, so you won't find documentation for them in the full IBM TCP/IP package.

arp

The *arp* (Address Resolution Protocol) command shows or changes the address translation table used for the address resolution protocol. The arp command collects information from Internet hosts to build a mapping table that translates Internet addresses into hardware addresses. Syntax can be obtained by entering **arp -?** at the OS/2 command line:

```
E:\>arp -?
Usage:
      arp hostname
            Look up arp entry for host <hostname>.
      arp -a
            Print out all arp table entries.
      arp -f
            Flush all arp table entries.
      arp -d hostname
            Delete arp table entry for host <hostname>.
      arp -s hostname hardware_addr [temp] [pub]
            Add arp table entry for host <hostname>.
            temp  - timeout this entry if not used.
            pub   - reply for other host.

            Example:
                arp -s olegps2 66:11:12:12:11:22 temp

      arp -? Help.
```

assist

The `assist` program is the basis for the Customer Assistance object in the IBM Internet Customer Services folder. This program is for IBM Internet Dialer users only.

finger

The `finger` command is used to locate individual users on the Internet. The self-help syntax is

```
E:\>finger -?
Usage: finger [-?] [user@]<host>
        [user] - user to finger on remote host
        <host> - remote host to finger
        Options -
                -?              Display this message
```

The Internet provider system I access is provided for my users' group through Digex. Let's see if I can use `finger` to see what's happening on Digex right now, late on a Saturday afternoon:

```
E:\>finger access.digex.net
[access.digex.net]
Login      Name              TTY Idle   When     Where
rhopkins  Robert Hopkins     p0        Sat 15:53  pm5.digex.net
dfeola    dfeola             p1        Sat 16:06  pm4.digex.net
paulh     Paul Houghton      p2     9  Sat 16:28  pm5.digex.net
wavecorp  Wave Corp. Systems p3    13  Sat 16:32  204.7.141.100
lynch         ???           *p5        Sat 15:32  pm4.digex.net
marra     Mary E. Lauer      p6        Sat 15:59  pm4.digex.net
chds      Capitol Hill Day Sch p7     Sat 16:46  pm4.digex.net
kariane   katrina ariane     p8        Sat 16:44  pm5.digex.net
jasperc   Jasper Corrigan    pa        Sat 16:19  pm5.digex.net
crtcorp   Erik D. McWilliams pb        Sat 16:23  204.91.7.5
rjeffrey  Robert Jeffrey     pc        Sat 16:46  pm4.digex.net
nightman  Luke               pd        Sat 15:12  pm4.digex.net
sbender   Scott Bender       pe        Sat 16:39  harmony-ds.com
frampton  adam frampton      pf        Sat 16:44  pm5.digex.net
tgrover   Todd Michael Grover q0       Sat 16:44  pm5.digex.net
ch        Cathy Hong         q1        Sat 16:44  pm5.digex.net
reavin    Harris Reavin      q2        Sat 16:45  pm4.digex.net
lizard    smouldering dog   *q5        Sat 15:27  stripes.tigr.org
```

Well, it's pretty busy. I wonder if my acquisitions editor is on the Internet right now. Let's see:

```
E:\>finger markt@dorite.use.com
[markt@dorite.use.com]
Login      Name          TTY         Idle    When     Where
markt     Mark Taber     pts/36            <Jan 28 16:07> iq-ind-ts3.iques
```

There he is! What happens if I finger myself, so to speak:

```
E:\>finger tyson@cpcug.org
[tyson@cpcug.org]
Login name: tyson                      In real life: Herbert Tyson
Last login Fri Jan 27 23:24 on ttyp1 from tyson.cpcug.org
Plan:
To sleep, perchance to dream... once I finish this book!
```

This last one is interesting. What exactly is a Plan? And why, the first time I did a finger on my e-mail address, did it say that I had no plan? Because, strictly speaking, I didn't. Some systems support the use of .plan and .project files that you can put onto your UNIX provider system. These files originally were intended to provide a way for users with distinct secure accounts to share information. If your system supports this use of finger, then you, too, could have a plan.

To find out, you should log on to your shell account (assuming you have one), and enter **help plan-project** at the command line. Or, try to find help on the finger command. Or, if you don't see anything, ask your provider. Through persistence, I was able to cajole the following information on my shell account, by entering **help plan-project** as shown here:

```
cpcug shell 1  4:59pm  > help plan-project
New accounts on Express Access are set up such that each user's
directory and files cannot be read by other users, thus affording
maximum privacy.  This is accomplished in two ways: by limiting access
to your directory, and by making all new files unreadable by others.

These defaults prevent others from reading plan and project files.
These are two files, .plan and .project, which you may create in your
directory; they are seen by other users who run the "finger" command.

To allow other users to see your plan and project files, while
prohibiting access to all other files, run the following two commands:

    chmod go+r .plan .project
    chmod go+x .

The first command allows read access to users in your group, and all
other users.  The second command allows other users to search your
directory for specific files.
For more information on file protections in Unix, use the man command
to read the manual pages on the following commands:
    finger
    chmod
    umask
```

Armed with this information, I created a file that I named .plan and FTPed it to my home directory. Next, I use the chmod command to make the file available for anyone who issues the finger command followed by my e-mail ID. It's not the same as having a World Wide Web home page, but it'll do for a start.

host

The host command translates between host names and IP addresses. For example, you could use the host command to find out the IP address of ftp.ibm.net:

```
F:\TCPIP\BIN>host ftp.ibm.net
ftp01.ny.us.ibm.net is 165.87.194.246
```

If you reverse the process, host displays the obverse:

```
F:\TCPIP\BIN>host 165.87.194.246
165.87.194.246 is ftp01.ny.us.ibm.net
```

The host command can be useful when you have one type of Internet location and you need the other. The host command also is useful for building a list of aliases into your hosts file. By default, the hosts file (in \tcpip\etc) usually contains just your own IP number and host name. However, you can include in the hosts file any number of additional IP numbers and short-hand names that you want to be able to use to access those hosts. Suppose, for example, that you would like to be able to refer to ftp01.ny.us.ibm.net simply as ibm. You can do it. First, you use the host command to learn the IP number for ftp01.ny.us.ibm.net (as shown earlier), and then you use a text editor to add the following line to your hosts file:

```
165.87.194.246 IBM
```

You can create other useful aliases as well. I use the following aliases for accessing several popular resources:

```
128.123.35.151 hobbes
198.105.232.1 msftp
198.105.232.5 msweb
192.216.191.11 walnut
```

One additional use for the hosts file is to fix an occasional problem that some users have when sending mail while running TIA (The Internet Adapter). Sometimes, you might find that mail queues up but is never sent. A frequent cause of this is a failure of TCP/IP to resolve your host name. This often can be fixed simply by including the dummy IP number you use for TIA in your hosts file along with your mail ID. For example, if your e-mail address is smith@jones.com, then you might have the following in your hosts file. Note that 192.0.2.1 is used by many TIA users, as is 0.0.0.0.

```
192.0.2.1 smith
```

hostname

The hostname command requests that your name server resolve your host name based on your Internet address. The hostname has no parameters.

For example, if I enter **hostname** at the OS/2 command line with a SLIP connection running, the following happens:

```
F:\TCPIP\BIN>hostname
tyson.cpcug.org
```

ifconfig

The ifconfig command is most often used to set your IP and destination IP addresses when connecting via SLIP. Complete syntax is available by entering **ifconfig -?** at the OS/2 command line:

```
E:/>ifconfig -?
Usage: ifconfig interface
        [ [af] [ address [ dest_addr ] ] [ up ¦ down ][ netmask mask ]
        [ broadcast brd_addr ] ]
        [ metric n ]
        [ mtu    n ]
        [ trailers ¦ -trailers ]
        [ arp ¦ -arp ]
        [ -allrs ]
        [ bridge ¦ -bridge ]      [snap ¦ -snap ]
        [ icmpred ¦ -icmpred ]
        [ 802.3 ¦ -802.3 ]
        [ canonical  ¦ -canonical  ]
```

Typical usage in OS/2 is automatic, as done either by slippm or by a REXX script file. The usual command looks something like the following, where *ipaddr* is your IP address, and *ipdest* is the IP address of your gateway:

```
ifconfig sl0 ipaddr ipdest netmask 255.255.255.0
```

ifolder

Use the ifolder command to rebuild the IBM Internet Connection for OS/2 folder structure. Don't do this unless your IBM Internet Connection for OS/2 folder has been either lost (such as through a system crash), or otherwise ruined. To run the ifolder program, open an OS/2 command-line session and enter **ifolder**. It will rebuild your IBM Internet Connection for OS/2 folder.

Depending on the extent of your damaged or lost objects, you might also need to rebuild your Ultimedia Mail/2 Lite directory structure and objects. You use the makeidx command for that; see makeidx later in this chapter.

inetcfg

The `inetcfg` command currently can be used to set a `keepalive` timer. Some Internet providers automatically drop the modem connection if no activity is detected after a certain interval. Depending on the provider, the activity check might be set at 5-, 10-, 30-, or 60-minute intervals, or not at all. Some providers just implement a check during peak demand hours. You can use `inetcfg` to set the `keepalive` timer to any value between 0 and 120 minutes (if 0 is specified, the default 120 minutes is used). NewsReader/2 uses the `keepalive` timer to prevent a SLIP connection from disconnecting. This is set in the Options|NewsReader/2 dialog box. To use `keepalive` without having to use NR/2, enter the following command:

```
G:\>inetcfg keepalive=5
```

This command causes the `keepalive` timer to be set to five minutes. At present, the `keepalive` variable is the only command implemented for `inetcfg`.

inetver

The `inetver` command returns the current version of Inet:

```
G:\>inetver
Inet Version: 2.05h
```

Inet is one of the control programs used by the OS/2 Warp IAK at boot time.

ipformat

The `ipformat` command is used to trace the results of an `iptrace` command. If you are having difficulties with the transmission or reception of data over the Internet, your provider or someone else might ask you to run an `iptrace` to see what's happening during the data transfer. `ipformat` can then be used to make the `iptrace.dmp` file more manageable. The whole syntax for `ipformat` can be obtained by entering **ipformat -?** at the OS/2 command line.

A typical use of `ipformat` follows, where `iptrace.dmp` was generated during a failed FTP attempt from the WebExplorer:

```
g:\tcpip\bin>ipformat <iptrace.dmp
 Reading input file....  Please wait

------------------------------- #:1 -------------------------------------
  Delta Time:  0.000  Packet Length: 59 bytes (3B hex)
 SLIP: Not Compressed
 SLIP:  Dest: 164.109.001.003.    Source: 164.109.215.016.
-------------------- IP HEADER --------------------------
 IP:   Version: 4 Correct    Header Length: 20 bytes
 IP:   Type Of Service: 00
 IP:      000. ....   Routine
```

```
IP:     ...0 ....   Normal Delay
IP:     .... 0...   Normal Throughput
IP:     .... .0..   Normal Reliability
IP:  Total Len: 57 (x39) bytes          Id: 471E
IP:  Flags: 0
IP:     .0..        May Fragment
IP:     ..0.        Last Fragment
IP:  Fragment Offset: 000
IP:  Time To Live: 30 sec    Protocol: 11 (UDP)
IP:  Header Checksum: 34A8
IP:  No Options
-------------------- UDP HEADER --------------------
UDP:  Source Port: 1088    Dest Port: 53 (Domain NameServer)
UDP:  Length: 37 (x25)
UDP:  Checksum: 90AD
---------------------- DNS ----------------------
DNS: ID:3
DNS: Query    Standard Query
DNS: FLAGS: 10
DNS:    .0. .... = No Truncation
DNS:    ..1 .... = Recursion Desired
DNS: Return Code: 0  (No Error)
DNS: Question Cnt:  1,    Answer Cnt:  0
DNS: Authority Cnt:  0,   Additional Cnt:  0
DNS:  Question Section
DNS:    Name: ftp.ibm.net.
DNS:    Type: 01    Class: 01


---------------------------- #:2----------------------------
 Delta Time:  0.281  Packet Length: 189 bytes (BD hex)
SLIP: Not Compressed
SLIP:  Dest: 164.109.215.016.    Source: 164.109.001.003.
-------------------- IP HEADER --------------------
IP:  Version: 4 Correct    Header Length: 20 bytes
IP:  Type Of Service: 00
IP:     000. ....   Routine
IP:     ...0 ....   Normal Delay
IP:     .... 0...   Normal Throughput
IP:     .... .0..   Normal Reliability
IP:  Total Len: 179 (xB3) bytes *ERROR*  Id: 91D2
IP:  Flags: 0
IP:     .0..        May Fragment
IP:     ..0.        Last Fragment
IP:  Fragment Offset: 000
IP:  Time To Live: 58 sec    Protocol: 11 (UDP)
IP:  Header Checksum: CD79
IP:  No Options
-------------------- UDP HEADER --------------------
UDP:  Source Port: 53 (Domain NameServer)    Dest Port: 1088
UDP:  Length: 159 (x9F)   (fragmented packet)
UDP:  Checksum: 0
---------------------- DNS ----------------------
DNS: ID:3
DNS: Query Response    Standard Query
DNS: FLAGS: 18
DNS:    .0. .... = No Truncation
```

```
DNS:    ..1 .... = Recursion Desired
DNS:    ... 1... = Recursion Available
DNS: Return Code: 0  (No Error)
DNS: Question Cnt:  1,    Answer Cnt:  2
DNS: Authority Cnt:  2,   Additional Cnt:  2
DNS:   Question Section
DNS:     Name: ftp.ibm.net.
DNS:     Type: 01    Class: 01
DNS:   Answer Section
DNS:     Name: ftp.ibm.net.
DNS:     Type: 1   Class: 1
DNS:     TTL: 49164    Len: 0005

------------------------------ #:3 ------------------------------
 Delta Time:  0.000  Packet Length: 42 bytes (2A hex)
SLIP: Not Compressed
SLIP:  Dest: 165.087.194.246.    Source: 164.109.215.016.
------------------- IP HEADER --------------------
IP:   Version: 4 Correct    Header Length: 20 bytes
IP:   Type Of Service: 00
IP:     000. .... Routine
IP:     ...0 .... Normal Delay
IP:     .... 0... Normal Throughput
IP:     .... .0.. Normal Reliability
IP:   Total Len: 40 (x28) bytes        Id: 471F
IP:   Flags: 0
IP:     .0..      May Fragment
IP:     ..0.      Last Fragment
IP:   Fragment Offset: 000
IP:   Time To Live: 30 sec    Protocol: 06 (TCP)
IP:   Header Checksum: 71E5
IP:   No Options
------------------- TCP HEADER --------------------
TCP:   Source Port: 1042        Dest Port: 21   (FTP)
TCP:   Sequence #: 964428801
TCP:   Ack #: 0
TCP:   Offset: 20 bytes
TCP:   Flags: 02
TCP:     ..0. .... Urgent bit Off
TCP:     ...0 .... Ack bit Off
TCP:     .... 0... Push bit Off
TCP:     .... .0.. Reset bit Off
TCP:     .... ..1. Synchronize bit On
TCP:     .... ...0 Finish bit Off
TCP:   Window: 4096        Checksum: 7A72
TCP:   No Options
TCP:   No data in this packet.
```

Because the display of ipformat is fairly long, users generally redirect it to a file and then use a text editor or browser to look at it. For example, the following command puts the formatted iptrace.dmp into iptrace.out, which can then be browsed or studied at leisure:

```
G:\>ipformat <iptrace.dmp >iptrace.out
```

iptrace

The `iptrace` command is used to check the transmission of IP packets. Use `iptrace` without any parameters.

As shown in the following example, the output to the screen shows the IP addresses of any exchange. The meat of the `iptrace` is sent to `iptrace.dmp`, which is a binary file that only makes sense when displayed using `ipformat`. A typical `iptrace` session goes something like this:

```
F:\TCPIP\BIN>iptrace
sl0: tracing enabled
  sl0:[  0.000]:  Dest: 164.109.1.3     Source: 164.109.215.16
  sl0:[  0.312]:  Dest: 164.109.215.16   Source: 164.109.1.3
  sl0:[  0.063]:  Dest: 164.109.15.31    Source: 164.109.215.16
  sl0:[  0.187]:  Dest: 164.109.215.16   Source: 164.109.15.31
  sl0:[  0.000]:  Dest: 164.109.15.31    Source: 164.109.215.16
  sl0:[  0.469]:  Dest: 164.109.215.16   Source: 164.109.15.31
  sl0:[  0.000]:  Dest: 164.109.15.31    Source: 164.109.215.16
  sl0:[  0.312]:  Dest: 164.109.215.16   Source: 164.109.15.31
  sl0:[  0.000]:  Dest: 164.109.15.31    Source: 164.109.215.16
  sl0:[  0.282]:  Dest: 164.109.215.16   Source: 164.109.15.31
  sl0:[  0.187]:  Dest: 164.109.215.16   Source: 164.109.15.31
q
sl0: tracing disabled
the ip trace taken
```

When you think the trace has run long enough, you can just press Enter to stop it. In the third line from the bottom of this example, I typed **q** and pressed Enter, but Enter would have been enough.

linkup

The `linkup` command is used to start OS/2 Internet client programs such as Gopher, UltiMail, FTP-PM, and NewsReader/2. `linkup` verifies that a SLIP or PPP connection is running before starting the other program. If you are not connected, `linkup` displays the dialog box shown in Figure 11.1. When a connection is lost, `linkup` pops up to let you know. To start an application from the command line using `linkup`, you must specify the complete name (including the `.EXE`). If the application is in your path, you do not need to specify the disk and directory. For example, to use `linkup` to start the text-mode version of FTP, enter the following command:

`G:\>linkup ftp`

Many OS/2 IAK users survive quite nicely without `linkup`. `linkup` uses approximately 800KB of memory. If you can find a way to get along without it, your applications will certainly start faster, and will probably run faster as well. To see how you can set up all of the major OS/2 Internet applications to run without `linkup`, see the sidebar titled "For Experts Only" in Chapter 2, "The OS/2 Warp Internet Access Kit."

FIGURE 11.1.

The linkup *command checks to see if you are connected before launching a SLIP client.*

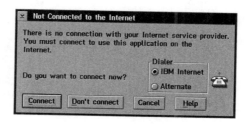

The only time when it might be useful to have linkup running is when you absolutely need to know when a connection drops. When linkup is running, it pops up a dialog box and sounds an audible alarm.

makeidx

Use the makeidx to rebuild the index for your mail directory. In the following, replace *userid* with your Internet login ID:

```
G:\>makeidx c:\tcpip\umail\mailstor\userid userid
```

Yes, you do type your user ID twice. For example, if your Internet login ID is gcsmith, then you would enter

```
G:\>makeidx c:\tcpip\umail\mailstor\gcsmith gcsmith
```

netstat

The netstat command gives a variety of network statistics. The syntax for netstat can be determined from the OS/2 command line as follows:

```
21:00:52(99) E:\>netstat -?
Usage: netstat [ -? ] ¦ [ -mtuisprcna ]

Where:
m - mbufs
t - tcp
u - udp
i - ip
s - sockets
r - routes
c - icmp
n - interfaces
a - address
p - arp
? - help
```

The parameters display various network statistics, as the name of the command implies. For example:

```
21:14:45(71) F:\TCPIP\BIN>netstat -r
   destination        router       refcnt        use flags    snmp  intrf
                                                               metric
   164.109.201.3  164.109.215.16      0           0   U         -1   sl0
        default    164.109.201.3      1          289  U         -1   sl0
```

Other parameters for the netstat command are as follows:

Parameter	Description
a	Address of network interfaces
c	Information about *Internet Control Message Protocol* (ICMP) statistics
i	Internet Protocol statistics
m	Memory buffer usage
n	Information about LANs
p	Shows the address resolution protocol table
r	Route information (as set by the ROUTE command)
s	Socket information
t	TCP connections
u	User Datagram Protocol statistics

nslookup

Use the nslookup (Name Server Lookup) command to resolve the IP addresses and names of Internet names and addresses. You can also use nslookup to get a list of hosts in a domain. This can be useful when you know the domain for an individual, but you don't know the host name. nslookup has two operational modes: single-command and interactive. To issue a single nslookup command, the syntax is:

nslookup [*options*] [*hostname*]

The following example shows the results of issuing this command for the host hobbes.nmsu.edu without any options:

```
F:\TCPIP\BIN>nslookup hobbes.nmsu.edu
Server:  kerberos.digex.net
Address:  164.109.1.3
Non-authoritative answer:
Name:    hobbes.nmsu.edu
Address:  128.123.35.151
```

To use nslookup in interactive mode, enter **nslookup** without any parameters. You will see the > prompt. While at the > prompt, you can issue any additional queries without having to enter nslookup again. You also can enter **?** at the > prompt to get a complete list of commands. For example:

```
F:\TCPIP\BIN>nslookup
>?
Default Server: kerberos.digex.net
Address:  164.109.1.3
> Commands:           (identifiers are shown in uppercase, [] means optional)
NAME              - print info about the host/domain NAME using default server
NAME1 NAME2       - as above, but use NAME2 as server
help or ?         - print info on common commands
set OPTION        - set an option
    all           - print options, current server and host
    [no]debug     - print debugging information
    [no]d2        - print exhaustive debugging information
    [no]defname   - append domain name to each query
    [no]recurse   - ask for recursive answer to query
    [no]vc        - always use a virtual circuit
    domain=NAME   - set default domain name to NAME
    srchlist=N1[/N2/.../N6] - set domain to N1 and search list to N1,N2, etc.
    root=NAME     - set root server to NAME
    retry=X       - set number of retries to X
    timeout=X     - set initial time-out interval to X seconds
    querytype=X   - set query type, e.g., A,ANY,CNAME,HINFO,MX,NS,PTR,SOA,WKS
    type=X        - synonym for querytype
    class=X       - set query class to one of IN(Internet),CHAOS,HESIOD or ANY
server NAME       - set default server to NAME, using current default server
lserver NAME      - set default server to NAME, using initial server
finger [USER]     - finger the optional NAME at the current default host
root              - set current default server to the root
ls [opt] DOMAIN [>|>> FILE] - list addresses in DOMAIN(optional: output to FIL
    -a            - list canonical names and aliases
    -h            - list HINFO (CPU type and operating system)
    -s            - list well-known services
    -d            - list all records
    -t TYPE       - list records of the given type (e.g., A,CNAME,MX, etc.)
view FILE         - sort an 'ls' output file and view it with more
exit              - exit the program
```

ping

The ping command sends an echo request to a remote system to find out if the system is on-line and accessible. ping stands for Packet InterNet Groper. Aren't you glad you asked? The syntax for ping can be obtained by entering **ping -?** at the OS/2 command line:

```
E:\>ping -?
Usage:  ping [-?drv] <host> [size [packets]]

Where:
d        - Turn debug on.
r        - Bypass the normal routing tables.
```

```
v        - Verbose output. Include all ICMP packets received.
host     - Destination.
size     - The size of data portion of the packet.
packets - The number of Echo Request packets to send.
```

ping commonly is used to try to determine why a particular login fails. For example, I just tried to connect to hobbes.nmsu.edu, but the connection was refused. Using ping, I can determine whether or not Hobbes is connected:

```
21:14:55(71) F:\TCPIP\BIN>ping hobbes.nmsu.edu
PING hobbes.nmsu.edu: 56 data bytes
```

After entering this command, nothing else happened, as is typical when a connection is not working for some reason. So, I tried a different address to make sure that my connection was okay:

```
21:29:39(0) F:\TCPIP\BIN>ping ftp.ibm.net 60 5
PING ftp01.ny.us.ibm.net: 60 data bytes
68 bytes from 165.87.194.246: icmp_seq=0. time=250. ms
68 bytes from 165.87.194.246: icmp_seq=1. time=250. ms
68 bytes from 165.87.194.246: icmp_seq=2. time=250. ms
68 bytes from 165.87.194.246: icmp_seq=3. time=250. ms
68 bytes from 165.87.194.246: icmp_seq=4. time=219. ms
— —ftp01.ny.us.ibm.net PING Statistics— —
5 packets transmitted, 5 packets received, 0% packet loss
round-trip (ms)  min/avg/max = 219/243/250
```

In the latter command, I told ping to send five packets of 60 bytes each. The output from ping shows that each packet took a quarter of a second or less for the round trip.

It's Ping Time!

Some users use ping to keep a SLIP connection alive. Unfortunately, the version of ping that comes with the IAK doesn't let you set a time interval for pinging. As a result, if you just enter **ping**, it will keep pinging continuously, often slowing down your session by using part of the bandwidth for pinging. You can use the following REXX program, however, to ping at regular intervals:

```
/* PingTime */
call RxFuncAdd 'SysLoadFuncs', 'RexxUtil', 'SysloadFuncs'
call SysLoadFuncs
parse arg host size numpak interval
if host='' then do
    say 'Syntax is: pingtime {hostname} {packetsize} {#-packets} {#-seconds}'
    say 'E.g.:    pingtime ftp.ibm.net 10 1 60'
end
```

```
else Do Forever
     'ping' host size numpak
     say 'Sleeping for' interval 'seconds—Press Ctrl+C to stop'
     call SysSleep interval
End
```

This REXX program uses the `SysSleep` function to wait after pinging. It then `pings` again at the interval you specify until you end the program (by pressing Ctrl+C, for example). Use any text editor to create a file called `pingtime.cmd` that contains the preceding code. To run it, enter the following (at the OS/2 command line):

```
pingtime hosthame size number time
```

In this command, the following placeholders are used:

`hostname`	The name or IP number for the host you want to ping.
`size`	The size of the data packet to use.
`number`	The number of packets per `ping` execution.
`time`	The amount of time to wait between successive `ping` executions.

For example, to ping xxx.yyy.com every 60 seconds with one 64-byte packet, enter

pingtime xxx.yyy.com 64 1 60

Having done that, `pingtime` will execute the following command once every minute:

```
ping xxx.yyy.com 64 1
```

To make this really useful, you might create an OS/2 program object where `pingtime.cmd` is the program, and use the parameters you want to generate the ping you need to keep your connection open. I created an object called Ping60 in my IBM Internet Connection for OS/2 folder. It just pings my nameserver once a minute. When I need it, I just double-click its icon.

PPP

The `ppp` command is similar in concept to the `slip` command, but it starts a PPP session. `ppp` command syntax is available at the OS/2 command line by entering **ppp -?**:

```
E:\>ppp -?
Usage: ppp [options], where options are:
        <device>        Communicate over the named device
        <speed>         Set the baud rate to <speed>
        <ip>:<ipdest>   Set the local and/or remote interface IP
                        addresses.  Either one may be omitted.
        asyncmap <n>    Set the desired async map to hex <n>
        auth            Require authentication from peer
        connect "cmd"   Invoke command cmd to set up the serial line
                           Ex. connect "slattach atdt9,999-9999 CONNECT"
        defaultroute    Add default route through interface
        file <f>        Take options from file <f>
```

```
idle <n>        Set the idle timeout period to <n> minutes.
modem           Set/Reset modem control lines
mru <n>         Set MRU value to <n> for negotiation
netmask <n>     Set interface netmask to <n>
notify          Display notification message when DCD signal drops
priority <n>    Set process scheduling priority to <n>
rtscts          Use hardware RTS/CTS flow control
silent          Don't send connect request to peer, wait for request
```

Note

When using REXX scripts with ppp, all SLIP functions must be changed to their PPP counterparts:

SLIP	PPP
SLIP_COM_OUTPUT	PPP_COM_OUTPUT
SLIP_COM_INPUT	PPP_COM_INPUT
SLIP_GETCH	PPP_GETCH

route

The route command is used to change the network routing tables. When running under slip or ppp, routing information is kept in memory as part of the TCP/IP stack. The route command ensures that your Internet gateway is correctly defined. Syntax for route can be obtained by entering **route -?** at the OS/2 command line:

```
e:\>route -?
Usage:
route [-fh?] (add ¦ delete) (net ¦ host ¦ subnet) (<destination> ¦ default)
     <router> [<metric>]

Where:
   -?         Displays this message.
   -f         Flushes network entries in the routing table prior to this entry.
   -h         Flushes host entries in the routing table prior to this entry.
   add        To add a route.
   delete     To delete a route.
   net        To add or delete a network.
   subnet     To add or delete a subnet.
   host       To add or delete a host.
   destination Is the destination host or network.
   default    All destinations not defined with another routing
              table entry.
   router     Is the next-hop in the path to the destination.
   metric     Number of hops to destination.  Metric is
              required for add commands.

Example:   route -fh add net 129.34.10.0 129.34.10.60 1
```

Under OS/2 Warp's IAK, the most commonly used form of the route command is something like this:

```
e:\>route add default 164.109.201.3 1
```

This example adds 164.109.201.3 as the default route for all destinations that aren't otherwise defined in the routing table. The metric tells the routing table how far this address is from your own IP address—one *hop* in this case. The hop count is the number of bridges a frame passes through on the way to its destination. A *bridge* is a connection between two computers, and a *frame* is the basic information unit sent over TCP/IP.

sendmail

The sendmail command can be used to send mail without Ultimedia Mail/2 Lite. The syntax for the sendmail command is:

```
sendmail -af letterfile -f [toaddress fromaddress][-t]
```

You can specify the addresses either in the -f section, or in the letter itself. If you specify the addresses in the letter, use the -t switch to tell sendmail to read the addresses from the file. For example, for jsmith@smith.com to mail the contents of message.dat to jjones@jones.net, he could enter this command (exactly as shown here, including the angle brackets (< >) and quotes):

```
e:\>sendmail -af message.dat -f "John Smith" <jsmith@smith.com> "Jim Jones"
➥<jjones@jones.net>
```

Or, if the to and from addresses are contained at the top of message.dat, as they are here:

```
From:"John Smith" <jsmith@smith.com>
To:"Jim Jones" <jjones@jones.net>
```

then he could enter the following command:

```
e:\>sendmail -af message.dat -t
```

If you're having problems with UltiMail, you might try sending yourself a message to see if anything is getting through. In order to use the sendmail command, you must have a sendmail.cf file in your etc directory. The sendmail.cf file uses the same format as sendmail.uml (also in the etc directory). So, you can create sendmail.cf simply by copying sendmail.uml. Once the file is copied, you then need to find and modify the following lines to insert the name of your mail relay and your mail hub:

```
# The unqualified (domain-less) name of the mail relay
Dvmail-relay
# The fully-qualified domain name of the mail hub
Dhmail-hub
```

For example, for my own setup, my *mail-relay* and *mail-hub* are the same as my domain— yours might be, too; but, possibly not. You can find out from your Internet provider. In my case, the two lines became the following:

```
DVcpcug.org
Dhcpcug.org
```

To send mail using `sendmail`, you create a text file with your message in it. The easiest way is to put the To and From addresses in it as well. For example, to test this, I put the following three lines in a file called TEST.LTR:

```
To: "Herb Tyson" <tyson@cpcug.org>
From: "Herb Tyson also" <tyson@cpcug.org>
Hi, Herb. This is a test. Didja get it?
```

I then sent it to myself with the `sendmail` command, and the session looked like this:

```
f:\tcpip\bin>sendmail -af test.dat -t
IBM OS/2 SENDMAIL VERSION 1.3.6)

reading f:\tcpip\etc\sendmail.cf 10
```

That's all. When the command finished, I refreshed the In-basket in Ultimedia Mail/2 Lite, and the letter was waiting for me.

slattach

The `slattach` command can be used to initiate a SLIP connection. When using the Dial Other Internet Provider dialer (SLIPPM), the `slattach` is most often used by SLIPPM when it issues the SLIP command. The syntax for `slattach` can be obtained at the OS/2 command line, as follows:

```
f:\tcpip\bin>slattach -?
slattach Version 2.0 Revision:   1.3  24 Oct 1994 10:24:58
Usage: slattach [options] <attach-script>, where options are:
-?               Usage options
-f <resp file>   Read attach-script from response file <resp file>
-l <lock-file>   Set lock-file on comport
-p <comport>     Use comport <comport>
-t <timeout>     Timeout comport read after <timeout> seconds (default 60)
-v               Verbose mode

<attach-script> [SendString ExpectString] [SendString ExpectString] ...
<esc-sequence>  [\d]    2 second delay
                [\n]    CRLF
                [\q]    toggle quiet mode
                [\r]    CR
                [\s]    space
                [^<c>]  Send Control <c>
```

When you put a script into the Login Sequence field in the Dial Other Internet Provider dialer, that script ultimately is fed to `slattach`. In order for `slattach` to work, `slip` must already have been started with the appropriate parameters. The most efficient way to run `slattach` is as a parameter to the SLIP invocation. If the following `slattach` command will connect and log in, it also can be combined with a `slip` command:

```
slattach -p com2 at&f OK atz OK atdt5551515 NNECT \r login: shexx assword: \r
➥login: smith assword: htims32 homeb tia \r
```

So, rather than first running `slip` and then running `slattach`, you could do it all at once:

```
slip -com2 -mtu 1006 -nocfg -connect "slattach -p com2 at&f OK atz OK
➦atdt5551515 NNECT \r login: shexx assword: \r login: smith assword:
➦htims32 homeb tia \r
```

This, alone, is not adequate to start a SLIP session. In addition, you would need to issue the appropriate ifconfig and route commands. Even then, it's possible that your mailer and other software wouldn't work, to the extent that they get information from tcpos2.ini, which is set by SLIPPM. In any event, if you *need* to delve into the workings of the OS/2 IAK, you'll need to look at `slattach`.

slcfg

The `slcfg` command is used to test the formatting of the `slip.cfg` file, as shown in the following example. If the `slip.cfg` file was set up incorrectly, `slcfg` should tell you pretty quickly.

```
f:\tcpip\etc>slcfg slip.cfg
Parsing file:
  INTERFACE:
    Name = sl0
    Device = com2
    MTU = 1006
    RTT (rtt,var,min) = 0, 0, 0
    Pipe (send, recv) = 0, 4096
    SSThresh = 0
    MaxQueue = 12
    MaxFastQ = 24
    UseFastQ = 1
    Compression = 0
    Attachcmd = '(None)'
    Attachparms = 'com2 38400'
    IPaddress = '164.109.215.16'
    IPdest    = '164.109.201.3'
```

slip

The `slip` command is used to start a SLIP session. You can get the syntax for `slip` by entering **slip -?** at the OS/2 command line, as follows:

```
f:\tcpip\etc>slip -?

    SL/IP     OS/2 TCP/IP Multiple Interface SLIP Driver
    2.00      Copyright(c) IBM Corp. 1993, 1994
              Revision:   1.23   28 Nov 1994 11:05:58

Usage: slip [options], where options are:
 -?                        Usage help.
 -com<n>                   Use com port <n> for interface sl0.
 -connect "command"        Invoke command to setup modem connection.
 -d                        Increase debug level.
```

```
-exit <timeout>              Exit SL/IP <timeout> minutes after line disconnect.
-f <config file>             Use <config file> instead of default: slip.cfg.
-hangup <command>            Send <command> to sl0 com port on exit.
-idle <timeout>              Exit SL/IP after <timeout> minutes of idle time.
-ifconfig <ipaddr> <ipdest>  Configure sl0 with the specified IP addresses,
          +defaultroute      optionally add a default route through <ipdest>,
          +proxyarp          make a proxy ARP entry for <ipdest> using <ipaddr>.
-modem <command>             Send modem <command> to interface sl0 com port.
-mtu <size>                  Set interface sl0 MTU to <size>.
-nocfg                       Ignore configuration file.
-notify                      Notify on termination of Data Carrier Detect.
-p<n>                        Run SL/IP at priority <n>, where <n> =1-4. If <n>
                             is ommitted run in time critical server mode, <n>=3.

-rtscts                      Use RTS/CTS hardware flow control.
-speed <baud>                Set sl0 com port speed to <baud>.
-t[i¦o]                      Trace input and output packets.
-vj                          Use VJ header compression for interface sl0.
```

To prepare for using `slattach` or `slipterm`, you might issue a command such as the following:

```
F:\TCPIP\BIN>slip -com2 -mtu 1006 -nocfg
```

When a SLIP session is successfully launched, you see something like this:

```
SL/IP        OS/2 TCP/IP Multiple Interface SLIP Driver
2.00         Copyright(c) IBM Corp. 1993, 1994
             Revision:   1.23   28 Nov 1994 11:05:58
Current bit rate is 57600

[MON ] SLIP Driver Running.  Exit with Ctrl-C or Ctrl-Break
```

When running `slip` manually, you should return to this screen to close the connection. When you press Ctrl+C, the connection is terminated.

sliphold

The `sliphold` command is used to hold a COM port connection open when the SLIP driver is stopped. This lets you start and stop SLIP without breaking the connection. A `sliphold` command is usually followed by with a `slipkill` command. The syntax for `sliphold` can be obtained from the OS/2 command line by entering **sliphold -?**:

```
F:\TCPIP\BIN>sliphold -?
Usage: sliphold [-f <config file>] [interface]
        -f <config file>  - Name of configuration file to use.
                            slip.cfg is the default.
        interface         - Interface name to select, sl0-sl9.
```

slipkill

The `slipkill` command is used to kill a running `slip` driver. Use the `slipkill` command without any parameters to remove the `slip` driver from memory (that is, to kill it). Enter **slipterm -id** to obtain the OS/2 process ID for any `slip` drivers that are open. Enter **slipterm -?** to find out the preceding:

```
F:\TCPIP\BIN>slipkill -?
slipkill [options]: Terminate SLIP driver.
where [options] are:
-?          Usage information.
-id         Return process ID of SLIP driver, do not terminate driver.
```

slipmsg

The `slipmsg` program is used by the system (by `linkup`, for example) to notify you that the SLIP connection has been broken. You can use `slipmsg` on the command line all by itself while SLIP is running to give yourself a bogus disconnection message.

slipterm

The `slipterm` program is a fully manual method for connecting with your Internet provider. The use of `slipterm` was discussed also in Chapter 3, "The IBM Internet Connection." As with `slattach`, `slipterm` requires that SLIP has already been started. The syntax for `slipterm` can be obtained by entering **slipterm -?** at the OS/2 command line, as follows:

```
F:\TCPIP\etc>slipterm -?
SLIPTERM 2.01.6  - OS/2 TCP/IP
Provides a simple terminal session with the COM port that is associated with
the SLIP interface defined in the slip configuration file.
Usage: slipterm [-d] [-w##] [-f config] [com<n>] [interface]
where: -d   - debug mode.  The SLIP driver does not need to be running.
       -w## - wait mode.   SLIPTERM will wait ## seconds for the SLIP driver
                           to have completed startup.
       -f <config file> - Name of configuration file to use.
                           slip.cfg is the default.
       com<n>           - Com port to access
       interface        - Interface name to select, sl0-sl9.
```

`slipterm` is most often used for diagnosing connection problems and developing logon scripts. Because `slipterm` requires that SLIP already be running, one way to start `slipterm` is in tandem with a `slip` command. For example, the following command starts a SLIP in a background window:

```
F:\TCPIP\BIN>start slip & slipterm -w 10 com2 interface sl0
```

It then starts slipterm, but instructs slipterm to wait for up to 10 seconds to give slip a chance to get started. Once slipterm is active, you can dial. A typical slipterm session might look like this:

```
F:\TCPIP\etc>start slip&slipterm -w 10 com2 interface sl0
 Waiting for SLIP - maximum wait = 30 seconds ]
————————————————————————————————————————+
 SLIPTERM 2.01.6  - OS/2 TCP/IP               (using com2) |
————————+——————————————————————————————————+
   Key   |        Action                                  |
————————+——————————————————————————————————+
  F10    | Successful exit (continues TCP/IP setup)        |
  ESC    | Unsuccessful exit (aborts TCP/IP setup)         |
  other  | Sent to COM port unchanged.                     |
————————+——————————————————————————————————+
 Requesting COM port access from SLIP driver ]
 SLIP driver granted access ]
 Startup Complete ]
atdt3012200258
CONNECT 14400/REL-LAPM-COMP
Express Access Online Communications Service 301-220-2020
         Communication settings are Eight bits no parity.
         Don't have an account?  Login as new (no password).

access login:s01356
Password:<suppressed>
SL/IP session from (164.109.201.7) to 164.109.215.16 beginning....
[ Shutdown Complete]
F:\TCPIP\etc>ifconfig sl0 164.109.215.16 164.109.201.3 netmask 255.255.255.0
F:\TCPIP\etc>route add default 164.109.201.3 1
```

Note that after I got the SL/IP session from message, I pressed the F10 key, whereupon the Shutdown Complete message appeared. The latter means a shutdown of slipterm—not of your OS/2 system.

tracerte

Use the tracerte command to find the path that IP transmissions have to follow to a given host or destination. For example, to trace the part from my IP to Hobbes:

```
F:\TCPIP\BIN>tracerte hobbes.nmsu.edu
traceroute to hobbes.nmsu.edu (128.123.35.151), 30 hops max, 38 byte packets
 0  * * *
 1  pm3.digex.net (164.109.201.8)  218 ms  188 ms  187 ms
 2  littleboy.digex.net (164.109.20.15)  219 ms  188 ms  187 ms
 3  enss230.digex.net (164.109.1.1)  219 ms  219 ms  188 ms
 4  t1-3.cnss59.Washington-DC.t3.ans.net (140.222.59.4)  218 ms  219 ms  218 ms
 5  mf-0.cnss56.Washington-DC.t3.ans.net (140.222.56.222)  219 ms  219 ms  219
    ms
 6  t3-1.cnss72.Greensboro.t3.ans.net (140.222.72.2)  219 ms  219 ms  219 ms
 7  t3-0.cnss104.Atlanta.t3.ans.net (140.222.104.1)  250 ms  219 ms  219 ms
```

```
 8   t3-2.cnss64.Houston.t3.ans.net (140.222.64.3)  250 ms  219 ms  250 ms
 9   t3-0.cnss112.Albuquerque.t3.ans.net (140.222.112.1)  281 ms  313 ms  250 ms
10   cnss116.Albuquerque.t3.ans.net (140.222.112.196)  281 ms  250 ms  250 ms
11   enss365.t3.ans.net (192.103.74.46)  250 ms  250 ms  344 ms
12   LAWR.NM.ORG (129.121.1.1)  281 ms  250 ms  250 ms
13   UNM-Technet.az.westnet.net (204.134.77.122)  282 ms  250 ms  250 ms
14   NRAO-UNM.az.westnet.net (204.134.77.130)  282 ms  250 ms  281 ms
15   192.65.78.9 (192.65.78.9)  281 ms  250 ms  250 ms
```

update

The update program is the engine for the Retrieve Software Updates program. Use the update program to list available updates to the Warp IAK on the IBM Gopher. You can obtain the syntax for update by entering **update -?** at the OS/2 command line. You will see a dialog box containing the following:

```
update [-h host] [-l path] [-l1:filename] [-p port] [-s sel] [-t path]
```

To start the default update for the Retrieve Software Updates object, you could enter the following from the OS/2 command line:

```
C:\>update -h  updates.gopher.ibm.com
```

As noted in Chapter 7, "Navigating with OS/2 Gopher," in order to access the software updates without using the update program, you need to set the port to 77 instead of the default Gopher port (which is 70). To access these files using the WebExplorer, you would specify the URL as gopher://updates.gopher.ibm.com:77.

CHAPTER
TWELVE
ADDITIONAL INTERNET APPLICATIONS AND RELATED UTILITIES

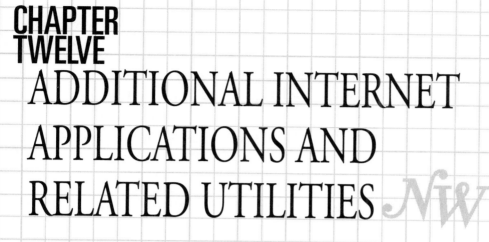

OS/2 Applications

DOS and Windows TCP/IP Applications Under OS/2

Does the OS/2 Internet Access Kit satisfy all of your wants and needs, or does it leave you wanting more? There is more! In this chapter, I'll survey some of what's out there, and try to give a mini-review of the alternatives and additions. Each of the shareware or demo versions of OS/2 programs mentioned is available at a number of Internet FTP sites.

For your convenience, nearly all these programs are available at the Sams *Navigating the Internet Software Library,* located at the Macmillan Computer Publishing Internet site, which is accessible through the World Wide Web or by FTP:

World Wide Web   `http://www.mcp.com/sams/software/netos2.html`
Look under "Internet" in the Software Library.

FTP   `ftp.mcp.com`
Look in `/pub/sams/internet/os2`.

When you go to retrieve a file, you may discover that a filename has changed. This usually happens because the software has been updated, and the version of the software is a part of the filename. You won't have to worry about this if you retrieve the files through our Web page. If you're retrieving files by FTP, read the `INDEX.TXT` file in the `/pub/sams/internet/os2` directory for updated information on these files.

Other popular Internet sites for OS/2 software are:

Hobbes   `hobbes.nmsu.edu`
Walnut Creek   `ftp.cdrom.com`
IBM Watson   `software.watson.ibm.com`
OS/2 Shareware BBS   `bbs.os2bbs.com` (FTP not available; direct dialup is 703-385-4325)

OS/2 Applications

As noted elsewhere in this book, the OS/2 Warp Internet Access Kit is largely based on IBM's TCP/IP for OS/2 package. Over the past several years, a trickle of shareware and commercial applications appeared on the OS/2 front to complement, augment, and even replace some of the TCP/IP SLIP client applications that come with TCP/IP for OS/2. With the advent of OS/2 Warp, that trickle has become more of a torrent in recent months. In this section, I'll tell you about some of what's available, and show you where to find it.

NetSuite 1.0 for OS/2 by NeoLogic Software

What began as the LA series of applications—LA Times, LA Gopher, and LA FTP—last year was renamed as NetSuite, featuring NetSuite News, Gopher, and FTP. This set of applications from NeoLogic Software offers alternatives to NewsReader/2, OS/2 Gopher, and FTP-PM. NetSuite is a commercial product. A 30-day demonstration version is available for downloading (see the name and location at the end of this section).

Each of the NetSuite clients has a control panel, as shown in Figure 12.1. You use the control panels to pop up a list of choices, or to access special Settings notebooks. For changing the appearance of the NetSuite applications, unlike the clients that come with OS/2 Warp, the NetSuite applications are more fully integrated into OS/2. For example, if you don't like the colors or fonts, you don't have to fumble around with limited choices. Just use the OS/2 font and color palettes to decorate NetSuite however you like.

FIGURE 12.1.

Each of the NetSuite applications has its own control panel.

As shown in Figure 12.2, the FTP client offers a different twist. Rather than having to clutter up a folder with a number of different customized FTP-PM objects (or clutter your brain remembering all of the different names), the NetSuite FTP program maintains a list of FTP servers. When you start NetSuite FTP, you choose the desired FTP from the list. The pulldown Type list also lets you connect to a variety of different types of FTP servers: UNIX, OS/2 IBM TCP/IP, PC/TCP, DEC VMS, IBM VM, Novell Netware FTP, and Microsoft Windows NT. Of course, if you don't have the foggiest idea what kind of server you're connecting to, there's always Auto Detect (a NetSuite FTP option that automatically determines the type of server).

FIGURE 12.2.

NetSuite FTP lets you choose FTP sites from a list.

NetSuite FTP also features a console window (shown in Figure 12.3) that shows you exactly what dialog is taking place between your system and the FTP site. No more guessing about what's happening. Another nice enhancement is a built-in *parent* directory icon that makes it easier than using the IAK's FTP-PM to return to the next-highest level.

FIGURE 12.3.

NetSuite FTP features a console for observing the dialog between client and server.

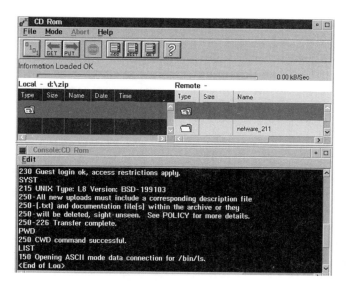

Product Information

Availability: At the Sams *Navigating the Internet* Software Library

Filename: NSUITE1B.ZIP

Note

The version of NetSuite that's available for download is a demo version of a commercial product—not shareware. When you install and use the components, a 30-day timer is started. After 30 days, the demo version can no longer be used. At this writing, NetSuite writes the starting reference date into the extended attributes for a file in your \os2\boot subdirectory on your root drive. This action does not affect your system's ability to run. The normally accepted vehicles for creating software expiration timers are *.INI files, such as OS2.INI. However, because many users have figured out how to use INI file editors to erase software expiration dates, companies such as NeoLogic have resorted to other methods for ensuring that software isn't used beyond the intended demonstration period.

IBM TCP/IP

The OS/2 Warp IAK's elder sibling, IBM OS/2 TCP/IP 2, might be considered either an alternative to the IAK, or a heftier foundation. If you want to run the IAK applications over a LAN, or if you want to run server applications, you need to obtain the full TCP/IP program. Like the IAK, TCP/IP comes with FTP, telnet, and a newsreader.

The mail application that comes with IBM TCP/IP—LAMAIL—is somewhat faster and leaner than Ultimedia Mail/2 Lite, but it lacks some of the features as well. It does, however, offer what many users find to be a much more useful approach to creating text notes. As shown in Figure 12.4, LAMAIL hijacks OS/2's Enhanced PM (EPM) editor for creating mail. If you acquire the EPM spelling and thesaurus extensions for EPM, this provides a way of ensuring fewer typos when composing e-mail missives.

FIGURE 12.4.

IBM TCP/IP 2's LAMAIL commandeers EPM as a mail editor, adding a Mail item to the menu.

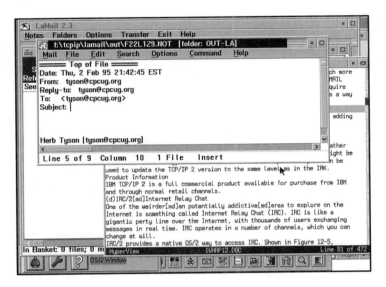

TCP/IP 2 does not have a Gopher client, nor does it come with the WebExplorer. However, it does work well with the IAK's Gopher and WebExplorer. The version of NewsReader/2 that comes with TCP/IP is rather different from the version that ships with the IAK. That, however, might be considered transitory, because the Retrieve Software Updates object can be used to update the TCP/IP 2 version to the same level as in the IAK.

According to IBM, using TCP/IP and the OS/2 Warp IAK together is not sup-ported. Many users, however, report success in combining the two if they first apply the TCP/IP 64092 CSD (August 1994 Corrective Service Diskettes) to TCP/IP version 2.0, and then install the Warp IAK on top of it to the same directory. I can-not attest to whether or not this works or how well it works, however. If you try it, make sure you back everything up before proceeding. Note also that the procedure very likely will change when TCP/IP version 3.0 and OS/2 Warp Connect (formerly known as OS/2 LAN Client) become available.

Product Information

IBM TCP/IP 2 is a full commercial product available for purchase from IBM as well as through normal retail channels.

IRC/2: Internet Relay Chat

One of the weirder—and potentially more addictive—areas to explore on the Internet is something called Internet Relay Chat (IRC). IRC is like a gigantic party line over the Internet, with thousands of users exchanging messages in real time. IRC operates in a number of *channels*, which you can change at will.

IRC/2 provides a native OS/2 way to access IRC. Shown in Figure 12.5, messages posted by other chatters stream above. Users exchange questions, comments, tips, and jibes in a fast-paced repartee. You compose your replies on the bottom line, and dispatch them with a press of the Enter key.

FIGURE 12.5.

Join the party with Internet Relay Chat. It's truly weird, and addictive.

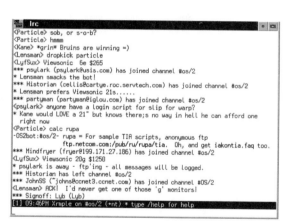

Product Information

Availability: At the Sams *Navigating the Internet* Software Library

Filename: IRC2_010.ZIP

HTMLGen 1.05: An HTML Script Generator

HTMLGen is a quick and easy way to create your own World Wide Web masterpieces—providing you have a way to make it available for public access (see Chapter 8, "Navigating the Web with the WebExplorer"). With HTMLGen, you won't have to learn the ins and outs of HTML. Using the simple menus, you can build an impressive HTML page in a matter of minutes.

HTMLGen provides an editable entry window (see Figure 12.6). Completely menu driven, HTMLGen offers support for the complete HTML tag set. To insert an inline graphic, for example, just click Images, Inline, and fill out the filename. You can even browse your hard disk to find it. Nothing could be simpler.

FIGURE 12.6.

HTMLGen 1.05—a Web page builder.

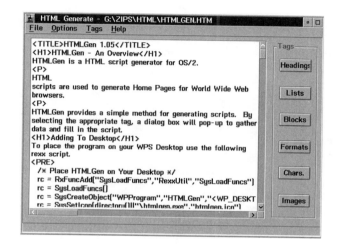

Product Information

Availability: At the Sams *Navigating the Internet* Software Library

Filename: `HTMLG105.ZIP`

SIO and Vmodem

Many OS/2 users long ago discovered that the default communications drivers—COM.SYS and VCOM.SYS (the latter for virtual DOS sessions running under OS/2)—do not always deliver peak performance, especially when attempting high-speed communications with DOS and Windows applications running under OS/2. In particular, when running DOS and Windows communications programs above 9600 baud without a 16550 UART-based COM port, users noted numerous errors due to dropped characters.

In response to this, independent programmer Ray Gwinn developed the SIO (Serial Input/Output) and VSIO (Virtual Serial Input/Output) drivers for OS/2. Mr. Gwinn's drivers are designed to work with 8250-type serial I/O devices, which embrace most PC-compatible systems using 8250, 9250A, 16450, 16550, 16550A, and 82510 communications chips. The SIO drivers deliver higher performance (for most users) than the default COM.SYS and VCOM.SYS drivers. These benefits are measurable for OS/2, DOS, and Windows programs running under OS/2. In exchange for an installation procedure that takes less than five minutes, OS/2 users discover that communications programs they had given up on suddenly work.

Note

Compatibility with the COM.SYS and VCOM.SYS drivers is not 100 percent (deliberately), and not all communications programs can use the SIO drivers. However, except as noted, most people who install and use the SIO drivers notice only benefits and experience few, if any, problems.

As noted in Chapter 3, "The IBM Internet Connection," some users need to add a line to set DTR to ON on their communications port in order to get SIO to work properly with the dialers provided with the IAK. A few users might find some incompatibilities between their modems (the Intel 144/144e, for one) and the SIO drivers when using certain programs.

However, because the demonstration versions of the SIO drivers have a reasonably long trial period, you should be able to evaluate whether they work for your system before you need to register them. Thus, unlike regular commercial software, you won't have to buy a *pig in a poke*.

In addition to the SIO and VSIO drivers themselves, Ray Gwinn's enhancements include the following:

PMLM   Poor Man's Line Monitor. This program, shown in Figure 12.7, monitors the state of the communications port and the flow of all data. PMLM enables you to see every byte of data that goes in and out of your COM port. Using the tools provided with SIO, this makes it possible to quickly track down problems with communications.

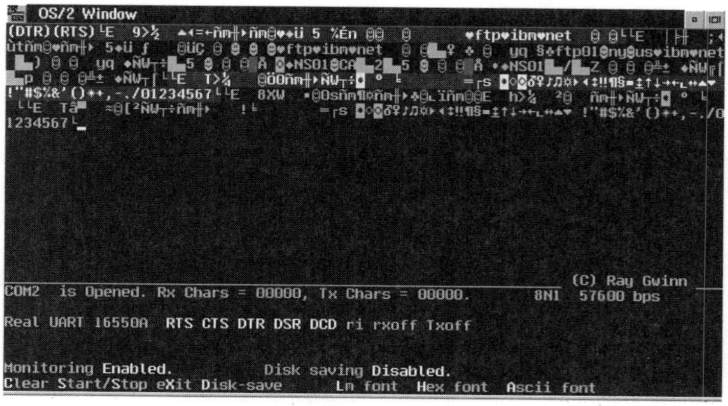

FIGURE 12.7.

The Poor Man's Line Monitor shows you what's really going through your COM port!

Vmodem   The Virtual Modem. Vmodem allows ordinary communications programs—such as HyperAccess Lite, PMComm, ZapOCom, and others—to operate as telnet clients. Chapter 10, "Connecting to Other Systems Using Telnet," mentions some of the limitations: the lack of a scrollable window, and the lack of file handling capabilities (Zmodem, Ymodem, Kermit, and so on). Vmodem lets your normal communications program communicate over the Internet with any Internet telnet host.

What does this mean? This means that you can use your normal communications programs—including the CompuServe Information Manager for OS/2—over the Internet. Moreover, a number of regular telephone-style BBSs are now using the server capabilities of Vmodem to make BBSs available over the Internet. This means that you can call some of your favorite BBSs while connected to the Internet—without having to reach them by long distance. The list of BBSs on the Internet that now support Vmodem is growing. At the time of this writing, the list includes the following:

`bbs.os2bbs.com`	Pete Norloff's OS/2 Shareware BBS
`199.248.240.2`	Ray Gwinn's SIO Support in Virginia
`199.100.191.2`	Bob Juge in Houston, Texas
`199.67.41.2`	PCBOARD, Clark Development
`198.69.157.10`	Steve Haynes in Virginia
`198.68.171.210`	File Bank BBS
`198.68.17.57`	Paul Breedlove, Multinet
`bbs.windstar.net`	Steve Schmidt in Chicago, Illinois
`198.96.20.209`	Steven Bonisteel in Canada
`194.70.36.10`	Jon Morby in England
`198.17.249.111`	Pete Link in USA
`199.165.149.4`	Pete Person in Washington State
`bbs.adam.anet.cz`	Tomas Kucera in Prague, Czechoslavakia
`202.12.87.130`	Russell Coker in Australia
`volvo.datacomm.com`	Tony Wagner, West Coast USA
`204.120.33.159`	Bob Palmer in Belton, Missouri
`199.190.72.11`	Patty and Roger Morris, LA
`203.4.149.97`	Dave Blears, Australia
`204.91.224.2`	Bridgewater, New Jersey
`tgax.com`	The Graphics Alternative
`bbs-ce.uab.es 666`	Universitat Autonoma de Barcelona

To use Vmodem, all that is required is a simple change to your OS/2 `CONFIG.SYS` file. The following, which just adds `(com3,internet:3e8,none:3)` to the end of the existing line, enabled me to use COM3 (which doesn't otherwise exist on my system) as a virtual modem port for using my OS/2 communications programs as telnet terminals:

```
device=g:\sio\sio.sys (com3,internet:3e8,none:3)
```

After you've added the virtual port definition (COM3, in my case) and rebooted, you start the Vmodem program (you might create an OS/2 program reference object for `vmodem.exe` in your IBM Internet Connection for OS/2 folder to make starting Vmodem easier). When Vmodem is running, you can use your OS/2 communications programs over the Internet to connect with Vmodem servers as well as ordinary telnet servers. When using an ordinary communications program, instead of telephone numbers, you use Internet addresses, which can be names or IP addresses.

In order to get updates for PMComm, I used to have to download over 500KB via a long distance telephone connection from a BBS that's over 2,000 miles away. Now, I and anyone else with Vmodem, can use ordinary communications programs to connect to Vmodem servers over the Internet from anywhere in the world, without having to call long distance.

To use the CompuServe Information Manager for OS/2 over the Internet with Vmodem, you need to make some settings changes. From the menu, choose Special | Session Settings. Now, make the following changes:

1. Set the Network to **Internet**.
2. Set the telephone number to **198.4.6.2**. (the IP address for compuserve.com)
3. Set the Connector to your Vmodem port; COM3, as set in the (com3,internet:3e8,none:3) part of your DEVICE=SIO.SYS line in your CONFIG.SYS file.
4. Set the modem Initialize string to nothing at all (click the Modem button from the Session Settings window).

Note

You also can use the regular telnet program that comes with OS/2 to connect to these BBSs over the Internet, even without having Vmodem on your computer. However, given that telnet lacks scripting, scrollback, Zmodem, and a number of other features that many consider essential on BBSs, using telnet to connect to these BBSs foresakes the Vmodem advantages. However, if you just need to dash off a quick message or read messages, rather than download or upload files, then you can telnet to any of the BBS sites shown above.

Product Information

Availability: At the Sams *Navigating the Internet* Software Library

Filename: SIO145.ZIP

The latest version can be purchased from Ray Gwinn's BBS on the Internet at 199.248.240.2, or by telephone at 703-494-0098.

TE/2—Coming Soon: Enabled for Telnet

Possibly a sign of things to come, Brady Flowers has enabled telnet capabilities in his popular TE/2 OS/2 communications program. In beta at this writing, the drivers will enable you to use TE/2 as a replacement for the telnet clients that come with OS/2. The telnet-enabled

TE/2 works with any Telnet host and will not require Vmodem. This provides scrollback capabilities, the use of standard BBS protocols (for those telnet hosts that support them), as well as the ability to write scripts for performing on-line chores. The telnet-enabled demo version of TE/2 will be placed on the Macmillan FTP server when it becomes available.

Product Information

Availability: At the Sams *Navigating the Internet* Software Library

Filename: `TE2_130T.ZIP`

PMMpeg: Movie Player

Many users find the multimedia browsers (`AB.EXE`, `VB.EXE`, and `IM.EXE`) to be very slow and memory-intensive. Fortunately, some shareware alternatives that can be used in place of those are available for some of the viewing formats. For Mpeg videos, the PMMpeg movie player provides excellent and fast performance. PMMpeg does not support as many formats as `VB.EXE`. However, if you do a lot of browsing of MPeg formatted movies, the extra speed might be worth the shareware registration fee and the disk space required.

Product Information

Availability: At the Sams *Navigating the Internet* Software Library

Filename: `PMMPEG21.ZIP`

PMJpeg: Graphics Browser

Like the video browser (`VB.EXE`), the default image browser (`IB.EXE`) that comes with OS/2 Warp is a bit slow and big. Many OS/2 users prefer to replace it with the shareware PMJpeg image display program. PMJpeg supports the following image formats:

JPG
GIF
TIF
TGA
PCX
BMP

Product Information

Availability: At the Sams *Navigating the Internet* Software Library

Filename: `PMJPG163.ZIP`

YARN/2: A Text-Mode Offline News and Mail Handler

One complaint that many Internet users have about the IAK's NewsReader/2 application is that you are confined to reading newsgroup articles while logged onto the Internet. If you have an account with unlimited time and a telephone you don't mind tying up, this might not present any particular problem for you. For those who have neither, however, this failing of NewsReader/2 is fundamental. They might be interested instead in the OS/2 version of YARN.

YARN/2 is a text-mode news and mail handler. Without using Ultimedia Mail/2 Lite or NewsReader/2, YARN gathers your mail and newsgroup articles for you quickly, so you don't have to spend tons of time "on the air," so to speak. Then, when the articles and mail have been downloaded, you can read and respond offline without being connected. When you are ready to send and post any replies, you go back onto the Internet. If newsgroup reading is a primary focus of your Internet activities, using something such as YARN can cut your on-line time dramatically. (Ultimedia Mail/2 Lite enables you to do offline reading and replying, too, but NewsReader/2 does not.)

Product Information

Availability: At the Sams *Navigating the Internet* Software Library

Filename: YRN2_076.ZIP

Archie for OS/2

One of the most aggravating Internet tasks is locating files. For example, I can tell you that a file named YRN2_076.ZIP exists on the Internet. Finding a site that has it, however, can be quite a problem. It's as if I were to tell you to search for a golden needle hidden in a haystack. It's worse than that, however, because the Internet isn't like a single haystack—it's hundreds of haystacks, all mixed together.

Archie is one approach to solving this problem. Using a number of Archie servers, you can search the Internet for files. Archie servers search numerous anonymous FTP sites around the world for files for you. Using Archie servers is somewhat cumbersome, however, because many of them are available only via telnet, with its limited capabilities.

Using Archie for OS/2, you can specify your search from the OS/2 command line, storing the results of a search in a file if you think the results won't fit onto a single screen of data (which often is the case). Let's take a look at a search for any files matching yrn2, because YARN/2 might exist in different places with different filenames.

```
G:\zips\test>archie -t -s yrn2
Host faui43.informatik.uni-erlangen.de
   Location: /mounts/epix/public/pub/pc/os2/hobbes/incoming
```

```
              FILE -r--r--r--      760  Oct 12 01:25  yrn2_073.txt
              FILE -r--r--r--   476165  Oct 12 01:13  yrn2_073.zip
Host nic.switch.ch
    Location: /mirror/os2/2_x/bbs
              FILE -rw-rw-r--   475968  Oct  3 02:36  yrn2_072.zip
Host faui43.informatik.uni-erlangen.de
    Location: /mounts/epix/public/pub/pc/os2/hobbes/new
              FILE -r--r--r--   475968  Oct  3 02:36  yrn2_072.zip
Host nic.switch.ch
    Location: /mirror/os2/2_x/bbs
              FILE -rw-rw-r--   472756  Jul 25 07:51  yrn2_069.zip
Host flop.informatik.tu-muenchen.de
    Location: /incoming
              FILE -rw-r--r--   478511  Jul 11 09:28  yrn2_068.zip
```

As you can see, the command line specified archie -t -s yrn2. The -t tells Archie to sort any *hits* (successful matches of the search text) in reverse chronological order. The -s yrn2 is the instruction to perform a case-insensitive search for the substring yrn2 in any filename. Thus, it would match any of the following filenames:

```
Z-YRN2.TXT
yrn2_073.zip
YRN2_071.ZIP
```

Using case-insensitive searching takes account of the fact that some FTP servers store all file-names in either all uppercase or all lowercase, and some use the case in which the file was de-livered. The substring search doesn't limit you to a precise filename. Substring searches can be useful for finding files related to a general topic, for which you don't know the actual filenames but you suspect that they might use a certain pattern of letters.

Product Information

Availability: At the Sams *Navigating the Internet* Software Library

Filename: ARCHIE.ZIP

Other Recent OS/2 Internet-Related Programs

As you learn about the Internet, you undoubtedly will develop your own likes and dislikes. You can use your FTP capabilities to find and use hundreds, if not thousands, of programs to enhance your use of the Internet and the Warp IAK. What follows is a short list of some of the recent programs for OS/2 that have appeared in public file archives. Because everything is moving *very* quickly, however, you should expect that many of the filenames have been replaced with more recent versions. The latest versions we can find will be placed on Sams *Navigating the Internet* Software Libary, located at the Macmillan Computer Publishing Web and FTP sites. You also can find many of these on Hobbes or Walnut Creek.

ELM23-2.ZIP	The Elm 2.3.11 mail front-end for OS/2.
FSP2-10A.ZIP	FSP is a protocol, a bit like FTP, for moving files around. It's designed for anonymous archives.
GOPHER.ZIP	Gopher v1.9915 is an OS/2 PM Gopher client.
HTMLWIZ1.ZIP	HTML Wizard for OS/2.
MINUET.ZIP	TCP/IP-based mail reader with Gopher.
OS2CHAT1.ZIP	Os2Chat is a smaller, faster, and easier method than IRC of communicating via UANet.
PMICS.ZIP	Playing chess through the Internet Chess Server under OS/2.
PMPREP.ZIP	PMPrep is a PM uudecoder, which can decode multiple files at the same time.
POPCL221.ZIP	Popclient 2.21 for OS/2 is a port of the UNIX Popclient version 2.21.
POPIT01B.ZIP	POP3 0.1 BETA mail client.
RTFTHTML.ZIP	OS/2 port of RTFTOHTML 2.7.5 (HPFS only).
SOUPER12.ZIP	Extract mail and news to SOUP format (a format that collects mail and news for offline reading).
TRN_196B.ZIP	TRN newsreader in version 3.5.
VXFTP42.ZIP	Multithreaded PM FTP client.

DOS and Windows TCP/IP Applications Under OS/2

Using the OS/2 Warp Internet Access Kit, you also can run DOS TCP/IP programs and Windows WINSOCK-compliant SLIP programs. The IAK comes with a special version of WINSOCK.DLL that is necessary for running Windows programs under OS/2. To use DOS and Windows program under the IAK, you need to do the following:

1. Ensure that x:\TCPIP\BIN\VDOSTCP.SYS (where x is the drive on which the TCPIP directory is located) is in your DOS_DEVICE setting for the WIN-OS/2 objects that you plan to use. This generally is taken care of by the line DEVICE=x:\tcpip\bin\vdostcp.sys in your OS/2 CONFIG.SYS file. Unless you explicitly remove that line or remove the DOS_DEVICE settings for specific DOS and WIN-OS/2 objects, the vdostcp.sys driver should be used automatically after installing the IAK.

2. Ensure that your OS/2 DOS AUTOEXEC.BAT file contains a SET statement for the ETC directory to use for VDMs (virtual DOS machines) running under OS/2. Like vdostcp.sys, this line is automatically added to your OS/2 AUTOEXEC.BAT file when you install the IAK: @SET ETC=f:\tcpip\dos\etc.

3. To run WINSOCK-compliant programs, you also need to ensure that WINSOCK.DLL is copied to your Windows or WIN-OS/2 SYSTEM subdirectory. Unlike vdostcp.sys and the ETC subdirectory, this step is not performed automatically by the IAK installation.

If you have an existing `WINDSOCK.DLL` file already, rename it as something else and copy the version from `\TCPIP\DOS\BIN` to your Windows or WIN-OS/2 `SYSTEM` subdirectory (for example, `OS2\MDOS\WINOS2\SYSTEM` or `\WIN\SYSTEM`, or whatever it's called on your computer). You also need to make sure that the OS/2 `WINSOCK.DLL` is the only version of that file in your DOS path (specified in your OS/2-DOS `AUTOEXEC.BAT` file). You might need to change your path or to rename other versions of `WINSOCK.DLL`.

In addition to `WINSOCK.DLL`, the IAK also provides `WPING.EXE`, which is a Windows version of Ping that you can run under WIN-OS/2. Shown in Figure 12.8, Windows Ping lets you select hosts (from among any previous hosts you've pinged) from a pull-down list. It also lets you specify the data length, number of iterations, and the time interval between ping attempts. It's very similar to `PMPING.EXE`, which comes with the full TCP/IP for OS/2 package, and it kind of makes you wonder why IBM chose not to include the latter in the IAK. It's almost as if they want OS/2 users to have a better pinging tool for Windows than for OS/2.

FIGURE 12.8.

Windows Ping, the only GUI Ping that comes with the Warp IAK.

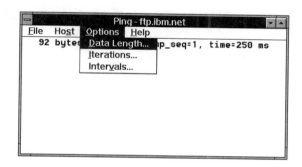

Netscape

You can run WinSock-compliant Internet applications, such as Netscape, using the OS/2 IAK. Some people prefer Netscape over the WebExplorer. Some don't. Fortunately, with OS/2 you don't have to decide. Use whichever one you want. In fact, you can compare the two side-by-side (as shown in Figure 12.9).

How do they compare? You be the judge. On the one hand, you don't need to have or use any WIN-OS/2 support in order to run the WebExplorer. Many users find that Netscape's graphics mode causes a palette shift with some video adapters and drivers, resulting in a distortion of other applications when running Netscape in seamless mode on the OS/2 desktop. Also, many users encounter a bland and uninformative `TCP Error` when using some of the Netscape options.

On the other hand, if you're using other Windows programs under OS/2 anyway, the necessary WIN-OS/2 subsystem is already running, and the incremental drag of running Netscape isn't significant. Also, you're probably one of many users who *don't* get a palette shift. Moreover, if you're one of many people who cannot use FTP under the WebExplorer, you'll likely find no such problem when using Netscape.

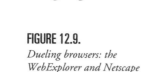

FIGURE 12.9.

Dueling browsers: the WebExplorer and Netscape duking it out on the Internet!

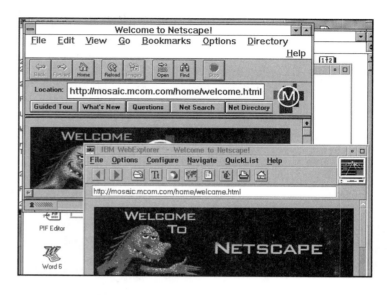

Your best bet is to try both of them to see which one gives you the best results. Personally, I prefer the WebExplorer. It's good and getting better. However, if you've already been using Netscape and want to run it, or if you use them both and prefer Netscape (or Mosaic), the choice is yours.

At this writing, there is a focus problem with Netscape version 1.0 when running in a seamless (windowed) WIN-OS/2 session. When you click on the title bar, or when you try to access menus, they don't stay highlighted. When used from a full-screen WIN-OS/2 session, however, Netscape works fine. This problem might have been fixed by the time you read this.

Eudora

The one application in the Warp IAK for which there appears to be nearly universal hatred is Ultimedia Mail/2 Lite. A number of OS/2 users have, in fact, chosen to use the popular Eudora POP mail client for Windows. Is it better? You be the judge.

Other Windows and DOS TCP/IP Programs

As a consequence of Windows' enormous popularity and DOS's head start, there are numerous other DOS and Windows programs that work under OS/2. They include FTP, Gopher, Finger, IRC, and virtually every other kind of TCP/IP application you might want. Here is a short list of recent entries that you might want to take a look at. Keep in mind, however, that most of these are shareware, and require payment if you decide to keep using them.

WSFNGR14.ZIP	WinSock Finger and Whois client in one application.
EUDOR144.EXE	Eudora for Windows.
NS16-100.ZIP	Netscape 1.0, WWW browser.
HTMLASST.ZIP	HTML Assistant for Windows.
WSARCH07.ZIP	Archie WinSock Client.
IRC4WIN.ZIP	IRC4WIN, a WinSock-compliant IRC client.
QVTWS398.ZIP	WinQVT/Net, a suite of TCP/IP client and server applications for Windows 3.1.
QWS3270.ZIP	Windows Sockets 3270 Telnet application.

APPENDIX A
INSTALLING THE OS/2 WARP INTERNET ACCESS KIT

Installing from CD-ROM

Installing from 3.5-Inch Diskettes

The Internet Access Kit (IAK) is located on the OS/2 BonusPak. If you have OS/2 on CD-ROM, you will need the compact disc labeled "BonusPak." If you have the diskette version, then you will need Internet Diskettes 1 through 4.

Installing from CD-ROM

To install the IAK from CD-ROM, follow these steps:

1. Insert the BonusPak CD-ROM into your CD-ROM drive, and then double-click the CD object in your Drives folder.
2. In the folder for your CD-ROM drive, double-click the Internet folder.
3. Double-click the object labeled INSTALL.EXE.
4. In the Install IBM Internet Connection for OS/2 dialog box, adjust the destination drive letter, if desired, to a location that has (optimally) 15MB free. You don't need a full 15MB. However, you won't regret having room for growth later on. At a minimum, you need about 10MB for installation.
5. Click Install.
6. The installation program will copy the necessary files to your hard disk and will tell you when installation is complete.
7. When you get the completion message, save any data in any applications that might be running, close the applications, and then shut down and reboot.
8. After you reboot, some additional parts of the IAK installation will be run automatically. These are necessary to complete the installation and create the OS/2 objects and folders. Wait until all disk activity has stopped before attempting to use the OS/2 Internet Access Kit.

Note

> On some systems, a bug in the CD-ROM drivers might prevent you from installing the IAK. You might see an error message that one or more of the .ZIP files could not be unzipped. If this happens to you, you can install the IAK by following these steps:
>
> 1. Create a working directory or folder on an OS/2 drive (call it INET, or something like that).
> 2. Copy all the files from the Internet directory on your CD-ROM to the working directory.
> 3. Run INSTALL.EXE from the working directory.
> 4. Pick up at step 4 in the preceding procedure (that is, perform steps 4 through 8), then continue with step 5 here.
> 5. When installation is complete, you can delete all the files in the working directory.

A fix for your CD-ROM driver is likely to be available on one of the IBM FTP or Gopher sites. Set your Gopher to the following to get an index of available files:

`ftp:software.watson.ibm.com@/pub/os2/ls-lR`

After you download the index file (`ls-lR`), display it (using the OS/2 System Editor, for example, or any text browsing program), and check under the `os2fixes` listing for items that resemble the manufacturer name of your CD-ROM (items that contain the word *sony*, for example). If you find something, click the `os2fixes` Gopher item, and then download the file. Make sure you also download any accompanying text files.

Installing from 3.5-Inch Diskettes

To install the IAK from 3.5-inch diskettes, follow these steps:

1. Insert Internet Diskette 1 into your diskette drive, and then double-click on the corresponding drive object in your Drives folder (that is, drive A or B, depending on where the diskette was inserted).

2. Double-click on the object labeled `INSTALL.EXE`.

3. In the Install IBM Internet Connection for OS/2 dialog box, adjust the destination drive letter, if desired, to a location that has (optimally) 15MB free. You don't need a full 15MB. However, you won't regret having room for growth later on. At a minimum, you need about 10MB for installation.

4. Click Install.

5. The installation program will copy the necessary files to your hard disk and prompt you to insert Diskettes 2, 3, and 4. It will tell you when installation is complete.

6. When you get the completion message, save any data in any applications that might be running, close the applications, remove any diskette from your A: drive, and then shut down and reboot.

7. After you reboot, some additional parts of the IAK installation will be run automatically. These are necessary to complete the installation and create the OS/2 objects and folders. Wait until all disk activity has stopped before attempting to use the OS/2 Internet Access Kit.

APPENDIX B
INTERNET ACCESS PROVIDERS

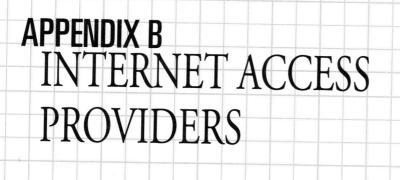

Geographical and Area-Code Summary of
Providers in the United States and Canada

Alphabetical List of Providers

Although the IBM Internet Connection provides a way of quickly getting onto the Internet, this may not be the most cost-effective way for you to get on the Internet. You may be better off with a provider in your area with a local phone number. This appendix lists companies and organizations that provide dial-up Internet accounts for individuals. This list includes providers in the United States, Canada, and other countries.

If you already are connected to the Internet but are searching for alternatives, check online at `ftp://nis.nsf.net/internet/providers/` or `http://www.internic.net/internic/provider.html` (open the WebExplorer and set the URL to either location). The National Science Foundataion (NSF) and InterNIC maintain lists of providers that are updated very frequently. Note, however, that Web addresses are subject to change, so it's possible that either or both of these addresses might have changed by the time you read this. If you're not already connected, other good sources are your local newspaper and yellow pages.

Geographical and Area-Code Summary of Providers in the United States and Canada

This section presents North American Internet provider names grouped by the state or province that the provider services, by area code, and then alphabetically by provider name. Details and contact information for each provider follow in the next section. The first (and largest) portion of this list presents providers that supply standard access. At the end of this list are the providers that supply packet/network or toll-free access.

Standard-Access Providers

Alabama — 205
interQuest Inc.
Nuance Network Service
Planet Access Networks

Alaska — 907
Internet Alaska

Alberta — 403
Alberta SuperNet Inc.
CCI Networks

Arizona — 602
ACES Research
CRL Network Services
Evergreen Internet
Internet Direct, Inc.
Internet Express
Network 99, Inc.
New Mexico Technet, Inc.
Primenet

Arkansas — 501
Sibylline, Inc.

British Columbia — 604

Cyberstore Systems Inc.
DataFlux Systems Limited
Wimsey Information Services

California — 209

Sacramento Network Access
West Coast Online

California — 213

CRL Network Services
CSUnet (California State University)
DHM Information Management, Inc.
DigiLink Network Services
Earthlink Network, Inc.
KAIWAN Corporation
Primenet

California — 310

CERFnet
CRL Network Services
CSUnet (California State University)
DHM Information Management, Inc.
DigiLink Network Services
Earthlink Network, Inc.
KAIWAN Corporation
Lightside, Inc.
Netcom On-Line Communication Services

California — 408

Aimnet Information Services
Best Internet Communications, Inc.
    (BEST)
CSUnet (California State University)
ElectriCiti Incorporated
Internet Connection
InterNex Information Services, Inc.
Netcom On-Line Communication Services
Portal Communications Company
Scruz-Net
South Valley Internet
West Coast Online
zNET

California — 415

Aimnet Information Services
APlatform
Best Internet Communications, Inc.
    (BEST)
CERFnet
CRL Network Services
CSUnet (California State University)
ElectriCiti Incorporated
Institute for Global Communications
    (IGC)
InterNex Information Services, Inc.
LineX Communcations
Netcom On-Line Communication Services
QuakeNet
Scruz-Net
The Well
West Coast Online

California — 510

Access InfoSystems
Aimnet Information Services
Best Internet Communications, Inc.
    (BEST)
CCnet Communications
CERFnet
Community ConneXion
CRL Network Services
CSUnet (California State University)
ElectriCiti Incorporated
HoloNet
HoloNet/Information Access
    Technologies, Inc.
InterNex Information Services, Inc.
Netcom On-Line Communication Services
Sacramento Network Access, Inc.
West Coast Online

California — 619

CERFnet
CSUnet (California State University)
CTS Network Services (CTSNet)
ElectriCiti Incorporated

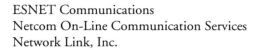

ESNET Communications
Netcom On-Line Communication Services
Network Link, Inc.

California — 707

Access InfoSystems
CRL Network Services
CSUnet (California State University)
Northcoast Internet
Pacific Internet
West Coast Online

California — 714

CERFnet
CSUnet (California State University)
DHM Information Management, Inc.
DigiLink Network Services
Digital Express Group (Digex)
KAIWAN Corporation
Lightside, Inc.
Netcom On-Line Communication Services
Network Intensive

California — 805

Dataware Network Services
KAIWAN Corporation

California — 818

CERFnet
CSUnet (California State University)
DHM Information Management, Inc.
DigiLink Network Services
Earthlink Network, Inc.
KAIWAN Corporation
Lightside, Inc.
Netcom On-Line Communication Services
Primenet

California — 909

CSUnet (California State University)
Digital Express Group (Digex)
KAIWAN Corporation
Lightside, Inc.

California — 916

CSUnet (California State University)
Netcom On-Line Communication Services
Sacramento Network Access, Inc.
Sierra-Net
West Coast Online

Colorado — 303

CNS
Colorado Internet Cooperative Association
Colorado SuperNet
DASH - Denver Area Super Highway
Internet Express
Netcom On-Line Communication Services
New Mexico Technet, Inc.
Nyx
Rocky Mountain Internet, Inc.

Colorado — 719

CNS
Colorado SuperNet
Internet Express
Old Colorado City Communications
Rocky Mountain Internet, Inc.

Connecticut — 203

Connix: The Connecticut Internet
    Exchange
I-2000
New York Net
PCNet
The Dorsai Embassy

Delaware — 302

SSNet, Inc.

District of Columbia — 202

CAPCON LibrARY Network
Capitol Area Internet Service (CAIS)
ClarkNet (Clark Internet Services, Inc.)
NovaNet, Inc.
US Net, Inc.

Florida — 305

Acquired Knowledge Systems, Inc.
CyberGate
Florida Online
Gateway to the World, Inc.
IDS World Network
SatelNET Communications

Florida — 407

Florida Online
IDS World Network

Florida — 813

CENTURION Technology, Inc.
Florida Online
PacketWorks, Inc.

Florida — 904

Florida Online
SymNet

Georgia — 404

CRL Network Services
Internet Atlanta
MindSpring Enterprises, Inc.
Netcom On-Line Communication Services
Ping

Georgia — 706

Mind Spring Enterprises, Inc.

Hawaii — 808

Hawaii OnLine

Idaho — 208

WLN

Illinois — 217

FGInet, Inc.

Illinois — 312

American Information Systems, Inc. (AIS)
InterAccess Co.
MCSNet
Netcom On-Line Communication Services
Ripco Communcations, Inc.
Tezcatlipoca, Inc.
WorldWide Access

Illinois — 708

American Information Systems, Inc. (AIS)
CICNet
InterAccess Co.
MCSNet
Ripco Communcations, Inc.
Tezcatlipoca, Inc.
WorldWide Access
XNet Information Systems

Illinois — 815

American Information Systems, Inc. (AIS)
InterAccess Co.
MCSNet
WorldWide Access

Indiana — 317

IQuest Network Services
Network Link, Inc.

Indiana — 812

IgLou Internet Services

Iowa — 319

INS Info Services
Planet Access Networks

Iowa — 515

Cyberlink Communications
INS Info Services

Iowa — 712
INS Info Services

Kansas — 316
Southwind Internet Access, Inc.
Tyrell Corp.

Kansas — 913
Tyrell Corp.
SkyNET Corp.

Kentucky — 502
IgLou Internet Services

Kentucky — 606
IgLou Internet Services

Louisiana — 504
Neosoft
Neosoft, Inc.
Tyrell Corp.

Maine — 207
maine.net, Inc.

Manitoba — 204
MBnet
Traveller Information Services

Maryland — 301
CAPCON LibrARY Network
Capitol Area Internet Service (CAIS)
ClarkNet (Clark Internet Services, Inc.)
Digital Express Group (Digex)
FredNet
NovaNet, Inc.
US Net, Inc.

Maryland — 410
CAPCON LibrARY Network
Capitol Area Internet Service (CAIS)
ClarkNet (Clark Internet Services, Inc.)
Digital Express Group (Digex)

Massachusetts — 508
Inter Access Company
intuitive information, inc.
Schunix
The World
UltraNet Communications, Inc.

Massachusetts — 617
BIX (Delphi Internet Services)
Inter Access Company
Internet Access Company
Netcom On-Line Communication Services
North Shore Access
Pioneer Global
The World
Wilder Systems, Inc.
Xensei Corporation

Michigan — 313
CICNet
ICNet/Innovative Concepts
Innovative Data (ID-Net)
MichNet
Msen
Msen, Inc.

Michigan — 517
ICNet/Innovative Concepts
MichNet
Msen, Inc.

Michigan — 616
ICNet/Innovative Concepts
MichNet
Msen, Inc.

Michigan — 810
ICNet/Innovative Concepts
Innovative Data (ID-Net)
MichNet
Msen
Rabbit Network, Inc.

Michigan — 906
ICNet/Innovative Concepts
MichNet
Msen, Inc.

Minnesota — 218
Minnesota Regional Network (MRNET)
Red River Net

Minnesota — 507
Millenium Communications
Minnesota Regional Network (MRNet)

Minnesota — 612
Cloudnet
Millenium Communications
Minnesota MicroNet
Minnesota Regional Network (MRNet)
StarNet Communications, Inc. (Winternet)

Missouri — 314
Neosoft
Neosoft, Inc.

Missouri — 816
SkyNET Corp.
Tyrell Corp.

Montana — 406
WLN

Nebraska — 402
INS Info Services
Internet Nebraska Corp.

Nevada — 702
Evergreen Internet
Great Basin Internet Services
Network 99, Inc.
Sacramento Network Access, Inc.
Sierra-Net

New Hampshire — 603
MV Communications, Inc.

New Jersey — 201
Internet Online Services
Neighborhood Internet Connection
New York Net
Planet Access Networks
The Dorsai Embassy
Zone One Network Exchange (ZONE)

New Jersey — 609
Digital Express Group (Digex)
New Jersey Computer Connection
New York Net

New Jersey — 908
Digital Express Group (Digex)
I-2000
New York Net
Planet Access Networks
Zone One Network Exchange (ZONE)

New Mexico — 505
Internet Express
New Mexico Technet, Inc.

New York — 212
Blythe Systems
Creative Data Consultants
CRL Network Services
Echo
Escape (Kazan Corp)
Ingress Communications, Inc.
Internet Online Services
Interport Communications Corp
Maestro Technologies, Inc.
Netcom On-Line Communication Services
Network 23, Inc.
New York Net
NYSERNet
Panix
Phantom Access Technologies, Inc.
Pipeline Network
The Dorsai Embassy
Zone One Network Exchange (ZONE)

New York — 315
NYSERNet

New York — 516
Creative Data Consultants
I-2000
LI Net, Inc.
Long Island Information, Inc.
Maestro Technologies, Inc.
Network Internet Services
New York Net
NYSERNet
Panix
Phantom Access Technologies, Inc.
The Dorsai Embassy
Zone One Network Exchange (ZONE)

New York — 518
Internet Online Services
NYSERNet
Wizvax Communications

New York — 607
NYSERNet

New York — 716
NYSERNet

New York — 718
Blythe Systems
Creative Data Consultants
Echo
Escape (Kazan Corp)
I-2000
Ingress Communications, Inc.
Interport Communications Corp.
Maestro Technologies, Inc.
New York Net
NYSERNet
Phantom Access Technologies, Inc.
The Dorsai Embassy
Zone One Network Exchange (ZONE)

New York — 914
Cloud 9 Internet
I-2000
New York Net
NYSERNet
Phantom Access Technologies, Inc.
The Dorsai Embassy
TZ-Link
WestNet
Zone One Network Exchange (ZONE)

New York — 917
Network 23, Inc.
New York Net
Zone One Network Exchange (ZONE)

North Carolina — 704
FXnet
Interpath
Northcoast Internet
VNet Internet Access, Inc.

North Carolina — 910
Interpath

North Carolina — 919
Interpath

North Dakota — 701
Red River Net

Ohio — 216
APK Public Access UNI*
Exchange Network Services, Inc.

Ohio — 513
EriNet Online Communications
Freelance Systems Programming
IgLou Internet Services

Ohio — 614
OARNet

Oklahoma — 405
GSS Internet

Oklahoma — 918
GSS Internet
South Coast Computing Services, Inc.

Ontario — 416
UUNorth Incorporated

Ontario — 519
Hookup Communication Corporation

Oregon — 503
Agora
Hevanet Communications
Internetworks
Netcom On-Line Communication Services
Teleport
Teleport, Inc.
WLN

Pennsylvania — 215
FishNet (Prometheus Information Corp.)
VoiceNet/DCS
You Tools Corporation (FAST.NET)

Pennsylvania — 412
Telerama

Pennsylvania — 610
FishNet (Prometheus Information Corp.)
SSNet, Inc.
You Tools Corporation (FAST.NET)

Pennsylvania — 717
You Tools Corporation (FAST.NET)

Rhode Island — 401
IDS World Network

Quebec — 514
Communications Accessibles
    Montreal, Inc.

South Carolina — 803
A World of Difference, Inc.
FXnet
Global Vision, Inc.
SIMS, Inc.
South Carolina SuperNet, Inc.

Tennessee — 615
Edge

Texas — 210
Freeside Communications

Texas — 214
DFW Internet Services, Inc.
Metronet, Inc.
NeoSoft, Inc.
Netcom On-Line Communication Services
Texas Metronet

Texas — 409
Info-Highway International, Inc.
Internet Connect Services, Inc.
NeoSoft, Inc.

Texas — 512
Eden Matrix
Freeside Communications
Illuminati Online
Internet Connect Services, Inc.
Netcom On-Line Communication Services
Onramp Access, Inc.
Real/Time Communications
Zilker Internet Park

Texas — 713
Black Box
Info-Highway International, Inc.
Internet Connect Services, Inc.
Neosoft
Neosoft, Inc.South Coast Computing
    Services, Inc.

Texas — 817
ACM Network Services
DFW Internet Services, Inc.
Metronet, Inc.
Texas Metronet

Texas — 915
New Mexico Technet, Inc.

Utah — 801
Evergreen Internet
Internet Direct of Utah
XMission

Virginia — 703
CAPCON LibrARY Network
Capitol Area Internet Service (CAIS)
ClarkNet (Clark Internet Services, Inc.)
Digital Express Group (Digex)
Netcom On-Line Communication Services
NovaNet, Inc.
PSI
US Net, Inc.

Virginia — 804
Global Connect Inc.
Widowmaker Communications

Washington — 206
Cyberlink Communications
Eskimo North

Netcom On-Line Communication Services
NorthWest CommLink
Northwest Nexus, Inc.
Pacific Rim Network, Inc.
Pacifier Computers
Skagit On-Line Services
Teleport
Teleport, Inc.
Townsend Communcations, Inc.
WLN

Washington — 509
Internet On-Ramp, Inc.
WLN

Wisconsin — 414
BINCnet
Exec-PC BBS
FullFeed Communications
Internet Connect, Inc.
MIX Communications
WorldWide Access

Wisconsin — 608
BINCnet
FullFeed Communications

Wisconsin — 715
BINCnet
FullFeed Communications

Packet Network/Toll-Free Access Providers

CompuServe Packet Network
IDS World Network

PSINet
HoloNet

SprintNet
Neosoft
Portal Communications Company

Tollfree/800 Access

AlterNet (UUNET Technologies)
American Information Systems, Inc. (AIS)
BIX (Delphi Internet Services)
CENTURION Technology, Inc.
CERFnet
CICNet
CNS
CRL
DASH—Denver Area Super Highway
Digital Express Group (Digex)
Exec-PC BBS
Freeside Communications
FXnet
Hookup Communication Corporation
IgLou Internet Services
Info-Highway International, Inc.
INS Info Services
InterAccess Co.
Internet Express
Internet Online Services
Interpath
IQuest Network Services
Msen
Neosoft
Neosoft, Inc.

Netcom On-Line Communications
    Services
Network Intensive
New Mexico Technet, Inc.
OARNet
Pacific Rim Network, Inc.
PCNet
Ping
Primenet
Rabbit Network, Inc.
Rocky Mountain Internet, Inc.
Sacramento Network Access, Inc.
Scruz-Net
South Coast Computing Services, Inc.
Traveller Information Services
Tyrell Corp.
UltraNet Communications, Inc.
VNet Internet Access, Inc.
VoiceNet/DCS
West Coast Online
WLN
Zone One Network Exchange (ZONE)

Tymnet

Holonet

Alphabetical List of Providers

This section presents an alphabetical list of providers grouped by country and then by provider name. Countries included are the United States, Canada, Australia, Germany, Netherlands, New Zealand, Switzerland, and the United Kingdom.

Providers in the United States and Canada

The following is a list of North American Internet provider names in alphabetical order by provider name.

A World of Difference, Inc.
Area code(s):   803
Voice phone: 803-769-4488
E-mail address: info@awod.com
Services provided: Shell, PPP

Access InfoSystems
Area code(s):   707, 510
Voice phone: 707-422-1034

E-mail address: info@community.net
Services provided: Shell, SLIP, PPP

ACES Research
Area code(s):   602
Voice phone: 602-322-6500
E-mail address: sales@aces.com
Services provided: SLIP, 56-T1

ACM Network Services
Area code(s):   National/International
Voice phone: 817-776-6876
E-mail address: account-info@acm.org
Services provided: Shell, SLIP, PPP, T1

Acquired Knowledge Systems, Inc.
Area code(s):   305
Voice phone: 305-525-2574
E-mail address: samek@aksi.net
Services provided: Shell, SLIP, PPP

Agora
Area code(s):   503
E-mail address: info@agora.rain.com
Dialup number: 503-293-1772
Services provided: Shell, Usenet, FTP,
                   telnet, Gopher, Lynx,
                   IRC, mail, SLIP/PPP
                   coming

Aimnet Information Services
Area code(s):   408, 415, 510
Voice phone: 408-257-0900
E-mail address: info@aimnet.com
Services provided: Shell, SLIP, PPP,
                   DNS

Alberta SuperNet Inc.
Area code(s):   403
Voice phone: 403-441-3663
E-mail address: info@supernet.ab.ca
Services provided: Shell, e-mail, Usenet,
                   FTP, telnet, Gopher,
                   SLIP/PPP

AlterNet (UUNET Technologies)
Area code(s):   All
Voice phone: 800-4UUNET4
E-mail address: info@uunet.uu.net
Services provided: telnet only, SLIP, PPP,
                   56, 128 T1, 10Mps

American Information Systems, Inc. (AIS)
Area code(s):   312, 708, 800, 815
Voice phone: 708-413-8400
E-mail address: schneid@ais.net
Services provided: Shell, SLIP, PPP,
                   leased lines

APK Public Access UNI*
Area code(s):   216
Voice phone: 216-481-9428
E-mail address: support@wariat.org
Services provided: Shell, SLIP, PPP

APlatform
Area code(s):   415
Voice phone: 415-941-2641
E-mail address: support@aplatform.com
Services provided: Shell, SLIP, PPP

Best Internet Communications, Inc. (BEST)

Area code(s):	408, 415, 510
Voice phone:	415-964-2378
E-mail address:	info@best.com
Services provided:	Shell, SLIP, PPP, Leased lines

BINCnet

Area code(s):	608, 414, 715
Voice phone:	608-233-5222
E-mail address:	ward@binc.net
Services provided:	SLIP, PPP, 56-T1

BIX (Delphi Internet Services)

Area code(s):	National/International
Voice phone:	800-695-4775, 617-354-4137
E-mail address:	info@bix.com
Services provided:	Shell

Black Box

Area code(s):	713
Voice phone:	713-480-2684
E-mail address:	info@blkbox.com
Services provided:	Shell, SLIP, PPP, ISDN

Blythe Systems

Area code(s):	212, 718
Voice phone:	212-348-2875
E-mail address:	accounts@blythe.org
Services provided:	Shell

CAPCON LibrARY Network

Area code(s):	202, 301, 410, 703
Voice phone:	202-331-5771
E-mail address:	info@capcon.net
Services provided:	Shell, SLIP, PPP

Capitol Area Internet Service (CAIS)

Area code(s):	202, 301, 410, 703
Voice phone:	703-448-4470
E-mail address:	dalston@cais.com
Services provided:	Shell, SLIP, PPP, ISDN, 56-T1

CCI Networks

Area code(s):	403
Voice phone:	403-450-6787
E-mail address:	info@ccinet.ab.ca
Services provided:	Shell, e-mail, Usenet, FTP, telnet, Gopher, WAIS, WWW, IRC, Hytelnet, SLIP/PPP

CCnet Communications

Area code(s):	510
Voice phone:	510-988-0680
E-mail address:	info@ccnet.com
Dialup number:	510-988-7140, login as guest
Services provided:	Shell, SLIP/PPP, telnet, e-mail, FTP, Usenet, IRC, WWW

CENTURION Technology, Inc.

Area code(s):	800, 813
Voice phone:	813-572-5556
E-mail address:	jablow@cent.com
Services provided:	Shell, PPP, 56, 128, T1

CERFnet

Area code(s):	619, 510, 415, 818, 714, 310, 800
Voice phone:	800-876-2373
E-mail address:	sales@cerf.net
Services provided:	Full range of Internet services

CICNet

Area code(s):	313, 708, 800
Voice phone:	800-947-4754 or 313-998-6703
E-mail address:	info@cic.net
Services provided:	SLIP, FTP, telnet, Gopher, e-mail, Usenet

ClarkNet (Clark Internet Services, Inc.)

Area code(s):	410, 301, 202, 703
Voice phone:	800-735-2258, ask for extension 410-730-9764
E-mail address:	info@clark.net
Dialup number:	301-596-1626, login as guest, no password:
Services provided:	Shell/optional menu, FTP, Gopher, telnet, IRC, news, Mosaic, Lynx, MUD, SLIP/PPP/CSLIP, and much more

Cloud 9 Internet

Area code(s):	914
Voice phone:	914-682-0626
E-mail address:	scottd@cloud9.net
Services provided:	Shell, SLIP, PPP, ISDN, 56 and up

Cloudnet

Area code(s):	612
Voice phone:	612-240-8243
E-mail address:	info@cloudnet.com
Services provided:	Shell

CNS

Area code(s):	303, 719, 800
Voice phone:	800-748-1200
E-mail address:	service@cscns.com
Dialup number:	719-520-1700, 303-758-2656
Services provided:	Shell/menu, e-mail, FTP, telnet, all newsgroups, IRC, 4m, Gopher, WAIS, SLIP, and more

Colorado Internet Cooperative Association

Area code(s):	303
Voice phone:	303-443-3786
E-mail address:	contact@coop.net
Services provided:	SLIP, PPP, 56, T1, ISDN

Colorado SuperNet

Area code(s):	303, 719
Voice phone:	303-273-3471
E-mail address:	info@csn.org or help@csn.org
Services provided:	Shell, e-mail, Usenet news, telnet, FTP, SLIP/PPP, and other Internet tools

Communications Accessibles Montreal, Inc.

Area code(s):	514
Voice phone:	514-931-0749
E-mail address:	info@cam.org
Dialup number:	514-596-2255
Services provided:	Shell, FTP, telnet, Gopher, WAIS, WWW, IRC, Hytelnet, SLIP/ CSLIP/PPP, news

Community ConneXion

Area code(s):	510
Voice phone:	510-841-2014
E-mail address:	info@c2.org
Services provided:	Shell, SLIP/PPP

Connix: The Connecticut Internet Exchange

Area code(s):	203
Voice phone:	203-349-7059
E-mail address:	office@connix.com
Services provided:	Shell, SLIP, PPP, leased lines

Creative Data Consultants

Area code(s):	718, 212, 516
Voice phone:	718-229-0489 x23
E-mail address:	info@silly.com
Services provided:	Shell

CRL

Area code(s):	213, 310, 404, 415, 510, 602, 707, 800
Voice phone:	415-837-5300
E-mail address:	support@crl.com
Dialup number:	415-705-6060, login as newuser, no password
Services provided:	Shell, e-mail, Usenet, UUCP, FTP, telnet, SLIP/PPP, and more

CSUnet (California State Unversity)

Area code(s):	All in California
Voice phone:	310-985-9445
E-mail address:	maryjane@csu.net
Services provided:	56, 128, 384, T1

CTS Network Services (CTSNet)

Area code(s):	619
Voice phone:	619-637-3737
E-mail address:	support@cts.com
Dialup number:	619-637-3660
Services provided:	Shell, e-mail, Usenet, FTP, telnet, Gopher, IRC, MUD, SLIP/PPP, and more

CyberGate

Area code(s):	305
Voice phone:	305-428-4283
E-mail address:	sales@gate.net
Services provided:	Shell, e-mail, Usenet, FTP, telnet, Gopher, Lynx, IRC, SLIP/PPP

Cyberlink Communications

Area code(s):	206
Voice phone:	206-281-5397, 515-945-7000
E-mail address:	sales@cyberspace.com
Services provided:	Shell, SLIP, PPP

Cyberstore Systems Inc.

Area code(s):	604
Voice phone:	604-526-3373
E-mail address:	info@cyberstore.ca
Dialup number:	604-526-3676, login as guest
Services provided:	E-mail, Usenet, FTP, telnet, Gopher, WAIS, WWW, IRC, SLIP/PPP

DASH - Denver Area Super Highway

Area code(s):	303
Voice phone:	800-624-8597, 303-674-9784
E-mail address:	info@dash.com, custserv@dash.com
Services provided:	Shell, SLIP, PPP, Leased lines

DataFlux Systems Limited

Area code(s):	604
Voice phone:	604-744-4553
E-mail address:	info@dataflux.bc.ca
Services provided:	Shell, e-mail, Usenet, FTP, telnet, Gopher, WAIS, WWW, IRC, SLIP/PPP

Datawave Network Services

Area code(s):	805
Voice phone:	805-730-7775
E-mail address:	sales@datawave.net
Services provided:	56

DFW Internet Services, Inc.

Area code(s):	214, 817
Voice phone:	817-332-5116
E-mail address:	sales@dfw.net
Services provided:	Shell, SLIP, PPP, 56 -T1

DHM Information Management, Inc.

Area code(s):	213, 310, 714, 818
Voice phone:	310-214-3349
E-mail address:	dharms@dhm.com
Services provided:	LAN, PPP, SLIP, T1-56, Shell

DigiLink Network Services

Area code(s):	213, 310, 714, 818
Voice phone:	310-542-7421
E-mail address:	info@digilink.net, bob@digilink.net
Services provided:	ISDN, PPP

Digital Express Group (Digex)

Area code(s):	301, 410, 609, 703, 714, 908, 909
Voice phone:	800-969-9090
E-mail address:	info@digex.net
Dialup number:	301-220-0258, 410-605-2700, 609-348-6203, 703-281-7997, 714-261-5201, 908-937-9481, 909-222-2204; login as new
Services provided:	Shell, SLIP/PPP, e-mail, newsgroups, telnet, FTP, IRC, Gopher, WAIS, and more

Earthlink Network, Inc.

Area code(s):	213, 310, 818
Voice phone:	213-644-9500
E-mail address:	info@earthlink.net
Services provided:	Shell, SLIP, PPP, ISDN, 56, T1, DNS

Echo

Area code(s):	212, 718
Voice phone:	212-255-3839
E-mail address:	info@echonyc.com
Dialup number:	212-989-3382
Services provided:	Conferencing, e-mail, shell, complete Internet access including telnet, FTP, SLIP/PPP

Eden Matrix

Area code(s):	512
Voice phone:	512-478-9900
E-mail address:	jch@eden.com
Services provided:	Shell, SLIP, PPP, T1

Edge

Area code(s):	615
Voice phone:	615-455-9915 (Tullahoma), 615-726-8700 (Nashville)
E-mail address:	info@edge.net
Services provided:	Shell, SLIP, PPP, ISDN, 56

ElectriCiti Incorporated

Area code(s):	619, 408, 415, 510
Voice phone:	619-338-9000
E-mail address:	info@electriciti.com
Services provided:	SLIP, CSLIP, PPP

EriNet Online Communications

Area code(s):	513
Voice phone:	513-436-1700
E-mail address:	info@erinet.com
Services provided:	Shell, SLIP, PPP

Escape (Kazan Corp)

Area code(s):	212, 718
Voice phone:	212-888-8780
E-mail address:	info@escape.com
Services provided:	Shell, SLIP, PPP, 56

Eskimo North

Area code(s):	206
Voice phone:	206-367-7457
E-mail address:	nanook@eskimo.com
Services provided:	Shell

ESNET Communications

Area code(s):	619
Voice phone:	619-287-5943
E-mail address:	steve@cg57.esnet.com
Services provided:	Shell

Evergreen Internet

Area code(s):	602, 702, 801
Voice phone:	602-230-9339
E-mail address:	evergreen@libre.com
Services provided:	Shell, FTP, telnet, SLIP, PPP, others

Exchange Network Services, Inc.

Area code(s):	216
Voice phone:	216-261-4593
E-mail address:	info@en.com
Services provided:	Shell

Exec-PC BBS

Area code(s):	414
Voice phone:	800-EXECPC-1, 414-789-4200
E-mail address:	info@earth.execpc.com
Services provided:	Shell

FGInet, Inc.

Area code(s):	217
Voice phone:	217-544-2775
E-mail address:	newuser@mail.fgi.net
Services provided:	Shell, SLIP, PPP

FishNet (Prometheus Information Corp)

Area code(s):	215, 610
Voice phone:	610-337-9994
E-mail address:	info@pond.com
Services provided:	Shell, SLIP, PPP

Florida Online

Area code(s):	407, 305, 904, 813
Voice phone:	407-635-8888
E-mail address:	jerry@digital.net
Services provided:	Shell, SLIP, PPP, ISDN, 56-T1

FredNet

Area code(s):	301
Voice phone:	301-698-2386
E-mail address:	info@fred.net
Services provided:	Shell, SLIP

Freelance Systems Programming

Area code(s):	513
Voice phone:	513-254-7246
E-mail address:	fsp@dayton.fsp.com
Services provided:	Shell, SLIP

Freeside Communications

Area code(s):	210, 512
Voice phone:	800-968-8750
E-mail address:	sales@fc.net
Services provided:	Shell, SLIP, PPP, ISDN, 56-T1

FullFeed Communications

Area code(s):	608, 414, 715
Voice phone:	608-246-4239
E-mail address:	info@fullfeed.com
Services provided:	Shell, PPP, 28.8, 56, 384, T1

FXnet

Area code(s):	800, 704, 803
Voice phone:	704-338-4670
E-mail address:	info@fx.net
Services provided:	Shell, SLIP, PPP, ISDN, 56, T1

Gateway to the World, Inc.

Area code(s):	National/International
Voice phone:	305-670-2930
E-mail address:	mjansen@gate.com
Services provided:	Shell

Global Connect, Inc.

Area code(s):	National/International
Voice phone:	804-229-4484
E-mail address:	info@gc.net
Services provided:	SLIP, CSLIP, PPP, DNS

Global Vision, Inc.

Area code(s):	803
Voice phone:	803-241-0901
E-mail address:	derdziak@globalvision.net
Services provided:	Shell, SLIP, PPP, ISDN, 56-T1

Great Basin Internet Services

Area code(s):	702
Voice phone:	702-829-2244
E-mail address:	info@greatbasin.com
Services provided:	UUCP, SLIP, PPP

GSS Internet

Area code(s):	405, 918
Voice phone:	918-835-3655
E-mail address:	info@galstar.com
Services provided:	Shell, SLIP, PPP

Hawaii OnLine

Area code(s):	808
Voice phone:	808-246-1880, 808-533-6981
E-mail address:	info@aloha.net
Services provided:	Shell, SLIP, PPP, 56-T1, DNS, ISDN

Hevanet Communications

Area code(s):	503
Voice phone:	503-228-3520
E-mail address:	info@hevanet.com
Services provided:	Shell, SLIP, PPP, telnet

HoloNet

Area code(s):	510, PSINet, Tymnet
Voice phone:	510-704-0160
E-mail address:	support@holonet.net
Dialup number:	510-704-1058
Services provided:	Complete Internet access

HoloNet/Information Access Technologies, Inc.

Area code(s):	National/International
Voice phone:	510-704-0160
E-mail address:	support@holonet.net
Services provided:	Shell, [C]SLIP, PPP, DNS

Hookup Communication Corporation

Area code(s):	519, Canada-wide
Voice phone:	800-363-0400
E-mail address:	info@hookup.net
Services provided:	Shell, e-mail, Usenet, FTP, telnet, Gopher, WAIS, WWW, IRC, Hytelnet, Archie, SLIP/PPP

I-2000

Area code(s):	203, 516, 718, 908, 914
Voice phone:	516-867-6379
E-mail address:	mikef@i-2000.com
Services provided:	SLIP, PPP

ICNet/Innovative Concepts

Area code(s):	313, 810, 616, 517, 906
Voice phone:	313-998-0090
E-mail address:	info@ic.net
Services provided:	Shell, SLIP, PPP, DNS, ISDN, 56K, T1

IDS World Network

Area code(s):	401, 305, 407, CompuServe Network
Voice phone:	401-885-6855
E-mail address:	info@ids.net
Dialup number:	401-884-9002
Services provided:	Shell, FTP, Gopher, telnet, Talk, Usenet news, SLIP

IgLou Internet Services

Area code(s):	502, 812, 606, 513
Voice phone:	800-436-IGLOU
E-mail address:	info@iglou.com
Services provided:	Shell, SLIP, PPP, ISDN

Illuminati Online

Area code(s):	512
Voice phone:	512-462-0999, 512-447-7866
E-mail address:	admin@io.com
Services provided:	Shell, SLIP, PPP, ISDN

Info-Highway International, Inc.

Area code(s):	409, 713
Voice phone:	713-447-7025, 800-256-1370
E-mail address:	smcneely@infohwy.com
Services provided:	Shell, SLIP, PPP

Ingress Communications, Inc.

Area code(s):	212, 718
Voice phone:	212-679-8592
E-mail address:	info@ingress.com
Services provided:	Shell, SLIP, PPP, 56-T1

Innovative Data (ID-Net)

Area code(s):	313, 810
Voice phone:	810-478-3554
E-mail address:	info@id.net
Services provided:	Shell, [C]SLIP, PPP, 56-T1

INS Info Services

Area code(s):	800, 319, 402, 515, 712
Voice phone:	800-546-6587
E-mail address:	service@ins.infonet.net
Services provided:	Shell, SLIP, 56-T1

Institute for Global Communications (IGC)

Area code(s):	415
Voice phone:	415-442-0220
E-mail address:	support@igc.apc.org
Dialup number:	415-322-0284
Services provided:	E-mail, telnet, FTP, Gopher, Archie, Veronica, WAIS, SLIP/PPP

InterAccess Co.

Area code(s):	312, 708, 815
Voice phone:	800-967-1580
E-mail address:	info@interaccess.com
Dialup number:	708-671-0237
Services provided:	Shell, FTP, telnet, SLIP, PPP, and so on

Internet Access Company

Area code(s):	617, 508
Voice phone:	617-276-7200
E-mail address:	info@tiac.net
Services provided:	Shell, SLIP, PPP, ISDN, 56

Internet Alaska

Area code(s):	907
Voice phone:	907-562-4638
E-mail address:	info@alaska.net
Services provided:	Shell, 56-T1

Internet Atlanta

Area code(s):	National/International
Voice phone:	404-410-9000
E-mail address:	info@atlanta.com
Services provided:	UUCP, SLIP, PPP, ISDN, 56, T1

Internet Connect Services, Inc.

Area code(s):	409, 512, 713
Voice phone:	512-572-9987, 713-439-0949
E-mail address:	staff@icsi.net
Services provided:	Shell, SLIP, PPP, ISDN, 56-T1

Internet Connect, Inc.

Area code(s):	414
Voice phone:	414-476-ICON (4266)
E-mail address:	info@inc.net
Services provided:	Shell, SLIP, PPP, ISDN, 56-T1

Internet Connection

Area code(s):	408
Voice phone:	408-461-INET
E-mail address:	sales@ico.net
Services provided:	SLIP, PPP, ISDN, 56-T1

Internet Direct of Utah

Area code(s):   801
Voice phone: 801-578-0300
E-mail address: johnh@indirect.com
Services provided: Shell, SLIP, PPP,
                    56-T1

Internet Direct, Inc.

Area code(s):   602
Voice phone: 602-274-0100,
                    602-324-0100
E-mail address: sales@indirect.com
Services provided: Shell, SLIP, PPP

Internet Express

Area code(s):   719, 303, 505,
                    602, 800
Voice phone: 800-592-1240
E-mail address: service@usa.net
Services provided: Shell, SLIP, PPP,
                    dedicated lines

Internet Nebraska Corp.

Area code(s):   402
Voice phone: 402-434-8680
E-mail address: info@inetnebr.com
Services provided: Shell, SLIP, PPP

Internet On-Ramp, Inc.

Area code(s):   509
Voice phone: 509-927-RAMP
                    (7267), 509-927-7267
E-mail address: info@on-ramp.ior.com
Services provided: Shell, SLIP, CSLIP,
                    PPP, leased line

Internet Online Services

Area code(s):   201, 212, 518, 800
Voice phone: 800-221-3756
E-mail address: accounts@ios.com
Services provided: Shell, SLIP, PPP,
                    leased lines, DNS

Internetworks

Area code(s):   National/International
Voice phone: 503-233-4774
E-mail address: info@i.net
Services provided: SLIP, PPP, ISDN,
                    leased lines

InterNex Information Services, Inc.

Area code(s):   415, 408, 510
Voice phone: 415-473-3060
E-mail address: sales@internex.net
Services provided: ISDN

Interpath

Area code(s):   919, 910, 704
Voice phone: 800-849-6305
E-mail address: info@infopath.net
Services provided: Full shell for UNIX,
                    and SLIP and PPP

Interport Communications Corp.

Area code(s):   212, 718
Voice phone: 212-989-1128
E-mail address: sales@interport.net,
                    info@interport.net
                    (autoreply)
Services provided: Shell, SLIP, PPP,
                    dedicated lines

interQuest inc.

Area code(s):   205
Voice phone: 205-464-8280
E-mail address: paul@iquest.com
Services provided: Shell, SLIP, PPP

intuitive information, inc.

Area code(s):   508
Voice phone: 508-342-1100
E-mail address: info@iii.net
Services provided: Shell, [C]SLIP,
                    PPP, 56

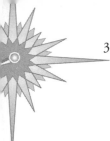

IQuest Network Services

Area code(s):	317
Voice phone:	317-259-5050, 800-844-UNIX
E-mail address:	info@iquest.net
Services provided:	Shell, SLIP, PPP, ISDN, 56, T1

KAIWAN Corporation

Area code(s):	714, 213, 310, 818, 909, 805
Voice phone:	714-638-2139
E-mail address:	sales@kaiwan.com
Services provided:	Shell, SLIP, PPP, 56, 256, 512, 768, T1

LI Net, Inc.

Area code(s):	516
Voice phone:	516-476-1168
E-mail address:	questions@li.net
Services provided:	Shell, SLIP, 56, T1

Lightside, Inc.

Area code(s):	818, 310, 714, 909
Voice phone:	818-858-9261
E-mail address:	lightside@lightside.com
Services provided:	Shell, SLIP, PPP, 56-T1

LineX Communcations

Area code(s):	415
Voice phone:	415-455-1650
E-mail address:	info@linex.com
Services provided:	Shell

Long Island Information, Inc.

Area code(s):	516
Voice phone:	516-248-5381
E-mail address:	info@liii.com
Services provided:	Shell, SLIP

Maestro Technologies, Inc.

Area code(s):	212, 718, 516
Voice phone:	212-240-9600
E-mail address:	staff@maestro.com, rlekhi@maestro.com
Services provided:	Shell, SLIP, PPP

maine.net, Inc.

Area code(s):	207
Voice phone:	207-780-6381
E-mail address:	atr@maine.net
Services provided:	SLIP, PPP, 56, T1

MBnet

Area code(s):	204
Voice phone:	204-474-9590
E-mail address:	info@mbnet.mb.ca
Dialup number:	204-275-6132, login as mbnet with password guest
Services provided:	Shell, e-mail, Usenet, FTP, telnet, Gopher, WAIS, WWW, IRC, Archie, Hytelnet, SLIP/PPP

MCSNet

Area code(s):	312, 708, 815
Voice phone:	312-248-8649
E-mail address:	info@mcs.net
Services provided:	Shell, SLIP, PPP, dedicated, ISDN

Metronet, Inc.

Area code(s):	214, 817
Voice phone:	214-705-2900, 817-543-8756
E-mail address:	info@metronet.com
Services provided:	Shell, SLIP, PPP

MichNet

Area code(s): 313, 616, 517, 810, 906
Voice phone: 313-764-9430
E-mail address: `recruiting@merit.edu`
Services provided: SLIP, PPP, host services, 56, T1

Millennium Communications

Area code(s): 507, 612
Voice phone: 507-282-8943, 612-338-5509
E-mail address: `info@millcom.com`
Services provided: Shell, SLIP, PPP

MindSpring Enterprises, Inc.

Area code(s): 404, 706
Voice phone: 404-888-0725
E-mail address: `sales@mindspring.com`
Services provided: Shell, SLIP, PPP

Minnesota MicroNet

Area code(s): 612
Voice phone: 612-681-8018
E-mail address: `info@mm.com`
Services provided: SLIP, SLIP, PPP

Minnesota Regional Network (MRNet)

Area code(s): 612, 507, 218
Voice phone: 612-342-2570
E-mail address: `sales@mr.net`
Services provided: SLIP, 56, T1

MIX Communications

Area code(s): 414
Voice phone: 414-228-0739
E-mail address: `sales@mixcom.com`
Services provided: BBS, SLIP, PPP

Msen

Area code(s): 313, 810, 800
Voice phone: 313-998-4562
E-mail address: `info-request@msen.com`
Services provided: Shell, e-mail, telnet, FTP, Usenet, Gopher, IRC, WAIS, SLIP/PPP

Msen, Inc.

Area code(s): 800, 313, 517, 616, 906
Voice phone: 313-998-4562
E-mail address: `info@msen.com`
Services provided: Shell, SLIP, PPP, ISDN, 56 to T1

MV Communications

Area code(s): 603
Voice phone: 603-429-2223
E-mail address: `info@mv.mv.com`
Services provided: Shell, SLIP, PPP, 56

Neighborhood Internet Connection

Area code(s): 201
Voice phone: 201-934-1445
E-mail address: `info@nic.com`, `combes@nic.com`
Services provided: Shell

Neosoft

Area code(s): 713, 504, 314, 800, SprintNet
Voice phone: 713-684-5969
E-mail address: `info@neosoft.com`
Services provided: Shell, Usenet, FTP, telnet, Gopher, SLIP/PPP, and so on

NeoSoft, Inc.

Area code(s):	800, 713, 409, 214, 504, 314
Voice phone:	713-684-5969
E-mail address:	jmw3@neosoft.com
Services provided:	Shell, SLIP, PPP, ISDN, 56, T1

Netcom On-Line Communications Services

Area code(s):	206, 212, 214, 303, 310, 312, 404, 408, 415, 503, 510, 512, 617, 619, 703, 714, 818, 916
Voice phone:	800-501-8649
E-mail address:	info@netcom.com
Dialup number:	206-547-5992, 212-354-3870, 214-753-0045, 303-758-0101, 310-842-8835, 312-380-0340, 404-303-9765, 408-261-4700, 408-459-9851, 415-328-9940, 415-985-5650, 503-626-6833, 510-274-2900, 510-426-6610, 510-865-9004, 512-206-4950, 617-237-8600, 619-234-0524, 703-255-5951, 714-708-3800, 818-585-3400, 916-965-1371; login as guest
Services provided:	Shell, e-mail, Usenet, FTP, telnet, Gopher, IRC, WAIS, SLIP/PPP

Network 23, Inc.

Area code(s):	212, 917
Voice phone:	212-786-4810
E-mail address:	info@net23.com
Services provided:	Shell

Network 99, Inc.

Area code(s):	National/International
Voice phone:	702-442-7353, 602-780-7533, 800-NET-99IP
E-mail address:	net99@cluster.mcs.net
Services provided:	56K-T3

Network Intensive

Area code(s):	714
Voice phone:	800-273-5600
E-mail address:	info@ni.net
Services provided:	Shell, SLIP, PPP, 56, ISDN, T1

Network Internet Services

Area code(s):	516
Voice phone:	516-543-0234
E-mail address:	info@netusa.net
Services provided:	Shell, SLIP, PPP

Network Link, Inc.

Area code(s):	619, 317
Voice phone:	619-278-5943
E-mail address:	stevef@tnl1.tnwl.com
Services provided:	Shell, NNTP, IDSN, 56, T1

New Jersey Computer Connection

Area code(s):	609
Voice phone:	609-896-2799
E-mail address:	info@pluto.njcc.com
Services provided:	Shell, SLIP, PPP

New Mexico Technet, Inc.

Area code(s):	505, 602, 303, 915, 800
Voice phone:	505-345-6555
E-mail address:	granoff@technet.nm.org
Services provided:	Shell, SLIP, PPP, leased line

New York Net

Area code(s):	201, 203, 212, 516, 609, 718, 908, 914, 917
Voice phone:	718-776-6811
E-mail address:	sales@new-york.net
Services provided:	SLIP, PPP, 56, 64, 128 to T1

North Shore Access

Area code(s):	617
Voice phone:	617-593-3110
E-mail address:	info@shore.net
Dialup number:	617-593-4557, login as new
Services provided:	Shell, FTP, telnet, Gopher, Archie, SLIP/PPP

Northcoast Internet

Area code(s):	707
Voice phone:	707-444-1913
Services provided:	Shell, FTP, telnet, Gopher, SLIP/PPP

NorthWest CommLink

Area code(s):	206
Voice phone:	206-336-0103
E-mail address:	gtyacke@nwcl.net
Services provided:	Shell, SLIP, PPP, 56 - T1

Northwest Nexus, Inc.

Area code(s):	206
Voice phone:	206-455-3505
E-mail address:	info@nwnexus.wa.com
Services provided:	Shell, SLIP, PPP, 56, T1

NovaNet, Inc.

Area code(s):	703, 202, 301
Voice phone:	703-524-4800
E-mail address:	sales@novanet.com
Services provided:	Shell, SLIP, PPP, 56-T1

Nuance Network Services

Area code(s):	205
Voice phone:	205-533-4296
E-mail address:	info@nuance.com
Services provided:	Shell, Usenet, FTP, telnet, Gopher, SLIP/PPP

NYSERNet

Area code(s):	212, 315, 516, 518, 607, 716, 718, 914
Voice phone:	315-453-2912
E-mail address:	info@nysernet.org
Services provided:	Shell, 56-T3

Nyx

Area code(s):	303
Voice phone:	303-871-3308
E-mail address:	info@nyx.cs.du.edu
Services provided:	Shell, semi-anonymous accounts

OARNet

Area code(s):	614
Voice phone:	800-627-8101
E-mail address:	info@oar.net
Services provided:	Shell, SLIP/PPP

Old Colorado City Communications

Area code(s):   719
Voice phone: 719-528-5849
E-mail address: thefox@oldcolo.com
Services provided: Shell, 56

Onramp Access, Inc.

Area code(s):   512
Voice phone: 512-322-9200
E-mail address: info@onr.com
Services provided: SLIP, PPP

Pacific Internet

Area code(s):   707
Voice phone: 707-468-1005
E-mail address: info@pacific.net
Services provided: Shell, SLIP, PPP,
                     56K-T1

Pacific Rim Network, Inc.

Area code(s):   800, 206
Voice phone: 206-650-0442
E-mail address: sales@pacificrim.com
Services provided: Shell, SLIP, PPP,
                     ISDN, 56K-T1

Pacifier Computers

Area code(s):   206
Voice phone: 206-693-2116
E-mail address: sales@pacifier.com
Services provided: Shell, SLIP, PPP

PacketWorks, Inc.

Area code(s):   813
Voice phone: 813-446-8826
E-mail address: info@packet.net
Services provided: PPP, ISDN

Panix Public Access UNIX and Internet

Area code(s):   212, 516
Voice phone: 212-787-6160
E-mail address: info@panix.com
Dialup number: 212-787-3100,
                     516-626-7863,
                     login as newuser
Services provided: Shell, Usenet, FTP,
                     telnet, Gopher, Archie,
                     WWW, WAIS,
                     SLIP/PPP

PCNet

Area code(s):   203
Voice phone: 800-66-4INET
E-mail address: sales@pcnet.com
Services provided: Shell, SLIP, PPP,
                     ISDN, %6, T1

Phantom Access Technologies, Inc.

Area code(s):   212, 718, 516, 914
Voice phone: 212-989-2418
E-mail address: info@phantom.com
Services provided: Shell, SLIP, PPP,
                     56-T1

Ping

Area code(s):   404, 800 (includes
                     Hawaii and Alaska)
Voice phone: 800-746-4835,
                     404-399-1670
E-mail address: bdk@ping.com
Services provided: Shell, SLIP, PPP, 56

Pioneer Global

Area code(s):   617
Voice phone: 617-375-0200
E-mail address: sales@pn.com
Services provided: Shell, 28.8, 56, T1

Pipeline Network

Area code(s):	National/International
Voice phone:	212-267-3636
E-mail address:	`staff@pipeline.com`
Services provided:	Shell

Planet Access Networks

Area code(s):	201, 908, 319, 205
Voice phone:	201-691-4704
E-mail address:	`fred@planet.net`
Services provided:	Shell, SLIP, PPP, dedicated lines

Portal Communications Company

Area code(s):	408, SprintNet
Voice phone:	408-973-9111
E-mail address:	`info@portal.com`
Services provided:	Shell, e-mail, Usenet, FTP, telnet, Gopher, IRC, SLIP/PPP

Primenet

Area code(s):	602, 213, 818
Voice phone:	602-870-1010, 800-4 NET FUN
E-mail address:	`info@primenet.com`
Services provided:	Shell, SLIP, PPP, 56, 128, T1

PSI

Area code(s):	North America, Europe and Pacific Basin; send e-mail to `numbers-info@psi.com` for list
Voice phone:	703-709-0300
E-mail address:	`all-info@psi.com`
Services provided:	Complete Internet services

QuakeNet

Area code(s):	415
Voice phone:	415-655-6607
E-mail address:	`info@quake.net` (autoreply), `admin@quake.net` (human)
Services provided:	SLIP, PPP, DNS, 56-T1

Rabbit Network, Inc.

Area code(s):	810, 800 (entire U.S. and Canada)
Voice phone:	800-456-0094
E-mail address:	`info@rabbit.net`
Services provided:	Shell, SLIP, PPP, leased lines

Real/Time Communications

Area code(s):	512
Voice phone:	512-451-0046
E-mail address:	`info@realtime.net`
Services provided:	Shell, SLIP, PPP, IDSN, Custom services

Red River Net

Area code(s):	701, 218
Voice phone:	701-232-2227
E-mail address:	`lien@rrnet.com`
Services provided:	Shell, SLIP, 56, T1

Ripco Communcations, Inc.

Area code(s):	312, 708
Voice phone:	312-665-0065
E-mail address:	`info@ripco.com`
Services provided:	Shell

Rocky Mountain Internet, Inc.
Area code(s):   303, 719
Voice phone: 800-900-RMII
E-mail address: `mountr@rmii.com,`
                     `jimw@rmii.com`
Services provided: Shell, SLIP, PPP,
                     56, T1

Sacramento Network Access, Inc.
Area code(s):   800, 916, 209,
                     510, 702
Voice phone: 916-565-4500
E-mail address: `sales@sna.com`
Services provided: Shell, SLIP, PPP

SatelNET Communications
Area code(s):   305
Voice phone: 305-434-8738
E-mail address: `martinson@satelnet.org`
Services provided: Shell, SLIP, PPP

Schunix
Area code(s):   508
Voice phone: 508-853-0258
E-mail address: `info@schunix.com`
Services provided: Shell, SLIP, PPP,
                     ISDN, 56, 128, T1

Scruz-Net
Area code(s):   408, 415
Voice phone: 800-319-5555,
                     408-457-5050
E-mail address: `info@scruz.net`
Services provided: SLIP, PPP, ISDN,
                     56, T1

Sibylline, Inc.
Area code(s):   501
Voice phone: 501-521-4660
E-mail address: `info@sibylline.com`
Services provided: Shell, SLIP, PPP, 56,
                     128, T1, DNS,
                     Advertising

Sierra-Net
Area code(s):   702, 916
Voice phone: 702-832-6911
E-mail address: `info@sierra.net`
Services provided: Shell, SLIP, PPP,
                     56-T1

SIMS, Inc.
Area code(s):   803
Voice phone: 803-762-4956
E-mail address: `info@sims.net`
Services provided: Shell, SLIP, PPP,
                     ISDN, 56, 128, 256

Skagit On-Line Services
Area code(s):   206
Voice phone: 206-755-0190
E-mail address: `info@sos.net`
Services provided: Shell, SLIP, PPP

SkyNET Corp.
Area code(s):   816, 913
Voice phone: 816-483-0002
E-mail address: `info@sky.net`
Services provided: Shell, SLIP, PPP,
                     56-T1

South Carolina SuperNet, Inc.
Area code(s):   803
Voice phone: 803-748-1207
E-mail address: `info@scsn.net`
Services provided: SLIP, PPP, 56, T1

South Coast Computing Services, Inc.
Area code(s):   800, 713, 918
Voice phone: 800-221-6478
E-mail address: `sales@sccsi.com`
Services provided: Shell, SLIP, PPP,
                     56, T1

South Valley Internet

Area code(s):	408
Voice phone:	408-683-4533
E-mail address:	info@garlic.com
Services provided:	Shell, SLIP, PPP, Dedicated, Leased

SouthWind Internet Access, Inc.

Area code(s):	316
Voice phone:	316-263-7963
E-mail address:	staff@southwind.net
Services provided:	Shell, TIA-SLIP

SSNet, Inc.

Area code(s):	610, 302
Voice phone:	302-378-1386
E-mail address:	info@ssnet.com, sharris@ssnet.com
Services provided:	Shell, SLIP, PPP UUCP

StarNet Communications, Inc. (Winternet)

Area code(s):	612
Voice phone:	612-941-9177
E-mail address:	info@winternet.com
Services provided:	Shell, SLIP, PPP

SymNet

Area code(s):	904
Voice phone:	904-385-1061
E-mail address:	info@symnet.net
Services provided:	Shell, SLIP, PPP

Teleport

Area code(s):	503, 206
Voice phone:	503-223-4245
E-mail address:	info@teleport.com
Dialup number:	503-220-1016
Services provided:	Shell, e-mail, Usenet, FTP, telnet, Gopher, SLIP/PPP

Teleport, Inc.

Area code(s):	503, 206
Voice phone:	503-223-0076
E-mail address:	sales@teleport.com
Services provided:	Shell, SLIP, PPP, ISDN

Telerama

Area code(s):	412
Voice phone:	412-481-3505
E-mail address:	sysop@telerama.lm.com
Dialup number:	412-481-4644
Services provided:	Shell, e-mail, telnet, Usenet, FTP, telnet, Gopher, IRC, SLIP/PPP

Texas Metronet

Area code(s):	214, 817
Voice phone:	214-705-2900
E-mail address:	info@metronet.com
Dialup number:	214-705-2901, 817-261-1127; login as info, with password info
Services provided:	Shell, e-mail, Usenet, FTP, telnet, Gopher, IRC, SLIP/PPP

Tezcatlipoca, Inc.

Area code(s):	312, 708
Voice phone:	312-850-0181
E-mail address:	ilixi@tezcat.com
Services provided:	Shell, TIA

The Dorsai Embassy

Area code(s):	718, 212, 201, 203, 914, 516
Voice phone:	718-392-3667
E-mail address:	system@dorsai.dorsai.org
Services provided:	Shell, SLIP, PPP

The Well

Area code(s): 415
Voice phone: 415-332-4335
E-mail address: info@well.com
Services provided: Shell

The World

Area code(s): 617, 508
Voice phone: 617-739-0202
E-mail address: staff@world.std.com
Services provided: Shell, DNS

Townsend Communcations, Inc.

Area code(s): 206
Voice phone: 206-385-0464
E-mail address: inquiries@olympus.net
Services provided: PPP, 56

Traveller Information Services

Area code(s): 204
Voice phone: 800-840-TNET,
204-883-2686
E-mail address: info@traveller.com
Services provided: Shell, CSLIP, PPP,
ISDN

Tyrell Corp.

Area code(s): 816, 913, 504, 316
Voice phone: 800-TYRELL-1
E-mail address: support@tyrell.net
Services provided: Shell, [C]SLIP, PPP

TZ-Link

Area code(s): 914
Voice phone: 914-353-5443
E-mail address: drew@j51.com
Services provided: Shell

UltraNet Communications, Inc.

Area code(s): 508
Voice phone: 508-229-8400,
800-763-8111
E-mail address: info@ultranet.com
Services provided: SLIP, PPP, ISDN, 56,
128, 384

US Net, Inc.

Area code(s): 301, 202, 703
Voice phone: 301-572-5926
E-mail address: info@us.net
Services provided: Shell, SLIP, PPP,
DNS, 56-T1

UUNorth Incorporated

Area code(s): 416
Voice phone: 416-225-8649
E-mail address: uunorth@north.net
Dialup number: 416-221-0200,
login as new
Services provided: E-mail, Usenet, FTP,
telnet, Gopher, WAIS,
WWW, IRC, Archie,
SLIP/PPP

VNet Internet Access, Inc.

Area code(s): 704, public data
network
Voice phone: 800-377-3282
E-mail address: info@vnet.net
Dialup number: 704-347-8839,
login as new
Services provided: Shell, e-mail, Usenet,
FTP, telnet, Gopher,
IRC, SLIP/PPP,
UUCP

VoiceNet/DCS

Area code(s):	800, 215
Voice phone:	215-674-9290
E-mail address:	info@voicenet.com
Services provided:	Shell, SLIP, PPP, ISDN

West Coast Online

Area code(s):	415, 510, 707, 408, 916, 209
Voice phone:	800-WCO INTERNET
E-mail address:	info@calon.com
Services provided:	Shell, SLIP, PPP, ISDN, 56-T1

WestNet

Area code(s):	914
Voice phone:	914-967-7816
E-mail address:	staff@westnet.com
Services provided:	Shell

Widomaker Communications

Area code(s):	804
Voice phone:	804-253-7621
E-mail address:	bloyall@widomaker.com
Services provided:	Shell, SLIP, PPP

Wilder Systems, Inc.

Area code(s):	617
Voice phone:	617-933-8810
E-mail address:	info@id.wing.net
Services provided:	Shell, pipeline, PPP, SLIP, ISDN, 56-T1

Wimsey Information Services

Area code(s):	604
Voice phone:	604-936-8649
E-mail address:	admin@wimsey.com
Services provided:	Shell, e-mail, Usenet, FTP, telnet, Gopher, WAIS, WWW, IRC, Archie, SLIP/PPP

Wizvax Communications

Area code(s):	518
Voice phone:	518-271-6005
E-mail address:	root@wizvax.com
Services provided:	Shell, SLIP, CSLIP, PPP

WLN

Area code(s):	800, 206, 509, 503, 208, 406, 360
Voice phone:	800-DIAL-WLN, 800-342-5956, 206-923-4000
E-mail address:	info@wln.com
Services provided:	Shell, SLIP, PPP, 56-T1

WorldWide Access

Area code(s):	312, 708, 815, 414
Voice phone:	708-367-1870
E-mail address:	support@wwa.com
Services provided:	Shell, SLIP, PPP, ISDN, Leased lines

Xensei Corporation

Area code(s):	617
Voice phone:	617-773-4785
E-mail address:	sales@xensei.com, terri@xensei.com
Services provided:	SLIP, PPP, ISDN, 56K

XMission

Area code(s):	801
Voice phone:	801-539-0852
E-mail address:	support@xmission.com
Services provided:	Shell, SLIP, PPP, leased line

XNet Information Systems

Area code(s):   708
Voice phone: 708-983-6064
E-mail address: info@xnet.com
Dialup number: 708-983-6435,
                     708-882-1101
Services provided: Shell, e-mail, Usenet,
                     FTP, telnet, Gopher,
                     Archie, IRC, SLIP/
                     PPP, UUCP

You Tools Corporation (FAST.NET)

Area code(s):   610, 215, 717
Voice phone: 610-954-5910
E-mail address: internet@youtools.com
Services provided: SLIP, PPP, ISDN,
                     56-T1

Zilker Internet Park

Area code(s):   512
Voice phone: 512-206-3850
E-mail address: info@zilker.net
Services provided: Shell, SLIP, PPP,
                     ISDN

zNET

Area code(s):   408
Voice phone: 408-477-9638
E-mail address: info@znet.com
Services provided: SLIP, PPP, ISDN,
                     DNS

Zone One Network Exchange (ZONE)

Area code(s):   800, 718, 212, 914,
                     516, 917, 201, 908
Voice phone: 718-549-8078
E-mail address: info@zone.net
Services provided: UUCP, SLIP, PPP,
                     56-T1

Providers in Australia

Aarnet

Voice phone: +61 6-249-3385
E-mail address: aarnet@aarnet.edu.au

Connect.com.au P/L

Areas serviced: Major Australian capital cities (2, 3, 6, 7, 8, 9)
Voice phone: 1 800 818 262 or +61 3 528 2239
E-mail address: connect@connect.com.au
Services provided: Shell, SLIP/PPP, UUCP

Providers in Germany

Contributed Software

Voice phone: +49 30-694-69-07
E-mail address: info@contrib.de
Dialup number: +49 30-694-60-55, login as guest or gast

Individual Network e.V.

Area serviced: All of Germany
Voice phone: +49 0441 9808556
E-mail address: in-info@individual.net
Dialup number: 02238 15071, login as info
Services provided: UUCP throughout Germany; FTP, SLIP, telnet and other services in
                          some major cities

Inter Networking System (INS)

Voice phone: +49 2305 356505
E-mail address: info@ins.net

Providers in the Netherlands

Knoware

E-mail address: info@knoware.nl
Dialup number: 030 896775

NetLand

Voice phone: 020 6943664
E-mail address: Info@netland.nl
Dialup number: 020 6940350, login as new or info

Simplex

E-mail address: simplex@simplex.nl
Dialup number: 020 6653388, login as new or info

Providers in New Zealand

Actrix

Voice phone: 04-389-6316
E-mail address: john@actrix.gen.nz

Providers in Switzerland

SWITCH - Swiss Academic and Research Network

Voice phone: +41 1 268 1515
E-mail address: postmaster@switch.ch

Providers in the United Kingdom

Almac

Voice phone: +44 0324-665371
E-mail address: alastair.mcintyre@almac.co.uk

Cix

Voice phone: +44 49 2641 961
E-mail address: cixadmin@cix.compulink.co.uk

Demon Internet Limited

Voice phone: 081-349-0063 (London)
                    031-552-0344 (Edinburgh)
E-mail address: internet@demon.net
Services provided: SLIP/PPP accounts

The Direct Connection (UK)

Voice phone: +44 (0)81 317 0100
E-mail address: helpdesk@dircon.cu.uk
Dialup number: +44 (0)81 317 2222

Note to Providers

If you would like to be included in future versions of this list, for use in subsequent editions of this book as well as other Sams Internet books, send an e-mail message to Mark Taber at mtaber@netcom.com.

APPENDIX C
INTERNET RESOURCES FOR OS/2

World Wide Web Pages of Interest

FTP Sites

OS/2-Related Newsgroups

This appendix provides you with Internet resources you can use to find out more about OS/2. The resources are divided into the following three categories:

◆ World Wide Web Pages of Interest
◆ FTP Sites
◆ OS/2-Related Newsgroups

World Wide Web Pages of Interest

This section contains a collection of URL (uniform resource locator) addresses for use in the OS/2 WebExplorer. To use these addresses, open the WebExplorer. Press Ctrl+D, type the URL exactly as you see it here, and press Enter. If you see something you like, just press Ctrl+A to add it to your WebExplorer QuickList. See Chapter 8, "Navigating the Web with the WebExplorer," for additional information.

CalTech OS/2 Home Page
http://www.ccsf.caltech.edu/~kasturi/os2.html

Carnegie Mellon University OS/2 Home Page
http://www.club.cc.cmu.edu:8001/~jgrande/cmuos2.html

Cleveland OS/2 User's Group Home Page
ftp://ftp.wariat.org/pub/users/cos2ug.html

GoHTTP
http://gopher.ag.uiuc.edu/DLM/goHTTP/GoHTTP.Html

HitchHikers Guide to OS/2
http://venus.ee.ndsu.nodak.edu/os2/mharmless/hhgos2/hhgos2.htm

IBM Kiosk for Information
http://ike.engr.washington.edu/ike.html

IBM OS/2 Warp Home Page
http://www.austin.ibm.com/pspinfo/os2.html

Internet Relay Chat OS/2 Home Page
http://venus.ee.ndsu.nodak.edu/os2/

Mid-Atlantic OS/2 User Group Home Page
http://www.pinn.net/~reaper/maos2ug.html

MIT OS/2 WWW Home Page
http://www.mit.edu:8001/activities/os2/os2world.html

Munich OS/2 Archive
http://www.leo.org/cgi-bin/leo-dls/pub/comp/os/os2/00-index.html

North Suburban Chicago OS/2 User Group Home Page
`http://www.mcs.com/~schmidtj/http/nscoug/home.html`

Northern NJ OS/2 Users Group
`http://www.intac.com/nnjos2/nnjos2ug.html`

OS/2 Information Page
`http://www.cen.uiuc.edu/~jt11635/os2/os2.html`

OS/2 Northwest BBS
`http://www.halcyon.com/os2_northwest/os2nw.html`

OS/2 Power Home Page
`http://www.salford.ac.uk/os2power/os2power.html`

OS/2 Software Library
`http://www.state.ky.us/software/os2.html`

OS/2 Stuff Worldwide Home Page
`http://tklab3.cs.uit.no/OS2/index.html`

OS/2 Web
`http://www.intac.com/nnjos2/os2web.html`

Raj's Urbana-Champaign Home Page
`http://www.cen.uiuc.edu/~rs9678/raj.html`

Stupid OS/2 Tricks
`http://index.almaden.ibm.com/nonibm/tricks/tricks.html`

Team OS/2
`http://www.cen.uiuc.edu/~jt11635/os2/Docs/TeamOS2.html`

The Warp Pharmacy
`http://www.zeta.org.au/~jon/WarpPharmacy.html`

Timothy Sipples Frequently Asked Questions List
`http://www.mit.edu:8001/activities/os2/faq/os2faq0000.html`

UIUC OS/2 Home Page
`http://www.cen.uiuc.edu/~rs9678/raj.html`

University of Texas OS/2 Home Page
`http://deputy.law.utexas.edu/os2homepage.html`

University of Warwick OS/2 Home Page
`http://www.warwick.ac.uk/~phueg/os2/`

Walnut Creek
`http://ftp.cdrom.com/pub/os2`

FTP Sites

The following is a list of anonymous FTP sites of interest to many OS/2 users. To use these, open FTP-PM. Specify the address shown here as the Host, use anonymous as the User name, and use your e-mail Internet address as the Password (for example, smith@jones.net). Once you're logged on, you can navigate to the online location shown here (or, explore for yourself). See Chapter 9, "Sending and Receiving Files with FTP," for additional information.

3Com (Network Adapter Cards)
Address: ftp.3com.com
Online Location: /binaries/nw_adapters/Drivers

ATI Technical Support (Video Card Drivers and Support)
Address: atitech.ca
Online Location: pub/support/OS2

Cirrus Logic (Video Card Drivers and Support)
Address: cirrus.com
Online Location: pub/support

Hobbes (Major OS/2 File Repository)
Address: ftp-os2.nmsu.edu
Online Location: /os2

IBM (Internet Access Kit Updates)
Address: ftp.ibm.net and ftp01.ny.us.ibm.net
Online Location: pub/

IBM (General IBM Files)
Address: ftp.pcco.ibm.com
Online Location: pub/

IBM Watson Research Lab (General IBM Files)
Address: software.watson.ibm.com
Online Location: pub/

Kai Uwe Rommel (General OS/2 Files)
Address: ftp.informatik.tu-muenchen.de
Online Location: pub/

Lexmark (Printer Drivers)
Address: ftp.lexmark.com
Online Location: pub/drivers

Mirror of Hobbes
Address: luga.latrobe.edu.au
Online Location: pub/

Usenet Newsgroup Archives

Address:	`ftp.uu.net`
Online Location:	`usenet/`

Walnut Creek (Major OS/2 File Repository)

Address:	`ftp-os2.cdrom.com`
Online Location:	`.1/os2`

OS/2-Related Newsgroups

The following are newsgroups that usually are available from most news servers. The ones beginning with comp are the major groups frequented by most OS/2 Internet users. If they aren't available on your news server, ask your news administrator (or your OS/2 provider) if they can be added. To use these groups, display the whole list of newsgroups in NewsReader/2 (choose File|List all newsgroups), click on the newsgroup you want to add, and then choose Actions|Add Groups. See Chapter 7, "Navigating with OS/2 Gopher," for additional information.

```
aus.computers.os2                    fido7.os2.comm
bit.listserv.os2-l                   fido7.os2.drv
comp.binaries.os2                    fido7.os2.faq.d
comp.os.os2.advocacy                 fido7.os2.marginal
comp.os.os2.announce                 fido7.os2.prog
comp.os.os2.apps                     fido7.os2.wanted
comp.os.os2.beta                     fiod7.su.os2
comp.os.os2.bugs                     ger.pc.os2
comp.os.os2.games                    git.os2
comp.os.os2.misc                     kiel.os2
comp.os.os2.multimedia               maus.os.os-2
comp.os.os2.networking.misc          maus.os.os2.prog
comp.os.os2.networking.tcp-ip        relcom.comp.os.os2
comp.os.os2.programmer.misc          sfnet.atk.os2
comp.os.os2.programmer.oop           tamu.micro.os2
comp.os.os2.programmer.porting       tp.pd-soft.os2
comp.os.os2.programmer.tools         tw.bbs.comp.os2
comp.os.os2.setup                    ucb.os.os2
de.comp.os.os2                       uiuc.org.os2ug
fido.ger.os2                         uw.os2-users
fido7.os2                            zer.z-netz.rechner.ibm.os2
```

GLOSSARY

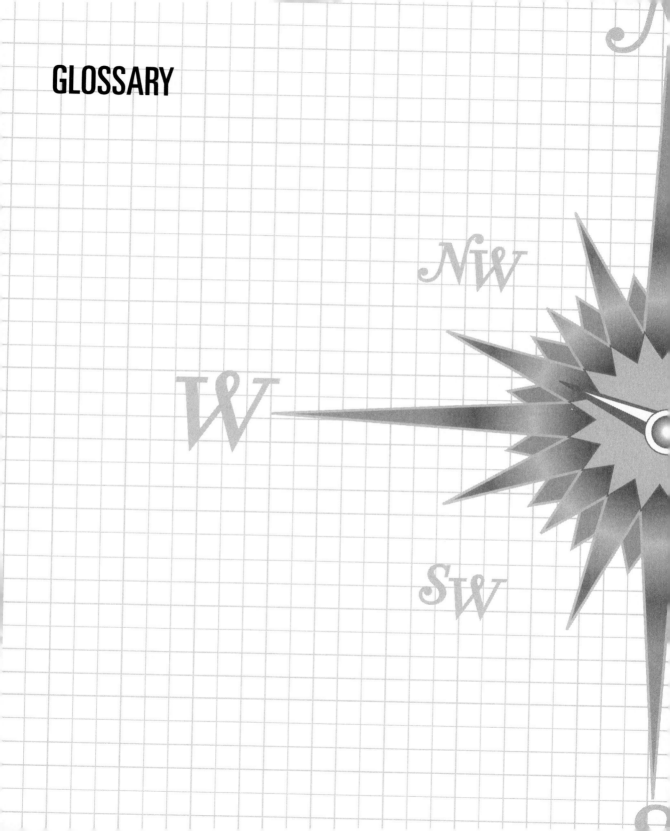

3270 or 3270 telnet Special version of telnet for full-screen-oriented connection to a mini-computer or a mainframe.

annex Loosely translated, it's a synonym for gateway or destination. It's a computer that connects other computers to the Internet.

anonymous FTP site An FTP server that permits users without accounts or passwords to download (and sometimes upload) files.

ANSI American National Standards Institute. In computerdom, it often refers to an enhanced character set or to the use of colors on a computer terminal.

any key Any key except for shift keys, that is, any key that does something when pressed all by itself. The Shift, Ctrl, NumLock, ScrollLock, and CapLock keys don't qualify. The Alt key usually doesn't qualify either. When told to press *any key*, press the spacebar, the Enter key, or a letter key.

arc Short for *archive*, arc is one of many file-archiving and file-compression formats, usually given the extension `.arc`.

Archie A tool for searching for files across the Internet.

archiving File compression.

article A message posted to a newsgroup.

ASCII American Standard Code for Information Interchange. It often refers to the first 128 characters (0 through 127) on an IBM PC-compatible computer. ASCII usually means plain text without binary or high byte (128 through 256) characters. It can also mean files that don't contain any control characters, such as ASCII 26 (Ctrl+Z) or ASCII 27 (Escape).

au A sound file format (*au* from *au*dio).

BBS Bulletin Board System, a computer connected to a modem in answer mode. It allows remote users to connect via modem to read and post messages. Most BBSs support uploading and downloading files using standard protocols such as Xmodem, Ymodem, Zmodem, and Kermit.

binary Refers to files that are intended for processing by a computer rather than for direct reading by a human. Often refers to files that contain all 256 characters. Binary is really a misnomer (because everything on a computer is actually binary).

chat Short for *Internet relay chat*, which is a kind of free-for-all Internet party line.

client A computer or program that gets information or services from a server. The programs in the OS/2 Warp Internet Access Kit are clients.

compression A method for encoding files so they take up less room on disk.

destination A synonym for gateway or annex, it's a computer that connects other computers to the Internet.

domain A network connected to the Internet; domains are the basic building blocks of the Internet. If your e-mail address is smith@smithville.net, then smithville.net is your domain.

download Receive a file from a remote system. In FTP-ese, a download is a get.

drag To move a mouse while holding down a mouse button.

dynamic IP address An IP address that can be different each time you log onto a SLIP or PPP provider.

e-mail Electronic mail. E-mail refers to personal—as opposed to public—messages passed over the Internet, CompuServe, BBSs, and other computer-based messaging systems.

e-mail address An address consisting of your e-mail ID and your domain name. For example, smith@smithville.net is an e-mail address.

FAQ Frequently Asked Questions list.

finger A program that uses the Finger protocol; it's a way to inquire about specific e-mail addresses on the Internet.

firewall A protective computer or computer program that isolates a domain or host from direct contact with the Internet.

flame A message (usually a newsgroup article) that expresses extreme anger or harsh criticism.

folder A directory or subdirectory.

freeware Computer software that has no associated licensing fees. Freeware is not the same as public domain.

FTP File Transfer Protocol. A protocol for sending and receiving files over a TCP/IP network, such as the Internet.

gateway A computer that connects two other computers; gateway usually refers to a computer that connects other computers to the Internet.

get An FTP term meaning to download or receive a file from a remote system.

GIF Graphics Interchange Format. A copyrighted graphics format for storing computerized images. GIF files usually have the extension .gif.

Gopher A simplified menuing system for accessing files and information over the Internet.

header The part of an electronic message that contains the sender, receiver, date, message title, message type, and possibly other information.

home page An HTML document for a particular Internet address. It also is used loosely to describe any HTML document that you use as a starting or entry point to the World Wide Web.

host A variously used term that seems to mean any computer that is connected directly to the Internet.

HTML   HyperText Markup Language. The standard format for World Wide Web documents.

hypertext   A document that contains links (URLs) to other documents, data, and programs.

image   A computerized picture.

INF   A file format used by OS/2's hypertext VIEW program, usually given the extension .INF (*INF* for *INF*ormation).

IP   Internet Protocol.

IP Address   A 32-bit Internet address that enables any computer to find any other computer that is online; for example, 122.335.301.66.

IPL   Initial Program Load. It's IBM-ese for booting your computer.

IRC   Internet Relay Chat. A computerized party line over the Internet.

jpeg   A graphical image file format, usually given the extension .jpg.

link   In Web-ese, a URL reference to a Web server, an HTML document, or a file.

local   Your own computer. Or, if you are logged to a remote computer and accessing an even *more* remote computer, then the less-remote computer becomes quasi-local.

login ID   The ID you use to access a specific system.

lurk   Usually refers to reading newsgroup articles regularly but never letting your presence be known. In amateur radio circles, it's called *reading the mail*.

mail ID   The ID you use to access mail from a mail server.

mail server   A computer that acts as a connection point for incoming and outgoing mail. Because many Internet users aren't connected to the Internet full-time, mail servers enable you to receive mail when your computer is offline.

MIME   Multipurpose Internet Mail Extensions. An e-mail format that permits the transmission of compound documents consisting of text, formatted text, graphics, and other binary files.

Mosaic   The original World Wide Web browser.

mpeg   A movie file format usually given the extension .mpg.

MUD   MultiUser Dungeon, a game usually played over telnet terminals.

name server   A computer that translates between Internet names and IP addresses. In order to use names like cpcug.org, there must be a name server that translates such names in 32-bit dotted IP addresses, such as 164.109.15.31.

netfind   An Internet protocol for locating people who have Internet e-mail addresses.

Netiquette   A coined word meaning net etiquette, which refers to the proper way of behaving on the Internet.

Netscape A Windows-compatible World Wide Web browser.

newsgroup A subgroup of Usenet that contains news articles (messages) relating to a specific topic; such as `comp.os.os2.networking.tcp-ip`.

NR/2 NewsReader/2. A newsgroup client application that comes in the OS/2 Warp Internet Access Kit.

NSF National Science Foundation. One of the foundation blocks of the Internet.

object The fundamental unit in an object-oriented environment. It's any *thing* you can do *something* to or with. For example, you can drag a file or a folder to a printer, shredder, program, or to another folder. File, folder, printer, and shredder are all objects. In OS/2's workplace shell, there are four general types of objects: data files, programs, folders, and devices.

offline Not connected to a remote system or to a network; for example, not connected to the Internet.

PING Packet InterNet Groper. A program that tests the accessibility of Internet addresses.

PM or Presentation Manager The graphical API (applications programming interface) for OS/2.

POP Post Office Protocol. A type of e-mail server.

port A number identifying a particular TCP/IP protocol or stack; for example, port 70 usually is used for Gopher, and port 21 usually is used for FTP.

PPP Point-to-Point Protocol. A method for connecting computers to the Internet over a serial line such as a modem.

protocol An information or process exchange format.

provider An organization that connects others to the Internet.

proxy An intermediate Internet destination (such as a firewall) that protects end-users from direct connection to the Internet.

public domain Owned by everybody, such that anyone can use it freely.

put An FTP term for upload.

remote A computer that is connected to your own computer over a network. Even in a peer-to-peer system, the computer you are using is local, and any other computer on that network is remote, with respect to your computer.

ROT13 An encoding scheme designed to prevent someone from unwittingly reading something they don't want to read (for example, the finale to a movie or a book, or the final score of a tennis match). ROT13 is a simple encryption method that rotates the letters of the alphabet by 13 characters: a becomes n, b becomes m, and so on.

RTF Rich Text Format. An enhanced text format for transferring word processing files between different word processors.

RTFM Read The [expletive deleted] Manual; a rude admonition to someone who poses questions that can be answered by reading a program's documentation.

server A computer or program that provides information or services to other computers. For example, a mail server acts as a storage-and-retrieval depot for e-mail; a Gopher server acts as a point of entry to Gopherspace; an FTP server acts as a file upload and download site for FTP clients; and so on.

shareware Try-before-you-buy software. You try it, and if you use it, you're supposed to pay a registration fee. People who use shareware without registering it are known as *weasels*.

signature The closing line(s) of an e-mail or article that tell others who you are and how you can be reached.

site Loosely, used as a synonym for *server* (see **server**), as in telnet site, FTP site, Gopher site, and WWW site.

SLIP Serial Line Internet Protocol. A method for connecting computers to the Internet through a serial connection such as a modem and telephone lines.

SLIP ID The login ID you use to connect to your SLIP account. SLIP IDs usually are different from mail IDs.

SMTP Simple Mail Transfer Protocol.

snd An audio file format (*snd* as in *sound*), often given the extension .wav.

spam Newsgroup articles designed to fill up new servers with useless messages.

stack A specific TCP/IP protocol. Each layer in TCP/IP is referred to as a stack, and each stack is addressable through a TCP/IP port number of some kind.

static IP An IP address that always stays the same.

tar A tape-archiving utility (*tar* for *t*ape *ar*chiving).

TCP/IP Transmission Control Protocol/Internet Protocol. The set of data exchange formats that are used by the Internet.

telnet A terminal-emulation program that enables a computer (such as a PC) to connect to a remote host.

twit Anyone whose newsgroup postings you don't want to read.

UNIX A family of multitasking operating systems including AIX, LINUX, and SunOS. Most of the major systems on the Internet are running UNIX operating systems.

upload Sending a file to a remote system (the FTP term is put).

URL Uniform Resource Locator. Simply put, a URL is a Web-ese address for anything you can access using a Web browser.

Usenet The collection of newsgroups.

uue An encoding scheme that converts binary (8-bit) files (such as programs and graphics files) into ASCII files (7-bit) to enable transmission over computer networks that don't allow 8-bit file transfers. You use uuencode to create uuencoded files (usually with the extension .uue), and you use uudecode to decode uuencoded files.

Veronica One of Archie's girlfriends (the other one is Betty). Veronica is also an Internet searching system for locating Gopher titles. Veronica stands for Very Easy Rodent-Oriented Net-wide Index to Computerized Archives. Rumor has it that they struggled for *weeks* to find a set of words to go with the already-chosen term Veronica.

virus Program designed to interfere with the normal operation of computers or computer programs. Computer viruses can be spread by running untested programs on unprotected systems.

WAIS Wide Area Information Server. An information system for searching and retrieving data.

Warp OS/2 version 3, soon to be known as Warp 1.

warp The speed of light, approximately 1.08 billion kilometers per hour (if you're going that fast, it might as well be metric).

wav A sound wave file format, usually having the extension .wav.

whois An Internet program for searching for information about entities on the Internet. Whois servers usually are specific to domains.

World Wide Web An HTML-based system for accessing text, programs, pictures, sounds, movies, and all kinds of neat stuff over the Internet. The WWW is an attempt to make most of the Internet's most popular resources available via a simple graphical interface.

WPS or Workplace Shell The graphical interface for OS/2 version 2 and higher.

X Window A graphical windowing system for the UNIX operating system.

zip A file-archiving and -compression format; it allows one or more files to be stored in a single file, consuming much less disk space than the uncompressed file(s). This reduces disk storage space as well as file transfer time with uploading and downloading. Zipped files usually have the extension .zip.

zoo A file-archiving and -compression format, usually having the extension .zoo.

INDEX

X-Y-Z

Add to Your Sams Library Today with the Best Books for Programming, Operating Systems, and New Technologies

The easiest way to order is to pick up the phone and call
1-800-428-5331
between 9:00 a.m. and 5:00 p.m. EST.
For faster service please have your credit card available.

ISBN	Quantity	Description of Item	Unit Cost	Total Cost
0-672-30520-8		Your Internet Consultant	$25.00	
0-672-30459-7		Curious About the Internet	$14.99	
0-672-30667-0		Teach Yourself Web Publishing with HTML in a Week	$25.00	
0-672-30545-3		OS/2 Warp Unleashed, Deluxe Edition (Book/CD)	$39.99	
0-672-30595-X		Education on the Internet	$25.00	
0-672-30617-4		World Wide Web Unleashed	$35.00	
0-672-30529-1		Teach Yourself REXX in 21 Days	$29.99	
0-672-30484-8		Your OS/2 Warp Consultant	$25.00	
0-672-30460-0		Absolute Beginner's Guide to UNIX	$19.99	
0-672-30413-9		Multimedia Madness! Deluxe Edition (Book/Disk/CD-ROMs)	$55.00	
0-672-30638-7		Super CD-ROM Madness! (Book/CD-ROMs)	$39.99	
0-672-30590-9		The Magic of Interactive Entertainment, Second Edition (Book/CD-ROMs)	$44.95	
❏ 3 ½" Disk		Shipping and Handling: See information below.		
❏ 5 ¼" Disk		TOTAL		

Shipping and Handling: $4.00 for the first book, and $1.75 for each additional book. Floppy disk: add $1.75 for shipping and handling. If you need to have it NOW, we can ship product to you in 24 hours for an additional charge of approximately $18.00, and you will receive your item overnight or in two days. Overseas shipping and handling adds $2.00 per book and $8.00 for up to three disks. Prices subject to change. Call for availability and pricing information on latest editions.

201 W. 103rd Street, Indianapolis, Indiana 46290

1-800-428-5331 — Orders   1-800-835-3202 — FAX   1-800-858-7674 — Customer Service

Book ISBN 0-672-30719-7

PLUG YOURSELF INTO...

THE MACMILLAN INFORMATION SUPERLIBRARY™

Free information and vast computer resources from the world's leading computer book publisher—online!

FIND THE BOOKS THAT ARE RIGHT FOR YOU!

A complete online catalog, plus sample chapters and tables of contents give you an in-depth look at **all** of our books, including hard-to-find titles. It's the best way to find the books you need!

- STAY INFORMED with the latest computer industry news through our online newsletter, press releases, and customized Information SuperLibrary Reports.

- GET FAST ANSWERS to your questions about MCP books and software.

- VISIT our online bookstore for the latest information and editions!

- COMMUNICATE with our expert authors through e-mail and conferences.

- DOWNLOAD SOFTWARE from the immense MCP library:
    - Source code and files from MCP books
    - The best shareware, freeware, and demos

- DISCOVER HOT SPOTS on other parts of the Internet.

- WIN BOOKS in ongoing contests and giveaways!

TO PLUG INTO MCP: →   WORLD WIDE WEB: **http://www.mcp.com**

GOPHER: gopher.mcp.com

FTP: ftp.mcp.com